STREET SOVEREIGNS

STREET SOVEREIGNS

Young Men and the Makeshift
State in Urban Haiti

Chelsey L. Kivland

CORNELL UNIVERSITY PRESS   **ITHACA AND LONDON**

First published 2020 by Cornell University Press

Library of Congress Cataloging-in-Publication Data

Names: Kivland, Chelsey L., 1979– author.
Title: Street sovereigns : young men and the makeshift state in urban Haiti / Chelsey L. Kivland.
Description: Ithaca : Cornell University Press, 2020. | Includes bibliographical references and index.
Identifiers: LCCN 2019011209 (print) | LCCN 2019012305 (ebook) | ISBN 9781501747007 (pdf) | ISBN 9781501747014 (epub/mobi) | ISBN 9781501746987 | ISBN 9781501746987 (cloth) | ISBN 9781501746994 (pbk)
Subjects: LCSH: Young men—Haiti—Port-au-Prince. | Street life—Haiti—Port-au-Prince. | Port-au-Prince (Haiti)—Politics and government. | Ethnology—Haiti—Port-au-Prince.
Classification: LCC HV1441.H2 (ebook) | LCC HV1441.H2 K58 2020 (print) | DDC 305.242/109729452—dc23
LC record available at https://lccn.loc.gov/2019011209

For my baz, near and far

The Spiral

The morning after Dou tells me the meaning of his name

Poise belies fury

We go to look at the spirals on the wall

Painted just the other day by the poet

The one who left Bel Air long ago

His face stoic, apart from the others

They are stuck in the whirlwind of the geto

Heads spinning, seeing red, yellow, and orange

The angry dizziness of hunger, chaos, and insecurity, I think

But of course, I got it wrong

Fury belies poise

It is the onlooker who is spooked

Pulled into the undertow of the people

Dou tells me: This is a zone that has a lot of

problems

but at the same time a lot of

force

"Vive Haïti, Vive Le Bel Air!"

Contents

Preface

This story takes place in the heart of Port-au-Prince, Haiti. The neighborhood is called Bel Air, named for the pleasant sea breeze that cascades over the hilltops from the Gulf of Gonâve. In many ways, Bel Air's history traces the story of Haiti itself (Laguerre 1976a). In the early seventeenth century, Monsieur Randot, a wealthy French colonist, claimed it as Habitation Randot, a sprawling sugar plantation on which, at any given time, over one hundred Africans toiled as slaves. In 1749, the colonial government purchased the land for the soon-to-be capital Port-au-Prince. The district then split along a social divide that would come to define colonial Saint Domingue. White colonists lived in the *ba* (lower) section near the city market and port, and a population of free and enslaved blacks settled *anwo* (up high) along the hilly landscape. The upper Belairians built makeshift shacks that overlooked the paved streets and privileged households below. Those *anba* perceived those *anwo* as a threat to the colonial order, casting them as violent criminals. Upper Belairians both embraced and subverted this projection by cultivating a reputation as *militan* (militants), as righteous defenders of their territory and community. When the colonists erected checkpoints and curfews to police what was perceived as a criminal district, upper Belairians rebelled by providing a haven for *mawon*, or newly escaped slaves, and orchestrating raids of colonists' homes and marketplaces. In November 1791, just months after Dutty Boukman launched the revolution in the northern region, Belairians attacked colonial administrators downtown, cementing the *anwo* district's role as a key front of the military that would declare Haiti independent in 1804.

Despite the promises of the new republic, the geographic divide of race and class—and the tensions it produced—persisted. In the nineteenth and twentieth centuries, lower Bel Air became populated by store owners, civil servants, and professionals who were classified as *milat* (people with African and European ancestry) and had typically been free prior to independence. In contrast to the privileged below, upper Bel Air continued to be home to the impoverished and downtrodden and a fount of protests and rebellions.

Recently, Bel Air's demographics have become more uniform. As the series of neoliberal "structural adjustments" took hold in the 1980s, rural peasants flooded the city and settled in the *katye popilè* (popular quarters) like Bel Air. As the district became crowded, the wealthier and lighter-skinned urbanites fled for the suburbs, turning all of Bel Air over to the impoverished—though destitution still slopes upward. Far from invoking the fresh air of a coveted locale, today the name Bel Air appears as a cruel joke, mocking the poor, congested, and dilapidated district. Yet the neighborhood's power to upset the order of things has remained. Adopting an idiom popular in the urban United States, residents have taken to calling the neighborhood a *geto* (ghetto)—expressing an awareness of the neighborhood's social problems, an appropriation of these problems as vehicles for social consciousness and political action, and a sense of solidarity with people of color *lòt bò dlò* (overseas) who have likewise mobilized for change in their marginalized urban enclaves.[1]

In this book, I follow a group of residents who reside in the uppermost part of Bel Air, on land infused with a long history of segregation, poverty, and exploitation. I was a daily presence in their zone—called Platon Bèlè, or Bel Air's Plateau—from 2008 to 2010 and have returned countless times since, often staying with friends there. My first days in the zone I was struck by the manifold tribulations surrounding me, by the rickety shacks that threatened to collapse with the next gust of wind, by the towering mound of garbage that obstructed the entrance to a dilapidated health clinic, and by the dejected faces of unemployed men with nothing to do and all day to do it. However, the more time I spent in Bel Air, the more I became attuned to the militant spirit that lurked behind the tableau of what Haitians call *mizè* (misery). I began to notice how those same unemployed men were inventing activities and coming together to furnish what they needed to make it through the day. They were sweeping the streets, making music groups, organizing press conferences and protests, setting up community patrols, and founding development organizations. And somewhat ironically, they appeared to be using the neighborhood's reputation for poverty and violence as not only the problem to be solved by their organizing but also the platform that enabled them to organize. They managed, in other words, to capitalize on societal perceptions of their potential for militancy and protest in order to contract with aspiring politicians, secure state jobs, and enter development economies. This book traces how they have done so by creating neighborhood organizations known as *baz*, or "base"[2]—a name that invokes the group's emplacement in territory, empowerment via social contacts, and ethos of militancy.

The baz is the sticky interface of insecurity and activism. The anthropologist Arjun Appadurai has observed that "locality," or the feeling of belonging to a place, cannot be assumed by residence alone. Its establishment often depends on ritualized activities that erect a boundary between an emplaced community and outlying zones of risk or danger. "The production of a neighborhood," he writes, "is inherently an exercise of power over some sort of hostile or recalcitrant environment, which may take the form of another neighborhood" (1996,

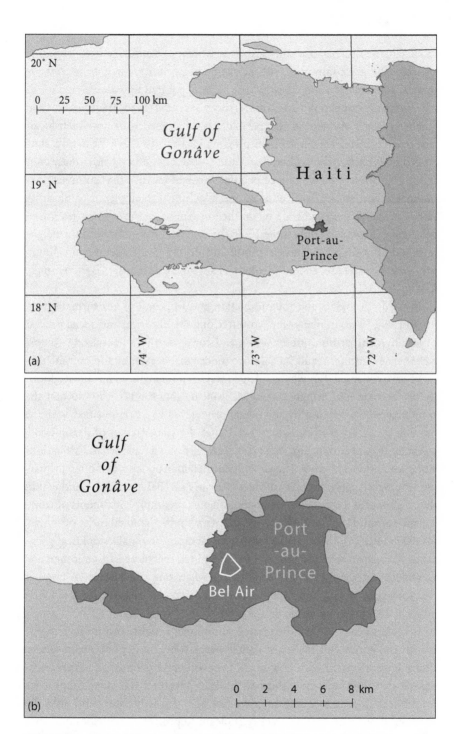

FIGURE 1. Maps of Port-au-Prince in Haiti and Bel Air in Port-au-Prince. Designed by Jonathan W. Chipman.

184). This was reflected in the term *baz*, which, as a military base, conjured a locale where a community was surrounded by, but secured from, outside threats. To be hailed as "my baz" was to be incorporated into a sovereign locality, a space of "our people" and "our territory" as opposed to "their people" and "their territory." Appadurai was particularly concerned with how such localized sovereignties have come under pressure in contexts where the nation-state faces destabilization from liberalizing and globalizing forces. Under these conditions, he observed a waning of people's sense of locality, the "complex phenomenological quality," or feeling of and attachment to emplaced community (1996, 178). What Appadurai saw on the horizon was a deterritorialization of belonging, in which people sought identity and connection beyond the neighborhood. "Put simply, the task of producing locality (as a structure of feeling, a property of social life, and an ideology of situated community) is increasingly a struggle" (1996, 189).

In trying to understand the production and workings of baz formations in urban Haiti, I was, in many ways, also tracking the historical and social process of locality construction, preservation, and conversion in a liberalizing context where state hegemony and its cohesive modes of integration and enfranchisement have collapsed. But whereas Appadurai found that, in such contexts, locality has become increasingly unleashed from neighborhoods, I found that the conjuncture between locality and neighborhood has in fact intensified, with the baz emerging as a key domain that mediates the construction of personhood, community, and citizenship. Belairians carried strong neighborhood affiliations alongside national identity. They identified as Haitian but also, and often primarily, with their neighborhood and zone, as *moun Bèlè* (Bel Air people), and within the neighborhood they were members, affiliates, or simply cohabitants of zones oriented around baz formations. And just as with the "national order of things" (Malkki 1992, 25), these attachments were far from optional. A political geography of rivalrous competition and conflict pitted one baz against another, one neighborhood against another, and dictated where one called home.[3] A popular rara song goes: "If you don't have a baz in Bel Air, do not come to Bel Air" (*Si ou pa gen baz nan Bèlè, pa monte Bèlè*).

Because of how the baz integrates communal, activist, and militant sentiments, and because of the many hats it wears, some more public than others, I have long struggled with how much to reveal and how much to keep confidential about the identity of those with whom I worked. It is standard practice for anthropologists to mask the identities of our collaborators and even the location of our studies. The practice is meant to protect our collaborators, but when I showed people in Bel Air early drafts of this ethnography, many took it instead as a failure to give them proper credit for their work.[4] The members of

FIGURE 2.   View of shacks lining a corridor along the mountainside of Plateau Bel Air.

Baz Zap Zap—the group that figures most prominently in this ethnography—were proud of their work as musicians, political actors, development workers, and defenders of the neighborhood, and they wished to be acknowledged. At the same time, both they and I wished to untether the criminal, illicit, and violent actions entailed in this work from identifiable persons. No one was naïve to the fact that in a place where *politik* (politics) denotes a violent game of one-upmanship, some things were best kept secret. Eventually, we agreed on a compromise. I would use the names of their organizations but mask their individual identities with pseudonyms.[5] I would also locate the neighborhood but withhold details that led to specific households. Although far from perfect, this compromise helped me include my collaborators in the making of this ethnography as recognized participants rather than objects of observation. It extended an ethic of mutual respect learned in fieldwork onto the page—or what I came to call "*fas-a-fas* research."

When I first began, in the summer of 2010, to focus my anthropological interests on the baz, the country swung between the extremes of discouragement and hope. It was still reeling from a massive earthquake six months prior that had claimed hundreds of thousands of lives, but it was also rapturous in the energy of an international rebuilding campaign and presidential election. In this space of uncertainty and anticipation, many Belairians began to traffic in a new slogan: *Fas-a-fas,* or face-to-face. Kal, a key member of Baz Zap Zap, wrote it in red and blue capital letters inside a picture frame and hung it over the handlebars of his motorbike. With his knack for lyricism and connecting with the cultural zeit-geist, the presidential candidate Wyclef Jean, formerly of the US hip-hop outfit The Fugees, picked up the mantra for his political motto, and, with the help of many at Baz Zap Zap, the tag soon dominated the political graffiti coating the cityscape. Awash in this motto, I began to see it as revealing how many felt a new and better society must begin with cultivating a forgotten way of relating to each other. It figured, in body and sentiment, the kind of honest, compassionate, and sincere interactions people longed to have with others, especially those with higher social standing and power in society. To many at Baz Zap Zap, it meant *respè* (respect)—a key value that undergirds the baz and about which I will have much more to say. *Fas-a-fas* meant standing before one another as equals, in full ownership of one's personhood and with full respect of another's personhood. As an ethnographer from a position of relative privilege, I took it to heart. Written in the cover of my field journals, it was my primary lesson in fieldwork etiquette, instructing me in a more socially engaged and methodologically collaborative anthropology.

Fas-a-fas recalls the Haitian anthropologist Michel Rolph Trouillot's plea for postcolonial anthropologists to "face the native" (2003, 133). Trouillot's concern with anthropology as traditionally practiced is that it casts collabo-rators as objects of observation that figure in but do not help construct the theories anthropologists formulate about the world. Thus anthropology has failed to attribute to collaborators a "competency effect" (2003, 133), or the ability to theorize their own action in ways that have analytical purchase for understanding their social milieu, let alone the global one beyond it. All too often the voices of gang members, peasants, or migrants appear in ethnog-raphies to provide limited or narrow understandings that anthropologists then correct or explain by way of broader structural or historical analysis. The correction to this, Trouillot argued, resides in a methodological pivot: by standing not behind but before collaborators. Rather than envision cul-ture as scripts that "the anthropologist strains to read over the shoulders of those to whom they properly belong," as Clifford Geertz memorably artic-ulated (1973, 452),[6] Trouillot aimed to position researcher and researched head-to-head in the act of interpretation, to grant them shared competency in the task of making sense of the cultural scripts in which they are both implicated—as partners in the field and as subjects of the globalized world.[7] The challenge, as another anthropologist who took up this call wrote, is to frame the ethnography "not as a story about an exotic *them* but as a story about and for *us*" (Bonilla 2015, xviii).

On the surface, this seems eminently doable. But does granting shared competency truly correct for the "epistemic violence" of the academy (Spivak 1988, 280)? Does this move risk ignoring how structural violence and poverty limit access to academic competency?[8] Consider, for example, an ethnography that very much inspires this book: Philippe Bourgois's *In Search of Respect.* Although his Nuyorican collaborators offered, in witty, thoughtful dialogue, their personal motivations for and reflections on selling crack-cocaine, being poor, and waging violence, they are, according to Bourgois, largely blinded to the structural factors influencing their agency and action: "They attribute their marginal living conditions to their own psychological or moral failings. They rarely blame society; individuals are always accountable" (1995, 54). This blind spot, Bourgois made clear, is tied to their structural position—a reflection of their embeddedness in the US culture of personal responsibility as well as their marginalization in the public educational system. Hence the question becomes: how do we grant our collaborators the right to speak (rather than be spoken for) without denying that that right has been systematically curtailed for generations?

Part of the answer lies in acknowledging the subjective nature of all knowledge. I am reminded of a talk I gave about my research not long after finishing this manuscript. I found myself on the defensive when a colleague questioned my heavy use of baz members' own thoughts and ideas. "These men are obviously cunning and crafty; how do you know their grand thoughts about democracy are not just efforts to best represent themselves and make their case?" she asked. "In the throes of poverty and hunger, isn't it more about getting by, doing what they have to do, saying what they have to say to make the right contacts?" I countered by saying that what I had learned from my conversations with these men was that to be successful at politicking one must also think politically.

My point was to challenge the presumption that what scholars do is objective analysis and what "natives" do is biased (read: flawed) interpretation. I saw in the comment an attempt to delegitimize the thoughts of those I study not only by casting them in the racial guise of the trickster but also by insisting they were incapable of theorizing because of the exigencies and limitations of their place in society. Yes, they had biases, and yes, they had ulterior motives. But don't we all? Theorizing is not an act performed outside society; countless inquiries into the sociology of science have shown just how dependent our theories are on the cultural and social contexts of their making.[9] Moreover, the comment implied that theorizing is an act best left to those with the luxury of unhurried, disinterested thought. Not only is this certainly not the case in the pressure-filled realms of "publish or perish," but moreover, it was clear to me that the demands of life in urban Haiti made theorizing an act of urgent necessity. Getting to the bottom of social problems and envisioning a world without them were obligatory for people in Bel Air in a way they had never been for me.

My rebuttal also made a more fundamental, if subtler, point about methodology. In many ways, I had learned how to tell fact from fiction from *diskisyon* (literally discussions but meaning argument) in which I had not just "faced the natives" but also allowed myself to be faced by them. The ethic of *fas-a-fas* was most apparent during those countless moments of fieldwork when collaborators and I debated what I was observing, what people had said, how they had said it, and what it all meant. Our *diskisyon* moved beyond passive listening or observation to embrace the rocky and contested terrain of argument and interpretation. In Haiti, *diskisyon* is an important sign of respect, reflecting a commitment to matters of mutual concern and an investment in the consequence of what others say about them. I carry these *diskisyon* out of the field and into my writing, by mobilizing my collaborators' ideas about poverty and insecurity, democracy and development, statehood and sovereignty as significant interventions in debates both on the streets of Port-au-Prince and in the halls of academia. I engage their "native categories"—from *mizè* (misery) to *respè* (respect), from *fè leta* (state making) to *filing* (pleasure)—not as illustrative of theory but as theories in themselves, theories that rethink critical issues of concern to all those interested in political failure and possibility. In the spirit of *fas-a-fas*, this involves elaborating and contesting these ideas as one would any institutionally accredited philosophy. The challenge is not simply to air the voices of the voiceless in an academic argument to which they are not privy, but rather to recast academic debates as public debates in which author and collaborator (as well as reader) are engaged as consequential theorists.

Acknowledgments

Men anpil, chay pa lou (Many hands make the load light).

Living in Haiti reminds you that life is a collective endeavor. This is not only because the days can be filled with struggles and setbacks, but also because a helping hand is never far away. The load of this book was eased by many hands in the field. My gratitude goes to my baz—my friends, colleagues, comrades—who accompanied me in the research, especially the people of Bel Air. I bear no minor guilt that you appear in this book under pseudonyms and without proper acknowledgment of your profound contributions to every query, word, and insight. I want to thank you for your willingness to accompany me on this research project, your steadfastness in seeing it to completion, and the vision, verve, and fun you infused along the way. A cold Prestige and an effusive toast to you awaits.

As a gesture of equal respect, let me also keep the many other helping hands nameless and instead acknowledge you via the bases, or spaces, of support you provided for this book. In Haiti, the list of people to recognize feels endless. I am especially grateful to my adopted family in Jacmel who introduced me to Haiti and sparked the interest that kept me coming back. Thank you to the people of Port-au-Prince—those I met and came to know as well as the strangers I walked among—for making the city a place of comfort amid the crowds. My gratitude extends to the Faculté d'Ethnologie of the Université d'Etat d'Haïti for opening its doors and welcoming an American student with a steep learning curve. My adviser, his many students, and the renegade psychology student who served as my research assistant offered unfailing support, both academic and personal. Thank you to my many hosts in Haiti who greeted me after long days with a reminder to eat, rest, and laugh, and to my uptown friends who made me feel a part of the club and introduced me to the city beyond Bel Air. Many local organizations and NGOs, especially Viva Rio and KOREBEL, provided crucial institutional homes. A special debt is owed to the other anthropologists whose fieldwork in Haiti coincided with mine, especially my roommate over the longest stint of research in Port-au-Prince. Our collective appreciation of the value of ethnography gave me the fortitude to keep on working and writing amid tragedies big and small.

Several scholarly communities conspired to make this book possible. It all began at the University of Chicago, where the erudition and enthusiasm of the

anthropology department convinced me to transfer from the sociology department and commit to an ethnographic frame of mind. Thank you especially to
my advisers for providing the theoretical scaffolding for me to ask good questions, and for maintaining, despite packed calendars, an open-door policy for
all matter of concerns and for time immemorial. Thank you also to my friends,
cohort, and the extended community of graduate students at U of C for swap-
ping reading lists, sharing ideas, and offering feedback, not to mention producing
the examples of scholarship that provided the personal motivation and theoretical inspiration I needed to finish this book. Several other scholars beyond U of
C have made a significant impact on how I carried out and interpreted my fieldwork in Haiti. Thank you to the fellow panelists and attendees of my (often early-
morning) presentations at the American Anthological Association and Haitian
Studies Association for the November jolts of intellectual energy and queries that
sustained me throughout the year. A final note of thanks is owed to my writing
coach, who kept me to a schedule, provided boosts of confidence, and celebrated
the minor accomplishments.

Many people carried me through the writing and rewriting of this book, especially those tied to the institutions where I was lucky to land postdoctoral fellow-
ships. For the time and support that enabled me to embark on this new book,
I am most grateful to my colleagues at Dartmouth College. Thank you for reading drafts, listening to talks, and offering the words of encouragement needed
to keep faith in this project. Thank you also to my fellow postdocs at Columbia
University for motivating me through the fateful stage of pitching the book, and
to my fellow Caribbeanists there for taking the time for afternoon coffee and
chats that enabled us to swap stories from the field and theories for interpreting
them. Another debt of gratitude is owed to the two anonymous readers from
Cornell University Press for careful readings, detailed suggestions, and uplifting
words, and to my editor, Jim Lance, for his early trust in the project and for his
commitment to it until the end.

Various institutions provided critical financial support for this project. The
generous grants of the Wenner-Gren Foundation, the National Science Foundation, and the Fulbright-Hays Program of the US Department of Education
funded my doctoral research. The University of Chicago's Anthropology Department and Dartmouth College's Claire Graber Goodman Fund supported critical
supplemental fieldwork trips throughout the research process. Various stages of
writing were given institutional support by the Charlotte W. Newcombe Doctoral Dissertation Fellowship and the TIAA CREF Ruth Simms Hamilton Fellowship, as well as the anthropology departments at the University of Chicago,
Dartmouth College, and Columbia University.

Nothing would be possible without my home base. Thank you to my ancestors and grandparents for founding and building such a far-reaching, supportive

family, to my parents for nurturing my instincts, instilling in me an ethic of social justice, and encouraging my adventures, and to my siblings for always being there to both lift me up and keep me grounded. My marriage brought me into a new family, whose immediate and unconditional affection, not to mention help with child care, I profoundly appreciate. My son, who came into my life in the final stages of this manuscript, gave me the force to live when I was most in need of it. My deepest debt of gratitude goes to my husband for your love through it all.

Cast of Characters

Baz Zap Zap

Zafè Pèp la, Zafè Peyi a

Street Sovereigns of Plateau Bel Air, includes Zap Zap rara, Chanpwèl Blada secret society, OJREB social organization, OJMOTEEB social organization (also called MLK), MOG *brigad vijilans*, Bèlè Masif rap group

Adam: Former member of Duvalier political bureau, sponsor of baz activities, director of baz's watering hole

Berman: *Sanba* and director of Zap Zap rara (until 2010), best friend of Kal, father of five, deceased in earthquake

Bernie: Member of Baz Zap Zap, *kone* player in Zap Zap rara, member of Chanpwèl Blada, director of art gallery and smoke shop, former Teleco employee

Blan Kouran: Member of OJREB, informal electrician for zone

Carl: member of MOG and OJMOTEEB, informal security agent for zone's market

Frantzy: Vice President of Zap Zap rara, President of OJREB, employee at Programme National de Cantine Scolaires, father of one son

Fritz: Former member of Duvalier political bureau, founder of the *katye komite* that became Baz Zap Zap, President of Zap Zap rara, employee at the Complexe Educatif du Bel Air

Jak: Member of Baz Zap Zap, *kone* player in Zap Zap rara, member of Chanpwèl Blada, motorcycle chauffeur, and former Teleco employee

Kal: *Pòt pawòl* of Baz Zap Zap, *banbou* player in and director of Zap Zap rara, *pòt pawòl* for OJREB, delegate of OJMOTEEB, Lavalas political organizer, former Teleco employee, husband of Sophie, father of two daughters

Manfred: *Oungan* for Zap Zap rara, cousin of Rémy

Michel: Secretary general of Baz Zap Zap, founding member of MLK, vice secretary for OJREB and secretary for OJMOTEEB, delegate for Bèlè Masif

Nadine: Singer in Zap Zap rara and Bèlè Masif rap group, hair stylist, best friend of Sophie, mother of one son

Nerlande: *Konseye fèt* for OJMOTEEB (until 2010), girlfriend of Berman, mother of one daughter, deceased in earthquake

Petit: *Sanba* and *kone* player in Zap Zap rara, Lavalas political delegate, leader of a neighborhood-wide federation of rara bands, former Teleco employee, godson of Fritz, father of six

Rémy: *Oungan* for Zap Zap rara, son of Ti Bout

Roland: Former leader of Bel Air Resistance Platform (1993–1994), founder of the Lavalas OP JPP, political organizer for various politicians

Samuel: Member of Baz Zap Zap, tailor, father of my godson

Sophie: Friend of Baz Zap Zap, hair stylist and entrepreneur, wife of Kal, mother of one daughter (Laloz)

Ti Bout: Head of Duvalier political bureau, father of Rémy

Yves: Leader of Baz Zap Zap, former *banbou* player in Zap Zap rara, public relations officer of OJREB, delegate and sponsor of OJMOTEEB, political organizer for Lavalas and other parties, holder of various posts and jobs in state and nongovernmental (NGO) offices, husband and father of five

Baz Grand Black

Street Sovereigns of Bel Air, rival of Baz Zap Zap, includes the armed faction Ling Di

Dread Mackendy: Founder and leader of popular army that fought Operation Baghdad following President Aristide's ouster in 2004, deceased in 2004

Manno: Popular delegate for mayor of Port-au-Prince, political liaison for Baz Grand Black and other baz in Bel Air

Marc: Member of Baz Grand Black, employee at Viva Rio

Paul: Member of Baz Grand Black, political candidate for deputy, brother of Ti Snap

Ti Snap: Leader of Baz Grand Black

Baz GNP

Street Sovereigns of Bel Air during Aristide's second mandate (2000–2004), usurped by Grand Black

Fred: Leader of Baz GNP, employee at Port-au-Prince port

Baz Pale Cho

Street Sovereigns of Bel Air valley, post-earthquake rivals of Baz Zap Zap and Baz Grand Black

Kamal: Leader of Baz Pale Cho, director of Carnival band

Baz 117

Armed group of youth that emerged post-earthquake in zone neighboring Bel Air that terrorized the area through petty crime, rape, and turf wars with other baz

CAMEP: Centrale Autonome Métropolitaine d'Eau Potable, former public water utility in Port-au-Prince

CIMO: Le Corps d'Intervention et de Maintien de l'Ordre, the anti-riot branch of the Haitian National Police

CNDDR: La Commission Nationale de Désarmement, Démantèlement et Réinsertion, disarmament campaign orchestrated by MINUSTAH after 2004 ouster of President Aristide

Fanmi Lavalas: the political movement and party led by Jean-Bertrand Aristide

Fondation Grand Black pour le Développement: the development organization led by Baz Grand Black

GNB: Gran Nèg Bèlè or Grenn nan Bouda, name of baz in Bel Air in early 2000s; Grenn nan Bouda also named national anti-Lavalas movement during same period

Groups des 184: regrouping of civil society organizations opposed to President Aristide's second presidential mandate, expansion of ISC

IADB: Inter-American Development Bank

ISC: Initiative de la Société Civile, regrouping of civil society organizations opposed to President Aristide's second presidential mandate

Kompleks (Complexe Educatif du Bel Air): neighborhood trade school run by MAST

MAST: Ministère des Affaires Sociales et du Travail, the Haitian government office for social affairs and labor

MINUSTAH: Mission des Nations Unies pour la Stabilisation en Haïti, multinational, UN peacekeeping force

MLK: Martin Luther King, name of staff, or clique, that founded MOG and OJMOTEEB

MOG: undefined but spells *mòg* (morgue), name of armed baz tied to Baz Zap Zap that runs area's *brigad vijilans*

NGO: Nongovernmental organization

OJMOTEEB: Organisation des Jeunes Moralistes Travaillant pour l'Enrichissement d'Education au Bel Air, youth development organization, partner/rival with OJREB, outgrowth of MLK and root of MOG

OJREB: Organisation des Jeunes pour la Renaissance et l'Education du Bel Air, youth development organization, partner/rival with OJMOTEEB

ONA: Office National d'Assurance Vieillesse, state-run social security office

OP: Òganyizasyon Popilè, community groups linked to the Fanmi Lavalas party

PNCS: Programme National de Cantine Scolaires, national school lunch program

RPK: rat pa kaka, the slogan of the Bel Air Resistance Platform, 1991–1994, and the title adopted by those fighting to uphold President Aristide's second mandate

SMCRS: Service Métropolitain de Collecte de Résidus Solides, the public sanitation company for Port-au-Prince

Teleco: Télécommunications d'Haïti, the former public telecommunications company

UN: United Nations

USAID: United States Agency for International Development

Viva Rio: Brazilian NGO focused on security and development and working in Bel Air

Note on Orthography

Although Creole (Kreyòl) has always been the common language of Haitian people, it was not until the 1987 constitution that both French and Creole were recognized as national languages. Following the 1987 declaration, the codification of Haitian Creole spelling established by the Institut Pédagogique National (IPN) in 1979 became the standard orthography for the new national language. This book follows the IPN orthography and uses the *Haitian Creole-English Bilingual Dictionary* of the Indiana Creole Institute (Valdman 2007) to resolve any discrepancies in spelling. In Creole, pluralization is marked by the article *yo* after the noun (e.g., *baz yo*) which does not translate easily into English. Hence I have not marked pluralization on the word but through the word's agreement with the verb (e.g., baz make the state). I have not altered Creole pluralization in quoted material, or Creole spellings in quotations of primary documents. There has been some debate about how to refer in English to the language—as Haitian, Creole, or Kreyòl. I am attentive to these debates, especially as they concern the need to elevate the status of the language. I use the term *Creole* when working in translation to follow common procedures of translation for other officially recognized languages. I quote and translate into English all speech, proverbs, songs, and writing with the intention of capturing the *pwen* (point) of the message— although, inevitably, I have lost in translation part of the discourse's complexity and eloquence. All translations are my own unless otherwise noted.

STREET SOVEREIGNS

THE BAZ

Hegel should not be astonished to discover that the *real person* appears everywhere as the essence of the state—people make the state.

—Karl Marx, Critique of Hegel's Doctrine of the State, 1843

***Nou fè leta. Nou se leta!"* (We make the state! We are the state!)**

—Bel Air resident and leader

In the fall of 2012, over two years after a 7.0 earthquake forced Frantzy to spend nearly a year sleeping under a blue tarp on Port-au-Prince's Champs de Mars plaza, he received the best news of his life. "They gave me a job!" he yelled. "You hear that?" He repeated the question four times, desperately trying to overcome the poor connection between a VoIP line in Haiti and my cell phone in rural New England.

"I do," I said. "I'm so happy for you!"

In an ecstatic burst, he told me he had been awarded a low-level post at PNCS, or Programme National de Cantine Scolaires, the national school lunch program. I pictured the smile that filled Frantzy's wide face, softening his strong jaw. His elation reminded me of when, months earlier, he had called to announce the birth of his first child, a son who was his spitting image and whom he named Lebron, after the US basketball star. After telling me his salary (about $120 per month), he explained how he planned to give something each month to his close friends Michel and Carl, his sister in the countryside, and Lebron's mother. "After I take care of my people," he said, "I will have about 250 goud ($5) to take care of myself. That means coffee with bread in the morning, a hot meal at noon, and Tampico and cookies in the evening." His projections did not seem to match the high cost of living in the Haitian capital, but the prospect of stable earnings inspired him to imagine a better life. "Everything's in shape now!" he exclaimed. "I worked to organize people in the geto, and it brought me something, finally! You see how all that work brought what I merit, how the baz gives me respect. *Nou fè leta. Nou se leta!*"

The final lines—a lyric from a neighborhood rap group—addressed how Frantzy's new job resulted from his work as a political organizer in Bel Air, a downtrodden and volatile district of central Port-au-Prince. Over the course of the 2010–2011 presidential election, Frantzy acted as a key figure in the baz, or social clique, that ruled their zone. He was the right-hand man to Yves, the leader of the baz since the mid-1990s. Under the auspices of their youth development organization, the group managed candidates' distributions of food aid to impoverished residents; in the name of their political organization, they arranged candidate-sponsored street parties and press conferences; and through their rara music group, they took to the streets to sing and stomp out their appraisals of the electoral process. For most of the election, the baz remained untethered to any one particular candidate, instead soliciting *frè* (fees) from all who wished to campaign in the area. That said, they remained broadly aligned with the political descendants of Lavalas, the movement begun in 1990 by the Catholic priest turned populist politician Jean-Bertrand Aristide. They mainly threw their weight behind the notary Jean-Henry Céant, a legal adviser and personal friend of Aristide. Céant and other Lavalas-linked candidates failed to advance past the first round of elections—a fate the baz, and the urban poor more generally, attributed to electoral interference from the international community. This setback dimmed Frantzy's political aspirations, but following the election, Yves was still able to redeem political credit for two state posts: Frantzy's in the school lunch program and another for himself at the newly reopened public health clinic.

After the tremendous loss and suffering of the earthquake, Frantzy's good news was extremely welcome. But concerns lingered. I wondered how the job might raise others' expectations of him and put stress on his relationships. Over the past few years, I had witnessed how Frantzy's organizing efforts made him vulnerable to neighbors' envy and anger—sentiments that resulted in ransacked living quarters and temporary periods of exile.[1] My mind traveled to payday at the end of the month and anticipated that his carefully calculated income distribution would not go smoothly. "Will people be jealous? You're not worried that this can bring problems for you?" I asked. "I am a leader of the baz. I find a place in the state, and now I will share with my baz," he countered confidently.

For the moment, Frantzy's concerns lay elsewhere.

Like anyone among the newly employed, he fretted about looking the part. He knew the job would require refashioning the hip-hop aesthetic he had cultivated in the zone into state standards of sartorial respectability. "With this job," he said,

"I must carry myself another way." I had often seen him recycle the same gray suit, white shirt, and red tie for church functions, and I asked if he would have to go to the office every day.

"Yes, that's right. I'll find some secondhand clothes, but when you come in December, you need to bring me a pair of shoes—not tennis shoes but shoes for an office. Size 9, you hear? If possible, bring me a hat too. Not a cap but a nice hat. You understand?!"

"And the hat size?" I asked.

"Whatever's normal," he replied, "but the shoes are more important, okay?"

"Okay," I said, before congratulating him again on his efforts and saying goodbye.

In December, I fulfilled Frantzy's request. Kal, a leader of Zap Zap, my closest friend in Bel Air, and a key figure in this ethnography, had arranged for a friend to pick me up from the airport. I made the trip to Bel Air in the back of a rusted-out pickup truck, with size 9 Oxfords in tow. The truck inched through the dust-filled streets crowded with cars and vendors. After an hour and with no more spare change for the boys who wiped our windshield with dirty rags, it was a relief to climb the hilltop to Bel Air. Perched on the district's highest plateau, the zone where Frantzy resided overlooked the Champs de Mars plaza to the south, an endless expanse of wood-and-tin shacks to the north, and the Gulf of Gonâve to the west. When we arrived, the zone appeared abuzz with camaraderie. A light sea breeze had lured residents out from the dirt corridors of their shacks and into the street. Several children played marbles along the curb, three old-timers gathered under the wood awning of the local watering hole, a young woman did her friend's nails under the shade of a jasmine tree, and a group of four young men sat curbside, playing a friendly game of dominoes, the current loser with a bag of stones over his shoulder in mockery.

All looked up as the truck clattered to a stop.

Kal leaned forward from the back seat and exclaimed in his characteristically thunderous baritone, "*Nou rive nan baz ou!*" (We've arrived at your base.) I quickly descended and began a string of long, gregarious greetings, as friends and acquaintances of five years asked about my mother, husband, siblings, friends, and any other relation I'd ever mentioned. After circling the zone, I noticed I hadn't seen Frantzy. This seemed odd as Frantzy was usually among the first to greet me, and I knew he'd heard the commotion. I asked Kal for his whereabouts and learned he was at his house.

When I found Frantzy, my suspicions were confirmed. He sat on the concrete stoop of the room he rented from one of the few homeowners in the area. He was passing the time by rhythmically flicking his feet and slapping his Nike flip-flops against his heels as he listened to songs played from his cell phone's speaker.

When he looked my way, I saw he had a fresh scar near his left eye and another across his neck.

"I brought you the shoes," I said, as I greeted him with a kiss on the cheek.

"Thanks a lot," he replied, as he took them out of the black plastic bag and inspected the size. "They'll work well! Now, I just need to wait until I heal. I don't want to look like a *bandi* (bandit) at the office."

"What happened?" I asked.

His eyes downcast, he told me that Carl, a good friend and ally in his political maneuverings, had attacked him with a machete and a brick.

"Why?" I asked.

"He was frustrated," he said. "He found nothing, and he became jealous of me. It's like that. We work with politicians, and we give them power, but they create divisions between us. I use them to find a little security in my life, but it is *ensekirite* (insecurity) that invades me. I don't feel at ease in my own zone anymore."

"So, what are you going to do?" I asked.

"Sometimes I question why I came back here after the twelfth [the earthquake]. But this is my zone, and I need to make it right. I am adding some new, young people to the baz. To defend ourselves. It's for that reason they call me Ti Makandal."

Frantzy then explained that he had begun to use a portion of his earnings to hire two young friends to patrol in front of his doorstep at night with machetes and rocks. For the makeshift *brigad vijilans* (defense brigade), Frantzy took inspiration from François Mackandal, the *mawon* (escaped slave) whose raids of colonial plantations in the mid-eighteenth century inspired the Haitian revolution. Yet despite his redemptive justifications, this intervention, I would later learn, was less than successful, resulting in heightened angst from his estranged friend and Frantzy's subsequent relocation to another zone before Yves eventually mediated an accord with Carl via a payout and the promise of a job. For the moment, I responded with the most obvious but also naïve inquiry.

"But you should bring a complaint to the police as well," I insisted.

"Oh, See-see," he began, using my nickname compassionately. "You know that will change nothing. For a long time, Haiti does not really have a state that is strong. We must defend ourselves from the bandits that run everything. There are people who think the state collapsed in the *goudou goudou* [an onomatopoeia for the earthquake], but for me, it was long before that. Now Haiti almost does not have a state office that can do anything at all. It can give a job here and there, but not for all those who need it, so everyone becomes frustrated. Me, I turn my frustration into an activity. It's up to me to make the state appear in Bel Air, and I can say I succeeded, but it gives me problems too."

What accounts for Frantzy's desire to take state power and duties into his own hands, despite the ever-present physical dangers and uncertain outcomes of governing with his limited authority and capacity as a local leader? This aspiration for state making—its historical roots, organizational manifestation, conditions of possibility, and paradoxical outcomes—is the subject of this book.

The story of Frantzy's job came at a critical juncture in my ethnography of Bel Air. I had come to Bel Air in 2008 to study the Carnival street bands known as rara and *bann a pye* (carnival bands "on foot") in urban Haiti. In August 2012, I finished my dissertation on this subject, with Frantzy's rara Zap Zap among the protagonists. But in the course of my research, and especially as I followed the postearthquake election cycle, my attention shifted elsewhere. The band, it appeared, was only one aspect of a much larger and more complex sociopolitical organization. I wanted to know more about this organization: the part-social clique, part-band, part-political association, part-development organization that residents called the baz, or "the base." For young men like Frantzy, the baz has become the *nomos* of their worlds, organizing where and how they socialized, their prospects for income and livelihood, the edifice of their security, and the form of their political participation. The baz, as the anthropologist Frederico Neiburg writes, is "a social form related to geographical space, multiple scales of belongings, affinities, and hostilities" (2017, 121; Braum 2014; Neiburg 2017).[2]

Gage Averill (1997, 9), writing in the wake of the Duvalier family dictatorship in Haiti, described Haiti as exhibiting a "spatial, radial vision of the distribution of power in society," where people on the margins of society extend their agency by allying with their peers as a means of "linking themselves to more powerful people who are in turn linked to others, all the way to the president or one of his rivals." Now three decades into the neoliberal democratic transition, the search for agency from the margins is stronger than ever, yet this search is characterized by an effort to enmesh oneself in multiple alliances and to reach for not the single site of the president but several sites of those who govern. If represented schematically, the baz would not configure a single, homogenous group but a complex network of affiliated, overlaping social cliques (often called *staff*). There was not a centralized leadership structure, but it was possible to ascertain a core network of leaders, countable on one hand, who led these various groups. And while rarely a settled matter, this and other baz were identified with a single prominent politcal leader, who acted as its political representative for outside groups and a main sponsor for its many activities, contracting with governmental agencies, political parties and leaders, powerful citizens, and NGOs and contractors.

Baz Zap Zap carried the name of the rara group that was its most public and publicly recognized face. Kal played the banbou in the rara, and although not the group's official president, he was its recognized leader.[3] The point of contact for the rara's political work, Kal often called himself the baz's *pòt pawòl* (spokesperson). However, despite his leadership role, the head of the networked baz was Yves, variously known as its *chèf* (chief), *dirijan lari* (street director), or *lidè kominotè* (community leader). Once a banbou player in the rara, Yves rose to power when he led the zone in its militant defense of former President Aristide's second presidency (2001–2004)—an undertaking for which he served two years in prison. Adept at shifting alliances, Yves has held posts under subsequent administrations, most recently working as the security guard at the public health clinic and as a liaison for the post-earthquake relocation committee. Yves used connections with state and NGO actors to broker jobs, services, handouts, and development projects for the two youth development organizations: OJREB, where he served in public relations, and OJMOTEEB, where he was named delegate and sponsor. OJREB's president was Frantzy, who acted as Yves's right-hand man and was the vice president of the rara. Kal was also the pòt pawòl for OJREB and a delegate of OJMOTEEB. OJREB and OJMOTEEB alternated as rivals and partners, at times fighting over events and projects and at others co-organizing them. OJMOTEEB grew out of a staff that called themselves MLK, for Martin Luther King, which formed as a friendship clique when its members were in grade school. Other baz activities included the armed brigade MOG and a rap group, Bèlè Masif, both begun by core MLK/OJMOTEEB members. There was also a secret spiritual society called Chanpwèl Blada (mimicking the word *brother* in Jamaican parlance), which was founded by the core rara members Jak, Kal, and Bernie.

The complex network of baz formations prefigured fragmentation. The baz was not organized as a well-defined hierarchy but a series of overlapping circles, held together but also differentiated by intersecting membership in various staff and divergent orientations to multiple leaders and their respective contacts in broader domains of power.

What intrigued me about the baz, however, was its ascendance as an organizing platform and how this platform connected to the shifting political landscape in Haiti. A relatively recent phenomenon, the baz emerged following the collapse of the Duvalier family dictatorship in 1986 and alongside the democratization and neoliberalization of the political economy. In my conversations with Frantzy and others, I was struck by how people implicitly (and often explicitly) viewed the baz as correcting an absence of governance that had accompanied the shift from an authoritarian state to a neoliberal democracy marked by a weak government. Instead of relishing the new absence of governmental

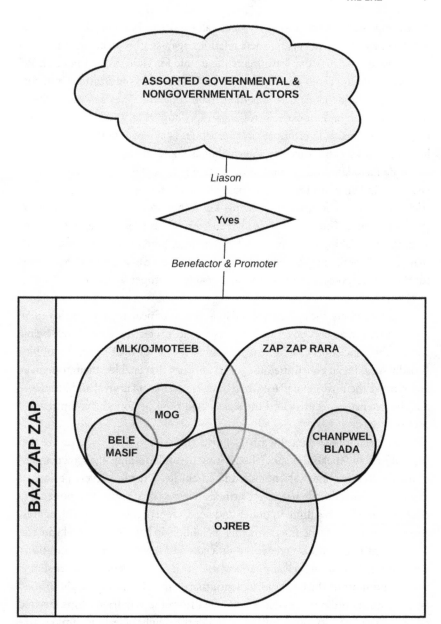

FIGURE 3.   Diagram of the overlapping organizations tied to Baz Zap Zap.

oversight or state intervention, as might be expected for a population on the heels of a repressive dictatorship, Belairians were busily organizing themselves into collectives aimed at "making the state" present and active in their lives. Why, I wondered, was this the case?

A compelling answer is what Haitians call *ensekirite*. For many in Bel Air, the baz defended its members and their relations against a broad array of physical and social insecurities that have made life unsafe for Haiti's urban poor. In Bel Air, ensekirite appeared everywhere. In both informal conversations and formal surveys, residents named it as their main concern.[4] They saw ensekirite in the rise of muggings, household robbery, rape, homicide, and kidnapping. But they did not sense it in criminal violence alone. They saw it in their dilapidated housing that so easily caved in the earthquake, and in the ever-present threat of the de facto landlord primed to oust them from squatted land. They sensed ensekirite in living "off the grid," in being forced to fend for themselves for electricity, trash collection, water, policing, and other social services neglected by the government. They also saw it in their lack of job prospects and, by extension, their vanishing opportunities for marriage, parenthood, and respectable manhood. Overall, they sensed ensekirite in the absence of a robust state apparatus that was responsive to the public and enabled a proper social life.

Enter the baz.

For its members, the baz intervened in a context of near-total unemployment, everyday violence, and governmental neglect to protect members' well-being, furnish their social needs and benefits, and advocate for their upward mobility. Broadly speaking, it constituted the social network that enabled them to remake and reorder their lives in a place where the very terms of survival and politics—and, by extension, security and the state—had been profoundly compromised over the years.

The more I followed baz members, however, the more I began to realize that their efforts to "make the state" had a way of undermining their own intentions. The baz, for one, was enmeshed in ensekirite. The most severe periods of ensekirite occurred when baz waged armed attacks against political opponents or rival groups, often resulting in police and peacekeepers countering with aggressive raids that put baz members and their neighbors in harm's way. Ensekirite was also evident in baz' brokerage with politicians and development organizations, which offered minimal inclusion at best and incited divisiveness and tension at worst. And most of the everyday violence that shaped life in the neighborhood and victimized ordinary residents emanated from the way friendships teetered on the verge of enmity, often collapsing under the weight of jealousy amid scarce resources. As the fallout from Frantzy's job makes clear, this was the case even when things went as planned, and even when the tensions did not come from outside but from within the baz. In addition to aggressive brinkmanship, the baz also had a way of intensifying the structured vulnerabilities resulting from governmental neglect and political disorder. Baz efforts to enact governance locally joined with those of NGOs and other community-based organizations in furthering the evacuation of state power and duties from the government (Kivland 2012; Schuller 2009). Moreover, the very phenomenon of localized political communities impeded the robust state apparatus and unified public that baz members envisioned as necessary for holding those in power accountable to them. In effect, the baz project appeared as much an attempt to replace a state perceived as largely missing from the lives of the urban poor as it was participating in the breakdown of the social contract that gave rise to the idea of an absent state in the first place.[5]

This book takes this paradox as its animating tension. It seeks to illuminate how the baz project captures both the profound achievements and grave difficulties of enacting sovereignty and governance "from below." Put in general terms, it asks: how—and at what benefit and cost—have people at the margins of society improvised political communities in the face of state collapse? This question has emerged across the globe as populations respond to the fallout of neoliberal reforms of state retrenchment and outsourcing. Since the United States and its allies began, in the second half of the twentieth century, to impose on peripheral countries structural adjustment policies for free and open markets, and governments became increasingly unable to control global flows of people, goods, and capital, much has been written about the "end of sovereignty" (Camilleri and Falk 1992). Most have sought proof of this "end" in the accelerated transformation of the Westphalian model, from states acting as the sole arbiters of their territory, to a new neoliberal regime, where transnational corporations and NGOs are increasingly assuming state powers and duties (see Nagengast 1994; Sassen 1996). The phenomenon of the baz, as I show, does not easily conform to this theory of state transformation. For one, the baz testifies not to the annihilation of sovereignty so much as the rehabilitation of it—as both a local practice and aspirational idea. In particular, I see the baz as illustrative of an attempt to enact governance locally as well as—and in so doing—to construct a new sovereign interface between fragmented sources of governance and street politics. In addition, the young men that I discuss here stand at the precarious center of this interface rather than the privileged apex. Unlike the transnational corporations and NGOs that are the focus of mainstream narratives of neoliberal transformations in governance, baz members are not capable of, nor do they aspire to, transcend the scale or power of the state. Instead, they mobilize local claims to leadership in order to both mimic and access state power—feats that elicit constructive and destructive consequences for them. For this reason, I refer to those in this position as "street sovereigns": leaders of their zones but marginal figures in elite power circles; community partners in electoral and development politics but criminal scapegoats in accounts of state corruption and inefficacy; respected by neighbors as local authorities but feared as sources of violence and exploitation. In chronicling the baz, I hope to dramatize its leaders' creative force and innovative tactics, as well as the political risks and institutional challenges of improvising the state from the margins of society, where the government and its centralized mode of rule and order have collapsed.

Beyond the Gang Narrative

The phenomenon of the baz came to international attention under stigmatizing labels long familiar to followers of street politics among poor urban black populations in Haiti and beyond. Startling accounts of street gangs run amok made headlines around the world in 2004, as Aristide's second presidential administration faltered and eventually collapsed.[6] Alleged news of pro-Aristide *chimè* who ruled their urban shantytowns as despots, waged violent attacks against political opponents, and engaged in robbery, rape, and kidnapping to finance their exploits cemented a narrative of baz leaders as baseless, vicious criminals. The term *chimè* invoked the fire-breathing, multi-animal monster chimera and had previously circulated in Haiti to name those unable to contain their anger or frustration. Yet international media largely ignored this meaning when translating the label for Aristide's urban loyalists, opting instead for "ghost." The shadowy, spectral figure of the ghost continued the "symbolic web built around *race*" that foreigners have long used to locate Haiti as a place of exotic, superstitious, and dangerous Others (Farmer 1992, 223, emphasis in original).[7] *Ghosts of Cité Soleil*, a widely watched documentary that detailed the lives and deaths of two of the capital's most prominent chimè crystallized this reading when it referred to the geto under their control as the "most dangerous place on earth." Similar tales of urban menace and mayhem resurfaced in the aftermath of the earthquake, with several headlines predicting the return of the spectral gangs: "Will Criminal Gangs Take Control in Haiti's Chaos?" asked *Time* Magazine; Reuters declared, "Gangs Return to Haiti Slum after Quake Prison Break"; and the tabloid *Daily Mail* admonished, "Machete-wielding Gangs Roam Streets!"[8]

Those who hail from the margins of the city, from geto such as Bel Air, are acutely aware of such ominous narratives, as well as the impact such depictions have on their lives. I was evacuated from Haiti four days after the earthquake, and shortly after I landed in New York, I began receiving news of the situation from Bel Air residents. "*Blan yo—the whites—*are afraid! They say we have *gang yo* [gangs], and the baz finds no help at all!" read one text message from Michel, the secretary for the baz's development organization. Another read: "We don't see the state. We don't see aid. We count on our baz to organize everything. *Pwoblèm!*" Like Michel, I resist conflating the terms *baz* and *gang* throughout this book. I do so because the term *gang* functions in Haiti, as elsewhere, to criminalize a type of group.[9] Foreigners, police, and state officials, as well as people like Michel, use the term *gang* as a mark of immorality and criminality—in short, to designate what they are not. I follow my interlocutors in using the term *baz* in order to reclaim the sociopolitical valences of the *baz* that often go unrecognized in the gang label. As Frederico Neiburg has argued, an understanding of the baz begins with "the realization that bases are much more than the immediate agents of violence, or the same thing as gangs, as they are so often described by experts" (2017, 130). Politically, the term *baz* referred both to the popular strata of society and the source of a leader's popular sovereignty. Baz leaders saw themselves as empowered by a local base of support and empowering *pèp la* (the people), or at least a subsection therein, in national politics. Yet I do not intend to ignore the violence at stake in the baz. Indeed, the term *baz* also conjured the unruly, lowly class of the electorate, or *moun sa yo* (those people), deemed unfit for liberal democracy or civil society. In grasping the tension between defense and delinquency, advocacy and criminality entailed in the gang label, I offer a more nuanced consideration of the contradictory entailments of baz politics: the productive conflicts and defiant potentials as well as the arrested ambitions and tragic outcomes entailed in poor urbanites' long-standing pursuit of organizational efficacy.

In working toward these goals, I have confronted a persistent ethical puzzle: how can I reclaim the self-organizing potential of those involved in the baz, without ignoring the real and grave *problems* with baz politics to which Michel alluded? And moreover, how can I address these problems while acknowledging that journalists and other outsiders might read the surfaces of the baz to construct an argument of urban Haitians as incapable of civil society, nonviolent organizing, or democratic politics? The stakes of this question are raised for ethnographies with black protagonists, since scholars and lay commentators have long framed sociopolitical problems in black communities in terms of an intrinsic cultural deficiency: a "culture of poverty" and "culture of violence."[10] Consider what *The New York Times* editorialist David Brooks wrote after the earthquake. Drawing on the work of Lawrence E. Harrison, a development scholar and long-time USAID mission director in Latin America, he argued that culture was the main driver of Haiti's poverty and lack of development progress.

> As Lawrence E. Harrison explained in his book "The Central Liberal Truth," Haiti, like most of the world's poorest nations, suffers from a complex web of progress-resistant cultural influences. There is the influence of the voodoo religion, which spreads the message that life is capricious and planning futile. There are high levels of social mistrust.

Responsibility is often not internalized. Child-rearing practices often involve neglect in the early years and harsh retribution when kids hit 9 or 10.

We're all supposed to politely respect each other's cultures. But some cultures are more progress-resistant than others, and a horrible tragedy was just exacerbated by one of them. (Brooks 2010, A27)

Here *culture* was imagined as sui generis and isolated from wider relations, the self-reproducing essence or ontology of the Haitian people or race. For Brooks, the earthquake's high death toll resulted *not* from Haiti's history of global marginalization, nor its destruction of state regulations and services under neoliberalism, nor its unbridled urbanization resulting from development plans. Rather, it was rooted in a set of poverty-causing, cultural proclivities, such as an inability to plan, social mistrust, and lack of responsibility, that Haitians have supposedly reproduced *among themselves* through poor child-rearing practices.[11]

The irony is that in mobilizing a decontextualized notion of culture, such readings actually prohibit a holistic social analysis, which is to say, a truly anthropological account.[12] Rather than grapple with how social patterns or phenomena have become *enculturated* at the evolving nexus of diverse structuring factors—from economic to political, material to ideological, local to global, historical to contemporary—an argument is made that the culture itself is pathological and, therefore, not worthy of understanding on its own terms. *Culture*, then, becomes a black box, inexplicable yet causal. Culture here acts less as a description of a particular form of life than a moral and political technology, defining what forms of life are worth redeeming or casting aside and sanctioning policies for multiplying some lives and eradicating others.[13] Echoing a discourse long rehearsed in international and national policy toward Haiti, Brooks's proposed solution was an "intrusive paternalism" aimed at creating "countercultures" of a supposedly more progress-oriented bent (2010, A27).

Although I am committed to debunking this argument, I do not want to lose sight of a cultural understanding of the baz, or how the baz, like all forms of human sociality and politics, exhibits a specific form as a result of the particular circumstances of its generation. Specifically, in pushing a reading of the baz beyond the gang label, I want to shift from interpreting it as an index of Haiti's intrinsic aversion to peaceful, effective organizing and governance, to acknowledging that its unique structure, ethos, and politics emerged and became entrenched in relation to when, where, and among whom it developed. Put differently, I see the baz not as indicative of a "culture *of* violence" but of a "culture *in* violence," a cultural response to a situation of structural, political, and social violence. With this change in perspective, I seek to capture how both the productive potential and the problematic consequences of baz politics are entangled in its contextual emergence. The agonistic, militant ethos embedded in baz politics arose in order to appropriate historical repertoires of authority as well as intervene in present configurations of power within and beyond the neighborhood. At base, what I am proposing is rather simple: namely, to theorize the political culture of the baz along both temporal and spatial axes of power, axes both historically deep and geographically broad. This is not a new proposal, but it is fundamental to understanding the baz as well as reaching the analytical and ethical ambitions of this book.

A starting point for work on political culture in Haiti (and the Caribbean more broadly) is the insistence that violence has mapped the contours of power relations in these societies since inception. From the Columbian conquest to colonial slavery, from the first government's imposition of militarized agriculture to the repressive decades of Duvalier dictatorship in the mid-twentieth century and its brutal afterlife in the 1990s, those in power have imposed their sovereign will through the force of arms.[14] At times the marginalized have joined their exploits as lowly soldiers or informal paramilitaries employed in their services. But they have also countered with popular armies and protest fronts of their own, from the slaves turned soldiers of the Haitian revolution to the series of nineteenth-century coups orchestrated by provincial armies, to the peasant armies that fought the US occupation in the early twentieth century, to the urban baz that defended Aristide's rule in the 1990s and 2000s and remain in postions of neighborhood leadership today.[15] This historical interchange of state despotism and popular militancy has inculcated what the Haitian political scientist Robert Fatton (2007, 2) terms an "authoritarian habitus," whereby violence has become the prime medium for exercising authority as well as challenging it. Tracing the historical development of this habitus is the first major axis of my explanation for baz politics. Throughout this book I am concerned with chronicling how baz' embrace of militancy, their violent rivalries, and the influence they have in the fragile democratic state revisit this history of the popular army as an icon and medium of sovereignty. As illustrated by Frantzy's identification as Ti Makandal, everyday struggles and political contestations over the ordering of persons and groups in the neighborhood often played out through appeals to historic militants and their sovereign aspirations.

However, I have some reservations about the explanatory power of history alone. Often an appeal to history can reinforce notions of cultural alterity, especially when that history is perceived as overly particular or unconnected to places beyond it—in short, when it is seen as *their* history.[16] This is especially the case in Haiti, a place mired, as Michel Rolph Trouillot (1990b) pointed out, in the fiction of historical exceptionalism. In modern history, Haiti is almost always cast as a place that is not just unique but fundamentally incomparable to the rest of the world—an aberrant, odd country.[17] This line of thinking forecloses applying to Haiti explanatory models applicable elsewhere, if not the task of explanation itself. But as with "culture-of" readings, the problem is as political as it is epistemological. "The idea that Haiti could fit no paradigm," the historian Brenda Plummer (1988, 6) argued, "prohibited the development of any but the most conservative policies" toward Haiti by the United States and allied foreign powers. Graver still was the fact that at the same time that it sanctioned aggressive international interventions, this trope of exceptionalism worked to obscure how international actors were at play in shaping Haitian realities, ultimately letting them and their policies off the hook: "The more Haiti appears weird, the easier it is to forget that it represents the longest neocolonial experiment in the history of the West" (Trouillot 1990, 7).

I have been struck by how entrenched the trope of exceptionalism remains in academic circles despite its shaky analytical grounds. Time and time again, colleagues working elsewhere in the world have responded to descriptions of the baz with remarks, such as, "This feels like a Haitian story. What about elsewhere?" or "This is such an intriguing case, but can it be generalized?" To be fair, many scholars of Haiti also hew to this line of thinking. The dominant academic analysis of the baz, for example, is that it is a contemporary instantiation of the paramilitaries that have long marked despotic rule in Haiti.[18] In such readings, the baz is seen as a contradiction rather than a product of democratization—a case in point that the Haitian political project is a failed or incomplete one when compared to the supposedly more evolved democracies found in North America or Western Europe. It is true that the baz is a unique sociocultural entity crafted in urban Haiti, but it is also true that its forms and implications are resonant in fragile cities across the democratizing, developing world—from garrison communities in Jamaica (Bogues 2006; Jaffe 2012a, 2013) to civil defense brigades in Liberia (Hoffman 2011), informal neighborhood courts in South Africa (Burr 2005), and street gangs in Chicago (Ralph 2014). In relegated urban territories worldwide, neighborhood associations, youth groups, and strongmen are partnering with a diverse cast of governing actors and assuming the work of politics and governance for their friends and neighbors. What is in need of explanation, then, is the baz as an analogue, not as a global outlier. The global proliferation of street sovereignties forces interrogation of how the baz is shaped by global political orders and forces as well as national and neighborhood political cultures. The challenge is to develop an analytical model that accounts for how street sovereignties align with both the dominant political logic and its counterforces, with both neoliberal democracy and poor urbanites' responses to it.

Here I take inspiration from urban ethnographies that have attempted to situate militant youth groups in multiscalar political configurations and explain their reproduction with reference to extant structural forces within and beyond the street. Among the most influential for my thinking was put forth decades ago by Philippe Bourgois (1995), who argued that the destructive practices he observed among "Nuyoricans" in late 1980s East Harlem—from drug dealing to domestic abuse—reflected the way societal repression becomes painfully internalized and reproduced through the very forms used to combat it. In particular, the "oppositional street culture" (1995, 141) his informants cultivated to resist societal exploitation and social marginalization proved ultimately and contradictorily destructive to themselves and their communities—precluding them from mainstream employment and leading to conflicts with friends and loved ones. Such an approach goes far in explaining the mutual reinforcement between different scales of violence, between the structural, interpersonal, and psychological. It can help explain, for example, how in the story about Frantzy's job, mass unemployment in the neoliberal era bred frustrations and jealousies that became expressed in rivalries between friends, which ultimately jeopardized future employment prospects.

However, this framework's focus on explaining violent proclivities and outcomes can also obscure the extent of entanglement between the precarious and productive aspects of the baz project and its street politics. Like the young men in *el barrio*, baz members often found that society-wide projections of their capacity for violence, coupled with their own embrace of militant identities, prohibited full inclusion in civil society, formal politics, or mainstream economies. Yet what struck me was how these very projections of ensekirite and militancy also provided them with the platform for organizing that forged their entry into both licit and illicit political economies and sources of livelihood. The young men I track in this book have been able to capitalize on their reputation for militant politics in order to control a lucrative protest economy, contract with aspiring politicians, secure state jobs, and forge development initiatives. Their success in these endeavors illustrates just how much the idiom of the gang constitutes a misreading of the baz. Rather than being reducible to senseless criminality or cultural despotism, the baz is instead rooted in a new mode of organizing that marginal urban youth have created to stake claims for representation and development in the neoliberal democratic era. The conditions of electoral politics, project-based governance, and community-based development have enabled the baz to emerge as a key player that negotiates and amalgamates relationships with global and national power structures. It is a project in localized, vernacular "state making," and it includes all the potential and problems of such an adventure in sovereignty.

On Street Sovereignty

The title of this book, with its invocation of "sovereignty"—that fixture of the modern state and international order—is an attempt to capture the ambitious claim to political authority and power entailed in baz members' assertions to *fè leta*, or "make the state." Yet framed here in terms of the *street*—that chronotope of urban margins, where poor, delinquent youth roam beyond and below the purview of the state[19]—the title reveals the tension between the force and the fragility of this project, its projection of territorial omnipotence and its relational and compromised performance of power in practice. This lived tension is, of course, operative in all sovereign projects. Indeed, in the Haitian context, the sovereign ideal appears as farcical at the level of the government as it does on the street. Hence in keeping force and fragility, sovereignty and marginality in my purview, my goal is not to subsume a local order of power under a dominant nation-state, nor to position the two in a political rivalry. Instead, it is to reveal a dialectical relation between a vitiated state that has further marginalized the urban poor and baz leaders' sovereign aspirations, efficacy, and struggles. In making this point, I develop two closely interwoven interventions into scholarly debates surrounding the changing dynamics of sovereignty today.

The first concerns a long-standing yet renewed anthropological concern with the structuration of power in the absence of formal and robust state institutions. In classic political thought, it has been customary to think of sovereignty as total autonomy and authority and to locate it squarely in the singular domain of the state—indeed, as the property that defines the state.[20] Such is the great dream of Westphalian sovereignty: that each state, no matter how small, is the ultimate arbitral agent and executor of force over its territory and the people residing therein. To quote Hannah Arendt, "sovereignty, the ideal of uncompromising self-sufficiency and mastership, is contradictory to the very condition of plurality" (1998, 234). But since at least the publication of *African Political Systems* in 1940, anthropologists have questioned both the necessary equivalence between the state and sovereignty and the idea of the singular state sovereign. In exploring how power and authority were constructed in the absence of recognizable governments, in so-called stateless societies, *African Political Systems* redefined sovereignty as embodied in people not states, in groups not governments. As A. R. Radcliffe-Brown wrote in his seminal preface to that volume, "Amongst some writers on comparative politics, there is a tendency to concentrate on what is called the 'sovereign state.' But states are merely territorial groups within a larger political system in which their relations are defined by war or its possibility, treaties, and international law. Political theory and political practice (including colonial administration) has often suffered by reason of this type of system being set up, consciously or unconsciously, as a norm" ([1940] 1955, xxi).

In many countries today, the norm of state sovereignty is no longer tenable, and anthropologists have marshaled alternative frameworks to grasp the plurality of actors now involved in governance. In postcolonial settings, sovereignties tend not to be organized around a highly centralized state but rather consist in "a horizontally woven tapestry of partial sovereignties" (Comaroff and Comaroff 2006b, 35), where plurality, incomplete control, and governing interdependence are the defining features of sovereignty. A range of governing actors, from NGOs to transnational corporations, from international financial institutions to civil defense brigades, now compete for control over the lives of people in any given territory or population. Such "*déplacement* of state functions" away from "national sites to infra-, supra-, or transnational ones," as Trouillot (2001, 132) argued, has demanded a more performative definition of sovereignty, where sovereignty denotes less a property of states than a repertoire of power—a form of practice and an orientation to others—that may be enacted by any agent within or beyond government (see also Hansen and Stepputat 2005). To use this flexible definition is not to remove the state from the equation but to see the ways in which sovereignty is tied to the state by virtue of a pattern and mode of action that state agents enact but which can be enacted by others beyond the state as well. Likewise, this definition is not intended to paint a picture in which all people are equally empowered and capable of being sovereign. Partha Chatterjee (2004, 4) opted for the term "those who govern," which I like for its ability to speak to an array of governing actors, while still recognizing the power these actors have vis-à-vis "the governed" in the moment of governance.

This way of thinking is nothing new in Haiti. The Haitian term *leta* (state) has long been used by the poor majority as a label for powerful individuals irrespective of their actual ties to the state apparatus—referring as much to the president, parliament, and military as to the class of commercial and professional elites that also govern through their alliances with political power. People use *leta* to name and define a kind of "power elite" (Mills [1956] 1999), forcing acknowledgment of all those who play a role in, and are thus responsible for, governing the country.[21] In a similar way, the phrase *fè leta* refers not simply to governmental workers but any agents, be they baz leaders or NGOs, who take on a role as more powerful than or in control of others in a state-like manner. In such usages, the state emerges as a performative power, a power that is produced by enacting it through repetitive acts of sovereignty, before audiences who recognize it as such.

For baz leaders, the sovereign project is also performative because it entails a degree of state mimicry. Throughout this book, I trace how baz leaders perform the sovereign acts and rituals of the state through the manifestation of force through violence, welfare, and pleasure, a range of undertakings that span the spectrum of control over life, from "necropolitics" (Mbembe 2003) to "biopolitics" (Foucault 2009) to what I call "hedonopolitics" (Kivland 2014). In particular, I trace in subsequent chapters the projection and enactment of an architecture of defense to ward off physical and social threats; the pursuit and management of political deals to advocate for and manage neighborhood electrical connections; and the promotion, organization, and enjoyment of annual street parties and beach days for the zone. I argue that this repertoire of sovereignty defines a political epistemology grounded in a cultural idiom of *respè* (respect). Invoking an interplay of defense as protection and advocacy, and fashioned through a gendered, racial, and class persona, *respè* guides my explanation for baz leaders' establishment of control over the zone and its source of legitimacy. If the power entailed in these activities relies on manifesting a degree of fear among outsiders and potential rivals, it is also dependent on legitimating this fear through practices that cultivate public welfare and pleasures, negating an everyday existence of misery, vulnerability, and insignificance. Though efficacious, this is a project that is never stable or complete. As a power constituted in performance, the state—whether made on the street or in government—is a project that is always in the process of being socially verified and challenged. Hence, it makes sense to say, as people in Bel Air often do, that the state does not make the state (*leta pa fè leta*) as much as the baz does.

Despite such pronouncements, it is important to remember that Haiti is not a stateless society in the manner envisioned by early political anthropology.[22] It has a government that aspires to, even if it fails to meet, the normative model. Keeping this in mind becomes critical to mapping the dynamic tensions and contestations among the many governing actors populating the political landscape. The notion that the capital-s State fails to perform statehood raises a key question animating scholarly debates on emergent configurations of sovereignties: what effect is the diversification of those who govern having on the governing capacity and authority of the State? Some anthropologists have shown how liberalizing democracies—especially those with centralized and robust governments—have extended their reach and powers by partnering with NGOs and transnational corporations capable of circumventing state regulatory regimes (Ferguson 1990; Ong 2006). However, the vast majority of anthropologists and political scientists working in Haiti and other aid-dependent countries have shown that the rerouting of funds, personnel, duties, and powers from governments to private organizations has weakened the state's governing capacity and its ability to exercise sovereignty over its citizens or in relation to international organizations (Étienne 1997; Ferguson 2006; Schuller 2007, 2012b; Trouillot 2001). Hence the now common characterizations of countries like Haiti as a "pseudo," "weak," or, most often, "failed" states.[23] These findings interest me, as they do baz leaders, who envision the vitiation of the state under neoliberal reforms and development economies as a hindrance to their political ambitions and economic livelihoods. But the approach I take here is somewhat different. I invoke a dialectical rather than an oppositional framework, in which state power is not presumed to exist and be challenged by a nonstate force but is rather in the process of being continually eluded, embraced, and constituted by it.

The need for this dialectical framework is clear when the political landscape is viewed from the vantage point of the baz. In much of the scholarship concerned with the end of state sovereignty, the idea of the "transnational" has been privileged to such an extent that the main subjects of research are those organizations, corporations, or social movements that are capable of transcending the national grid and forging globally networked linkages. Unfortunately, this has meant that less attention has been placed on the role of groups that are both more marginalized and more localized. When such groups have been brought to the fore, the discussion has often pivoted on the exacerbation of inequities and the reduction of citizens to "bare life."[24] Yet it is clear that groups on the urban margins are playing an empowered if precarious role within the dispersed structuration of sovereignty and governance. My question thus becomes: how are street organizations creating localized repertoires of governance and authority that provide both a counterpoint to and a means of entry into fragmented sovereignties?

Responding to the growth of neighborhood polities under democratization and development policy, as well as to the pressing needs of urban populations to secure political and economic survival in situations of entrenched poverty and precarity, a new wave of scholarship has explored what I call "street sovereignties"—informal, often criminalized, associations that provide a structure of leadership and conduit for representation and governance in poor, urban neighborhoods. From an analysis of the "subaltern governmentality" practiced by the localized cells of an outlawed populist political party in Peru (Nugent 2004, 211) to the squatter associations that enact a "politics of the governed" and organize for public services in urban India (Chatterjee 2004, 4) to the urban gangs that become "partners-in-governance" with sate actors in policing, service provision, and construction (Jaffe 2013, 737), anthropologists have argued that amid the decline of state systems and the fragmentation of governance have emerged informal sovereigns, particularly in impoverished urban enclaves, who are staking claims as both brokers and agents of governance.[25] This work has revealed a symbiotic relationship between state vitiation and the rise of street sovereignties. It is also clear that the neoliberal rollback and privatization of state services in Haiti has enabled baz leaders to become key political brokers in the management of marginal urban populations.

Yet my focus here extends beyond the political niche baz leaders fill to grapple with their statist aspirations. What I have found intriguing, and indeed paradoxical, is how despite the existence of the baz being predicated on the weakness of the state, baz leaders see their actions as part of an effort to bring the state into being. Contrary to neighborhood defense brigades and local courts in South Africa, for example (Burr 2005; Jensen 2005), baz leaders did not position themselves as substitutes for the state, nor did they seek to establish "zones of local sovereign power not entirely 'penetrated' or governed by the state" (Stepputat 2005, 30–31). Insofar as the baz sees itself as governing in conjunction with the government and NGOs, it makes little sense to position it in a tug-of-war with these entities. Hence, rather than ask how the baz strengthens or weakens those in power, I ask how this fragmented political configuration has enabled the baz to emerge as a collaborator in governance who aspires to make present the duties and services of the state—both in the zone and among those in power. This is the double move within baz leaders' claim to "make the state": to simultaneously perform state-like power and reconstitute vanishing state-citizen relationships.

In Want of the State

This statist aspiration may surprise students of political anthropology and political theory in general, and it brings me to my second intervention. If it has become customary to think of the state and sovereignty together, it has become almost obligatory to think of state sovereignty as defined by a repressive and violent form of power. Indeed, much of early political anthropologists' fascination with stateless societies had to do with a romanticization of them as utopian sites of freedom and revolutionary possibility. On the heels of European fascism, the French anthropologist Pierre Clastres imagined his indigenous informants of South America as constituting a "society against the state," a society whose heterogeneous composition and egalitarian values represented a challenge to the homogenizing and hierarchizing power of the modern state (1987, 1). The anthropologist was here enlisted in the task of warding off the "inevitable and ghostly presence" of the state, because it threatened the existence of indigenous society and of righteous politics globally (Das and Poole 2004, 5). From twentieth-century "salvage anthropology" to contemporary "ontological anthropology," this viewpoint has inspired anthropologists to treasure indigenous society as proof that "another world was possible" (Viveiros de Castro 2010, 15; see also Langer and Munoz 2003; Pallares 2002).

Another contemporaneous body of scholarship, influenced by indigenous ethnography but finding its bearings in European philosophy, likewise constructed the state in haunting terms and argued for its demise. Centering Max Weber's iconic definition of the state—as a "human community that (successfully) claims the *monopoly of the legitimate use of physical force* within a given territory" (Gerth and Mills 1946, 78)—the postwar generation of Marxist and postcolonial scholars constructed the state as the organization of repression. Seminal studies of large-scale peasant resistance (e.g., Mintz 1974; Paige 1975; Scott 1985; Wolf 1969), sought to reveal how the modern state furthered the domination of citizens and colonial subjects through coercive strategies of militarism and capitalism. Out of this work came a corpus of studies that mapped the relationship between the state and the people as one of domination and resistance, and that traced how the lowly were, through clandestine and subversive methods, challenging or escaping governmental and military power (Miller, Rowlands, and Tilley 1995; Scott 1985, 1990). This way of conceptualizing the state has enjoyed new life in several recent attempts to define the essence of sovereign power as violence and to, thereby, highlight the exercise of violence by actors within and beyond the state as an act of governance. The equation of sovereignty and violence is a centerpiece of the post-9/11 zeitgeist that resurrected Carl Schmitt's oeuvre and analyzed how a multitude of de facto sovereigns exercised state power by taking or flouting the lives of refugees, terrorists, political rivals, and others caught in "states of exception" (Agamben 2005) by war or social conflict (Das and Poole 2004; Hansen and Stepputat 2005).

These scholarly traditions can easily be applied to the history of Haitian statecraft as well as of popular resistance in Haiti. *Leta*, or the power elite, has, for much of its history, utilized brute force, repressive taxation, and social discrimination to maintain the subjugation of the majority of Haitians. At the same time, the rural and urban poor have cultivated, since independence in 1804, sophisticated strategies to ward off the encroachment of state power as well as overthrow particular regimes—from the semiautonomous homesteads known as *lakou* to the peasantry's *kako* armies. This historical record, coupled with the dominant theoretical understandings of statehood, poses a question of great relevance to this study. Why would people in contemporary urban Haiti seek to "make the state"—not just in terms of local governance but also by structuring relations with those in power? Why, in other words, do they *not* pursue what James Scott (1998, 78) calls "the art of not being governed," instead favoring the art of being governed?

I seek to address this question by reframing the relationship between localized domains of governance and the overarching political configurations that encompass them as strategies of political engagement rather than antagonistic opposition. Whereas popular forms of self-governance are often presumed to represent a quest for total autonomy from the state, I see it instead as a search for relative autonomy, a desire to mobilize control over a local domain in order to gain entry into and influence within broader domains of power. When citizens such as Frantzy lament, "Here, there is no state!" their words speak as much to the failings of the Haitian state as to their aspirations to summon it into existence and make it responsive to their needs. They speak, in large part, to the ideological attachments to Haitian statehood and its promise of racial and class redemption that took root during the revolution and have not wavered—indeed, may have even grown stronger—with the faults and failings of existing political institutions. At the same time the declaration also reflects political pragmatism. In the neoliberal context of the geto, where the government has progressively retreated from the landscape of governance; where basic services (from security to water, food aid to garbage collection, electricity to schooling) are increasingly provided through one-off development projects or neighborhood initiatives that fail to meet citizens' long-term needs or expectations; where NGOs and other nonstate entities that perform governance are unaccountable to customary practices of political redress (such as the vote or popular protest); and where government and politics remain among the only venues through which marginalized young men can seek a source of livelihood, a degree of social power, and a sense of respect, state making—understood as the infrastructure of governance as much as the ideal of the social contract—becomes a project well worth undertaking, or so I argue.

A Place Betwixt and Between

Bel Air, the neighborhood where this book takes place, inhabited an exceptionally contradictory place in the city. It exhibited the social contours of the geto: poor, crowded, derelict, insecure, and neglected. Yet unlike other geto, it was not located at the edges of the city but in its very center. A stone's throw from the National Palace, city port, commercial district (including the city's largest open-air market), and the middle-class district Lalue, Bel Air thrust itself into the purview of politicians, merchants, and well-heeled urbanites alike. Its strategic location, coupled with its penchant for protest, has lent it an outsized impact as the country's political barometer. "As goes Bel Air, so goes the country!" instructs the neighborhood motto.

The volatile status of the neighborhood carries over into residents' own senses of place and power in the city. At once peripheral and well-connected, socially deviant and respected, people in Bel Air embodied social positions that often seemed to contradict dominant schemes of social classification. They certainly did not fit the privileged side of the city folk/rural folk (*moun lavil/moun andeyo*) or uptown/downtown (*anwo/anba lavil*) divides that have long defined the country's class structure. Yet as movers and shakers in urban and national politics, Belairians also defied the position of the destitute and helpless victim that has dominated popular imaginaries of the poor in Haiti. Falling between social categories cast them into the precarious subjectivity that Victor Turner (1967, 95) called the "liminal persona," an unsteady state in which the categorically unclear become the socially unclean, their indefinability exposing them to stigmatized projections of danger and menace.

People in Bel Air and especially the young men I track here were acutely aware of how their power from the margins positioned them as objects of fear and derision among outsiders. Frantzy, for example, switched high schools twice as a result of being ridiculed as chimè by classmates from other districts, and when temporarily employed as a community health worker with an NGO he kept his place of residence a secret for fear of being identified as a bandit. However, despite the limitations this stigma placed on residents' outward and upward mobility from the geto, it could nonetheless be a source of residents' empowerment. It could become the basis for ensuring their necessary inclusion in political contests and processes (otherwise: *There goes the country!*), their exercise of authority over others (including women, the elderly, and other non-baz neighbors), and their security as they traversed the city. When accompanying me on excursions outside the neighborhood, Frantzy often fashioned himself in the guise of a *nèg geto* (geto black)—replete with sunglasses and red bandana tucked in an oversized cap—in order to out-bandit others and act as my (and his own) bodyguard. As we boarded public transport, he would often remark, "Don't worry. I'm the biggest *bandi* here." Still, his appropriation of a deviant identity spoke as much to his reclamation of self-authorized agency as it did to his circumscription within a subaltern status group. As I came to learn, Bel Air residents' articulations of urban difference did not conform to rigid binaries between the privileged and the powerless or the villain and the victim, but rather troubled the boundaries between them, reworking the categories as a result.

My attunement to the "betwixt-and-between" status of residents grew as I became increasingly aware of my own contradictory embodiment of power in Haiti as a white American woman. The baz is a space of *nèg*, a space of and for men who aspire to claim status as *gran* nèg (big men, also called *gwo nèg*). The term *nèg* comes from the derogatory French label for "blacks" (*nègre*), but today it functions less as a designation of skin color than as a generic label for Haitian manhood. Akin to the American usage of "guy," it can refer to Haitian men of any skin pigmentation, though it is rarely, if ever, used for foreigners. The label for them would be *blan,* from the French word for "white" (*blanc*). Even more than its counterpart, blan supersedes racial distinctions. In everyday life, when voiced by Haitians, it serves as a designation of national or communal belonging, marking any foreigner or outsider regardless of skin color. Dark-skinned Brazilian peacekeepers, my African American husband, and even Frantzy when he visited neighboring districts were hailed as blan—much to their chagrin.

Yet race or color is not irrelevant to these terms. Their current usages date to article 14 of the 1805 constitution, in which Jean-Jacques Dessalines attempted to undo the colonial color hierarchy by using nomenclatural fiat to strip whites and the often light-skinned "free people of color" (*gens de couleur*) of their racial distinction and incorporate them into the fold of the nation alongside the black, formerly enslaved residents: "Any exception of color among children of one and the same family, whose father is the head of State, must necessarily cease; Haitians shall henceforth only be known by the generic appellation 'blacks.'" The gesture was bold, but it did not erase the privileges of having light skin in a world ordered by slavery. Nor has it done so amid the extant global racial hierarchy. Today the meaning of blan enfolds notions of color, nation, class, and power. When I am hailed as a blan, I am not merely being marked as a foreigner or as a white but as someone with the influence and privileges that accompany my racial citizenship. As Mark Schuller (2009), writing of his own experiences as a white anthropologist in Haiti, put it, "no amount of acculturation or rapport building could take away the mark of privilege I carry around with me." Or as Kal once said, "*Blan vle di pouvwa*"! (*Blan* means power). Yet like Kal's own power from the margins, my status as a white/outsider functioned in ways that were often at cross-purposes with the dominant ordering of society.

Bel Air residents' first impressions of me varied dramatically. At times, I was perceived as a spy or CIA agent, someone to be met with caution and secrecy, if approached at all. Not without merit, such perceptions were rooted in a history of residents' experiences with such figures as well as their knowledge of "the anthropologist" as a favored disguise among foreign spies. Most of the time, however, I was welcomed with the enthusiasm of a sought-after friend or contact. I attribute this in large part to the culture of hospitality and mutual aid for which Haitians are famous. But I cannot deny that it also derived from the fact that I was seen as the potential source of a development project, visa, much-needed cash, or merely the sense of distinction of associating with a foreigner. This "blancophilia," as the Nigerian author Chinweizu Ibekwe (2010, 120) has sarcastically called it, lent me an ease of acquaintance with strangers unknown to most Haitians. But despite the benefits, I often resented it. With each "ask" came the reinforcement of racial hierarchies, of my enrollment in the slot of the wealthy and powerful. Over time, however, I came to understand how these "asks" were actually working with and through hierarchy. Beneath the surface of blancophilia was a certain recognition and even appropriation of my status and privilege among my interlocutors. As with *leta*, the assignation of blan interpellated me in a relation of power but also reciprocity, in a category of power that entailed duties and responsibilities. This was apparent, even though I did not fully grasp it, when I met Baz Zap Zap.

Our paths fortuitously crossed on my first bona fide research trip to Bel Air, in July 2008. Although I had been visiting Haiti since 2006, I was still unfamiliar with the city and did not yet speak Creole like a *rat*, or spy, as people wryly say of foreigners who have mastered the language. I owe much of my fortuitous entrée to the intellectual instincts and social savvy of Lizette, a psychology student who moonlighted as my all-purpose research assistant: guide, interpreter, confidant, and social coordinator. She and her circle of friends helped situate me in terms familiar and reassuring to residents: as a student with a budding social network of my own.

I vividly recall our first excursion to Bel Air together. We hopped in a *tap-tap*, or public bus, from my homestay in the middle-class area of Lalue and made the five-minute trip to city center. In the bustle of the crowd, Lizette, always quick on her feet, decided Plateau Bel Air was the place to go and led the way up the steep mountainside. I struggled under the weight of an overpacked backpack and demanded a rest when we reached the summit. We squatted on a raised rotunda planter stamped with the signature of a USAID development project. Its inaugural tree had already withered under the hot sun into a scratchy stump. A weathered man selling straw hats in the dirt bed quickly offered one as a substitute for the absent canopy. Probably attracted by my heavy accent, a crowd soon gathered. I rambled something about my interests in popular politics and the organizing activities of Carnival bands and other groups in the area. "A student, not a journalist," I recall Lizette saying, as if to fend off their potential reservations about a political inquiry. She clarified that I was an anthropology student working on a *memwa*, or thesis, and I wanted to learn more about the bands as a cultural but also a social and political phenomenon. A few of the men's eyes lit up, and we were quickly off the street and into a curbside dirt enclave. They ushered away some lounging boys and insisted we sit on a concrete bench tagged with the name and logo of Zap Zap. After a short wait, four members of the group joined us for our first conversation. I learned then about the interweavings of their musical, social, and political activities as the men readily bragged about their role in building the bench with an engineer who was involved in the last campaign for the area's *delege lavil* (urban delegate).

Manfred, the acting *oungan* (Vodou priest) for the group, a sixty-year-old man with a thin face and long braids, followed the scene with great interest, remarking a few times about how "serious" (*serye*) I was while he mimicked

FIGURE 4. View of decorated bench identifying Baz Zap Zap.

my note taking. As I prepared to leave, he circled the zone and enthusiastically boasted that I was a "good contact." "She plans to write a book about the
group!" he announced. A similarly aged man, whom I would learn was another
spiritual leader and potential rival of Manfred, chided, "CIA were known to
write books." The comment was a joke, but it stung, casting an air of suspicion
on my visit. I began to sweat as Manfred looked at me. But before I could react,
he retorted, "Yes, it's true! But she'll be *our CIA!*" Our eyes met as he continued:
"We give her our story, and she will carry it far . . . in the offices of the blan
and in the streets of the blan. Like that, she'll be become a bigger force for us.
Marenn nou! [Our godmother]."

"Oh-oh, oh-oh!" reverberated in the crowd. The sardonic astuteness of Manfred's remarks was instantly clear to all.

And I felt the weight of its message too. He was not denying the reality of
blan privilege but rather suggesting that, given the right approach and skill, such
privileges could be leveraged and put in the service of interests counter to their
customary hegemonic ends. I may have had the resources and advantages to produce a book, but I was still beholden to the cunningness of its main animators

to shape its narrative in ways that furthered their own quests for recognition, power, and respect. The remark also foreshadowed the social obligations that would ultimately commit me to the project of the book more than anything else. By welcoming me into the baz and sharing their lives with me, people in Bel Air obligated me to make good on our time together. This meant more than sharing their stories widely. In a twist of anthropological ethics, it also meant using them to achieve my professional goals. While I fretted about power imbalances, they were concerned with the practical matter of how to manipulate them. They were aware of the exploitation at stake in the anthropological project, but as they saw it, my success could be linked to their success. Here was baz politics at work: the empowerment of the group by entangling privileged outsiders in social relations of responsibility. The *CIA* becomes the godmother.

As elsewhere in the region, in Haiti the *marenn,* or godmother, is a social role reserved for the better positioned.[26] The honor often serves to incorporate and make use of the resources of another. As fate would have it for those in Bel Air, godmothers tend to be rather distant relations, whether socially, geographically, or both: the powerful neighbor, wealthy aunt uptown, cousin overseas, or foreign friend. This is not to deny the sentimental aspects of the godmother/godchild relationship. The godmother is, as people say, a kind of "second mother," a surrogate who provides for the child what or when the actual mother cannot. As the godmother for two young boys in Bel Air, I have learned that such provision is not optional. But insofar as it is an obligation, a godmother's gift of school tuition, birthday outfits, or Christmas gifts should stem from the love and care she has for the child. This is why the not-too-far, not-too-near relation is the ideal godmother. I view my fieldwork as a never-ending project in managing—by me as much by my informants—my role as a godmother.

As a *godmother*, my attachment and gifts were coded as maternal. It is significant that this is a kind of power particular to women. In Haiti, where women are seen as both the *poto mitan* (central pillars) and *dezyèm sèks* (second sex) of society, being marked as a woman served to qualify my role as a blan. I use the word *qualify* carefully. Being not just a white but a white woman shaped my fieldwork in profound ways.

Early readers of my work have often wondered how I, as a woman, gained access to the baz. For many reasons, they have assumed my sex/gender would have been an obstacle to overcome.[27] Yet I never felt that my womanhood prevented my research agenda. No doubt this had something to do with my corresponding status as a blan. Unlike nèg, blan is not a gendered category; it refers to white men and women. The androgyny of blan exposes how whiteness can overpower womanhood in Haiti, even in highly gendered arenas. Put differently, blan-ness can enable certain advantages often denied to non-blan women. For instance, I found that being a blan gave me access to and even a degree of influence in the male-dominated world of the baz—a world in which Haitian women were marginally incorporated at best or excluded at worst. Where it would be seen as sexually presumptuous to engage a Haitian woman visiting the neighborhood, baz leaders could approach me with a degree of neutered professionalism. After all, they viewed "managing the whites" (*jire blan yo*) as a natural extension of their role as the public representatives and political brokers of their zones. My status as a blan also aided the nuts and bolts of fieldwork. It freed me from some of the limitations and vulnerabilities experienced by the women I knew, granting me the freedom to circulate widely in the neighborhood, stay out late, and converse with many different men without facing repercussions for my reputation or safety. Alternatively, I found that my gender also worked to my benefit by tempering racial privilege. Being of the "second sex" undercut some of the potentially alienating or threatening aspects of my blan-ness: my elite education, my US citizenship, and my research into sensitive issues. Such was evident in the shift from CIA to *marenn*.

Of course, my race/gender did not always work in my favor. Most significantly, my status as a blan woman seemed to complicate my relations with Haitian women. Despite assumptions of gender affinities, the immediacy and ease I had befriending men in Bel Air was not replicated with local women. I attribute this, in part, to the less public sociality of many women. But I suspect it was also a consequence of my interest in a masculine phenomenon and the men who could elaborate it. This was clear in my relationship with Sophie, Kal's wife. Because we spent so much time together, Kal often referred to me as *madam mwen* (my wife). Sophie—his common-law wife—would often counter by instructing me to be careful lest she become jealous. All was said in jest; nonetheless, it was clear to me that she questioned my intentions. In response, I made a concerted effort to both demonstrate trustworthiness as I followed her husband and to express interest in her own life and views. Eventually, I became close with Sophie and a handful of other women in the zone—so close that they included me in the baz of their own, founded in 2014 (a worthy subject of another ethnography).

That July day in 2008 extended into daily visits over an eighteen-month stay in Port-au-Prince, two month-long return visits in 2010 following the earthquake, one subsequent one-month stay and two three-month stays in Bel Air proper in 2012 and 2013, and ongoing follow-up work over phone conversations, social media chats, and shorter return trips. In this time, I have come to know every street and back corridor in Bel Air, especially the hilltop zone that locates Baz Zap Zap. Here I have followed the lives of the local leaders and their political exploits, attending community events, socializing with various households, and collecting oral histories of baz members, elderly neighbors, and their kin.

Many other residents (and nonresidents) have offered insights and become collaborators in this research—other baz leaders, rara musicians, youth organizers, chatty street vendors, and resourceful wives and mothers. I became particularly close to a number of musicians I taught English in a class sponsored by an international NGO and one by a neighborhood organization. In this role, I learned much about the development activities of these organizations and affiliated baz in the area. While many of these people appear in this book, they do not figure as largely in the political narrative and neighborhood dynamics that provide the basis for my analysis.

Manfred's initiation of me into godmotherhood instilled in me an ethical commitment to long-term, if not lifetime, ethnography. Over the course of a decade, I have shared in manifold experiences in the zone, experiences both delightful and heartbreaking, intimate and public, from gatherings of family, friends, and neighbors to events that grappled with national politics and world-historical forces. We count births and funerals, state-sponsored Carnivals and public protests, street parties and cross-zone turf wars among our shared memories. Together, we felt the tremors of the 2010 earthquake and the heartache when it took so many we knew, and we have rejoiced in the collective effort to rebuild the zone from the rubble. Through these experiences, we have grown into a group bound together by a shared sense of affection and solidarity. Perhaps this is the most significant meaning of the word *baz*.

I passed nearly a year in the zone before I was greeted with the phrase that I now eagerly anticipate when I return to Haiti. As I descended from a motorbike on June 13, 2009, Kal yelled to me, "*Baz mwen! Sa k ap fèt la?*" (My baz, what's going on there?). The greeting and our simultaneous exchange of the word *respè* and a fist bump made me feel as I imagine it makes most residents feel: welcome and protected. I had found my baz: a place to call home and a network of support to navigate the contested and, at times, volatile neighborhood, nation, and world. This baz and its complex negotiations are the subject of this ethnography.

DEFENSE

The trimmed-down argument stresses the interdependence of war
making and state making and the analogy between both of those
processes and what, when less successful and smaller in scale,
we call organised crime. War makes states, I shall claim. Banditry,
piracy, gangland rivalry, policing, and war making all belong on the
same continuum—that I should argue as well.

—Charles Tilly, 1985

Ki jan ou ye? M ap goumen! (How are you? I keep fighting!)

—Popular greeting in Bel Air

In ostensibly familiar ethnographic fashion, I began this ethnography with car-
tography.[1] That map situated my field-site within the city of Port-au-Prince and
the country of Haiti. Here I turn to a different kind of map—one that captures
both the emplacement of the baz in the neighborhood and how the baz organizes
sociality and security for Bel Air residents. Drawn for me by five members of Baz
Zap Zap at the start of fieldwork in 2008, this map also serves as an artifact of
residents' initial efforts to render their neighborhood legible to me.

In a neighborhood school, on a warm November Saturday, I laid a piece of
poster board on an unsteady desk and handed out a collection of markers, which
soon ended up in the hands of Frantzy and Michel, the most formally educated
and, as such, steady of hand. Per convention, they began with a neat and tidy street
grid. But once the map was complete, they realized the rigid black-and-white
lines would not work. Part of the problem was that the majority of residents did
not dwell streetside but in the vast labyrinth of back alleys and corridors that cut
across the area's dirt hilltops. But even more problematic was that the grid did
not include the most critical geography in Bel Air. They quickly located a box on
the grid and labeled it "Baz Zap Zap." From there, they identified other significant
landmarks, including local schools, churches, and, of course, other baz. Most significantly, they marked the major crossroads adjacent to their baz with a bold red
dot, indicating it as a *cho* (hot or dangerous) area. It is there that stands L'église
de Notre Dame du Perpétual de Secours, the bullet-ridden Catholic church in

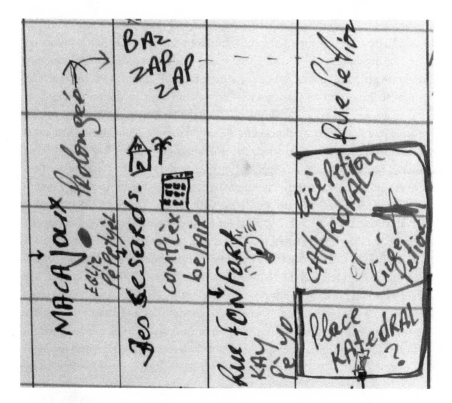

FIGURE 5. Map of Bel Air drawn by members of Baz Zap Zap.

front of which many city protests begin and where, in turn, most confrontations between residents and police and peacekeepers occur. It is also the location of the baz formation with which Baz Zap Zap is locked in competition, at times respectful, at others hostile. At this time, this rival baz, called Grand Black, was in a conflict with another nearby baz known by its Carnival group Samba the Best, which is why it was identified on the map. The dispute involved the handling of Carnival funds, and by this point, death threats had been exchanged. "There's too much ensekirite. The things have become cho. Between them, you won't hear 'my baz'!" Michel jokingly remarked when darkening the red dot. His comment underscored how the baz demarcates social affiliations and attachments against the complex of social threats known in Haiti as *ensekirite*.

A primary aim of this chapter is to make sense of the connection between that red splotch on the map and what may be called, following Pierre Bourdieu, the baz's defensive "habitus," the set of "durable, transposable dispositions, structured structures predisposed to function as structuring structures, that is, as principles that generate and organize practices and representations" (Bourdieu 1992, 53). The red dot highlights the many ways in which the baz is indicative of and in dynamic tension with ensekirite. The dot marked physical violence but also the physical burdened by the structural. The mapmakers, for example, thought it important to place a light bulb at the church, the only neighborhood space with twenty-four-hour electricity. The lone light cast the rest of the zone in a blanket of darkness and potential danger. "*Blakawout* (blackout) makes violence increase," Kal remarked, as Frantzy drew the bulb. An interesting choice of words, a blackout suggests not merely darkness but darkness where there should be light. With it, the mapmakers invoked a sense of danger tied to the physical and social obscurity of living with informal and rarely functioning electricity. Yet as much as the mapmakers framed the neighborhood as beyond city services, they also situated it at the center of city life. They identified the National Palace, Grand Rue (the city's main commercial road), Mache Tèt Bèf (the historic market), and the National Cathedral, among other landmarks. It is Bel Air's liminal position as politically central yet socially peripheral that staged the drama of the baz project. It raised the possibilities and the problems, the fortunes and frustrations of attempting to protect and advocate for the neighborhood from a marginal sociopolitical slot, a place within yet beyond the heart of the state.

The New Insecurity

In the popular US imaginary, Haiti conjures not only a very poor but also a very dangerous place. In addition to perpetual travel warnings listing the risk of theft, murder, and kidnapping of US citizens, Haiti (along with countries such as Iraq, Afghanistan, and Syria) was listed as an "imminent danger area" by the US Department of Defense until 2014. For Bel Air and other poor urban districts, the United States and Canada have special regional advisories, which strongly advise travelers to avoid them due to the prevalence of "armed gangs." In 2004–2006, Bel Air baz waged an armed resistance against the forces that ousted Jean-Bertrand Aristide from the presidency. Since Baghdad, as this period is called, the UN has designated Bel Air a "red zone."[2] The classification barred diplomatic and aid staff from entering the area unless under military escort. During my research, police and peacekeepers routinely patrolled the neighborhood and manned checkpoints surrounding its borders, allowing residents in and diverting other traffic. Such labels and barricades enforced a high degree of "inner-city apartheid" (Bourgois 1995, 32), cordoning off the neighborhood as a *zone de non-endroit* (no-go zone), a place where outsiders are afraid to enter and residents are unable to get out. Most foreigners in Haiti were bewildered at my decision to frequent the area on a daily basis, seemingly convinced that I would be robbed, kidnapped, or otherwise victimized by gangs savagely roaming the streets. Many of my middle-class Haitian friends shared their concern and have refused, for some time now, to travel farther downtown than the borderlands that mark entry into the Bel Air and Delmas 2 neighborhoods.

These perceptions stigmatized residents of these areas, while at the same time obscuring the burden of risk faced by them. The censorious North American and UN labels, in particular, overstate the risk to foreigners, especially white foreigners, who often benefit from racial and national privilege. I was reminded of this when security agents at checkpoints appeared overly concerned with my safety, instructing me to "make a quick visit" and "leave before dark." My friends in Bel Air also reminded me of the heightened level of protection I enjoyed. On my early trips to Bel Air in 2008, Berman, a late friend of Kal's, often informed me that my security was assured because most likely people assumed that I was connected to the Embassy, "the biggest baz of all!" Kal, attuned to the global media landscape, grasped my privilege in allied terms: "No one can do anything to you because if anything happened it'd be on CNN in no time!" he often joked.[3] In fact, during all the time I spent in Bel Air, walking around during the day and at night, and eventually living there for six months, I was never assaulted.[4] But this is not to say that violence was not a fact of life for Belairians. Indeed, in this same span of time, Kal's house was robbed twice, his motorbike vandalized, his estranged daughter raped, his face slashed with a razor, and his left eyelid split open from a fight. If this weren't enough, three of his good friends were killed, two in gun violence and one in the earthquake.

While the urban poor have long lived precarious lives, Kal's experience reflected an intensification of ensekirite induced by new forms of violence closely linked to baz formations.[5] Invoking US idioms, this violence is often glossed in official and lay accounts as gang violence—with crime and policy reports citing *afwontman antre gang* (gang confrontations) and *aksyon gang* (gang actions) for the muggings, carjackings, and kidnappings that have swept the country since the early 1990s.[6] The label of gang violence can mislead one into thinking that this violence is tied to criminal, rather than political, economies. For one, much of the so-called gang violence has been explicitly political. During Baghdad, rates of criminal violence skyrocketed in large part because some baz resorted to kidnapping and theft (usually targeting residents of neighboring geto) in order to acquire the weapons and ammunition they needed to wage daily battles with police and peacekeepers. Second, the economy of the baz has not revolved around the drug trade but rather the trade in political and development goods and services. The majority of baz conflicts I witnessed stemmed from disputes over access to or distribution of political funds and resources. Third, political instability and governmental neglect have provided a platform for criminal violence to flourish, affording the license (righteous cause) as well as the cover (widespread disorder) that have driven individuals to exploit and injure their neighbors in pursuit of wealth and power. "The majority of soldiers deviate from the battle," lamented a popular rap song about Baghdad; another commented on the rise of petty thievery during elections and warned, "When there's campaigning, don't leave your sneakers out to dry!" Many baz began—and still act—as brigad vijilans that protect against such broad and interconnected forms of ensekirite.

The Creole term *ensekirite* that Bel Air residents used to refer to the threat of violence in their lives identified more than an elevated crime rate. It marked an overarching sense of vulnerability. Neither entirely one's own nor entirely outside of oneself, ensekirite articulated, as the anthropologist Erica James put it, an "embodied uncertainty" (2010, 8). It reflected an epistemology of violence premised on the seamless integration of a range of threats. Insecurity could imply being under personal attack, whether waged by physical force, verbal threat, or sorcerous spell. It could also suggest the presence of impersonal, communal hazards, such as those that dwell in the environment beyond one's control, like the threat of being caught in the crossfire of another's battle or in the mayhem of a political protest when going about daily errands. Insecurity could further imply the menace of poverty. The greatest worry for Bel Air residents often stemmed from the most ordinary of exigencies: fear of a nighttime fire from rigged electrical connections, eviction from squatted housing, and the constant threat of hunger. As James, quoting a Belgian priest and social activist based in Port-au-Prince, wrote, "In Haiti, misery is a violence" (2010, 7). The phrase rang true not only because misery produced its own wounds, but also because efforts to circumvent it drove an ethos of defensive positioning and social brinkmanship that multiplied violence.

When asked what they do, baz leaders usually responded, "We defend the zone!" or "We defend our people!" As a result, a pivotal term for my analysis here is defend, or in Creole *defann*. The term *defann* comes from the French *défendre*, via the Latin roots *de*, meaning "away from," and *fend*, meaning "to strike." In Creole, as in colloquial English, notions of defense usually refer to the acts of "fighting off" or "protecting against" harmful persons, animals, or things. But, as in legal discourse, the notion of defense can also refer to the act of "coming to the aid of" an ally at risk or in danger. In phrases like "We defend the zone," baz leaders drew on both meanings of defense, asserting that they not only protected the zone *against* outside threats but also advocated *for* its needs and desires. In this sense, their defensive project was aimed at mitigating the twofold situation of insecurity represented by the red dot—that is, both social conflicts and exacting sociopolitical realities. In bringing these two dimensions together, the notion of *ensekirite*, I argue, can undo a false dichotomy between social violence and what scholars have called "structural violence," or the violence resulting from the unequal ordering of persons in society (Galtung 1969; Farmer 1996, 2004). In particular, ensekirite, with its multivalent connotations, can provide a rich analytical tool for exploring how multiple forms, scales, and temporalities of violence intertwine in the production of vulnerability. By speaking of ensekirite, I aim to show how acts of violence spiral into each other in ways that resist categorical, scalar, or temporal partition.[7] Baz leaders saw themselves as simultaneously defending against an ensekirite that was physical and structural, interpersonal and societal, and episodic and durational. In what follows, I show the inventive and often productive strategies used by the baz to defend against manifold threats. However, I also show how their efforts to defend the zone propagated new vulnerabilities. What was often not captured in leaders' claims to defend the zone, but readily apparent in their actual attempts to do so, was how their efforts to protect against threats or advocate for much-needed resources all too often incited rivalries and conflicts that put themselves and their neighbors at risk—as I trace in the following snapshot of a day in Bel Air that was cross-cut by multiple and entwining vectors of ensekirite.

Defense I: A Day against the World

In December 2012, I began a monthlong stay in the two-room shack where Kal, his wife, Sophie, and their teenage daughter have squatted since the earthquake in 2010. Kal was born in 1980 in a Bel Air house rented by his mother, a seamstress, and father, a low-ranking soldier in the Haitian army. But, at thirteen, after his mother died of tuberculosis, his father left the area, and he began staying at a friend's house. Handsome, musically inclined, and politically connected, he was able to overcome his meager financial situation and court several women. In 1998, at age eighteen, he had two women pregnant at the same time, ultimately committing to Sophie because she was, in his words, a "good woman" (*bon fi*), and because she took him into the house she shared with her sister. Ever since I met Kal in 2008, his goal was to have a job and his own house. With this, he said, he could "*fè* (become) *the man*." In 2010, at age thirty, Kal achieved the second half of this goal by capitalizing on the destruction of the earthquake.

He built his house on a sliver of land left unoccupied after a family, whose house collapsed in the tremors, left for the Dominican Republic. Using plywood, tarps, and Styrofoam, which the baz leader Yves had attained as a result of his engagement with the government's postearthquake relocation committee, Kal constructed a two-room shack on the salvaged concrete platform. A six-by-six-foot front room served as a kitchen, bathing area, and nightly motorbike garage. We all slept in the slightly larger backroom, with Kal and Sophie on the concrete floor and their daughter, Laloz, and me treated to a lumpy mattress stacked atop clothes and other belongings. A small freezer, defunct television, and wooden hutch consumed the space, and Sophie had to stack the items to make room to sleep. Each night, she removed from atop the hutch an impressive collection of trinkets and baubles, from Precious Moments porcelain angels to plastic Arthur and Mickey Mouse dolls to faux flowers; and each morning, she carefully rearranged them. "You can live in a little house," she often remarked as she performed the ritual, "but that doesn't mean you can't make it nice."

Despite her efforts, Sophie could not stop a myriad of hazards from impinging on her quaint living quarters. Most urgently, a spate of armed robberies had targeted the young men who make small change ferrying people around on their motorbikes in the city. The thefts of cell phones, cash, and motorbikes were largely blamed on a new group of youthful bandits known as Baz 117 and based in the Delmas 2 area adjacent to Bel Air. As a safety measure, some moto-chauffeurs, including Kal, limited their routes, and others stopped working altogether. This diminished their livelihood but did little to remove the threat, as Baz 117 had taken to exploiting the new routes as well as mounting the zone to steal the motorbikes. When I arrived that December, the first news I heard from Kal was about the *ti kouri* (little runs) Baz 117 was causing—moments of panic when a sighting or rumor of an approaching bandit caused people to scurry from the streets and take cover in their rickety houses. The panics were happening so often that the food vendors who usually crowded the streets now packed up at dusk, leaving them without essential earnings. Most residents, who were dependent on street food, went to sleep hungry.

It took only a few days before Kal and I came face-to-face with Baz 117. On his way to pick me up from a meeting in Delmas 2, two teenagers, one wielding a handgun, forced Kal's motorbike and all other traffic to a stop at a busy intersection. Observing the action from the doorway of a corner store, I watched as the teenagers approached a local couple in a rundown S.U.V. and demanded their cash and cell phones. The action unfolded rather seamlessly, and with the goods in their hands, I expected the young men to run off, and Kal and I to get on with our day. Instead they turned to Kal.

"Start the moto!" they yelled.

Kal started to climb off his motorbike but stopped when the teenagers began to climb on.

"*Ale!*" they yelled—*Go!*

When Kal returned to pick me up on the corner, he stared blankly and said nothing. But when we returned to his house, he launched into a tirade, explaining, amid huffs and puffs, that the bandits made him take them to their safe house in Delmas 2. He had refused the money they offered for his service, hoping this would untangle him from the theft. But he now worried that it was taken as a sign of contempt, especially given an earlier incident. Months earlier, Kal had approached a 117 affiliate in the street and punched him because he was part of a group that had recently raped his estranged daughter. Fearing retribution, Kal called on a few friends to revive the MOG brigad vijilans. The brigade erected makeshift barriers to block the corridors leading to the zone. They also formed a nightly patrol armed with two handguns. Contributions from Kal and other neighbors financed the operation. In addition to Baz MOG, the peacekeeping mission MINUSTAH also increased its patrols of the area.

One evening, about a week after the run-in with Baz 117, as Sophie and I brushed our teeth curbside, a few Brazilian peacekeepers passed by and asked out loud, "*Isi, no bandi?*" (Here, no bandits?), to which Sophie perfunctorily replied, "*Non.*"

"What am I going to say?" she chided as they left. "Oh, down there in Delmas 2. And then they come after me!"

Her admonishment raised not only the futility of the patrols but also the fear of being locked in a rivalry with Baz 117—a worry that resurfaced that evening. Not long after we were sound asleep in Kal's house, loud bangs against the tin door jostled us awake. Kal immediately grabbed a cement block and moved toward the door. Sophie seemed to apprehend the threat immediately.

She whispered, "117, they've come for the moto!"

This was plausible, but another fear popped into my mind. Earlier that day Kal had told me about how the owner of the land where he squatted had threatened to reclaim the plot. Kal responded by telling the landlord's cousin, who lived in the area, that he was "a Bel Air man with a baz that would turn chimè on him if [the landowner] tried to do anything to him." "'*Kal* does not mean calm!' I had them understand," he explained.

Kal translates as "calm," but, like many nicknames in Haiti, its meaning was other than it appeared—highlighting less his everyday steady demeanor than the temper that threatened to erupt at any moment.[8] Kal had also secured permission to use one of MOG's two handguns if confronted by the landlord. Though the weapon was not kept in his house and unlikely to assist him in the event of a raid, certainly not one in the middle of the night, he made his access to it known throughout the zone. "I don't want to touch a weapon, but people must know I have soldiers; like that, they give you more respè," he proclaimed as he paced back-and-forth in the intersection. The assertion was questionable, with Adam, an elderly man who the local rum and tobacco shop, countering, "What are you doing there? Talking tough like that? You'll invite disorder!" As the knocks grew louder, my suspicion rose that Kal's fearsome signals did not have their intended effect.

We were relieved when we heard the voice on the other end of the door. It turned out to be one of Kal's baz mates in need of a place to crash after a nasty fight with his girlfriend over funds earned from a recent baz project and earmarked for their daughter's school tuition, but which he had squandered in a dominoes match.

In the morning, my nerves were still on edge as I drank a cup of coffee outside Kal's house. I tried to follow the conversation at Kay Adam—the name for Adam's house and shop. Sipping homemade rum, three elderly men and one woman debated the character of a local politician by questioning whether he was the kind of person who would give someone a fruit picked from a tree or one that had already fallen to the ground. Joining the debate was a steady stream of young dreadlocked men who bought rolling papers from Adam and then a small amount of marijuana from Kal's baz mate Bernie, who ran an art gallery that doubled as a marijuana dispensary. "On the ground does not mean bad," one proclaimed to Bernie. Another young man seconded with a proverb: "A little does not mean cheap." Bernie shook his head, as if they had missed the point. He retorted: "Spoiled fruit is as strong as poison. The question is not what he gives but do you take it? First protect yourself!"

The comment brought me back to the night before, and I began to wonder about the multiple ways people protected themselves from the dangers in their lives. Between sales, Bernie, for example, was carving a potent sign into a nearly leafless tree next to his art gallery. He chiseled a snake coiled around the trunk in honor of Danbala, the venerable Vodou spirit who models perseverance despite formidable odds. "Like a snake, which can survive in even the hottest and most arid environments," as the Vodou scholar Karen McCarthy Brown wrote, "Danbala also models the persistent will to live that will not surrender to an inhospitable environment" (1991, 274)." So perhaps did the tree. In the sequin flags Bernie made (but rarely sold) in his gallery, both Danbala and a withered yet living tree were recurrent motifs. Recently, Bernie had also endured a couple of scares: one with a belligerent customer in need of credit and another with a relative attempting to reclaim the land where he lived. The arboreal engraving appeared to testify to Bernie's defiant spirit and his willingness to defend himself against formidable odds. The message was not lost on neighbors. Sophie, who shared coffee with me, eyed the carving suspiciously. She called to her friend Nadine across the street, in a voice loud enough for Bernie (and everyone else) to hear, "I hope no one will be working with *Maji* (magic) by my house." Bernie quickly reminded Sophie that he only "served *Ginen* and did not work with *Maji*"—rehearsing a common refrain for distinguishing benevolent, defensive spiritual work (*Ginen*) from offensive, malevolent sorcery (*Maji*).[9]

Soon afterward, our attentions shifted. Paul, the thirty-something aspiring politician whose character the folks at Kay Adam were debating, arrived. Paul was hoping to mobilize his local clout to become the district's deputy in Haiti's parliament. Paul was the brother of Ti Snap, the leader of Baz Grand Black. The chief baz in Bel Air, Grand Black maintained its ascendant status in the zone in part by enforcing a protection racket on the organizing activities of other baz in the area, especially their neighbors and rivals down the street. Paul had appeared in the zone that day to request a portion of the payment that the Organization of Moral Youth for the Enrichment of Bel Air (OJMOTEEB)—a youth development organization run by MOG members—had received from a senatorial candidate to host an HIV awareness seminar. Paul usually made such calls in a white jeep he used for his security job at the Ministère de la Justice et de la Sécurité Publique, but today he was on foot, taking the route of the dirt corridor that weaves through the hillside shacks lining the street. When he emerged from the hidden passageway, the young men seated curbside immediately took note and began greeting him with nods, fist bumps, and utterances of respè. I likewise rose from my seat, and Paul quickly greeted me—with a more gentlemanly kiss on the cheek. He then clapped twice. As if on cue, Kal, Bernie, and two other baz members called him into the gallery. After a short but boisterous discussion, they emerged, and to mark the successful negotiation, Sophie began distributing the pumpkin soup she had prepared for lunch.

The rest of the day easily slid into the slow and sluggish rhythm of life common to Bel Air. In the late afternoon, a handful of baz mates and I gathered under the canopy of the corner's most verdant tree and tracked passersby venturing around the corner. Jak and Kal were awaiting the opportunity to chauffeur a neighbor on their motorbikes, and Sophie and her best friend Nadine, skilled hair stylists, were awaiting friends looking to have their hair braided. When it was clear we would all be there for a while, I asked about the events earlier that day. It must have struck my interlocutors as excessively ignorant, and, truth be told, I was playing dumb in the hopes of gaining some clarification: "Why did Paul come to the zone today?" I asked.

"He came to get his cash," Jak responded. "Because we're doing an activity, we have to pay the chèf of the zone, so they don't do anything against us."

"That's how it is?" I asked.

"It's how it is," Nadine clarified. "The *machann* (market women) who makes the coffee has to pay, and to do development, the men must pay as well. It is not supposed to be like that. That can make them upset, but that's how it is."

"That's not the same thing," Jak responded. "We provide a service! Look, what's happening to the machann in Delmas 2!" he said, taking on a righteous tone. "They take, but they don't give."

He was implying that Baz Zap Zap worked to protect the local cooperative of female vendors from Baz 117, rather than exploit them for the group's economic gain. Nadine seemed unconvinced and looked away. The claim threatened to instigate an argument, but Kal soon interjected with a closing point. "*Se mizè ki fè nèg rayi nèg*" (It's misery that makes nèg hate nèg).

The curt phrase left a wake of silence.

"What does that mean?" I eventually asked.

"I don't want those who don't know the geto to see the youth in the geto as just criminals, as mean people," he began.

"They go into bad things because they do not find another way to make their life. There's no work. There's no activity. So they search to find something. That's a normal thing. For that to change, we need the state to make a real development, that which brings jobs for all the people, not just a small group of leaders! But right now, each group does its own little project. Some walk straight, others not straight, but in any case, the country cannot develop correctly. It's one against the other. Like we say, 'It's misery that makes nèg hate nèg.'"

"That means poor people engage in crimes because they are poor?" I asked, expecting this to be the end of our conversation.

But Kal surprised me: "No, it's not everyone who is in misery that does crimes. I can even say most don't. But it is misery that can make a young man look for respè in all places and find it in carrying weapons, doing crimes, all sorts of things. People are always saying, "Ever since *Ginen* (Africa), nèg have hated nèg but that does not mean forever, since people existed. No, that means ever since slavery. That's what we say here because that is misery itself, and that is what makes the little nèg hate the little nèg, because everyone wants to be chèf after that. They go crazy to be chèf. They have *foli chèf* [obsession with chiefdom]. They want to be chèf of the biggest baz, but there's no chèf that likes another chèf, and, I tell you, no chèf without people on the bottom. But like that even the leader remains in misery; he can be broke too. The chèf is in misery too. He'll ask to borrow money too. You know why Paul needed the money today. Because he has no gas in his car! He tries to make the state but he has no gas! Misery only! That's right! . . . And ensekirite all the time. He never escapes from that, because on top of the chèf is always a bigger chèf, and on bottom, there are a lot of little ones that want to be big."

The Structuration of Ensekirite

In the late 1960s, Johan Galtung, a Norwegian peace activist and critic of US Cold War policies toward socialist states, coined the term "structural violence" to refer to the harmful effects of the uneven distribution of wealth and resources in society. He used the term to capture the physical and psychological tolls endured by those on the wrong side of a social structure characterized by steep inequality. According to him, structural violence, like interpersonal violence, concerns matters of life and death; but unlike interpersonal violence, structural violence lacks a definite social agent and target, as well as an observable sequence of events enacted between them. It is, Galtung wrote, the kind of violence "built into the structure that shows up as unequal power and consequently as unequal life chances" (1969, 171). The concept has proven immensely useful for theorizing the suffering and disadvantage caused by neoliberal capitalism, xenophobia, racism, misogyny, and heteronormativity, among other systems of inequality.[10] But while diversifying what qualifies as violence, the concept as originally conceived can fall short of explaining the interrelationships between different kinds of violence. Addressing this limitation, Paul Farmer, the medical anthropologist whose writings about Haiti popularized the concept, has argued that structural violence must be seen as not only coeval with but also generative of "episodic" forms of violence (2003, 350). In his reports from Haiti in the fall of 2002, for example, he showed how violence exhibited an autopoietic drive, with one form of violence giving birth to another: a political crisis had yielded hikes in taxi fares, which yielded political protests, which drove "gang wars" over control of the protests (Farmer 2003, 351).

In many ways, it was this spiralistic fallout of structural violence that Kal invoked when he said, "Misery makes nèg hate nèg." These words were far from his own expression; they constituted the most common reply to my inquiries about the causes of ensekirite. Repeated by residents, politicians, and aid workers alike, the axiomatic claim offered a general critique of poverty and unemployment by underscoring how conditions of scarcity necessitated illegal or illicit tactics of survival. On this occasion, however, Kal complicated this economically essentialist reading. His correction of my perfunctory interpretation that everyone in misery turns to crime alluded to the stigmatization that can occur when structural violence is seen to predetermine deviance among the poor. As other observers of ensekirite in urban Haiti have claimed, invocations of structural violence can echo culture-of-poverty theory when they explain malicious social acts as directly caused by individuals' class positions. Erica James (2010, 51–52), for example, suggests, "violence cannot be regarded solely as the product of social structures of inequality or brutal cultures of poverty," since in "many cases of political conflict few members of a population may resort to physical or direct violence."[11] Still, it is important not to minimize the limited and precarious routes available to those who make their lives from less privileged structural locations.

One way around this analytical impasse—which, after all, rehashes age-old structure/agency debates—is to focus on how the urban poor's defensive maneuverings against their structural conditions can unwittingly become a source of their own vulnerability. Kal and others were engaged in a continual effort to cast themselves in an elaborate scenario of defense: to present themselves as prepared in sentiment; positioned in relations; empowered through spiritual, corporeal, and technological force; and equipped with plausible scripts for militant action. But this defensive habitus could reset the relations of competition and conflict even as it provided a degree of protection against immediate threats to life and personhood.

To judge from commentary surrounding the events on that typical December day, Kal had engaged in four cardinal acts of disrespect that open one up to counterattack: disparaging, threatening, attacking, and exploiting another. By his own account, he had undermined the authority of another group when he refused to accept their token of appreciation. Second, as Adam asserted, Kal had threatened others by boasting of his reputation as a "Bel Air man" that could "go chimè." Third, he signaled an attack by employing Baz MOG and displaying a command of spiritual power, access to weapons, and loyal soldiers. Finally, he participated in baz activities that accumulated wealth at the expense of others, owing a debt to Baz Grand Black and, as Nadine reminded him, effecting a protection racket over his area's street vendors. In witnessing this feedback loop of ensekirite, I was reminded of how Philippe Bourgois, drawing on Primo Levi, described street violence as a moral "gray zone," a place where victims befall villains, as "the oppositional street culture of resistance to exploitation and social marginalization" becomes "contradictorily self-destructive to its participants" (2002, 303). Kal's ensuing elaboration of why I was wrong, in fact, directly grappled with this tragic irony, offering insight into how baz members' struggles for a life beyond misery can often, if not inexcorably, perpetuate a pattern of social antagonism and conflict.

To make his point, Kal compared the saying "Misery makes nèg hate nèg" to the age-old Haitian proverb, "Ever since Ginen, nèg have hated nèg." Typically, this proverb is used to assert that social antagonism has always existed and is, therefore, inevitable.[12] But as Kal emphasized, it is possible to interpret Ginen, which indicates Africa more broadly, not as generic human history but the specific history of slavery, and to further qualify *slavery* as the paradigm for *misery*. There are two key theoretical points worth stressing about this revision. The first is that social rivalry can be seen as the outgrowth of the historically specific oppression of slavery and its legacy—an oppression more complex than economic deprivation. Indeed, the term *mizè* (misery) in Haiti invokes not merely poverty but a life world premised on social exclusion, everyday suffering, and emotional despair. An index of holistic oppression, the condition of misery identifies a structural slot that is, to invoke Pierre Bourdieu, structured and structuring of an agonistic habitus. The second point, then, is that agonism is constructed as not as a fact of life but as the consequence of maneuvering from a marginal position within the social structure. The defensive habitus was not inevitable but it was patterned: while the product of social structuration and, therefore, open to transformation, the habitus also structures—or, as Paul Farmer (2004, 315) put it, *strictures*—perceptions and practices that conditioned the possibility and potential for transformation.[13] Insofar as misery primed people for aggressive claims for income, power, and status, it also rendered them vulnerable to attacks from others whom they subjugated or further immiserated in pursuit of their claims. The result was the paradoxical category of a "chèf in misery," where baz leaders were caught between strivings to overcome misery and their reproduction of the groundwork—the unequal relations—that enabled it. The autopoietic logic linking misery to violence configured less a fixed cycle of causality than a complex, open-ended coil of accumulation.[14] The chèf entangled in the misery of the geto—where he remained embroiled in financial and social insecurity, far from a stable, predictable livelihood, and facing threats from above and below—did not invoke a linear trajectory from one form of violence to another or one scale of violence to another. Rather, it echoed what the Haitian artist and author Frankétienne, among others, has theorized as the "spiralist" dimension of life in Haiti, the self-inverting and unruly trajectories of insecurity, where one trauma enfolds into the next in ways that defy uniformity but nonetheless attest to repetition.[15] What Kal ultimately recognized through the revised proverb was the contradictory outcomes that accompanied the baz's defensive ethos, the ways in which configuring a reputation for violence had the potential to enable quests for empowerment at the same time that it propelled a tailspin of power plays and conflicts.

These dueling outcomes were made even more explicit when baz leaders shifted from the first to the second axis of defense, when they moved beyond reacting to outside threats toward proactively addressing the structural forms of vulnerability that accompanied life at the margins of the city.

Defense II: The Bends of Street Advocacy

When baz leaders claimed to "defend the zone," they also referenced their "state-making" project to represent and advocate for the zone, or to fè leta. Their notion of fè leta stood in opposition to the unethical domain of fè politik (doing politics), mimicking, in some ways, the moral division between Ginen and Maji. On the surface, to do politics meant to engage with or as a politician. But this usually conjured the more sinister and violent act of politicking—that of taking part in a violent competition for personal wealth and power at the expense of the people. To make the state, in contrast, suggested the altruistic act of governing. A communal endeavor, it implied providing state services for the benefit of the people. Yet insofar as the assertion of fè leta reflected a moral claim, it was one more aspirational than actionable. Baz leaders were the first to admit that making the state entailed doing some politics. Contacting and making claims on politicians entailed jockeying for position and power in the neighborhood and in the larger political field, and it meant exercising control over limited political resources. In this way, to make the state and to do politics were mutually constituted, and the baz, like the government, embodied a site of power that had the makings of a *marenn* (godmother) as much as an *agresè* (bully), to use local parlance.[16] Indeed, many formal politicians perceived the baz as unfit for civil society or liberal democracy because of the way in which baz politics led to turf wars between zones and violent affronts between political parties. That said, it is not that baz leaders were unskilled or unsavvy politicians. To the contrary, they were quite successful at using their political clout, connections, and reputation to advocate for the zone. The problem was rather that they were limited in their abilities to make lasting or far-reaching improvements given the precarity afforded by their base structural position.

In the summer of 2014, I returned to Kal's residence in Bel Air for another monthlong stay. On arrival, I was thrust into the thick of an unfolding political drama. A parliamentary election, postponed for over two years, was scheduled for the fall, and campaigns for the 2015 presidential election were heating up. Shortly after I arrived, Kal, ever the host, ran out to get some ice for the Coca-Cola he had been saving for my arrival. Laloz and I immediately began sharing our respective news. Nicknamed for the fun-filled dance style that was popular in her youth, Laloz had passed her final exams and was promoted to the eleventh grade. I congratulated her, and she asked after my niece and nephew. As I showed her their recent pictures, Kal's telephone rang. In the rush, he had left without it. I would have let it ring, but Laloz—my strictest language instructor, who regularly forced me to speak in challenging situations—insisted I answer it. I was stunned to find on the other end Maryse Narcisse, the coordinator of Aristide's political party and a candidate for president. Unfazed by the strange, accented voice, she simply asked that I have Kal call her back. "There are some important mobilizations coming up," she told me. After hanging up, I immediately went to tell Sophie, who was doing laundry in the street. "You speak too loudly," she said matter-of-factly. And then in a softer voice and with a wry smile, "You see how Kal is a *gran nèg* (big man). He *fè politik* . . . too much! And what does it bring? Heads together? No! Even a good job? No! Disorder, only disorder!"

Sophie's words provided the perfect commentary for the surrounding cityscape. The outside of Kal's home was covered in Fanmi Lavalas posters of Aristide and Maryse Narcisse. Flags supporting Jean-Henry Céant, another presidential candidate, hung from twine that stretched from the street to the corridor where Frantzy lived. Posters for presidential hopeful Jean Celestin dotted the outside of Bernie's gallery. And in the distance, I spotted a banner for Moïse Jean Charles, yet another candidate, hanging above the street leading to Grand Black's territory. For the most part, Fanmi Lavalas maintained a privileged negotiating position in Bel Air and with Baz Zap Zap in particular. But at this early stage of the election, Kal and others were more interested in establishing contact with whoever wished to campaign in the area. It was to their benefit to act as the zone's political gatekeepers, able to negotiate multiple candidates' access to the zone's populous and impassioned electorate in exchange for political favors. Yet to Sophie, it was already clear that the pull of opposing candidates had the potential to stoke divisions within the group as well as with other zones. Through the networked and overlapping collectivities of the baz, baz mates practiced a politics of contact and connection, rivalry and division, continually remaking unity amid factions, factions amid unity, as people vied for influence among and beyond their peers. These spiralistic dialectics of connection and competition were put on bold display during the election period I witnessed.

As I was resettling into Bel Air, another outsider was attempting to gain access for the first time. Daniel Belcourt—a middle-aged, cherubic man with a short, broad build, plump face, and sympathetic eyes—sought to strengthen his pursuit for a senate seat by securing contact with Baz Zap Zap and, in turn, a foothold in the neighborhood. Monsieur Belcourt, as he was respectfully called, worked most of his life as a teacher at a private school in Port-au-Prince. He had recently spent a few years in Brooklyn as a taxi driver, before returning to Haiti to launch his political career. He had encountered the Zap Zap rara one evening in June, while they performed at a restaurant in his middle-class neighborhood of Lalue. Soon after, Kal and Yves arranged a meeting with the candidate at his house. Kal requested that I accompany him to the meeting. He hoped that I, as blan, would counter common prejudices of the group as bandits and provide them with more legitimacy in their dealings. "Those people are afraid of Bel Air men, but as soon as they see you, they'll be at ease, and give us more respect" he told me nonchalantly. On a hot summer afternoon, Kal, Jak, three other baz members, one of their girlfriends, and I climbed onto the back of three motorbikes and made the seven-minute trek to the candidate's house.

Monsieur Belcourt was not a rich man, and his modest house reflected that. But as he ushered us onto his plant-filled patio and offered us drinks, the distance that separated the Bel Air residents from their middle-class compatriot was palpable. Dressed in street fashions of loose-fitting jeans, bejeweled t-shirts, and wide-brimmed caps, the baz members took their seats next to Monsieur Belcourt, dressed in his khaki slacks, a linen button-down shirt, and fedora. Hesitant to speak first, the Belairians hastily downed bottles of Cola Couronne.

"*Bon!*" Monsieur Belcourt began, breaking the silence with a pleasant, upbeat tone, "I'll tell you about my program." He spoke of broad goals for education and jobs but not did offer specifics on platform or his stance on recent political scandals. And because he was probably aware of Zap Zap's alliances with Aristide, he mentioned that he was a "child of Lavalas" but did not offer any party affiliation. One of his aides, a former student of his who was visiting Haiti from Miami, told the group he wanted to build a professional school in Bel Air that resembled the one he attended in the United States. The young men listened attentively, but when he finished they were silent. After a long pause, Kal said he'd help with the campaign because he "believed in education," but that he was tired of "candidates making promises to the zone and then not delivering." He then told Monsieur Belcourt that it would mean a lot if he came to the baz locale. "You have to understand the situation before you can offer a solution," he said. Monsieur Belcourt, leery of making the journey, told us he had another meeting. But Kal persisted, telling him it was a short trip and he would protect him. "*Ou p ap gen anyen!*" he kept repeating. (Nothing will happen to you.) Eventually, Monsieur Belcourt agreed, and he and his aides climbed into his pickup truck and followed the motorbikes back to Bel Air.

FIGURE 6.   Meeting of baz members with senatorial candidate in the courtyard of his house.

When we arrived in the zone, Kal asked Bernie to gather people in the Ton Malè—a temple that had been built in the wake of 117 to ward off ill will and harm as well as provide a pleasant seating area for neighbors to gather. Joining the symbolic scheme of the group's defensive project, the temple signaled its emplacement in the community and its influence over surrounding force fields, both social and spiritual. We gathered under its palm fronds in a ring of chairs surrounding the *poto mitan*, the central pillar of all Vodou temples through which the spirits travel to reach their human servants. Hung on this *poto mitan* was the spirit Bawon Samdi, the presider of the dead. At the spirit's feet were several *tèt mò*, or skulls that Rémy, the oungan of the temple, used to fashion protective charms for the rara band, chanpwèl, and others in need of curative powers. Rémy was, however, also aware of the menacing signal the temple sent to outsiders, especially potential criminals or political rivals. Aware of the dramatic display, he once told me: "Some of the skulls are from people we didn't even know. For the magic to work, you have to know their names. But the outsiders who see this ... they don't know the difference!" As Monsieur Belcourt took his seat, a soft chant about being "*mèt kalfou, mèt beton*" (masters of the crossroads, masters of the concrete) rippled through the crowd, interlocking Mèt Kalfou, the spirit of crossroads, with the urban zone. Monsieur Belcourt appeared struck by the mystical symbolism, and now it was his turn to cautiously take his seat, which he did near the temple's entrance.

Once settled, the conversation picked up where it left off, with Monsieur Belcourt repeating his general, noncontroversial political agenda, before floating the idea of a professional school. Frantzy, who introduced himself as "president of OJREB, who does development in the zone," dismissed the plans for the school. "I see you have not spent time in the zone," he scoffed. "We have had a professional school since Jean-Claude [Duvalier], and we have several training programs. The problem is they are all for women because that is what NGOs do. What we need is a program for young men. The guys only have two activities around here: do politics or motorbike-taxi, and both are not good!"

The few women present (including me) grimaced at the suggestion that aid economies exclude men, which was a common perception that reflected unemployed men's frustrations with a rise in women-centered projects among NGOs but failed to account for baz leaders' control over local development economies.[17]

Perhaps sensing this, Frantzy asserted that he could not speak for everyone, and he asked for all present to offer their opinion on the major problem in the zone. About twenty-five residents, speaking in steady succession, offered their

FIGURE 7. The Ton Malè at Plateau Bel Air where baz members relax, socialize, and hold meetings.

opinions. A few people demanded a police station, but most complained about electricity. The closest electrical transformer had exploded a few weeks before, burning two houses to the ground and sending the zone into perpetual blackout. With nearly all households tapped into the electrical lines illegally, transformers were often overwhelmed. In lieu of electricity, residents used kerosene lamps and candles, known fire hazards. Carl, another baz member, boldly made his case for a new transformer. He nudged toward Mr. Belcourt his eight-year-old daughter whose face had been irreparably scarred when, as a toddler, a candle tipped over and sent her bed sheet up in flames. Another advocate for the transformer was Blan Kouran. Nicknamed for his light complexion (*blan*) and facility with electrical currents (*kouran*), Blan Kouran rigged and maintained residents' informal electrical connections for a small but nonetheless burdensome fee. For those not incorporated into baz networks, the fee far exceeded that which residents in middle-class neighborhoods serviced by the public utility paid for electricity.

Once everyone had offered their ideas (including me, who joined the consensus), Monsieur Belcourt agreed that he would help restore electricity by acquiring and installing a new transformer. In exchange, Yves and Kal would arrange a local press conference announcing the group's support of him and compile two hundred ID numbers to deliver as votes in the election.

Many residents expressed their gratitude to Monsieur Belcourt, but it was clear that several core baz members were not satisfied. Kal, as if to excuse the discouraged expressions of his friends, explained to Monsieur Belcourt that the problem was that a new transformer was only a provisional solution and a subpar one at that. Kal explained to Monsieur Belcourt that the problem was that the transformer was only an *ed pèpè*, an aid that was junky, flimsy garbage—like the imported, secondhand clothes resold in Haiti and called *pèpè*. He explained that in no time the transformer would be scarred with burn marks, function only sporadically, and devolve into a source of fires. Jak, taking the cue from Kal, said that what the group really wanted was for the state to install electrical meters in households, connect the zone to the electrical grid, and to employ five baz mates at the state electrical company to administer payment. "This is better," he said, "because it would make the state appear in the zone. It would give us a social service and also more security for the zone." But Monsieur Belcourt's aide insisted this was the only option, as he would secure this transformer through an Inter-American Development Bank (IADB) program that directed funds not toward large-scale, public infrastructure (such as metered electricity for the city) but rather toward community-based, micro-projects in slum areas. "Unfortunately," the aide lamented, "development thinks small for small countries like Haiti."

A week later, after the IADB had contracted with OJREB as a "community partner," Monsieur Belcourt returned to the zone with an engineer from an upper-class

FIGURE 8. The meeting with the senatorial candidate in the Ton Malè.

family and an employee from the electrical company. While the engineer talked with the baz about a possible USAID-sponsored canal construction project, the electrician installed a new transformer, to which Blan Kouran immediately began reconnecting hundreds of households. Monsieur Belcourt had me take a photo of him and his aide, with several of the young men involved in the negotiation, toasting the electrical power with swigs of rum from Kay Adam. Later that evening, the baz hosted a celebratory street party with a D.J. sponsored jointly by Yves and Monsieur Belcourt. Hip-hop rhythms filled the air with an unmistakable good feeling, and Kal, clad in a dragon-emblazoned polo shirt, matching long cargo shorts, and shined Adidas high tops, overlooked the scene with proud contentment. However, even with the new transformer, electricity was only present for the few hours a day that the public utility switched it on. Unable to count on the state electrical company sourcing the zone, the party relied on a generator to power the sound system.

Well past midnight, Kal and I retired to his house. As if to mark the successful day, the electricity turned on as he collapsed in exhaustion next to Sophie on the concrete floor. Taking advantage of the light, I grabbed my notebook to record the day's events. After a moment of reflection (and noticing my note taking), Kal told me he had something to say. "If we manage this election well, we can bring some benefits to the zone," he began.

"I'll give Monsieur Belcourt a few votes, because he did something for the zone. That's a little democracy. But if he would commit to making us state employees, we could do a lot more for him. Like that, we could become partners, each with his own domain but working together to make the state present in the zone. I can even be a city delegate. That's real democracy. That's what I had to say."

With this statement, Kal anticipated the disappointment he would feel as the transformer shifted from resolving insecurity to instigating it. In the week that followed the installation, two members of OJREB that partnered with IADB got into a fist fight over the money distributed to residents who helped install the transformer. One of the concerned ended up with a slashed cheek. Around the same time, Blan Kouran kicked in his neighbor's front door and threatened him at gunpoint after he refused to pay for the new electrical connection. Not usually armed, Blan Kouran had been storing MOG's two handguns and, as residents anticipated, put them to use to enforce his business. Soon after the confrontation, a small but influential group of elderly neighbors led by Adam organized to confront Blan Kouran. In the midst of the confrontation, Adam sliced open Blan Komen's wrist with a machete. Later that evening, Blan Kouran returned to Kay Adam and demanded Adam's earnings from the day. Adam refused, and Blan Kouran threatened to return with the weapon. Fortunately, he never got the chance. The following day, Yves, in an attempt to calm the mounting tensions, exiled Blan Kouran from the zone for a month. He took up residence less than two intersections away, at a new baz recently founded by two men deported from the United States.

Over the weeks that followed, as I passed Blan Kouran on my way to Baz Zap Zap, I could not help but notice that his weight was rapidly declining. When I asked around about this, most residents figured it was Adam's sorcerous revenge, especially since Adam had recently visited his native Kentscoff, a rural area above the city, where he served the spirits. But to me, Blan Kouran's declining health seemed more likely to be due to the loss of his makeshift job and social safety net, which forced him to go without meals and adequate shelter. Immiserated, Blan Kouran largely stayed away from the zone, although he did venture back one night to tear down the political posters affixed to Kal's house and the electoral wires powering a large swath of the area.

In many ways, the new transformer was a feat that highlighted Kal's and others' command over baz politics and their ability to make it work for them. A handful of leaders outperformed other baz for a political contact, secured a degree of neighborhood consensus, demonstrated this consensus at meetings and celebrations, and mobilized baz members to hold politicians accountable and fulfill political promises to them. Yet their politicking also laid bare how baz leaders' attempts to assert power and make political claims stoked divisions at worst and provisional solutions at best. Insofar as baz leaders reinforced their role as political brokers for the urban poor, they also assumed the burden of governance—both the responsibility for it and conflicts over it, which they were not adequately prepared to handle. Without the authority, salary, and protections of state employees, Blan Kouran was put in a position where he extorted neighbors by force and faced their anger as a result. And while the alliances with multiple politicians enabled a steady stream of income-generating political activities, they also exposed baz leaders to the threat of violence from political factionalism. This became even clearer on Election Day.

I returned to Bel Air the subsequent summer to follow another round of parliamentary elections. Though still functioning, the transformer appeared on its last leg, with two charcoal-gray stains on its white drum evincing chronic overstress. The night before the election, on August 8, 2015, Monsieur Belcourt visited the baz again. At this point, Kal had committed to supporting Fanmi Lavalas candidates, but he was still willing to offer tepid support for his other political contacts. When Monsieur Belcourt appeared, Kal ushered him and one of his aides into the house, where Laloz and I were taking shelter from a light rain outside. After greeting the candidate, Laloz and I returned our attention to some housework (laying out laundry dampened by the rain), though we both continued to follow the interactions.

"Everything is good for tomorrow?" Monsieur Belcourt asked.

"My friend, we cannot make miracles. The people are not in line behind you," Kal replied, reflecting on the lack of support for the relatively unknown candidate.

"I know," Monsieur Belcourt offered resignedly.

"But you did something for the zone, and I'll help you in the way I can."

At that moment, Monsieur Belcourt awkwardly pulled a revolver from his trouser pocket in order to access some cash underneath it. I caught Laloz's eyes, and we both stayed still.

"Oh no! I am not about weapons! I don't like that!" Kal repeated. He looked my way, and I realized he was as much alarmed by what might ensue as mindful of his daughter's and my presence.

As if surprised by Kal's correction, Monsieur Belcourt chuckled and shook his head. "Me, neither, but here, you have to defend yourself, isn't that right!" he said.

"I told you you're not in danger in this zone," Kal responded, as he took the handful of Haitian currency from Monsieur Belcourt.

"We'll stay in contact," Monsieur Belcourt mumbled and turned to leave. Kal followed him into the street, yelling for Bernie and Jak.

As soon as they left, Sophie entered the house. Looking dismayed, she asked Laloz what happened. Whispering, Laloz said, "He had a firearm!"

"Oh oh!" Sophie responded.

And then in an even lower voice, Laloz told her, "He gave him money."

"Oh, OK! I'll have [Kal] pay for something now," she said, pleased to be made aware of the handout. But then addressing me, she said, "See-see, don't think because a little money enters, that doing politics is a good job. All his activities, that amounts to nothing. OK, we have a little electricity now, that's good, but that will not send our child to school. It's me who pays for that . . . with the little means I make in my [hair braiding] business. Those things, it's never enough!"

That night, a series of loud bangs again stirred the household. But unlike Bernie's visit a year ago, there were no knocks, only the sound of hands slapping and scratching the aluminum siding. After a second, it was silent. Without looking, we knew what happened: the political posters dotting the house had been torn down. In the morning, with shredded paper strewn about, rumors abounded about the culprits. Some suggested it was Blan Kouran again; others accused a rival group; most suspected Frantzy, who had thrown his weight behind another political party, which was faring poorly.

In any case, Kal appeared unfazed, or at least he said nothing of the matter. He proudly went about his work, organizing, with renewed energy, over twenty baz members to cast votes for Monsieur Belcourt as well as two other candidates with whom they were working. Using multiple ID numbers and solvent to wash the ink off the thumbnails of those who cast ballots, each of the young men voted about five times. In the end, though, it did not matter. By midday, youth presumed to be working for Tèt Kale, the party of acting president Michel Martelly—which enjoyed little support in the area—had ransacked all three of the local voting bureaus. Later Kal drove me around on his motorbike to survey the damage. As we took in the upended polling boxes and ballots blowing in the wind, I expected Kal to be upset, but he appeared indifferent. When I asked why he was so calm, he casually remarked, "Elections that never happen . . . bring activities that never stop!" And then, in a more serious tone, "It's not good, but it's how it is." Indeed, the electoral commission soon annulled the vote for the district and rescheduled it for October, when presidential elections were to be held. Marred by more fraud, the rescheduled vote was also annulled, forcing Haiti to go another year without a legitimately elected and fully functioning legislature or executive branch.

After observing these electoral machinations, I found it hard to take seriously Kal's earlier pronouncements about "real democracy." Perennially delayed elections, as he made clear, had their benefits: namely, keeping politicians, baz activities, and electoral cash circulating in Bel Air. But at the same time, this politicking did little to ameliorate feelings of being under threat of others' aggression or animosity, let alone address his group's political goals. Kal and others were painfully aware of how their utility for politicians (or state agents or aid workers) depended on both their electoral significance and their marginal status—that their place as power brokers at the base of society enabled their political services to be negotiated without much expenditure or sacrifice—without, for example, metered electricity or stable state jobs. Two text messages Kal sent me after the October vote underscored this point: "Election was not good. A lot of disorder! And all the big guys are doing *mawonaj* (marooning). They've abandoned the zone. The transformer is already finished. We're in blackout." And weeks later, as he began to organize for another vote, he wrote, "When there is no state, we defend a little activity after little activity. The things are not stable. Doing politics is not the same as making the state. A lot of disorder!"

Who Answers for the Broken Skin/Pots?

The central question returns: why did baz efforts to defend the zone not only fall short of their ambitions but, more often than not, spiral into antagonisms in ways that exacerbated senses of insecurity?

A casual reading of structural violence can conjure an image of an invisible hand, an impersonal force that isolates a sector of the population into the less privileged space of the geto through the perfunctory workings of the economy, government, or policy. There are two problems with this image. The first is that the image of isolation, of a geto detached from the larger social and political fields in which it is embedded, misses their interdependent and dialectical relationships.[18] Michel Laguerre once described Bel Air an "internal colony," in order to characterize the geto "not as a separated and isolated entity, but as integrated at the bottom of Haitian society" (1976b, 1). In this model, the relations of economic exploitation, racial subjugation, and political decency between the geto and the state were comparable to those between colonial nations and their colonies. He further argued that there was a cascading effect linking the marginal position of Haiti in the world to that of Bel Air in Haiti. The violent fallout of baz activities had less to do with their exclusion from the polity than their marginal inclusion in it, their position on the disadvantaged side of uneven interdependencies between the baz and national politicians (like Monsieur Belcourt) and the international community (like IADB).

The second problem has to do with the fact that social marginalization may be impersonal, but it is not a disembodied practice. One of Paul Farmer's key theoretical interventions was to argue that structural violence is not the effect of "accident or of *force majeure*" but "the consequence, direct or indirect, of human agency" (1996, 271)—such as a development policy to address recurrent blackouts with one-off replacements of transformers rather than the installation of metered electricity. There were also human decisions at play in how baz leaders deployed their position of dependency, often turning against their peers in defending themselves. "Being dependent," as Lagurre noted (1976b, 20) of the then local leaders, "also implies the possibility for a segment of a dependent sector to exploit the system at its advantages"—and I would add, bear its consequences: social feuding in the wake of the transformer's installation and harassment in the wake of voter mobilization.

The efficacy and dilemmas of the baz's efforts to defend themselves and the zone emerged from their empowerment in marginality, marginality in empowerment. This defensive effort was not pursued by sovereigns acting out a comprehensive, coherent strategy from the apex of the power hierarchy. Rather, it was pursued by street sovereigns at the critical yet volatile base of power, where they were both enabled and burdened by the helix of sociopolitical forces that encompassed them. From there they pursued a series of defensive, tactical maneuverings that carved out a space of partial and provisional security and advocacy. My phrasing takes inspiration from the French philosopher Michel de Certeau, who famously distinguished between the "strategies" of the powerful and the "tactics" of the powerless: whereas a strategy fulfills the systemic plans of those with the power to determine them, a tactic "insinuates itself into the other's place, fragmentarily, without taking it over in its entirety, without being able to keep it at a distance" (1984, xix). The successes as well as consequences of baz politics were, as de Certeau put it, a matter of "making do," of carving out a degree of agency from a marginal position of power and in the face of insecurity (1984, 30). Yet while the baz often proceeded by securing short-term, immediate needs, this did not prevent its members from thinking, in de Certeau's terms, "strategically"—imagining a political future in which they would move beyond defensive maneuverings to occupy a more offensive and empowered positionality.

Shortly after the election, Kal drew on the words of the Bel Air native, rap artist, and political historian Blaze One to capture his thwarted aspirations. "The situation of the people in the geto is a whirlpool of illusion," he told me. "It's like Blaze One put it: '*Andan geto, se bagay sal./Nèg yo sousite divizyon./Yo aji sou ti vizyon nou./E nou toujou peye po kase nan illisyon nou.*'" A wealth of signifiers in four curt rhymes, the stanza is impossible to translate. I can offer only a rough gloss: Inside the geto it's dirty things. The nèg [in power] catalyze our division. They antagonize our vision. And we always pay for the broken *po* (skin/pots) of our illusions. The last line plays on the double meaning of *po*—skin and pots— to raise again the specter of slavery as a lens for critiquing the here and now.

The line refers to how it was the lash, the violence of broken skin, that maintained the staunchest of hierarchies the island has known. It also observes that it was the enslaved that bore the blame when the master's kitchen pots turned up broken—the shards of French porcelain, a metaphor within a metaphor, symbolizing chaos in the corridors of power. Together, the image affords a most poignant summation of how those "at the base" bear the brunt and the blame of the violence that consolidates relations of power in society. But most striking about this lyric was the provident subjects it projected—subjects in whose eyes the future emerged at a crossroads between a vision and illusion, between aspiration and fantasy. Crisscrossed in the baz's defensive project was the recognition of the mutual constitution of its limitations and its potential. Kal and others held a defiant belief that another world was worth fighting for even if that alternative was continuously being undone. As the next chapter shows, this defiant political philosophy was nothing new but rather took root, decades ago, among the generations of the urban poor who adopted a militant posture in their usurpation of a dictatorial legacy and the founding of the contemporary democratic movement in Haiti.

HISTORY

> The tradition of all dead generations weighs like a nightmare on the brains of the living.
>
> —Karl Marx, 1852

> Dialect of hurricanes. Patois of rains. Language of storms. Unfolding of life in a spiral. In its essence, life is tension. Towards something. Towards someone. Towards oneself. Towards the point of maturation where the ancient and the new unravel. Death and birth. And every being finds itself—in part—in pursuit of its double. A pursuit that might even seem to bear the intensity of need, of desire, of infinite quest.
>
> —Franketienne, 1968

It was a quiet July morning at Baz Zap Zap. Dawn passed without any sleep-rousing political debates among the old-timers at Kay Adam's watering hole. No lively discussions animated a crew of four young men seated curbside. Everyone was recovering from the 2013 Carnaval des Fleurs, a summer festival inaugurated by the dictator François "Papa Doc" Duvalier in the 1950s and recently revived by the current president, Michel Martelly, who many in Bel Air derided as one of the dictator's long-lost *tonton makout*—the moniker for the dictator's militiamen. With a cup of sweet coffee in hand, I joined the crew relishing the rare silence. But Joel, a skinny, bald, middle-aged man, was intent on keeping things interesting. He began pacing vigorously in the middle of the road, spilling his cup of rum as he ranted indecipherably to me. I had grown used to Joel's bouts of drunken madness, but this seemed different.

My friend Max, an unemployed man in his twenties, spotted me and headed over, presumably to chat. Max was recently shot twice in his right leg after he had publicly accused an acquaintance in the armed group MOG of thievery. Not yet stable on his crutches, he had trouble getting past Joel's frenzy. He lost his balance and fell, cursing Joel as he hit the ground. Once he composed himself, I asked him if he understood what Joel was saying. He laughed and said I must be foolish to want to understand that. Sensing my interest, however, he called Joel over. Excitedly, Joel spouted some phrases at us. "The master of the society.

Your friend, Kriminèl. He burned it! He made us burn it! Red, red, red, red fires! September 1988! A lot of crying. Everybody runs. Out of the church. Everything red: red fires, red blood! They burned them too. But not all. His *petwo* [spiritual force], too mean. It'll consume you. Red, all red!"

Max straightened his back and stared at Rémy Ceus, sitting across the street. Rémy ran a secret society presided over by the Vodou spirit Bawon Kriminèl, so named for the ability to pronounce judgment on crimes and act criminally if merited. Rémy, a quiet, seventy-year-old man was seated out front at Kay Adam, sipping homemade rum and twiddling a pink campaign bracelet for Martelly on his wrist. Perhaps Rémy didn't hear, I thought. But after he finished his drink, he picked up a large rock, chased Joel down the street, and smacked him to the ground.

Joel had accused Rémy of leading and enlisting him in one of Haiti's most notorious crimes: the attack on Saint Jean Bosco. On September 11, 1988, a band of a hundred young makout forced their way into the church during Sunday mass and massacred the defenseless parishioners. Sporting red armbands and armed with rocks, machetes, and pistols, they slashed their way through the pews in search of Jean-Bertrand Aristide, the staunch anti-Duvalierist and leader of the popular wing of the democratic movement. They shot, stabbed, and beat parishioners as they grabbed handbags, wallets, and jewelry. Thirteen people died, and over seventy were wounded—"even a pregnant woman!" as Bel Air residents often stressed.

Joel's repeated reference to the color red produced a nightmarish tableau of fire, blood, and fury. It also drew attention to the assailants' red armbands, which signaled they had been ritually protected with magical force. Raising the specter of Bawon Kriminèl as a violent force indicted Rémy's father as the one who spiritually enforced the attack, for making a sorcerous deal that traded political power for the lives of the parishioners as well as the youthful assassins. We all knew that Rémy had inherited his spiritual powers and political contacts from his father, who was an influential oungan and a major makout under Duvalier.

A saying about the attackers goes, "There are those who passed, those who fled, those who killed themselves, those who became crazy." Several died at the hands of vengeful youth; others, like Rémy, went into exile in the Dominican Republic, returning to Haiti only after Martelly's election. Joel, of course, drank himself into madness.

Given this incrimination, I did not dare ask Rémy what had happened when he returned. I turned instead to Fritz, another old-timer and Kay Adam regular. He glared at Max, who was now hunched over his crutches smoking a cigarette. In a perturbed tone, he told me, "See-see, look at that *rat pa kaka* [pro-Aristide militant]! What have they ever done for this zone?! *Dezòd, dezòd!* [disorder].

FIGURE 9. View of Kay Adam displaying Fanmi Lavalas campaign posters from 2016 presidential election.

Those rats never did anything for this zone! Shoot, shoot, shoot! The only people who ever did anything for this zone, the person who gave us these hexagons [paved the streets], Edner Day, who gave us the *Kompleks* [Complex Educatif du Bel Air, a local state-run trade school], Ernst Bros, big makout!"

Fritz then joined Rémy at Kay Adam, and they shared a swig of five-star Barbancourt rum together. Not wanting to take the sides, I entered my friend Kal's house. I found him, his friends Jak and Petit, and his wife, Sophie, whispering about what had happened. I asked them if what Joel said was indeed true. Kal put a finger to his mouth and nodded. Jak, his fellow rara member, sprang into an old song: "Everyone is *mmm*, is *mmm*!"[1]—the *mmm* had substituted for Lavalas, the name of Aristide's movement, at a time when it was too risky to say it aloud. We captured the message—to be silent now as then about the truth—and changed the subject.

Later that day, when Kal, Jak, Max, and Petit settled into a game of dominoes across from Kay Adam and in full view of Fritz and Rémy, they broke into another rara song. It was the battle cry from the day Lavalas youth tracked down and killed Gwo Schiller, the leader of the church attack and six accomplices, and burned their bodies in the road before the church. "The Schiller Family./If you're there, Schiller will die./It's in the plan./Tomorrow at 4 pm, march with the patriots./Go before St. Jean Bosco, you'll find Schiller."[2] Signaling the age-old conflict between Duvalierist makout and pro-Aristide militants, the verse hung over the block as a testament that these four men, all members of Baz Zap Zap, were currently in command.

Multiple and complex histories of power and violence inhabit Bel Air's life world. That day, two generations collided and with them two moments of political violence. The dictatorial and democratic ages in Haiti prove to be *mêlée,* or entangled, in the spiralistic way theorized by the Haitian artist, novelist, and Bel Air native Frankétienne.[3] The movement of life, Frankétienne asserted, "does not progress along a straight line which would symbolize the sterility of nothingness, nor does it follow a circle, which would symbolize death. It is rather a movement in the shape of a spiral which reproduces some aspect of the past but at an infinitely superior level" (1992, 389–90). Frankétienne clarified for me this quotation in an interview I conducted with him at his uptown home in the fall of 2008: "Everywhere but especially where life proceeds despite great obstacles, like in the Bel Air quarter, history is not simple but *mêlée.* Tomorrow reproduces yesterday but in a way that enlarges what came before, and thus, it also expands the arc of what matters and is possible in the future." He also stressed that in a spiralistic view of history, "there is no great difference between the people today and the ancestors of the past," or, as he put it in the article, "no impenetrable barrier nor essential difference between the material and the spiritual" (1992, 390), since both are implicated in the energy of creation. Such mutual entanglements require, as Frankétienne instructs, a narrative that embraces the tension between the lived, the remembered, and the imagined, capturing the "contradictions between dream and reality, between instinct and reason, between tasks and desire of space, between speech and silence" (1992, 391).

In this way, the *mêlée* of time describes not only a theory of history but also an art to making it. The history maker must fabricate the present scene with, among, and over history's ruins. These "scenarios," to invoke the language of the performance theorist Diana Taylor, extend beyond any material archive to include holistic, embodied memories of the scene for action or reaction: the material, affective, and spiritual infrastructures that gave it significance.[4] Scenarios are the scenes of action—the settings, characters, roles, objects, values, and myths—available to people for elaboration or reprisal, embellishment or contestation, in order to animate the present from the past. Scenarios are, therefore, neither fixed nor invented, but rather define a repertoire of action characterized by variations on a theme. Comparing scenarios to Pierre Bourdieu's concept of habitus, Taylor writes, "They are passed on and remain remarkably coherent paradigms of seemingly unchanging attitudes and values. Yet, they react to reigning conditions" (2003, 31). This vision of making history invokes a single-set play, a set that has been rearranged over and over again to bring to life different scenarios, with each new scenario imperfectly supplanting the previous, so that each remains partially present.

Therefore, it is the task of the historian, the history teller, to decipher these layered scenarios by tracing how people both undo and redo the past in the lives they are making today. Such histories of conflict are to be found not only, or even primarily, in the dominant structures or narratives through which the present order of things shows itself, but rather by tracking the material, oral, and embodied layers of meaning that have been "silenced" or kept behind the scenes. Only by excavating this buried, ethnographic archive is it possible to understand what was at stake that July morning—to understand, that is, how dictatorial hauntings and democratic visions are entangled in the political making of the baz. To set the stage for this history, I begin with the story of Baz Zap Zap's creation, as recounted by the founding member Fritz.

Founding the Baz

The pro-makout sentiments of Fritz that opened this chapter belied his once fervent and still latent allegiances to Aristide and the Lavalas movement. Indeed, Fritz was a founding member of Foundation Zap Zap: the rara band, football club, and *komite katye* (block committee) that many credit with leading Bel Air's resistance to the de facto regime that ousted Aristide from power in 1991 and ruled, in brutal fashion, until 1994. Fritz was the elder to whom people turned for knowledge about the early democratic movement in the neighborhood. Soon after I ingratiated myself in Baz Zap Zap, Kal set up a meeting with Fritz to tell me the history of the baz. Fritz was among the few men with formal employment in Bel Air, but like others who worked, he held a political job. Since the mid-1990s, he has worked as an assistant secretary at the area's public professional school, called Kompleks, run by the Ministère des Affaires Sociales et du Travail, the state social work offce. Though he had few duties at work, spending most of the day seated at an old desk near the front entrance, watching the street, he approached his job with great professionalism. He dressed in pressed suits and reported for the full day, every day. This demanded our first meeting to be precisely scheduled, set for 4:30 pm on an otherwise uneventful Thursday evening some time before that July morning.

Fritz approached the meeting as he did his job, lending it an air of formality beyond what was necessary. After work, he usually changed into a white tanktop and shorts, reclined on a straw chair at Kay Adam, and sipped green *kleren* while listening to *konpa* songs on a plastic wind-up radio. On this day, however, he stayed in his white polyester suit and matching faux leather shoes. He received me in the street-side porch of his landlord's cinder-block house, not his one-room wooden shack. There his wife, Janice, draped a flower-printed sheet over a card table and set up two plastic chairs borrowed from the school. Fritz cemented the official tone with his opening remarks. "Now, See-see," he told me, "take all of your effort, all of your will, to understand what I am telling you, because it is very important."

He paused, and then continued: "When you arrive over there, and people ask where you were, it's important for you to not just say, 'I was in Haiti,' but 'I was in Bel Air, in Bel Air proper, in Baz Zap Zap!' And they'll try to demonize the zone, because they think that it's an evil zone, a place where people die. And you'll say, 'No, it's not like that.' You'll say, 'When something at the level of the state does not treat them well, and the zone has a grievance, they can shoot weapons; that's a demand they're making to deliver a message. But after that passes, everyone is normal, just like all other people.' The history of Bel Air, you must understand it very well. It's a history that's long—a history of militants, of revolutionaries. That's why I ask you to concentrate on what I am telling you."

I took his advice seriously, and checked the tape recorder, to which he responded, "Very well, okay, let's start."

He began by informing me that the rara Zap Zap was founded on March 23, 1992, six months after the coup d'état against President Aristide in 1991, during Aristide's exile in Venezuela. It was a "terrible, terrible time in the zone," he said. "The army took to the streets, and made a lot of abuses in Bel Air, in La Saline, in all the popular quarters."

He paused, shaking his head, and then started again. "Let me go further back. Now, in Bel Air, we wondered: all those big forces—United Nations, Organization of American States—`oversaw the election [of Aristide] in 1990, and a single general [Raul Cédras] can make a coup? That makes no sense! That stunned us. But George Bush, Papa Bush, was afraid. And he did not make a move. Instead they tried to negotiate with the army. Huh! So we knew, after that, it would be a long fight! We followed all the diplomatic work, but we knew too that we would have to fight against it."

Speaking of an international commission that was scheduled to enter Haiti in 1992 but ended up retreating, Fritz went on: "When they, the United States, was ready to send the commission, we got everyone together to go to the airport. We got all the big and little guys, men and women to show who our president is! But [the commission] never happened. And anyway, we would not have been able to go without a lot of deaths! Michel François and General Cédras [the coup leaders] prepared for us. They set the army on our block committee, and they broke down our door, and beat me and the other organizers.

"It was like that then. They'd swing the baton each night we tried to take to the streets: "*Makak!* (monkey) Get inside your house! *Makak!* Pow Pow!"

"So, we looked for another strategy. Now I tell you the story of Zap Zap's founding."

He picked up my pen, pointed it at me, and tapped my notebook.

"So, on the night of 23 March, we entered our houses, and we sent the children, the boys, to organize a meeting in the corridor, where the *demanbre* [sacred plot of land and hut holding instruments] is, and we brought everyone, all the youth together, and Monsieur Jean, the founder, said like this . . ."

Fritz looked around, made eye contact with a small crowd who had gathered to listen to the story. He then dropped his voice to a faint whisper and incarnated the late founder's raspy voice: "My neighbors, you know what happened. We cannot *revandike* [protest] if we do not have a weapon in our hands, and the people have no weapons. It's a rara in our hands. When they see the rara, they can't do anything. The people are thirsty for a series of things, for several demands to be heard, for us to raise our feet.

"It was in that optic that we founded Zap Zap. It was to replace the makout rara with a rara of the people, the affairs of the people, affairs of the country. It was the people who gave us that name. It was the foundation of the people. The people thirsted for change, and we let it speak for them. That's where the baz comes from.

"At one or two in the morning, we would take to the streets and sing for the people, all the youth singing for the country. When Zap Zap was before someone, it was, just let [the rara] speak for me. It was the biggest weapon in our hands. That's the Zap Zap foundation, and it stays today. It keeps growing—with social organizations, development organizations—but it's still that that is at the base. It's *militan* we are for all time!

"When Aristide returned in 1994, he knew Bel Air was for him, because of Zap Zap. In the place of the big makout, Zap Zap mounted the biggest baz for Aristide. It all began in the city, in the popular quarters. Here was the heart of democracy."

Petit, a diminutive forty-year-old man who had played with the rara during this epoch, agreed. "During the de facto," Petit insisted, "it was Zap Zap that brought the movement! We said, 'We're still here, and there are more people behind us!' We, the nèg geto, spoke for the whole zone, the whole country. It was the youth that brought changes, that *dechouke* [uprooted] the makout."

Fritz nodded in agreement as Petit spoke. But when he finished, Fritz shifted in his seat and smirked. "We had, we still have, a fight for us to do, really," Fritz complained. "I can say we did not meet the political challenge. I can say at the end our president did not bring forth respè for us. But the youth also did not demand it. We were supposed to have a community store, a restaurant, a radio, a good health clinic in the zone. You look at the lack of development in the zone now, and we have reason to be frustrated. I still have the little job from a project they did under Duvalier. Huh!"

Pointing at Kay Adam, he went on, "They were going to build a community radio there, in that old makout bureau, right here at Kay Adam. I sit there each night, and I don't forget. My father, he was a fan of Daniel Fignolé, who hated Duvalier and almost beat him in the first election, and when Duvalier came to power, they beat my father there and took him to prison. He never returned. Aristide said it was going to become a radio for the people. In the place they used to beat people, there would be a place to speak about all that abuse. But look, that never happened. It's not our fault, but I can say everyone is involved. They let the state fall to the level of the geto, but we wanted to arrive at the level of the state. They believed too much in individualistic things, and there were too many crimes, too much *dezòd, dezòd!*"

By the time I heard Fritz's story, I was accustomed to its tragic plot lines. The story of Baz Zap Zap began with a violent break from the dictatorial past, moved through the triumphant founding of a new democratic movement, but ended with the missed opportunities and broken promises of this movement. In recounting this tragedy, Fritz, like others, vacillated between contempt and nostalgia for the dictatorship, deriding its violence and social repression while also endorsing the public works—paved roads, professional school, and jobs—the local makout were able to bring to the zone. At the same time, Fritz expressed both hope for and frustration with the democratic movement, reliving the dream of popular rule while scorning the unfulfilled promises and increased *dezòd* of the past decades. His references to "disorder" specifically called out the youth in the district who backed Aristide, and others since, through force of violence. But it also more generally signaled how democratization did not usher in an era of peace but rather a shift in forms of political violence—a shift from the dictatorship's centralized, integrated, and identifiable network of sovereign enforcers to the shifting and competing networks of local power brokers that have emerged with the collapse of authoritarian rule and the rise of dispersed centers of power. The tragedy was that within this shift lurked an incomplete break from past scenarios of political violence.

The First Set: The Makout Bureau

The pattern of conscripting bands of militants from the poor majority to contest or maintain state power certainly predates the Duvalier dictatorship. In fact, many baz leaders in urban Haiti take inspiration from the nineteenth- and twentieth-century kako peasant bands that effectively controlled local territory and were regularly mobilized by regional or national politicians for regime changes, as well as to resist foreign interventions (Trouillot 1990a; 1995). When US troops landed in Haiti in 1915 to begin a twenty-year occupation, the kako armies took up arms against the US forces and, though ultimately defeated, their leader Charlemagne Péralte remains a national hero and an inspiration to many baz leaders.[5] However, despite taking up the mantle of these historic localized sovereignties, the baz's foundation was laid during Haiti's apex of centralized sovereignty. Unlike earlier political movements, the Duvalier dictatorship did not merely utilize local leaders for armed insurgency but transformed them into surrogates of state power. This surrogation of state power reached an unprecedented level of institutionalization in poor urban districts, and, for this reason, it has had an outsized impact on their political geography and structure.

When I asked Fritz about the Duvalier dictatorship, he began not with Papa Doc but with the downfall of his political rival Pierre-Eustache "Daniel" Fignolé. On the periphery of Bel Air stands a high school named after the beloved teacher and gifted orator who rose to power in the 1940s. Daniel Fignolé led the Mouvement Ouvrier Paysan (Movement of Workers and Peasants), the largest and most organized labor party in Haitian history (Smith 2009). The party's chief constituencies hailed from Bel Air and La Saline, and when Fignolé ran for president in the 1956–1957 campaign, residents offered their fervent support. "If it's Fignolé, put him on my heart! That's right, Papa!" they chanted (Laguerre 1976a).[6] François Duvalier had a plan to neutralize Fignolé. After the election, he agreed to name Fignolé provisional president; then, nineteen days later, he ordered, with backing from the Eisenhower administration in the

United States, top army officers to storm a cabinet meeting, arrest Fignolé, and send him into exile in New York.[7]

"When people heard that," Fritz recalled, "everyone in Bel Air took to the streets like what they call a *woulo kompresè* [steamroller], and we—not me but my father—made a lot of damage. The army fired on us, but we did not stop. Even when people came back to Bel Air, they did *bat tenèb* [to beat back the darkness by banging pots and pans] all night. That was when we learned that the zone could defend itself against the army. But the makout, I can tell you, were too strong!" In fact, the next day, soldiers and an independent network of secret police (called *cagoulars* for the black ski masks they wore) laid siege to Bel Air, killing hundreds of residents.[8] Backed by US support, Duvalier became the head of state in a sham election four months later.

Once elected, Papa Doc formalized the *cagoulars* into a civil militia twice the size of the army (Pierre-Charles 1973). Officially, they were the National Security Volunteers, but people preferred to call them makout, invoking the protagonist of a fable used to chastise unruly children. Tonton Makout identifies a cruel and callous uncle who abducts unruly children in his straw *makout* sack. The all-powerful uncle was the perfect referent to capture the extreme model of paternalistic violence and patronage the Duvalier regime brought into being. The uncle's enactment of excessive punishment drew particular attention to how Papa Doc enforced discipline not by punishing enemies of the state for their infractions but by sacrificing them in spectacular rituals of violence that symbolized the totality of the dictator's power (Trouillot 1990a).[9] The phantom of Tonton Makout also symbolized the expansion of the dictator as a presence that penetrated all spheres of life, from public institutions to the intimate corridors of religion and the family. Duvalier banned all civic organizations and brought any collective that could not be banned under the control of makout, including the army and the church.

The folkloric moniker also highlighted how Papa Doc, a country doctor and ethnologist by training, appropriated Vodou's symbolic repertoire and organizational structure as mechanisms for control and repression. His uniform of a dark suit, top hat, and glasses invoked Bawon Samdi, the affiliate of Bawon Kriminèl, who is chief spirit of the cemetery and the dead; likewise, the makout uniform of dark denim accented by a red bandana recalled the agricultural spirit Kouzen Zaka. But more concretely, Papa Doc subsumed the spiritual and ancestral communities that had long organized local life into the regime. In an effort to squash latent support for Fignolé, Papa Doc conscripted over five hundred makout in Bel Air, among them civic and cultural leaders, as well as all Vodou priests and priestesses (Laguerre 1983). The neighborhood was also home to three major *bureaux politiques* (political bureaus), the name for makout bureaus one grew out of a prominent literacy society, another from an association of civil servants, and the third from the Vodou temple and lakou run by Rémy's father, Saint Louis Ceus (Laguerre 1983). The bureau of Ceus exercised control over the same space as Baz Zap Zap today—a geographic implantation that was not by accident but a pointed signal of the usurpation of power.

Not unlike baz leaders today, Saint Louis, better known as "Ti Bout," for the stump that formed his right hand, invoked ambivalent feelings among residents. Most remembered him as a makout and, therefore, a source of fear and repression. Yet many also held a good deal of respect for him, especially in opposition to Rémy and his reputation for criminal exploits. Ti Bout was widely referred to as the "original *gran nèg*," a designation that highlighted his leadership of the zone. Ti Bout established his Bel Air lakou—the name for the common yard that houses an extended family[10]—in the mid-1940s after purchasing land with money borrowed from family in the countryside. He grew his lakou by acquiring two additional plots from neighbors and fathering three sons who eventually lived with their families there. On the land, he built a *perestil* (Vodou temple), where he held spiritual ceremonies and saw clients seeking ritual treatments. By all accounts, Ti Bout was a powerful oungan who wielded great spiritual force. If compelled, he could cure ailments, solve problems, protect against sorcery, and advance fortunes. Ti Bout also oversaw a secret society that channeled the spirit Bawon Samdi to defend its members and the zone against malevolent forces as well as provide a fair degree of camaraderie and fun for its male members. A robust, cheerful man who lived to old age, he fittingly called his society Lese koule m, jou longè (Letting Loose Yields Long Days).

Recognizing his social standing and large following, Papa Doc made Ti Bout the head of a political bureau in 1957. Political bureaus in Bel Air participated in quelling at least one insurgency against the regime, but, for the most part, they oversaw local policing, intelligence gathering, and campaign duties (Laguerre 1983).[11] "The state's eyes," as people often put it, Ti Bout's bureau was used to detain criminals or dissidents awaiting transfer to prison, to inform political leaders about residents' activities, and to mobilize voters for sham elections. A handful of officers oversaw these duties, including Ti Bout's ritual partner, Boss To, and an electrician named Anòl. Residents remember Boss To for his artistic talents and many wives, and Anòl for his fearsome displays in front of the bureau. "He used to do shows, like what [baz member] Bernie does today. He could bite live electrical wires, burn cigarettes into his bare skin, and chew glass bottles, and lay on them too, just like Bernie." Fritz recounted. "People loved the shows, but

FIGURE 10. Funeral Card of Ti Bout, gift of his son.

they were afraid of him too." Indeed, many adult males in the zone—including the baz members Kal, Petit, and Yves—have among their childhood memories a blood-drawing beating at the hands of Anòl. To this day, "*di* [tough] like Anòl" remains a popular boast among the men.

As bureau chief, Ti Bout received a small salary of ten dollars per month; his staff members Anòl, Rémy, and Boss To were also on the government payroll, though at a lower wage tier.[12] The bureaus' volunteers were unpaid, but they benefited from affiliating with it. Ti Bout used his political contacts to offer volunteers rewards and to resolve the qualms they brought to him—such as landing a state job, freeing people from jail, or securing school placements (Laguerre 1976b). For example, Adam, who left his poor peasant household and came to Bel Air in 1977, ingratiated himself in Ti Bout's bureau by shining shoes, and in 1980, he was added to the payroll at five dollars per month. Fritz earned his current job by running errands for a top makout at the bureau run by civil servants.

Beyond personal favors, bureau bosses occasionally secured public benefits—such as paving the hilltop street or building the Kompleks. The bureaus were also centers of neighborhood festivity and political celebration. Ti Bout founded the La Sainte Rose rara in 1953, but it achieved prominence—or, as Rémy put it, "started to fight"—only under Duvalier. The rara partook in the annual Lenten processions as well as serving as a sponsored participant in political campaigns and *kouday* (rallies) hosted for Duvalier. During Carnival season the rara doubled as a *bann a pye* (band on foot) called Raboday, which was also on the state payroll. Both the rara and carnival band were remembered in Bel Air for avoiding the coded political critiques that traditionally dominated such festivities to perform ritual fanfare for their political sponsor. Its most popular lyric was "Ceus pi bon!" (Ceus is best!)—which is still used by Zap Zap during the ritual performed before they take to the streets. In addition to the bands, Ti Bout's bureau organized a youth football squad, which played teams associated with other political bureaus. "*Ti Bout pa t gen ti bout aktivite*" (The little stump did not have a little bit of activities), as Fritz joked. This circulating web of private and public patronage, with economic and extra-economic benefits extending across a wide social network, helps explain why Fritz harbored nostalgia for the dictatorship despite fighting against it.[13] Whereas he regretted "all the abuse," he, like many, wished the democratic state would integrate today's baz to the same degree as the dictatorship integrated the bureaus.

Despite such claims, it is important to recall that the makout network functioned not like a hierarchical chain of command but like a convoluted web of informants encircling the dictatorial hub. The cornerstone of the Duvalierist state was that it replaced, as Trouillot notes, "the pyramidal structure of the traditional dictatorship with a centrifugal structure in which those who held power enjoyed it only on the basis of their direct link to the executive" (1990a, 171; Hurbon 1979). The regime was maintained not through the power of a few high-ranking makout as much as through the singular loyalty of the masses of low-ranking makout, who were pitted against each other in their efforts to sur-rogate the executive. "The ferocious competition at the bottom of the ladder, which evokes the image of a basket of crabs, neutralized the potential for mass revolt" (Trouillot 1990a, 155). The neighborhood bureaus as well as the staff of each bureau competed for political favors, power, and reputation.

Edner Day, a former civil servant, acted as the city prefect under Duvalier. His bureau was larger and, in some respects, more powerful than Ti Bout's bureau. Rémy recalled with regret being forced to run through the streets with the rara singing, "Edner Day *double!*" when the city prefect was "reelected." Ti Bout's bureau, however, was not subservient to the prefect but rather pitted against it. As Rémy told me, Ti Bout reported on the prefect to the head of the makout and the warden of Fort Dimanche prison, Madame Max Adolphe. The prefect, in turn, reported on Ti Bout's bureau to the police, which had a post in Bel Air. The bureau derived from the literary society and run by the major makout Ernst Bros, reported directly to the National Palace, as did a bureau in the nearby zone Delmas 2. Competition also permeated the inner workings of bureaus. Anòl and Rémy, for example, were believed to be card-carrying members of Duva-lier's secret service. The prestigious and secret "SDs"—born from the original *cagoulars*—reported to the executive and close associates about activities in the bureau and in the zone. Despite his low rank, Adam acted as an informant to Franck Romain, the mayor of Port-au-Prince, who, by all accounts, was deathly afraid of Ti Bout and regularly bribed him with cash.

Taken together, the political bureaus laid the foundation on which today's baz were both built and differentiated. Bureaus established the expectation of state-to-neighborhood patronage and the system by which the state channels funds and resources through local "big men" and their diverse "activities." The bureaus also mapped a geography of violence premised on political competition between rival neighborhood blocks. Edner Day's political bureau was on Rue St. Come, near where Zap Zap's rival Grand Black is now based. When Fritz chided the dis-order of the baz on that fateful July morning in 2013, Baz Grand Black had just initiated a partnership with another baz led by Martelly's presidential delegate for the zone, who was Edner's son. However, it should be remembered that contem-porary baz are also distinct from political bureaus. A critical difference, as Petit reiterated in the story of Zap Zap, was that the baz was not only *post*dictatorial but also *anti*dictatorial. The baz did not continue but rather usurped the power of political bureaus, appropriating the dictatorial set—its physical structures, geographic locales, and localized sovereignty—in order to deploy them toward the new scenario of democracy. To do so, the baz coalesced social networks and a model of organizing that echoed by opposing Duvalier's political bureaus. Most significantly, rather than traditions of elder authority and rural community, the baz turned to the emergent site of the geto and its impoverished *jenès* (youth) for its model of authority and power.

The Second Set: Democratic Organizing on the Block

In 1971, after the death of François Duvalier, his son Jean-Claude took over the dictatorship, promising an "economic revolution" in the wake of his father's "political revolution" (Trouillot 1990a, 209). Although foreign investment and large-scale economic restructuration did take place under "Baby Doc," the revolution did not radically alter the situations of the poor majority—at least not for the better. Rather, the divide in wealth and standards of living between the elite and the poor widened. In the 1980s, as support for the dictatorship waned amid high unemployment, rapid inflation, and soaring food prices, civic organizations sprouted in rural villages and urban neighborhoods to challenge the longstanding prohibition against assembly outside political bureaus and to explicitly advocate for democracy and development (Pierre-Charles 1988).[14] A major part of this grassroots efflorescence was the *ti legliz*, or "little church," movement. Inspired by mid-twentieth-century liberation theology, the little church redefined the Catholic Church's social doctrine as the preferential option for the poor and called on followers to treat the poor as God's "elect," whose salvation would liberate all people from living contrary to God's will.[15] Emphasizing praxis over doctrine, it also urged clergy to work alongside the poor in their search for social justice.[16] Ecclesiastical base communities (*ti kominote legliz*, or TKL) emerged within and beyond Haitian churches to discuss social issues and advocate for social change. When Father Jean-Bertrand Aristide, a devout liberation theologian, returned to Haiti in 1982, following his ordination as a Salesian priest, he became a leading member of the TKL based at Saint Jean Bosco in La Saline, another geto bordering Bel Air.

Aristide was unique among liberation theologians in that he gave the movement an explicit political intention, directing his ire at the Duvalier regime. Instead of focusing on an apolitical poverty, Aristide foregrounded inequality, redefining the suffering community as those at the bottom of an unjust sociopolitcal hierarchy. He called this community *pèp la*, or "the people." Unlike in common democratic discourse, the category of *pèp la* designated not all Haitians but the poor majority, *mas la* (the masses), exploited by what he called the *ti minòrite zwit* (slick little minority). Calling this class "the people" was a deliberate move that empowered the poor as the source of democracy and countered a long legacy of denigrating the poor as an inferior social class and even an inferior class of people, as less than human. Aristide called his movement Operation Lavalas, a phrase that paired the word used for military campaigns with the term for rain waters that race down Haitian mountainsides, washing away large boulders and uprooting trees along the way. The aquatic metaphor captured how, when indivisible, the people are a force that can overpower a powerful minority that stands in their way.

When recalling the early Aristide epoch, people in Bel Air often simply said, "*Li te pale pou nou*" (He spoke for us)! In one memorable conversation, Kal and some friends recounted Aristide's many slogans that illustrated who "the people" were and why their respect and humanity needed to be reclaimed.

"Titid spoke for all the little poor people. He would say that 'the *boujwa* [bourgeoisie] treat their dogs better than they treat the poor, and we are people!" Kal began.

"*Analphabèt pa bèt* [Those who are illiterate are not beasts]!" his friend Jak seconded.

"That means that even if you did not go to school, you are still a person, and you can vote," Yves affirmed. "*Pa fòme pa vle di sòt* [Not educated does not mean stupid]. For me, he is still king of the country! But Lavalas was stronger then. If he were here in power, he'd have us clean up the streets. Give us a job to do today."

"What I remember," Bernie added, "is how he spoke about how the people collect the crumbs under the table. The *boujwa* sit at the table and the poor are under it, like the dogs, eating crumbs.[17] And it's like how we collect the garbage washed down from *moun anwo*—[those up high—i.e., in the wealthier suburbs above the city]. It's their garbage, but then they call us dirty animals. You understand, See-see? You see, yes, there is garbage in the streets, but our houses are clean. We are a people that is clean!"

"Let me tell you something," Kal interjected. "Titid spoke for us! When you can speak with the people, you can carry an election. Listen: for the way he spoke to me, for the way he spoke for me, for the youth in the geto, I even abandoned my father! My father was a soldier. He was in the army, and I left him because the army used to beat the people—Makak! Pow Pow! I stood with the people, with Titid who was with the people! Now, everyone says that they are with the people, but it was Titid who spoke for the guys of the geto first."

Although Aristide captivated people at all levels of society, he found his staunchest followers among the youth living in impoverished urban neighborhoods. Just as TKL upturned traditional authority structures in the Catholic Church to empower lowly parishioners, Aristide's movement upended Duvalier's appropriation of elder authorities to empower young people instead. He particularly encouraged his youthful urban followers to form block committees, which would be later be formalized as Òganizasyon Popilè (Popular Organizations, or OPs) and linked to the Lavalas political network (Clother 2001; Smarth 1997, 1998).

FIGURE 11. Sketch of Fanmi Lavalas logo; the image shows different sectors of Haitian society (peasants and professionals) gathered around a common table.

In 1986, at Bel Air's plateau, Fritz and his friend Nene, then in their late twenties, took up the call to organize a block committee. A few friends and neighbors met at Nene's house to discuss and organize small projects to improve the neighborhood, such as garbage collection, road repairs, and a lending association. After Fritz recounted Zap Zap's origin story, he went on to detail—with a fair degree of nostalgia—the founding of the block committee.

"Before we even had the rara we had the block committee. The block committee was a thing we made to build a new group in the zone. Then it was only the political bureaus, so we began to say, "We're not with that fully. So, let's make something where everyone is included." We made the block committee, and we used it to do *devlopman lakay* [homegrown development]. When a tree fell after a storm and crushed my neighbor's house, a telephone poll did not work, or the road had a pothole, we got together to fix it. The block committee was part of the project to develop the zone.

"[The committee] worked very well! For any problem, we would ask all the neighbors for a little contribution, and they would give maybe one or two goud. Then five goud was one *bon* [good, meaning US] dollar. And with that, we would buy the materials and pay a team of youth, and they would work for a day. After the work was finished, everyone ate a hot meal together."

Similar forms of solidarity persist in the baz, but I surmised that Fritz was distinguishing this communal organizing from today. "People had no problem giving money?" I asked.

"Back then, everyone gave! Because they saw that we did things! . . . That is how the whole thing with tolls started. Now, the baz will set up a toll and ask for money for a project, but sometimes it's not even honest. Long ago, when there was a problem with the road, we would block the street and ask for tolls, and we fixed the road with that money. It was for the whole district."

Perplexed by how this organizing took shape under the nose of Ti Bout, I asked Fritz whether they were connected with the political bureau. "No, it was a thing for the youth!" he responded. "But they did not stop us either."

"Ti Bout did not have a problem because it was a different thing, and they were losing their force then too. Ti Bout would give contributions, and Adam was a delegate of the committee. We had alliances with the old guys, but the youth made a thing apart. We were with the makout but against them, because we did politics too. It was a *ti kominote legliz* too. We would talk about changes, and it was this group that began to organize protests, to take to the streets for democracy. We mobilized the people for Titid all the way until he became president."

Fritz and others called Aristide *Titid*—a diminutive for Aristide that played on his small stature and the French word for street urchin, *titi*. The moniker was fitting, as at the same time that Aristide promoted block committees all over Port-au-Prince, he courted a following of *ti moun lari* (street kids) that would become key players in his movement. Within the category of *pèp la*, Aristide routinely singled out a particular cohort as the vanguard of his popular democracy: "the loungers, hungry young men who had never had a job and who will never have a job if my country goes on as it has done for the last half century," to quote from one of his earlier sermons (Aristide 1990, 4). He founded a youth group at his church called Solidarite Ant Jèn (Solidarity among Youth), which held weekly mass and organized social and political events.[18] He also founded a youth center called Lafanmi Selavi (Family Is Life).[19] The program, also based at Saint Jean Bosco, worked to provide food, shelter, and opportunities for employment and education for wayward youth. The most frequent visitors to Solidarite Ant Jèn and Lafanmi Selavi were male teenagers from the geto surrounding the church.[20] Petit, now a key leader of the rara and political organizer for Baz Zap Zap, was among the cadres of youth who frequented, as a grade schooler, both Solidarite

Ant Jèn and Lafanmi SeLavi. As part of this involvement, he was encouraged to found a children's group that was linked to the block committee and organized activities for the youngest in the zone, like games and toy drives. Petit often stressed that what set Aristide apart was that he gave the youth hope that they could rise above their lowly social situations and, as he often put it, *fè yon lòt jan* (make another way). "When you look at why we fought for Titid," he once told me, "it is because he spoke for the youth who have no future, no jobs, nothing. That is why the zone is still for Lavalas, because we are still youth, with no jobs, who cannot take care of our children, send them to school, who cannot live as people ought to live, as grown people. We are still searching for the support so we can become people, grownups!"

I was about to interrupt, because I knew Petit was neither young (now in his forties) and that he had held a political job. He nodded, and then addressed my skepticism, describing how without a "good job" he was not yet fully grown.[21]

"I speak for all the little guys, but yes, I have had a state job in Teleco [the state telecommunications company] because of Aristide, and that was when I felt like a grown man.

"It is something simple: *chen grangou pa ale kay taye* [The hungry dog does not go to the tailor's house (but the butchers, where it finds a meal)].

"We went to Lavalas, in relation to the development of the zone's youth group; we became a part of Lavalas. Because Aristide supported the youth groups, he gave the youth support. He believed in us. At first it was not for money, because all we found was a little respè and a little support. We wanted to be part of the movement and the new state too. We could find a little something [some money or food] and make good dialogue about a future Haiti, where the youth would have good jobs. So we joined what Titid was doing. We made block committees and social committees of youth who wanted to bring social change. When you look at all the big political chèf in Bel Air, La Saline, Cité Soleil, Martissant, they all were poor folks who went to Lavalas because they found support for the young people. Sometimes, people forget this, but the whole question of the baz began with youth that ran behind Aristide."

In drawing this connection between the baz and the pro-Aristide block committees and youth groups. Petit was making not only a historical but also moral point. The popular movement had several influences on the formation of the baz, including reclaiming urban makout territory as the hotbed of the Lavalas movement, defining a youthful cast of urban political leaders, and orienting them around the political goal of popular democracy and development. Moreover, this movement found its moral compass in opposition to the economic and political repression of the Duvalier regime, which had excluded marginal urban youth. "Making another way" promised for unemployed youth a paycheck and a place in society. It also aspired to a livelihood rooted in honest, respected work rather than in administering state terror or organizing criminal exploits. However, as the democratic movement faltered under an unrelenting dictatorial legacy, a militant orientation to social change took hold among the nascent youth groups. The starting point for this shift was what Haitians call the *dechoukaj*.

The Third Set: The Opening of Militant Democracy

The term *dechoukaj* described the "social weeding" that occurred after the fall of the dictatorship in 1986, when enraged citizens—many affiliated with block committees—tracked down notorious makout, looted and destroyed their property, and often murdered them in a brutal spectacle. Many makout died by *Pè Lebrun* (Father Lebrun), a practice of necklacing borrowed from apartheid South Africa and named after a Port-au-Prince tire dealer, in which a tire filled with gasoline was forced around a makout's neck and set afire. The term *dechoukaj* derived from peasant life, where it denoted the collective effort to pull a tree out by its roots so it would never grow again. Urbanites, however, were also familiar with its usage in spiritual contexts, where it referred to the collection of medicinal plants with roots attached (Brown 1991). This method of plant extraction enables use of the plant's full power but it comes at a cost; coins are to be dropped at the spot of extraction. Such ritual practice suggests that the dechoukaj was a highly effective but also costly means of social change. If not fully extracted, "the weed" could return to avenge the one who pulled it.

Many of the most powerful makout escaped the worst of the dechoukaj. Bel Air makout Edner Day and Ernst Bros fled under protection, as did the head of the makout militia, Madame Max Adolphe.[22] Given the sheer quantity of makout, it was also impossible to uproot them all. The only makout at Ti Bout's political bureau who was killed was an underling who was charged with watching suspects in detention. He was seized, stabbed thrice, and burned by Pè Lebrun.[23] Ti Bout, in contrast, survived unscathed. This was due to the respect he had acquired as a conduit of state protection and benefits, but also because he, as his son Rémy put it, "managed his role in the makout and popular camp." Throughout this period, Rémy recalled, "my father and I carried makout badges in our shoes but we would always say, 'We stand with *pèp la!*'"

The duplicity of Ti Bout reflected how dictatorial power and violence lingered despite, or because of, the dechoukaj. The provisional government—the National Consul of Government—that took power in 1986 inaugurated what many derisively termed "Duvalierism without Duvalier" (Hooper, McCalla, and Neier 1986;

Trouillot 1990a). In the run-up to the new elections, the army, working in concert with undercover makout, gunned down countless political candidates, organizers, and supporters. The army specifically targeted the newly organized urbanites, conducting raids and arranging bombings of block committee meetings. In call-and-response fashion, many block committees repositioned themselves as local defense forces prepared to defend themselves and finish the dechoukaj against the makout.

"It was at this hour," as Fritz continued his narrative, "that we began to turn the committees into brigades. We worked at night. We would illuminate the whole quarter, with candles, lamps, flashlights. And we would do *bat tenèb* to show the army that we are here and alive and ready to defend ourselves! We were hiding too with rocks and what we could find to throw at the army trucks that sped through the neighborhood—shooting all over! They came after us because we were socially engaged, and we showed them that we would stay engaged until the makout power is finished. This is why we say militants for all time."

When Election Day came on November 29, 1987, Fritz's brigade, which now counted over fifty participants, joined others in patrolling the nearby polling station at the local Dumarsais Estimé public school. Their efforts proved successful, with many casting ballots. But a mile away at Ecole Argentine, a group of makout gunned down eighteen voters and injured several others. Under diplomatic pressure, the provisional government annulled the elections.

"After the massacre, a lot of people became chimè [angry]," Fritz continued. "I remember one young man—we called him Gasoline because he would do Pè Lebrun. He was very mean. He mounted a brigade that killed the makout. After the election, he attacked two guys who had celebrated the massacre. He killed one, with a tire, the whole thing, and burned the other's house. A lot of people saw that as malicious because that touches a lot of innocents too. But we had to send a strong sign because the army would keep returning even stronger than before."

Over the next three years, a spiral of makout action and dechoukaj reaction unfolded, embodied by a pattern among the newly organized urban poor of sequential shapeshifting between block committees and brigades. Fritz's block committee, for example, regrouped two foot patrols to monitor polling stations for the rescheduled election on December 16, 1990, when Aristide captured the presidency in a landslide victory.[24] But a month later, when the old makout guard made a last-ditch effort to stop Aristide's inauguration by seizing control of the National Palace, Fritz and thousands of others stormed the streets and attacked the cars, homes, businesses, and churches of suspected makout and the lawyers, businessmen, politicians, and priests who supported them. With the coup halted, the brigades were again retrofitted into block committees for Aristide's historic inauguration on February 7, 1991. Fritz's brigade swept trash from the streets, painted colorful murals on concrete walls, and decorated the streets with ribbons, flags, and plastic bottles painted in patriotic red and blue.[25] Fritz and Petit attended the inauguration and listened as President Aristide proclaimed, in his proverbial discourse, that his followers would have a new role in the state. "With our second independence, the Haitian people must bring about a social revolution by ceasing to equate the state with the interests of the oligarchy. . . . Would you like everyone, brothers and sisters, to be seated at the table?" Aristide asked. "Yes!" the crowd responded. (Farmer 2003, 139). The following day Fritz and Petit—and hundreds more—attended breakfast at the National Palace and then went on a march to the Fort Dimanche prison, where Aristide declared it a *salon pèp la* (people's museum) that would document makout abuses, much like the community radio pegged for Bel Air. Petit recalled the chant of the day: "The people are innocent! Call the *san manman* [motherless, meaning shameless and referring to makout] to come and talk! We won't take another coup d'état."[26] But seven months later, in one more turn of political violence, army soldiers seized President Aristide at his house and army chief brigadier general Raul Cédras declared himself president, beginning three years of rule by a military junta during which the militant scenario for the baz would become entrenched.

The Fourth Set: Zenglendo and Militantization of the Block Committees

In the first few days of the coup, soldiers stormed Lavalas strongholds, torching large swaths of shacks, killing an estimated fifteen hundred urbanites, and forcing thousands to flee to hiding places in Haiti or abroad (Farmer 2003; Haiti Commission 1991).[27] The army tightened its grip on those that remained, instituting an evening curfew, banning all nonstate radio stations, and outlawing any expression of support for Aristide (Fuller and Wilentz 1991). After two years of brutal repression, the international community, in an effort to pressure the military regime into resignation, implemented an international trade embargo against Haiti. But in a tragic twist, the embargo exacerbated suffering among the urban poor. While military leaders and elites largely circumvented its restrictions, the vast majority felt its effects acutely—an estimated one thousand Haitian children died monthly as a result of food shortages (Berggren 1993).[28] Summing up the compounding effects of state terror and famine, Petit told me, "During the de facto, you would pray all day for someone to give you five goud so you could buy a little bit of cornflakes to put in your house, because at five, six in the evening you had to be inside. The army would pass by, and if they found people, they would arrest you, and then kill you. If you did not die from hunger, you died looking for something to eat."

Another consequence of the embargo was the entrenchment of the army in criminal economies. Involved in drug trafficking since Jean-Claude Duvalier, the army made Haiti into a main transport point for drugs during the de facto period (Girard 2004). Regional army bases became operational hubs that organized both the international trans-shipment of drugs and petty drug sales locally. Smuggling of mundane goods (such as oil and food) also skyrocketed, as the embargo increased demand and created lucrative incentives for unlawful trading (Kemp, Shaw, and Boutellis 2013). In an effort to capture the depth of entanglement between criminal opportunism and political persecution, Haitians developed a new moniker for the executioners of de facto rule: *zenglendo*.[29] Like Tonton Makout, the term *zenglendo* derives from Haitian mythology. The Zenglendo (literally shattered-glass back) appears in fables as an elder whose sore back transforms into broken glass when an unsuspecting villager offers a massage. The shards of glass pulverize the villager's hands as the zenglendo snickers at the well-played ruse. If makout acted as excess-prone surrogates of state power, zenglendo embodied sovereigns run amok of state order—the elder enforcer turned decrepit bandit.[30]

In Bel Air, the army quickly claimed the old makout police post adjacent to the professional school as its local base of operations. It also created a post on a large lot in neighboring Delmas 2—which then housed the army's engineering corps and is now a park called Plas Lape (Peace Plaza—Aristide renamed it this on his return in 1994). Here the army built an *anakoutik*, an ostensible detention center for drug users and drug enforcement training grounds. In reality, the *anakoutik* was a hub of drug trafficking and a site of political indoctrination and detention. There the army offered a daily meal of rice and cabbage to those willing to fight Lavalas and the blan who threatened to restore democracy. Recounting the story of "rice-and-cabbage attachés" is a favored pastime at Baz Zap Zap, since the whole episode bordered on the absurd. Amid the hunger of the embargo, it was evident that most people trained merely for rice and cabbage, a bare-bones variant of the well-liked dish *diri jadinyè* (garden rice). The army enforced outlandish initiation rituals aimed at igniting nationalist pride against the blan. Kal, who was ten at the time, recalled eating the meal and being forced to chant, "I would eat a blan. If they come by land, we'll grab them! If they come by air, we'll grab them!" Laughing hysterically, Jak, who overheard Kal, recalled how for his meal he learned how to "tie up blan with various knots as though the [US] marines were an army of goats. But when the marines came, all the rice-and-cabbage attachés just ran and hid! That thing was *dwòl* [strange]."

Less humorous were the stories about the detention center, which claimed the lives of many Bel Air youth and democratic activists. Among them was Gasoline, the dechoukaj participant, and his family. In July 1993, soldiers raided his house of valuables and apprehended him, his brother, and a housemate and interned them in the center. They never resurfaced.

Because the de facto regime killed or forced into hiding countless Lavalas leaders, several scholars have emphasized its annihilating effects on the popular democratic movement (Ferguson 1993; Hallward 2007; James 2004; Schuller 2012b). Erica James, for example, has described the de facto regime as embodying what Achille Mbembe calls "necropower," a mode of order premised on "the subjugation of life to the power of death" (Mbembe 2003, 39). The way in which the regime targeted places like Bel Air exemplified the processes of segregation and terrorization that Mbembe, following Frantz Fanon, has identified as the modus operandi of necropower. De facto operatives cordoned off whole neighborhoods and plunged them into fear and deprivation through attacks that were indiscriminate (targeting anyone and everyone), intimate (penetrating communal and family life), and public (displayed for all to see). Destruction of houses, public beatings, and rape were among the army's favored tactics (James 2010; Jefferson et al. 1994). Such attacks, as James observed, "silence and disempower the individual victim but also the social community in which he or she is temporally and spatially embedded" (2010, 80).

But what stood out to me in the stories Bel Air organizers told of the de facto period was that, intentions aside, the zenglendo army did not succeed in destroying their political power, even if it did reground their militant ethos. Despite, or perhaps because, the zenglendo army outpaced the makout's death toll, they did not attain the degree of consent the makout had. As Kal put it, "The makout were chèf; they could *manje* [consume] you. But Ti Bout and the others, they protected the zone! The zenglendo army was different. They had no respect, none! They stole, and the people were so hungry they made them steal too, from even their families." With a defiant chuckle, he continued, "They made rice-and-cabbage attachés. They should have made nice vegetable with beef and crab attachés. It was just a bunch of bandits!" Instead of controlling the urban poor through a balance of violence and patronage, the zenglendo enforcers imitated the bandit and asserted a claim to power through superior force, not legitimacy. This method paradoxically reaffirmed for particular activists as well as for whole communities Lavalas's power and moral authority as righteous defenders of the people. For Kal, Petit, Fritz, and others, it led not to their annihilation but what may be called "militantization." In fact, as Fritz chronicled, it motivated in the stead of the makout bureau a cadre of local militants. Among these militants was Fritz's godson, Petit, whose story of coming to be a Zap Zap militant illustrates a broader pattern of radicalization among urban youth during the de facto.

Petit's nickname, referring to his tiny stature (at 5 foot 7 inches, 120 pounds), belies his political prowess and power in the zone. He has held many political posts in the neighborhood, from his debut as a *kone* player in Zap Zap during the mid-1990s, to his role as a Lavalas political delegate in the early 2000s during Aristide's second term, to his current posts as the Sanba of the Zap Zap rara, director of a federation regrouping the area's rara bands, and the head of a neighborhood gambling hall. When I met him in 2008, he underscored his politicization by introducing himself as a "militant, a Lavalas militant who was born in the rite of Sanba people who fought for democracy in Haiti. It's Sanba Petit!" In rara and other folk song traditions, the title of Sanba acts as an honorific for the lyricists charged with shaping the group's collective voice and social messages (Averill 1997; McAlister 2002). In 1990, when Petit adopted the title of Sanba, it was to identify himself politically with Lavalas and culturally with the *rasin* style. He grew short dreadlocks, wore a Jamaican tam, played in a rara band, and listened to popular *rasin* bands like Boukman Eksperyans. Perhaps for these reasons, or perhaps because his mother attended mass at Saint Jean Bosco, the army apprehended him, his little brother, and a friend, all teenagers at the time, shortly after the coup.

"It all began with *lom a grenad* [the man with the grenade]," as Petit began the story of his apprehension, citing the name residents gave to army officers who patrolled in front of the Kompleks with Uzis and grenades in hand. "They arrested us and had us follow behind them and walk to the office. When we arrived, the zenglendo army asked us to choose the baton. They made us choose the baton they would use to beat us."

Twisting his mouth into a pained grimace and raising he voice, he went on: "They beat us with the baton. Pow Pow, Pow Pow! They beat me everywhere, on my back, stomach, legs, knees, everywhere. They beat me, my penis, my ass, but my penis, Pow, Pow, Pow! I cried out loud. . . . The man with the grenade said my mom was Lavalas, that she could follow Titid's sermons, and that our house had pictures of Aristide in it. They beat us without reservation that day.

"But what was worse, I tell you, they cut up our heads. They emptied our pockets and made me use the change to buy a razor. They tore up our heads [with the razor], and then they beat us, blood oozing from my head, and they threw us, like *kaka* [shit], into the street. My mother was there, with the soldiers, and she carried me home. But it was not over. At eleven o'clock that evening, they came for us again.

"By that time, my mother had time to give us to the neighbor, who put clothes on my brother and me and took us to my mother's natal village, Ti Gwav [Petit-Goâve], where my grandma still lived. Afterward, the zenglendo army sent a group to look for us in Ti Gwav, and they said, "Those people display Aristide's photo," but my grandma had put *gad* [magical guards] around the yard, and they did not find us."

This account traces a standard "narratology of torture" (Feldman 1994, 410; see also Feldman 1991), whereby the infliction of pain and suffering unfolds as "the creation and acknowledgement of dominance." The acts of walking behind the soldiers, choosing the baton, and paying for the razor effected a hierarchy between the torturer and the victim. This hierarchy, paradoxically and erroneously, worked to position Petit and his brother and friend as not only meriting but also controlling the violence. Making the youth shave their own dreadlocks furthered their disempowerment by erasing the youths' political subjectivity and making them into common criminals or simple drug users. No less symbolic was the beating of the youths' genitalia, which participated in a contestation of gender. The torturers aimed to emasculate the young men in that moment and beyond it, by forever appropriating their reproductive capacity. Likewise, the mother's witnessing of the acts undermined her motherhood and infantilized the men as it emphasized her inability to protect the children.

After hearing about this torture, I was stunned when Petit went on to recast the story as a sign of his indestructible power. "That day, I became a militant," he told me. "They saw the power I have in the zone. They wanted to take it out of my hands, but they failed. Point for me. Zero for them. That gave me more respè. Look at the way I got six children now. How many do they got? Not six!" he told me. Such a "narratology of redemption," to invert Feldman's phrase, did not contest the army's creation of Petit as the author of his torture. Instead, it transformed this authorship into a sign of strength, salvaging his manhood and proving his destiny as a militant.

After two years in hiding, Petit returned to Bel Air in September 1994, a month before the United States initiated Operation Uphold Democracy—a UN-authorized military intervention—that returned Aristide to power and led to the disbandment of the army. Reflecting on that moment, Petit continued, "When I returned to Bel Air, I put *gren nan bouda m!*" using the phrase "testicles in my behind" to signify, as he put it, "force and courage."

"When the Americans came, I found a few comrades, those who were older than me, and we worked together to make Molotov cocktails, gas, wicks with red cloth, that we also kept on us to protect us, and we waited until midnight, and then we ambushed the army post, and there were two soldiers, man with the grenade, inside but they could not take the pressure, and they ran away. With the Americans there, and God, they could not do anything. That was a big force behind us. But [the marines] did not want to act [attack the army]. So, it was us who crashed the post; we crashed it entirely, until we took out all the bricks, and we sold them all. The *anakoutik* too. With that money, we bought rum to make [good] feeling, and we bought some machetes to protect the party, and we sang that song: "We call them, the UN./Captain Shelton, arrest them./We are not afraid of the army's big guns./We will still arrest them./Go ahead and give salvation./The man with the grenade panics./Those who aren't Lavalas are panicking./We call them, Titid./Arrest them, Signor!"[31] It was a good battle we made for democracy, for justice in Haiti."

He concluded: "It's a nice power I have now, but even nicer was what I had under Aristide, that was a nice power, a real militan, but it's also a power, look, for me to get that chance, I had to suffer something. I can even die for that still. That means in all those things, I arrived at the place where I can fight in the way of liberating Bel Air."

The Fifth Set: The Formalization of the Resistance

Petit's story is not unique. Fritz also traced his complicated break with the makout system to abuses he suffered from the zenglendo army. In the fall of 1992, two off-duty soldiers broke into his house and demanded that he show them where his photo of Aristide was hung. "I gave them my tin with my money, but when I did not produce the photo, they broke a beer bottle on my head." The soldiers then molested his wife at the time, grabbing her breasts and crotch before throwing her on the broken bottles. The soldiers then took his wife into the corridor behind their house, and the group's leader raped her outside the latrine. "I heard her cry!" Fritz wailed. Soon afterward, his wife fled to her natal village, and she and Fritz separated. It was then that Fritz and Zap Zap became involved in the Bel Air Resistance Platform (Platfòm Resistans Bèlè). During this time, resistance platforms developed in several poor neighborhoods of Port-au-Prince, as well as in regional cities such as Gonaïves. Straddling the language of populism, liberation theology, and the military, the platforms were known as the "Baz of Operation Lavalas"—originating the use of the term *baz* for both local organizations and nodes in the Lavalas network. "The platform brought its own army, a *lame popilè* [popular army], that battled for Baz Bel Air," as Fritz put it.

Beyond transforming newly politicized youth into self-declared militants, the platforms redefined local defense brigades as popular armies whose structure and methods of resistance would have a lasting impact on the baz. Specifically, the popular army employed a repertoire of resistance premised on the politics of *mawonaj* (maroonage), or a series of guerrilla tactics that enabled the disruption of the order of rule from a position of hiding or concealment. Inspired by the colonial-era maroons, the enslaved Africans who ran away from plantations, this repertoire employed "infrapolitical" (Scott 1990) methods such as transmitting covert political messages, spontaneous riots, civil disobedience, and other rebellious acts. "The people did not yet have weapons to make *rat pa kaka* [pro-Aristide militants] in front of the army at that point," Fritz explained. "It was disorder, throw leaflets, make garbage, put the rara outside, burn tires, do a mission and run, all that makes disorder! That's how the people's army makes a battle: act, act, act, then flee. We're there, we're not there. We had to find a little corridor to make our route." Like the maroons, who terrorized plantation masters and then the French army from their mountainous hideouts, the resistance platform avoided head-to-head confrontations with the army and its superior weaponry (Fouard 1972; Manigat 1977). But what set this repertoire apart from earlier incarnations of *mawonaj* was how they adapted these tactics to the urban context, honing what the Haitian politician and scholar Leslie Manigat has termed the "counterpower of the streets" (Danner 1987, 39).

Three of the tactics Fritz mentioned were particularly innovative in this regard, as well as significant for the development of baz politics. The first built on block committees' practice of street sweeping—a key feature of baz activities today. Faced with mounting garbage, residents were forced to fully take over trash collection, but rather than removing it from the streets they used it to blockade key intersections and construct *zil fatra* (garbage islands), or enclaves cordoned off by dumpsites. As Fritz explained, "We put the garbage in the street, to stop [the army's] walk-abouts each night, while we used the corridors." In addition to preventing passage, the garbage islands functioned at a symbolic level to belittle the army soldiers in an inversion of the dehumanizing acts which the army had leveled against them. As Fritz explained: "The baz was surrounded in garbage. It was not good; we suffered under that, but it stopped them from coming. No soldier wanted to be seen climbing over our garbage, and they knew we put our shit at the top!" Laughing, he went on. "So it became our fort, and we put all the garbage there, all of it. It was a little humiliation. I liked to watch that. Soldiers walking in shit!"

A second key tactic was the adaptation of rara for the urban milieu and its conversion from the makout band to democracy's vanguard. A whole cohort of rara bands linked to neighborhood resistance platforms emerged during this time, with six appearing in Bel Air and its surroundings.[32] While each group represented its block, together they lyrically expressed their solidarity as a collective platform by sharing the same politicized songs.[33] Their choral singing, as well as the large crowds with which they took to the streets, signaled their popular mandate while simultaneously providing a degree of anonymity.[34] "This was the epoch of the rara," Fritz recalled. "We were a real force. Anywhere from fifty to a hundred people would go out every Thursday night, Saturday too. We would make such a big crowd, the army could not stop us!" Still, the groups employed silences, substitutions, and double meanings to deliver their critiques. Fritz, for example, recalled how the band elaborated the song "Everyone is *mmm*" as they navigated the urban topography to avoid the army's gaze but also reach the people. They usually played only the melody, but "when the army was not there, we sang all the words, and when we were deep in the corridors with all the people, we would erupt like a cannon and sing loud: 'Everyone is *mmm*! We can't speak./ The army wants to kill us./Corridor, corridor, corridor.'"[35]

The third pivotal development involved the formalization of the brigade tradition into a popular army with constituent *kò* (corps). The corps of the Bel Air Resistance Platform included several young men who were armed with machetes and rocks and a few small caliber revolvers, as well as a few disaffected mak- out and a prominent ex-military officer. A makeshift, adaptable army, the corps served multiple purposes. It supplied bodyguards for platform leaders; it walked with Zap Zap and other raras on their night runs through the neighborhood; and it plotted surreptitious political missions such as throwing Molotov cock- tails into businesses, banks, and army posts; pelting rocks at car windows and unsuspecting soldiers; and blocking major streets with barricades of flaming cars and tires to shut down the city and prevent army vehicles from entering the neighborhood. The corps also held flash protests and disrupted gatherings of de facto leaders or partisans by breaking in and *voye trak* (throwing leaflets) that had pro-Lavalas slogans on them: "Long Live Aristide," "Aristide Will Return," or "Down with the Army." All these activities exemplified the active organization of residents into its own militant force primed to fight the zenglendo army and secure Aristide's return. In fact, when reflecting on the platform, many in Bel Air expressed regret that Aristide and other Lavalas leaders did not raise the stakes and declare war against the de facto regime (cf. Beckett 2008). "They could have given us weapons and supported the people's army in the de facto," Kal once told me, "because that was when all the people were behind us, and, with real weap- ons, we could have really fought the zengendo army, and not suffered for three years under Cédras."

Statements like these raise the question of how much the resistance plat- form came to reproduce the scenario of political violence that it opposed. After Petit recounted his story of torture, I asked him about whether the difference between the corps and the army was so great since they both were violent. He responded: "Two men have guns; they both are in Bel Air. I hear you ask, 'What's the difference between a corps and a band of zenglendo?' And I suspect you forgot what *defans lejitim* [legitimate defense] means. I'll tell you. It's respè. If you defend me, I respect you, and you need a weapon to defend against a weapon. It was machetes against the army's big guns. Force and courage makes justice. We're not afraid!" Here the concept of legitimate defense invoked something similar to but broader than self-defense. For one thing, it justified force within a moral framework of reciprocity, vindicating the corps because it defended against the corrupt and cruel zenglendo army. But it went even farther. The corps was justified because the danger was clear and present, and because it wielded the inferior power and weaponry of the subjected. Nonetheless, I countered and told Petit, "'But two wrongs don't make a right,' as we say in English."

Petit had the final word: "But we're still the people," he said.

When Aristide was returned to the helm of the state on October 15, 1994, he called for reconciliation—"no to violence, yes to reconciliation." But the calls from the streets of Port-au-Prince were, "Reconciliation yes, but justice first!" (Farmer 2003, 324). The future of the democratic movement would have to contend with Petit's and others' ideology of militancy and their belief in their right to use the counterpower of the street.

Layered Scenarios of the Baz

The Haitian anthropologist Michel Rolph Trouillot famously detailed how the histories we find in the archives can "silence the past." His key example is the tale of how Henry Christophe, the revolutionary soldier turned king of Haiti, expunged his rival Sans Souci from the historical record. King Christophe not only murdered his rival but also built his most famous palace at the murder site and named it Sans Souci. By supplanting his palace over the body of Sans Souci, Christophe "erased [Sans Souci] from his future, what has become the historians' present" (Trouillot 1995, 59). But the palace surely did not erase Sans Souci from Christophe's memory. Building the palace, in fact, attested to how much his rival weighed on his mind.

Baz Zap Zap stands to the makout bureau in the same way the palace stood to Sans Souci, with the edifice of the makout bureau buried deep beneath the present overlay of baz activities, hidden from common view. But at the same time, the bureau's legacy has lived on in the baz, in the ways it established local leaders as contested mediators of state power, in the ways it provided the ground figure against which the baz constructed its political identity, and in the militant tactics it used to contest ongoing dictatorial assaults and secure popular sovereignty. The baz both reproduced and altered established historical scenarios, emerging as both the copy and the converse of what came before. Insofar as these scenarios acted as entrenched patterns of action, or habitus—"meaning-making paradigms that structure[d] social environments, behaviors, and outcomes" (Taylor 2003, 28)— they also set the terms of dialogic reprisal.

To be sure, as Fritz, Petit, and others redeployed specific scenarios, they also responded to ever-changing exigencies and opportunities. As the story of Petit suggests, specific scenarios were elaborated through situations and practices that in their extemporaneity had a way of exceeding the habitus and its "generative schemes of regulated improvisations" (Bourdieu 1977, 78). A spiralist history is still a "realm of possibility," a space with a constant tension between the "subject as potentiality and the staging as actualization" (Frankétienne and Taleb-Khyar 1992, 391). Petit's emergence as a militant defied any predictable extension from the past, while still being grounded in it. My point is that unfolding outcomes were not replications of what came before but rather improvised responses to the reigning conditions, crafted from and implanted over the available material and ideological scripts for action. Like the bends of the spiralistic dialectic, they attest to multiple trajectories and valences, though in a "constant state of againness" (Taylor 2003, 21). Indeed, when I asked Petit about his personal trajectory, he asserted both the happy accident and inevitability of it all.

"My luck, they came after me, and, my luck, I came through that, and, my luck, I became a militan with lots of little guys behind me," he said. "But I tell you ... from the moment you are born in Bel Air, you are politicized. That means you can be born on the territory of Bel Air, or in the general hospital, or in the countryside, but if your mother takes you back to Bel Air, you are already politicized. That's because the zone for a long time has been a political zone, a zone of makout, a zone of Lavalas. That means each little pawn must have his camp. You can make your camp, or you can fall into one, but you must have a camp. The camp is how you *chache lavi* [make your life] in the geto."

RESPECT

What matters today, the issue which blocks the horizon, is the need for a redistribution of wealth. Humanity will have to address this question, no matter how devastating the consequences may be.

—Frantz Fanon, 1963

Bwè dlo nan vè; respekte vè (Drink water in the glass; respect the glass).

—Haitian proverb

My tailor in Bel Air was Samuel. The father of a young son, who became my godson in 2010, Samuel ran a workshop on the second floor of an abandoned building that teeters on the steep, dirt hillside below Baz Zap Zap. Samuel, who learned to sew from his deceased father, specialized in *deziyn* (designing) fashionable hip-hop attire from imported secondhand clothes. He took his trade very seriously, working long hours on new designs that he hoped would make him a renowned urban fashion designer. One day, in August 2010, I visited his workshop. The earthquake had put large holes in the concrete walls, which he covered up with posters of Bob Marley, TuPac Shakur, and LeBron James. Surrounding his manual sewing machine was a pile of scraps, out of which his son and neighborhood children were building ropes, dolls, and other amusements. While I watched him magically design a button-down, collared shirt into a sleeveless vest with embroidered graffiti tags, I asked him if he ever considered taking a factory job in the offshore garment industry. Wiping the sweat from his face, he slid back from his machine and let out a huff. He told me that he had worked at a factory in the mid-2000s. He earned just over 125 goud ($3/day) assembling Hanes t-shirts and undergarments. He said he could not tell me much about the job because he left after only a few weeks. "Why?" I asked "That job, that's not a good activity," he replied. "You find a little money, but after that, what else? It's for animals! Not Bel Air men. *Travay pou ou, manje ak lòt!* [Work for yourself, but eat with others.] Like that, people give me respè!"

In early 2001, just after Aristide was inaugurated as president, several people at Baz Zap Zap took part in a clandestine plot to win jobs in the then state-run telecommunications company Teleco. On the day the Teleco truck containing the local branch's payroll passed through the zone, they set up a barricade of burning tires and wood to prevent its passage. Two men stormed the blocked truck with machetes, dragged the driver from the vehicle, stole his keys, and secluded him in a hillside shack. They then arranged for Roland, the local Lavalas leader at the time, to alert party leaders. As Roland recited the story, "We told them Baz Zap Zap, the baz of the whole party, has seized the Teleco truck, and we demand ten jobs in Teleco, for all that we've done in the zone! They sent us only five jobs, but we were happy, and we released the driver, and he was fine." I grimaced in an attempt to communicate my realization that this amounted to kidnapping and that the driver, a blameless bystander, was likely not fine but traumatized by the affair. But Roland continued: "OK, it was like that, you see. We did a lot to organize for Lavalas, and we saw we were not going to get jobs, that they were not appreciating our work, and they were playing with us too much. So we had to seize the machine and show them that we were serious. This was a movement, a popular movement, to find a good job with respè, because people in the geto need good jobs!" Samuel, a participant in the ploy, reiterated: "We fought a lot for Aristide, but we lost our jobs. That's why we delivered the message, 'The state must give us what we're owed in severance,' when [President] Martelly visited Bel Air in December [2011]."

In March 2009, I witnessed a candidate for deputy in parliament visit Baz Zap Zap in an effort to secure the leaders' commitment to getting out the vote for elections. The candidate approached the meeting with Kal, Frantzy, and Yves in a no-nonsense way. He said how he would like to pay four young men 500 goud (then $12.50) to serve as election monitors for him. The monitors were to mobilize fifty votes each, manage the voting process, and, as he put it, "watch out for corruption." His calculated approach rubbed the men the wrong way, and they told him that it appeared that he lacked respè for them and the zone. Yves told him: "Don't forget Bel Air men are a proud people. And we can create disorder if you don't respect us." The statement was a threat to disrupt the voting process by blockading the streets with barricades, and a riotous argument followed. But this was only a rhetorical show of force. Eventually, the group agreed to help organize another visit in which the candidate would hand out some gifts to residents. "It is something small," Yves told him, "but for us democracy is not made in searching for votes. You are obliged to do something for the zone. You have to start with that. We can help you win a role in the state, but you have to give us a place in the state too." When the candidate was leaving, I approached his SUV to say goodbye. As I shook his hand, he told me, smirking: "You know, this is not a good zone. They all have guns here. That's how they do democracy! You should take care of yourself." Though reluctant to promise state jobs, the candidate later helped sponsor a mini-street party with a DJ who blared pop music from a pickup truck, treated the men to beers and the youth to a few cases of champagne cola, and distributed about fifty toy trucks and robots to children.

These examples of political critique and organizing in Bel Air—from the denouncements of factory work to the truck seizure to secure state jobs to the insistence on a fair exchange between politicians and poor, urban constituents—illustrated a complex political philosophy that both extended and challenged

FIGURE 12. Two baz members surveying activity at Plateau Bel Air.

commonplace understandings of democracy. As Samuel, Roland, and Yves made clear, this philosophy often found conceptual expression in the social value that Haitians call *respè*. Calls for respè expressed longings for a society where people treated each other with mutual understanding and appreciation. At the level of political society, respè envisioned the kind of polity that promoted egalitarian relations between citizens and reciprocal obligations between those in power and the people they serve. At the same time, however, these men's demands for respect expressed a particular stance that politicized the people in radical ways and spoke to a perceived right to utilize militant street power in order to reclaim the respect they have long been denied—as manifested in basic dignity, the right to public goods and services, gainful employment, and clout in the political process. Invoking a history of racial discrimination, class repression, and social emasculation, their discourses of respè modeled a paradigm of popular power grounded in the spirit of the revolutionary soldier who bravely fought for freedom and sovereignty. The paradigm had the potential to redeem the militant politics baz formations had cultivated in their efforts to defend themselves and the interests of their zones. Yet by embracing violence, it simultaneously offered the grounds on which political parties, development agencies, or upper-class civic groups— constituents of Haiti's budding *sosyete sivil* (civil society)—could denounce baz politics as beyond the pale of respectability and exclude its adherents from liberal democratic participation.

This chapter unpacks the divide between civil society and baz politics in order to reveal some of the ideological and practical tensions in Haiti's transition from a dictatorial regime to a democratic polity pursuing an international plan for neoliberal development. Building on the previous chapter's analysis of the history of the baz and the forces that shaped it, this chapter explicates the philosophical groundwork of baz politics—situating their political goals and strategies in light of the idea of respè. The end of the Duvalier dictatorship took place in Haiti at a time when the country was transitioning from a predominantly rural to an urban country, and the baz, as the popular leaders of the voter-dense geto where the new urbanites settled, emerged as key players in the popular movement for democracy. Yet unlike elite civil society and their allies abroad, baz leaders envisioned this democratic order in contrast to not only the Duvalier regime but also neoliberal paradigms of democratization and development. For the urban poor, neoliberal democracy was seen to contradict the radical democratic vision that took root, centuries ago, in the lived experience of political and social exclusion under slavery (Beckett 2008; Dubois 2013; Sheller 2000). This was because it produced material and symbolic forms of disrespect, from unemployment to inhumane living conditions to hunger. Indeed, the relation between neoliberal and popular visions of democracy proved dialectical in that the conditions of the former created the conditions for militant pursuits of the latter. Hence taking respect seriously as a democratic value—on a par with liberty, fraternity, and equality—teaches us larger lessons about democracy and popular politics. The politics of respè represent a kind of "alter-politics" (Hage 2015), a politics that neither directly opposes nor simply appropriates established democratic institutions but rather expands the very category of democracy by pushing our conceptual criteria toward alternative value systems. Yet insofar as respè provides a framework for understanding the role militancy plays in populist struggles for state inclusion, it also illuminates the role that rival discourses of peace and civility play in constituting civil society. As a disclaimer, in considering respè, I do not wish to read Haiti as a failed or uncivil democracy.[1] Because of an apparent contradiction between the democratic ideal of civil society and the rise in militant politics in Haiti, many have considered Haiti's democracy to not quite measure up to the purportedly more "successful" and "secure" democracies in North America and Europe (e.g., Gros 2012; Shamsie and Thompson 2006). Yet as I show here, the militant politics associated with democratic failure results not from any procedural incompetency or ethical deficiency among citizens but an uncompromising quest for representation and respect in the face of social and political marginality—a key goal of any democratic state.

Of Two Democratic Minds

> The western democracies are more convinced than ever before that there is only one possible model: their own . . . I do not believe that liberal and parliamentary democracy is in itself the indispensable corollary, the sole result and unique end of the movement for human rights. The democracy to be built should be in the image of Lavalas, participatory, uncomplicated, and in permanent motion.
>
> —Jean-Bertrand Aristide, 1992

When the Duvalier family dictatorship fell in 1986, calls for democracy resonated across all levels of society in Haiti. The 1987 democratic constitution, approved by 99.81 percent of voters in a nationwide referendum (Wilentz 1989), attested to a compromise between the visions of the wealthy and the hopes of the poor. While the constitution's private property clause and interdiction against nationalizing businesses preempted radical redistribution, it also recognized social inequality as the major problem facing the country. Haiti is regularly described as the poorest country in the Western Hemisphere, but what is less remarked is that it is also the most unequal.[2] By the end of Jean-Claude Duvalier's rule, the top 2 percent of the population appropriated 44 percent of the national income, with a mere twenty-four thousand people owning 40 percent of the country's wealth and the Duvalier family seizing over $500 million in public assets (Dupuy 2007, 51). In response, the constitution called for the "elimination of all discrimination between urban and rural populations"—a metonym for rich and poor. Invoking the country's 1804 Independence Act and the 1948 Universal Declaration of Human Rights, the constitution enshrined a broad array of basic rights: "the right to progress, information, education, health, work, and leisure for all citizens" and to "social peace, economic equity, [and] the concerted action and participation of all the people in major decisions affecting the life of a nation." While the constitution guarded against authoritarian rule—going so far as to sanction "armed self-defense" within the context of the home, it also prefaced the declaration of citizens' rights with the "reestablishment of a strong and stable state capable of protecting national values, traditions, sovereignty, and independence."[3]

Crucially, however, the constitution treated the democratic state and the rights it bestowed as decrees whose constitutional articulation constructed their existence. It did not lay out the manner, method, or timeframe of their actual fulfillment. Hence much hinged on how one conceptualized democracy as well as how one imagined the democratic state forging a pathway toward a more egalitarian society. Fundamental differences on these questions fomented a vast divide in Haiti's democratic movement.

The democratic movement, as the Haitian political scientist Alex Dupuy (2007) has argued, diverged into two camps. On one side was the new civil society. This included business associations, private clubs, civic groups, and political parties that regrouped members of the intellectual, professional, and business classes living in Haiti and abroad who had opposed the Duvalier family dictatorship but feared the common people and popular rule. These groups sought to establish a "minimalist" democracy, based on a minimal state apparatus, a minimally regulated economy, and a minimal set of civil liberties, mainly the freedom to vote, assemble, and speak freely (Dupuy 2007, 18). The minimal order found policy expression in what became widely known—in the corridors of power and on the streets of Bel Air—as the *plan neyoliberyal*, a series of structural adjustments promoted by the United States and its allies, which sought to reorient the domestic agricultural economy around agro-exports and, moreover, put poor Haitians to work in US offshore garment and light assembly factories (DeWind and Kinley 1988; Dupuy 1997). The plan proposed privatizing state industries and streamlining governmental ministries in order to create a "modernized state" that unleashed "the energy and initiative of Civil Society, especially the private sector" (Republic of Haiti 1994).[4] The idea was to create an open and free market for foreign trade, where low trade tariffs would ease both the exportation of assembly goods, which would benefit the elite class, and the importation of US crop surpluses, which would feed the new urban factory workers.

The other camp assembled a wide range of groups among the rural and urban poor—including peasant associations, trade unions, women's groups, church groups, student associations, and leftist intellectual and professional associations—and advocated for the kind of democracy being articulated by the rising leftist, populist leader Jean-Bertrand Aristide. In contrast to civil society, the popular movement envisioned a "maximalist" democracy, a democracy that bestowed the broad array of social, economic, and political rights that the constitution presupposed for a more egalitarian society (Dupuy 2007, 19). Popular groups also seized the constitutional call for a "strong and stable state," recognizing it as necessary to stand up to the national and international power elite and implement a political economy that incorporated the poor majority as valued participants. As a prevalent democratic chant for Aristide's 1990 campaign went, "*Chanje leta!/Bay li koulè revandikasyon pèp la* [Change the state!/Give it the color of the people's demands]!"[5]

The divide between minimal and maximal democracy, civil society and the popular movement, reflected what Arjun Appadurai (2007) has identified as a recent intensification of the age-old democratic conflict between liberty and equality. The conflict is most marked, he writes, "in the gap between the market orientation of *liberty* articulated by the Republican Right in the United States along with its allies elsewhere and the welfare orientation toward *equality* as stressed by many popular social movements throughout the world" (Appadurai 2007, 31). On one hand, neoliberalism constructs minimal government and deregulated markets as vehicles to individual liberty, which is understood as a kind of equality. Liberty, in this scheme, is the "natural" form of human equality that is thought to eventually redress, via economic growth, socioeconomic inequality—when the profits of the few "trickle down" to the masses.[6] On the other hand, popular movements, he writes, not only prioritize equality over liberty but add to equality's "original meaning of common humanity and popular sovereignty" a "powerful secondary meaning having to do with the elimination of poverty" (Appadurai 2007, 31). As Greg Beckett argues, writing of this new "politics of hope" (Appadurai 2007, 29) in Haiti, "the lived experience of suffering, poverty, and misery in the slums and in the countryside served as the ground for claims of equality and membership in the nation" (Beckett 2008, 24).

Constructing equality as individual autonomy versus social parity has far-reaching consequences for imagining the state in society. The neoliberal ideology, which measures liberty in terms of the protection of markets and civil society *against* the state, has inaugurated a noted evisceration of public sectors in much of the world, with state services cut, privatized, or outsourced to corporations or nongovernmental organizations—moves that have exacerbated divides in wealth and standards of living. By 2002, following a decade of far-reaching reforms to reduce the size and power of the Haitian state, a mere 1 percent of the population appropriated more than 50 percent of national income (Dupuy 2005b, 54). In contrast to neoliberal ideology, global popular movements have asserted the necessity of a robust state *for* equalizing society. The demand for equality and state power might appear contradictory, because of the long-standing tendency to posit the state against the people and to view popular movements through the lens of resistance against the state.[7] But the Haitian case reminds us that the two are not mutually exclusive—indeed, they can be mutually constitutive. To understand the philosophical groundwork that makes state-led equality possible, it is useful to draw on a social value beyond, or perhaps between, liberty and equality. That is respè.

Politics of Respect

In the 1990s, when the anthropologist Jennie Smith accompanied Haitian peasants in their political organizing, she learned that their visions of democracy centered on the idiom of respè, which they found lacking in liberal democracy. "American democracy, that's not real democracy, how can you have democracy if you don't have respect! The Americans, they come here to tell us what democracy is, but as for me, I don't see that they truly understand the thing," a peasant organizer told her. Playing on the word "democracy," he continued, "That's not *demokrasi* (democracy). That's *demo-krache* (demo-spit)!" (Smith 2001, 5). Respè, as they saw it, was an essential element of democracy because of its ability to reconcile what Smith called the dilemma of *chèf-tèt ansanm* (head honcho-heads together). The rural organizers, like their urban compatriots, routinely insisted that for a group to function effectively they needed two things: *chèf ak moun* (chief and people). The chèf was necessary to *ankadre* (support) the group and effectively represent its interests, while the large following was necessary to provide the power base for the leader. Without a strong leader who could succeed in larger political spheres, the group would be weak or discouraged. "*Nou manke chèf*" (we lack a chief), the rural organizers often complained.

At the same time, however, respè was not a social value meant only for the leader or those with particular social standing, as in staunchly hierarchical societies, but rather a social value all were owed by virtue of their common humanity.[8] In fact, when Smith's interlocutors described a democratic society imbued with respè, they often invoked human rights discourse and asserted claims to the vast set of rights enshrined in the constitution: a decent livelihood, basic social services, the right to speak and be heard, and recognition of their full humanity, including their needs for security, love, and leisure (Smith 2001, 180–81). They also went beyond the individual rights of human rights discourses (Asad 2000, 2003; Comaroff and Comaroff 1999b) to invoke a socially constituted citizen and solidaristic political community.[9] Unlike liberty, the value most revered in liberal democracies, respè was unthinkable at the level of individuals, outside of a relationship between people. In a respectful polity people—whether family, friends, or citizens—were to "come to one another's aid not out of charity but out of a recognition of its members' profound interdependence" (Smith 2001, 185).

This model of respè was very much operative in the life of the baz. When Yves, for example, insisted that the politician who campaigned in Bel Air "do something for the zone" in addition to paying baz leaders to act as election monitors, he implicitly entangled notions of redistribution and interdependency. As a leader, he recognized that the status he enjoyed was dependent on his ability to manage relations with both powerful outsiders and local followers by facilitating, in the fashion of "big-man politics" (Sahlins 1963), a continuous exchange of tangibles (jobs, money, food aid, toys) and intangibles (belonging, prestige, and pleasure). The ability to accrue as well as show respè took shape through his ability to navigate and activate nested spheres of power, between the block and the politician, the politician and the state, and the state and the international community (Glick Schiller and Fouron 2001). Shortly after the toy distribution, Yves held a community meeting to address mounting complaints: that the distribution benefited a small group of baz insiders, that it was a one-time event that did not lead to a lasting commitment, and that the toys were a poor substitute for what the zone really needed. In an effort to resolve the tensions, he opened the meeting by addressing the breakdown of respè that began at the top and spiraled down to the baz.

"You know what the biggest problem is here? [Pause.] It's that we get no respè! None! After Duvalier, Haiti became a democracy, but it's a fake democracy. Why? Because . . . it still lacks respè. The international community does not respect the government. The state does not respect the people. Especially in the geto, we don't find any respè. If one does not respect the other, if one does not appreciate the other, that means it's not a real democracy! We need a leader that's strong, who can fight for the people! Look at the word demo-krasi. It's not eleksyon-krasi [election-ocracy].[10] It means the state and the people make one. My vision since I started this political battle in Bel Air is to give each person dignity and respè. You have to vote, it's true, but that's not enough. I don't ask you to be okay with everything I say. But I ask you to walk with me to continue the fight for the people's movement. Respè for everyone! It's people we are, not animals!"[11]

Such usages of respè in Bel Air resonated with much of what Jennie Smith observed in the countryside. Yet, to recall Yves's threat of disorder if the politician did not respect him, Belairians used respè in a significantly different way as well. Urban discourses of respè additionally invoked the symbolic duality between the value systems of respectability and reputation that Peter Wilson (1973) famously identified in postcolonial Providencia and Caribbean societies more generally. Wilson showed how poor black men's pursuits of "reputation," or respect, countered the "respectability" of elite civil society, a value system that excluded the lower classes.[12] Wilson documented how socially marginalized men rejected the rigid class hierarchy that defined respectability in favor of the more "egalitarian" value of respect for which they could compete among themselves based on how well they fought, argued, sang, seduced women, played cards, and held their liquor, among other manly feats (cf. Sahlins 1963). Unlike in high society, where respectability derived from social distance from the people, these contests configured a model in which power resulted from exemplary expressions of shared human capacity, expressions that won popular acclaim precisely because of men's presumed commonality. The respected, as Wilson wrote, appeared as a "man of the people not as a separate class of man" (1973, 228).

A traditional greeting, common when visiting a house in the Haitian countryside, is for the visitor to call out onè (honor) and for the host to respond with respè. This exchange, which signals the elevated status of the host while still respecting the visitor, was rarely heard in Bel Air. Much more often I witnessed people, and especially men, greet each other by saying respè and then bumping fists together (cf. Thomas 2011). Put in a Wilsonian framework, this exchange of respè positioned the men as equals to each other, as well as status equals in a black counterculture set apart from the culture of respectability (in Creole, respektabilite) as exemplified by an elite, often lighter-skinned, class and their foreign, often white, allies. Indeed, when I asked residents about the greeting's origins, most cited Jamaica, as representative of a broader black diasporic culture. "Li sòt Jamyak. Se bagay black yo" (It comes from Jamaica. It's a thing of the blacks), as Yves clarified, using the English word black to affirm its Afro-diasporic resonance.

Unlike in the honor-respect model, these exchanges of respè on the street seemed to engender a space of belonging and competition simultaneously. Because the urban matrix of respect established egalitarian relations between men, it also set the stage for conflicts to define the most respected among them.

Perceptions of disrespect—from, for example, being ignored by a young affiliate, insulted by a rival, double-crossed in a love affair, or shafted in the distribution of funds—drove most violence in the life of the baz. Winning, or winning back, respect meant prevailing in contests of *fòs* (force), which entailed controlling or overpowering others through symbolic, spiritual, or material powers, including violence. Since expressions of respè responded to limitations placed on access to respectability, from employment to legal marriage to state recognition, young men's quests for respè often entailed embodying a street identity and mobilizing deviant or disreputable acts as indices of popular power and mediums for resistance to elite society (Bourgois 1995; Thomas 2011). Far from indexing harmonious social relations, the battle for respè often led to the use of violence to promulgate fear as a source of power. Of course, the use of force by itself was not a pathway to respè and people qualified such incarnations as *respè nan pè* (respect in fear). However, the skilled and justified use of force in a balanced conflict—one between two well-matched opponents—promised much respè. A disrespectful competition, in contrast, involved mismatched opponents, though much respect could be earned by overcoming a more powerful opponent, as when Roland held up the Teleco payroll truck or when Yves bullied the candidate for deputy into hosting a street party for the zone. Still, despite these qualifications, many at Baz Zap Zap were deeply aware of how the politics of respect could all too often preclude the political society they desired.

Dessalines on Respect

People in Bel Air often go back—way back—in time to explain current predicaments, and it was no different with the politics of respect.[13] I often learned about the contradictions within the politics of respect through the tales baz members recounted about Jean-Jacques Dessalines, the final, triumphant leader of Haiti's revolutionary army and the country's first head of state. Dessalines embodied the urban value of respè more than other famous revolutionaries, such as Alexander Pétion or François-Dominique Toussaint Louverture, and in turn, Belairians revered him the most. Samuel, in particular, often told me about Dessalines's legacy as a way of reflecting on his ideas for making Haiti right.

Samuel was an anxious person. He had a deep-seated paranoia of the many forces believed to be conspiring against him—from his overbearing in-laws to jealous neighbors to business rivals to political foes. His long face and stoic gaze somewhat masked his anxiety, but it was often betrayed by nervous twitches. He tapped his leg ceaselessly and rubbed his chin stubble so often that it was thin around his jaw. But he enjoyed talking about Dessalines, and when he did, his nerves abated slightly, lending him a professorial, dignified air. One afternoon in the summer of 2011, we sat in his sewing room, catching up on his affairs. He came to the topic of Dessalines by way of a lamentation about his most recent effort to connect himself to those in power. He had designed a pair of low-slung, jewel-emblazoned jeans for the son of then President Martelly, but like other people on the block, his attempt to curry favor with the new first family was unsuccessful. When he delivered the jeans at a political rally (via Yves), the president's son politely accepted them but ended up leaving them behind. This might have been due to the chaos of such events, but Samuel attributed it to the changing aesthetic of the president and his son. Both had attained mass popularity as pop musicians, dispelling accusations of elitism through their raunchy, norm-defying music. But as politicians, they also strove to embody the respectability of elite society. The slight from the young Martelly jumpstarted another airing of a "discourse on Dessalines," as Samuel called these musings.

As he retraced the story of Dessalines, who lived more than two centuries prior, I was reminded of the violent becoming and afterlife of statehood that Frantz Fanon articulated in the mid-twentieth century struggles for sovereignty among many Caribbean and African nations. In tracing these decolonizing movements, Fanon identified in them a dialectical tension between force as an equalizer and force as subjugation. The reality, wrote Fanon, is "that the last can be the first only after a murderous and decisive confrontation between two protagonists (2004, 3)." And yet, as Fanon also cautioned, "obviously the violence channeled into the liberation struggle does not vanish as if by magic after hoisting the national colors" (2004, 35). The forceful commitment to equality born in the struggle against slavery and against racial and economic subjugation sheds much light on the political projects that continue to take shape on the margins of urban Haiti.

"If we have respè in the geto today, it's not because we go to school or speak French," Samuel began. "No, it's because of Dessalines. But Dessalines died, yes, Dessalines died because he was brutish. He was a man who was very mean. That was because of his experience, as a slave, but not just that, with how he lived, like an animal. They whipped him, cut his wrists, put him in a hole and put syrup on his head so little animals could eat him. How he suffered made him mean.

"But, See-see, what killed Dessalines *really*? Because the thing that killed him was not because he was brutish. Pétion invited him to dine at his house, and [Pétion] poisoned him because he stood in his way. But the poison, maybe, did not kill him, so Pétion's people chopped him into small pieces, put him in a bag, and threw him into the canal. They threw away the first president of Haiti like garbage. You can say he died because there can never be two chèf.

"But when I say the thing that killed Dessalines was not because he was brutish, I don't mean [the duel with Pétion] alone. Now, I also mean because his mission was finished. See each mission has a beginning and an end. That means as soon as your mission is over you begin to lose your intelligence and your understanding. You turn against the people, and then you lose power. Pétion killed him, but he could not have killed him if the people had not abandoned him. Did he have another option than to turn against the people?"

"Did he?" I asked.

"That's a question for another time, because it's the same system that is still in Haiti today." He slapped the backs of his hands together in frustration.

"We hear a lot of people talking about how they'll save Haiti, but that's because there are people who don't understand that no one can change a system without dying because there are lots of interests at stake, and people in those positions are managing their interests. They'll kill you!

"Immediately after you want things to change you must decide to die for that to change. Dessalines died for that. Boukman died for that. Makandal died for that. A lot of people in Bel Air died for that too! For the people's revolution! There are people who say that was Aristide's problem. He gave us force with his speeches, but he did not manage it well. He could not direct the battle, because the *boujwa yo* [upper classes] and especially the *gran pisans yo* [foreign powers] were against him, and then the movement diverted, man against man . . . and when it diverted, the egg did not just rot in the geto, it exploded. . . .

"Look, look now at the men in the geto. After all the battles, they're still at the same level, under the table, without food, without work, nothing at all, and you just look up the hill at the *gran manjè* [big eaters], but downtown here, people are still in hunger or they're dead already . . . Me, I'm a *mò pale* ["talking dead," meaning facing imminent death].[14] But better I die in battle than in hunger. My dream is that I would become a revolutionary that fights against corruption, against a government that does not care for the people."

Unlike Pétion, who was born a free man of color, or Toussaint Louverture, who was freed as a young man and worked as an overseer, Dessalines spent most of his life as a field slave on a sugar plantation. Historians have documented the brutality of plantation life, including the very methods Samuel referenced. Elaborate rituals like burying people to the neck, dousing them in syrup, and letting flies eat them gave form to an environment of fear and terror, where colonists wielded total power over the lives of the enslaved. These methods of punishment exceeded the disciplinary modes of domination often identified with the modern state, but they were no less connected to the regimented extraction of wealth from human labor. In the century before the revolution, when Haiti was France's most profitable colony, one-third of Africans brought to the colony died in the

first few years, and over half in less than a decade (Fick 1990). Samuel asserted
that it was the total destruction of his life for profit that transformed Dessalines
into a "mean man" bent on revenge. It was why Dessalines fought without reservation in the revolution's final battles, and why, after independence, he ordered a
massacre of the remaining white population. With the call *"koupe tèt, boule kay"*
(sever heads, burn houses), his soldiers and followers killed an estimated four
thousand white people and destroyed countless properties (Girard 2011; Popkin
2007).[15] Samuel admired Dessalines' fearlessness and militant prowess, honoring
the revolutionary in his worship of the god Ogou Desalin. When possessed by
this god of war and politics, Samuel donned a red handkerchief and jacket with
epaulets and brandished a ritual sword (see Brown 1991; Hurbon 1995)—often
carrying the kerchief beyond the temple as a sign of force and a means of protection. But while honoring the valiant soldier, Samuel also saw how his "mean"
spirit fed an insatiable drive for power over others.

On October 17, 1806, after only two years in office, Dessalines was ambushed
following a meeting at the Port-au-Prince residence of his fellow-revolutionary-
turned-political-rival Alexander Pétion. As Dessalines headed home, a band of
youth, presumably hired by Pétion, ambushed him with machetes and killed
him. They dismembered his body before throwing it into the Pont Rouge canal
just north of Bel Air. Haiti soon separated into two territories, the south ruled
by Pétion and the north by another revolutionary Henry Christophe. For people
in Bel Air, the lethal rivalry exemplified how the politics of respè can devolve
into what Wilson (1973, 9) called "crab antics," invoking crabs in a barrel, each
attempting to rise from the bottom, but clawing and pulling at those who have
climbed ahead of them.[16] But as Samuel asserted, the rivalry also demonstrated
how Dessalines had been rendered vulnerable to the chiefly challenge because
he had lost the popular base of his sovereignty. After assuming office, Dessalines
faced much popular dissent for instituting a policy of "militarized agriculture"
(*caporalisme agraire*), whereby the military forced the newly freed population
back into a life of servitude on plantations little different from the slavery they
had just escaped.[17] For Samuel, this act disrespected the people, and without their
support, Dessalines could be disposed of without much consequence.

Nonetheless, Samuel recognized how Dessalines's implementation of militarized agriculture was not an unmitigated wrong. I awoke to many boisterous
debates about this policy among folks at Kay Adam. The policy was a tried-
and-true conversation starter because it invoked a timeless double bind. As
the ruler of independent Haiti, Dessalines faced the dilemma of integrating
the country into a world economy that had constructed its role as a producer
of cheap raw goods through slave labor. Dessalines may have chosen militarized agriculture, but his choices were limited by economic dependency. When

Samuel asserted the same system remained today, he indicated not only how the founding father's failings were reflected in contemporary leaders' feuds among themselves but also how those battles reflected the consequences of the sub-jugated slot Haiti still occupied in the global order. The pressure to fit into a global neoliberal economy that has constructed the cheapness of Haitian labor as its "market advantage" has compromised the ability of Haiti's contemporary leaders to govern in ways that treat the Haitian people with dignity and respect, ultimately stoking political crab antics.[18] This is why Dessalines's story, Samuel asserted, was Aristide's as well.

In August 1994, as a condition of his reinstatement as president of Haiti through the US-led, UN-authorized mission Operation Uphold Democracy, Aristide reluctantly agreed to implement the remaining elements of the post-dictatorial neoliberal reform package. Once in power, he attempted to stall it, but his successor, René Préval, acquiesced when faced with a blockade on inter-national aid—which, at this point, financed over 90 percent of the state budget (Morton 1997). When the reform bill passed in 1996, Aristide blamed allied party members in parliament, and he quickly founded a new political party, named Fanmi Lavalas (Lavalas Family), beginning years of infighting among factions of Lavalas.[19] Aristide's new party largely excluded civil society lead-ers who facilitated his entry into formal politics, and they, and many analysts (Dupuy 2007; Fatton 2002; White 1997), saw it as evidence of his thirst for the authoritarian power he once eschewed. But his reorientation of the party was in no small part a strategic response to his popular following's increasingly staunch stand against the neoliberal agenda. The 1996 World Bank country report acknowledged as much when it wrote, "a broad spectrum of grassroots organizations and members of parliament," if not "ideologically opposed to structural adjustment," are at least "skeptical of the executive as well as of the role of donors in the reform process, and need yet to be convinced of the benefits of economic reform and a revised role for the state" (1996, 5–6). With the 1994 plan stipulating layoffs for half of the state's forty-five thousand civil servants and for the sale of the state-owned flour, cement, electric, and telecommunica-tions companies (the state cooking oil and sugar industries were privatized in 1987), the "revised role" for the state precluded the political entitlements of jobs, social programs, and public services that people like Samuel envisioned of democracy. He and others also resented this revised role because it evidenced how Haitian leaders were becoming more responsive and accountable to inter-national dictates than to the people who had elected them (cf. Dupuy 2005b). Whereas Aristide's political platform was often too extreme for elites and their allies abroad, it could also be too moderate for those who felt a show of popular force was necessary for radical social change. For Samuel, this was the tragedy of Dessalines all over again: the inability of the revolutionary struggle to mount a sovereign, black nation-state capable of transcending the global order and realizing the "people's revolution."

How to Do Democracy: An Uncivil Debate

One of the more important messages Samuel conveyed through Dessalines's legacy was that the long denial of a respectful life justified the disreputable, or disrespectable, means by which it would need to be achieved. His enunciation of "the people's revolution"—with its nod toward war and upheaval—and his repeated references to a "fight" and "battle" identified a militant democratic praxis starkly different from the civil norms touted in global democratization campaigns. As the anthropologists Jean and John Comaroff (1997, 2006b) have pointed out, international financiers and evaluators of democratization in the developing world have championed minimalist forms of democracy. Rather than the substantive ends of democracy, democratization programs have championed democratic procedures, touting an idea of democracy based not on the *content* but rather on the *mechanisms* of popular sovereignty. "The political birth of a Brave Neo World," they write, has led "to reanimation—or more precisely, to the fetishizing anew—of old panaceas from the history of liberalism"—namely, the ballot box and civil society (2006b, 3). Democratization programs in Haiti have focused on strengthening what political scientists term "civil society," meaning nonstate civic and private interest groups. And the success of these programs has been largely assessed on the basis of whether "those who govern are selected through contested elections" (Przeworski 2000, 15).[20] The reduction of democracy to its most basic procedures has overlooked the goal of democracy: the respectful, egalitarian society routinely articulated by Belairians. What is more, by naming civil procedures as the criteria of democracy, these programs have stigmatized, if not criminalized, the militant methods many have felt necessary to achieve their democratic aspirations.

Reflecting on this divide between meanings of democracy, Partha Chatterjee (2000, 2004) has theorized how people in India and other developing countries have pursued "democracy" through two very distinct modes of political organizing—what he calls "civil society" and "political society." Questioning mainstream definitions of civil society as any nonstate organization, Chatterjee suggests that, in actuality, civil society is restricted to the legal domain whereby private citizens assert their civil liberties of speech and assembly to pursue their political and economic interests. Elite groups' mobilizations for enhanced liberty from the state by way of lobbies, civil suits, business associations, and political parties compose the politics of civil society. Political society, in contrast, concerns the ways in which populations excluded from civil society claim material and moral goods from all those who govern (including state and nonstate agencies). Though constitutions may recognize all citizens and grant them equal rights, in reality most people in the developing world, he writes, are only "tenuously, and even then ambiguously and contextually rights-bearing citizens" (Chatterjee 2004, 38). However, despite living at the margins of formal state structures, these populations are also not "outside the reach of the state or even excluded from the domain of politics," nor do they seek to be. Rather than engaging in the "art of not being governed" (Scott 2009, iv), squatters in urban India, Chatterjee's main example, form political associations dedicated to claiming the right *to be* governed. Such associations operate in a gray area between legality and morality, "mak[ing] a claim to habitation and a livelihood as a matter of right" despite acknowledging that "their activities are often illegal or contrary to good civic behavior" (2004, 59). In fact, there is often a "dark side" of political society, that zone where "criminality or violence are tied to the ways in which various population groups must struggle to make their claim to governmental care" (Chatterjee 2004, 75). Echoing the symbolic dualities invoked by Samuel and others, the differences between civil society and political society draw the line between minimal and maximal democracy, between respectable politics and the politics of respect, and between the power elite and the people.

What is fascinating about the Haitian case is that the ideological, methodological, and social divides between civil society and political society—the latter of which may be more appropriately termed "popular society" for this case—not only described the rift in the democratic movement from an analytical point of view but, over time, became the official titles for the main political constituencies. The popular democracy camp initially included groups from a broad range of grassroots organizations; however, by the mid-1990s, it was largely associated with urban baz formations. As the previous chapter shows, baz formations adopted a particularly militant platform following the 1991 coup against Aristide and subsequent three years of de facto military leadership. They formed neighborhood-based resistance platforms, defensive coalitions led by militan who actively engaged in clandestine attacks against the army. On Aristide's return to power in 1994, baz formations formally entered the Lavalas party network as local subsidiary political groups known as OPs (Clother 2001; Smarth 1997, 1998). Baz organizations' transmutation into OPs reflected their efforts to impinge on "civil society" by registering as official political organizations. However, baz/OPs' increasingly militant orientation restricted their abilities to claim full membership in civil society. In fact, their militancy not only widened the gap between civil society and popular society; it also caused a new rift to emerge within popular society. The move toward militancy limited the participation of women's groups, student associations, church groups, and leftist professionals and elites. Though many of these latter groups desired a more egalitarian society, they resisted the turn toward militancy—either because they (as women, elites, or nongeto residents) were excluded from its modus operandi or because they (as students or professionals) viewed themselves as aspiring members of civil society and advocated for civil pathways to reform. As a result, baz/OPs became increasingly defined (and increasingly defined themselves) as popular activists militantly opposed to civil society.

In fact, "violence"—as a sign and practice—became the decisive issue dividing popular society from civil society, and the goal of minimal versus maximal democracy. In light of the ties between baz leaders and Aristide's administration, the militancy of baz formations, and heightened level of insecurity, many in civil society complained that Aristide "gave the people too much democracy" (Beckett 2008, 187). This is apparent in the genealogy of the term *sosyete sivil* as a signifier for elite politics in Haiti. The political scientist Robert Fatton (2002) has traced the term's emergence to the "Demonstration Against Violence" held on May 28, 1999, in the run-up to Aristide's second presidency. Olivier Nadal, president of the Haitian Chamber of Commerce, ordered the demonstration to condemn "insecurity and anarchy" and to denounce popular groups for "disrupting and silencing civil society" (Fatton 2002, 41). The leaders of forty-two private organizations donned t-shirts emblazoned with "No to Violence" and called for "peace and order" in national politics as they addressed a crowd of two thousand on the Champs de Mars plaza in Port-au-Prince. On the periphery of the crowd were baz/OP members. They surrounded the site with flaming-tire barricades, drowned out the speeches with chants of "*jistis*" and "*defans lejitim*", and when an agitator of the 1991 coup called Aristide a "murderer," they threw fruit, rocks, chairs, and urine-filled plastic bottles onto the podium, causing the business leaders to brandish their white plastic chairs as shields. Fearing violent confrontation, the departmental police chief took to the stage, stopped the demonstration, and ordered everyone to go home (Human Rights Watch 1999; Haïti Progrès 1999).

In the wake of this demonstration, the civil society groups became formalized in a seventeen-member collective called the Initiative de la Société Civile (Civil Society Initiative), or ISC. The ISC members largely grew out of democratization programs sponsored by the United States, Canada, and the European Union. Such programs supported emergent politicians and civil society groups by linking them to elites, business organizations, and foreign aid, and providing training in campaign skills, organizational outreach, and media messaging.[21] The group's founder and leader, Rosny Desroches, led a USAID partner organization, which focused on the private education system.[22] Other member organizations included the Chamber of Commerce, pro-business interest groups, elite family foundations, evangelical organizations, and liberal political organizations. The ISC supported the anti-Lavalas political party coalition, the Convergence Démocratique (called "Convergence"), which engaged in a concerted destabilization campaign against Aristide's second presidency. The group boycotted the presidential election in 2000, then disputed Aristide's victory, and, finally, refused to negotiate with the elected government, precipitating a blockade of international aid and crippling the public sector.[23] At a democratization training session in December 2002 at the elite Hotel Santo Domingo in the Dominican Republic, Andre Apaid and Charles Baker, ISC members, garment factory owners, and brothers-in-law, expanded the ISC into a new civil society group that included select peasant groups, women's associations, and student organizations. The Group 184, so named for its 184 private organizations, eventually became a tacit political ally to the former army soldiers who waged an armed takedown of the Aristide government in 2004, after three years in office.[24]

The story of the ISC shows that the difference between civil and popular society was not that the former used violence and the latter did not. Rather, it was that both groups appealed to violence to make distinct moral arguments about their movements, with civil society locating its "civil" identity and moral superiority in its stance against violent political methods, and popular society locating its "militant" identity and moral superiority in its stance against the repression of the unequal social order. On one hand, civil society's appeals to nonviolence evidenced how its leaders envisioned a political order in which private citizens engaged in civic organizations and peaceable democratic procedures to mediate political differences and conflicts. In fact, their usages of *civil society* revealed the term's historical roots as a discourse set against not only dictatorial repression but also Hobbesian barbarism, the precivilized "condition of *warre*, one against another" (Hobbes 1968, 187). *Civil society* invoked the civic arena for mediating political and economic interests without recourse to despotic rule. It also called to mind a "civilized" domain of politicking distinguished from the "uncivilized" tactics of the street and "the savage people" more generally (Comaroff and Comaroff 1999b).[25] Yet in making these appeals, civil society leaders not only legitimated the class hierarchy that popular leaders often called a form of "economic violence"—what I would call "structural violence"—but they were also willing to covertly embrace the use of force if it stopped the popular revolution threatening to dissolve the class hierarchy.

On the other hand, baz/OPs pictured themselves working toward a peaceful society free of violence by advocating for the end of structural violence. Furthermore, baz/OPs viewed the call for civility as a deterrent to the radical action they felt was required to create a just society. In line with the politics of respect, many went so far as to assert that the people had a right to engage in "legitimate defense" against not only the superior weaponry of the former dictatorial army but also the superior resources of elite civil society. In this way, *civil society* and *popular society* functioned as moral-legal signifiers that did not so much describe their adherents as performatively construct their "Others": rhetorical sleights of hand that delimited the proper participants and methods of democratic engagement.

Disrespect of Neoliberalism

Among those leading the May 28 counterdemonstration was the Bel Air–based baz/OP best known as JPP. Adopting a common strategy, the group used a versatile acronym to place itself squarely in popular society while also deflecting accusations of criminality from civil society by registering, with the Lavalas party, as an official OP. JPP was alternatively rendered in Creole as *Jan l pase, l pase* (the way it goes, it goes) for the baz formation and in French as Jeunesse Pouvoir Populaire (Youth Popular Power) for the OP.[26] JPP was headed by Roland, a native of the southern city of Jacmel, whose family had moved to the city in his youth and settled in a modest house in Delmas 2, before moving to Rue Tiremasse, just down the hill from Baz Zap Zap. In 1985, when he was only fourteen, Roland joined the Heads Together Block Committee of Delmas 2, one of many groups in the area organizing to overthrow the Duvalier dictatorship. During the de facto period, he went into hiding in the north of the country, but returned in 1993 to help lead the area's resistance platform. On Aristide's return in 1994, and the disintegration of the resistance platform, Roland took over Lavalas leadership for the Bel Air neighborhood, with JPP becoming one of the area's most prominent OPs. He soon became the spokesperson for the United Fund of Spokespersons for Popular Organizations, a federation regrouping 160 OPs throughout the city.

On November 14, 2014, my friend Frantzy, then a rising local leader, arranged a meeting for me with Roland. Frantzy was close to Roland due to their organizing efforts on behalf of Jean-Henry Céant, the Lavalas-associated politician who ran for president in 2010 and was at this point preparing for a second campaign. We met in the Hotel Oloffson, a location I suspected Roland recommended because he associated me with its eclectic crowd of foreign journalists, artists, and anthropologists. But when I asked, he pointed to the large wrap-around porch that provided a clear view of traffic into the hotel. "After all this time in politics, I am like a soldier who is never at ease," he said. We sat at a table tucked in the porch's corner, Roland's back to the wall and his imposing bodyguard watching the hotel's entryway from the table in front of us. A short man with an oval face accentuated by a receding hairline, Roland spoke in a soft yet fast-paced voice, straddling a vibe of secrecy and urgency. "I'm interested in how Lavalas formed OPs like JPP," I began.

He said: "JPP took birth *with* Fanmi Lavalas, *not after*! It was our initiative! We took the initiative! It was the militan that made the movement. It was our demands! It was us who asked to be included in the political structure, who asked for the launch of the new party. The party that had the same demands as the baz organizations, that means it was against civil society and privatization. Fanmi Lavalas had to follow the people's route or we'd take to the streets! It's always the political base that makes power! That is what people don't really understand. The whole movement of the OPs, the reason JPP became a force in the political scene, began with the battle against the neoliberal plan.

"We began with a series of demonstrations. I recall that very well. We made many nice demonstrations. . . . On an early June morning, in 1997, hundreds of street children and people from the popular quarters gathered before the green gates of the National Palace and sat silently with empty plates in hand. At noon, the national lunchtime, they stood up, and banged the plates, hit them against the gates, and hundreds of other protesters joined them chanting for an end to hunger and *lavi chè a* [the rising cost of living]. We did that, the empty plates, because the neoliberal plan was supposed to be about development but we saw how it made the situation of the poor even worse. Now, the people, those in the countryside and city, were hungry. So we held the empty plates . . . we said, 'We're hungry!' But then, the CIMO [the SWAT-like branch of the national police] had just been formed under US direction, with donated antiriot materials from Madame [Madeline] Albright, and they abruptly intervened. They threw tear-gas canisters, and one hit the hand of my cousin. It was during that moment, that was when we launched the antineoliberal movement with a lot of force and we took the name JPP. It was a way for us to say, "Whatever happens to us, we'll fight. Whatever they do to us, we'll make it into a battle. The way it goes is how it goes," he said as he raised his fists.

Roland let me know that he was acquainted with the pains of hunger. He claimed that most in the geto have felt this pain so acutely and so regularly that they have become intimately aware of its power to incite frustration and anger. Thus it is not surprising that the empty plate came to represent both the structural violence of the neoliberal plan as well as the potential for popular aggression against it. When the protesters raised the empty plates, they were identifying themselves as the poor majority *nan grangou* (in hunger), set against the *gran manjè* (big eaters) among the elites. The idea of hunger for many, plenty for a few, raised inequality as not only a fact of life but also an act of violence stemming from the greed of those in power.[27] Whereas the country's power elite had once profited from predatory taxes on peasant produce (Trouillot 1990a), under the neoliberal plan they were capitalizing on the exploitation of cheap factory labor and the resale of cheap food imports. One of the tragic outcomes of the trade-off between domestic food production and cheap imports was that over time it drastically raised the cost of living for most Haitians. While the initial wave of imports succeeded in decimating the agricultural economy, the imports did not remain cheap for long.[28] As the Haitian currency lost value and the prices of staple foods such as rice, corn, and flour became newly sensitive to global markets, the burgeoning urban population was increasingly priced out of its daily meals—a phenomenon people called "*lavi chè a*," literally "the expensive life."

Yet in an important way, the empty plate invoked not a poor, helpless victim, as is the norm in international famine relief campaigns, so much as a desperate and aggrieved victim primed to lash out in the interests of survival. There is a strong sentiment that the high cost of living is not accidental but the product of forces benefiting from the plight of the poor. A song popularized by a Bel Air rara in the mid-2000s went, "*Bwe dlo nan vè, respekte vè*" (Drink water in the glass; respect the glass). Furthermore, the experience of hunger is signified through a structure of feeling premised on violence. On the streets of Bel Air, hunger is often referred to as "battery acid" (*asid batri*), "paint thinner" (*tinè*), or "Clorox" (*klowòks*), suggesting pains so intense and disorienting that it is like being poisoned. Hunger here figures as a lethal weapon wielded by opponents in a social conflict, making a revolt against the inflictors justified.[29] Indeed, the banging of plates was a classic *bat tenèb* that signaled the vastness and steadfastness of the population that could rise up against the neoliberal plan.

I suggested as much when I asked Roland if the protest turned violent. Afraid I had misinterpreted the narrative, Frantzy raised his hand and interjected, "That doesn't mean we were for violence. It was CIMO that intervened!"

"Yes, I understand," I said. "But doesn't it mean something like, 'By any means necessary. It's not exactly against violence . . .'"

"Let me explain this very well," Ronald began, now speaking in a steady, doctrinaire tone. "We founded the democratic movement in 1985 with a clear objective. How can the people participate in the development of our country, to *revandike* [demand] what they need in the public sector, to make those in power remember they exist, that the problems exist, and that there's a popular way to solve the problems? After the 1991 coup d'état, we still were in the fight, but the neoliberal plan had a different objective. It was to diminish the state, to fire people and turn it into a business. So, we founded JPP to save people from losing their jobs or at least to prevent the application of the neoliberal plan in a savage manner. That is the biggest thing!"

"But the development plans are always about jobs?" I queried.

"It's always *djob, djob, djob*! But a lot of *bon djob* [good jobs] were eliminated too. It was a savage development . . . but they called us savages! We live without electricity, even without toilets, but why? Not because we are not clean. Not because we don't know how to do things. Some houses have five toilets, electricity 24/7. No, it's because with that little job, we cannot live another way. That's not development. There are people who say, 'We were less free, but we lived better under the dictator Duvalier.' My father would say you could walk in the street at any hour, without any fear! The street was cleaner too. Not full of garbage. There were not all these people in the city. Now, we live one on top of each other! The blan say democracy is about choice. I say, *this* democracy is about making us *choose* poverty."

Roland's comments echoed Samuel's reasons for abandoning his factory job and seeking state employment by attaching himself to baz networks. The issue was not jobs per se but rather the kind of jobs (Katz 2015). Overall, the assembly industry has been unappealing to young men in Bel Air. This is, in large part, because of its reliance on low wages. But it also has to do with how factory work, which is highly regimented and managed, undermines a tendency fostered in Haiti since the days of slavery to place great value on control over the labor process (Trouillot 1990a). In addition, these jobs are coded as "women's work." The assembly industry's explicit desire for cheap labor and tacit desire for nonmilitant, nonunion workers have led to a predominantly female workforce.[30] The toil, low status, and gendered nature of these jobs, coupled with the volatility of the industry, have meant that few men stay on the assembly line long enough to alter their position in life. Indeed, the rate of formal unemployment in Haiti since the 1980s has steadily hovered at 70 percent and above 90 percent in places like Bel Air. Nonetheless, just about everyone I met, men and women, were doing some kind of *aktivite*—that is, bartering a good or service in the informal market.[31] While these jobs provided the flexibility and autonomy lacking in factory jobs, the problem was that, like factory work, driving a motorbike-taxi or selling cell-phone cards did not provide stable or sufficient income, let alone the respectability of a position in government. The challenge was, therefore, not only putting people to work but elevating earnings and the social value of their work. As Axel Honneth has argued, it is not labor per se but the "organization and evaluation" of labor that plays a central role in the "societal framework of recognition" (2007, 76).

Hence Roland's point was not just about the undesirability of factory jobs; it was also about the valorization of state jobs, which promised independent work as well as power and prestige. The issue of state job loss had high stakes for Roland. At the time of the neoliberal protests, he was hoping to parlay his leadership role in the OP movement into a political post within the top tiers of the next Lavalas administration. The potential to distribute political jobs to his followers from this post formed the basis of his power and respect as a local baz/OP leader. As the Teleco carjacking made clear, these jobs, if not provided, would be demanded by force. But it would be wrong to dismiss Roland's point as merely an exercise in self-aggrandizement or self-protection. State jobs also symbolized the norms of respectful redistribution. Akin to the reciprocal logic of the gift (Mauss 1954 [1990]), state jobs were considered payments for debts accrued through political service—for rara music at political marches, for organizing voting and press conferences, and for putting oneself at risk at boisterous counterdemonstrations. Furthermore, holding a job of this kind promised the unattainable marriage of respect and respectability. Being a rightful political leader was a personal quest for political power as much as it was a stance against the trend of "savage development" since Duvalier.

Roland came of age well after the most brutal years of the Duvalier dictatorship. He learned of the dictatorship from his father, a food wholesaler who, keeping his head in his business, had few run-ins with the heavy hand of the regime. His father's memories, in fact, reflected a fair degree of nostalgia for the secure, orderly, and clean life under Duvalier, as well as for the countless posts open to loyal servants of the dictatorial apparatus. At the same time that *bon djob* were declining in Bel Air, so were living conditions. The developmental shift from an agricultural economy to one premised on export factories drove hundreds of thousands of rural Haitians to leave the countryside for the city in search of jobs as factory workers, household servants, and petty merchants. In three decades, Haiti, once the most rural Caribbean country, became predominantly urban, with 58.6 percent of the population living in cities as of 2015.[32] Port-au-Prince's population has skyrocketed, from half-a-million inhabitants in 1971 (Locher 1978), to two million in the mid-1990s (Manigat 1997), to over three million in 2012 (United Nations Office of the Secretary General 2012). Marked by the unbridled expansion of existing geto and the "ghettoization" of formerly working-class areas, the city has transformed from the domain of the country's tiny elite class to that of the poor majority (Manigat 1997).

In places like upper Bel Air and its surroundings, where 135,000 people reside in households averaging five inhabitants (Fernandez and Nascimento 2007a), there is not enough room for everyone to sleep simultaneously, so instead people sleep in *relev* (shifts), with the working adults (usually women) and children sleeping first and unemployed men second.[33] Democracy has also not provided public services. Less than 4 percent of households are on municipal water or electricity lines, and all residents manage their own waste and trash (Fernandez and Nascimento 2007a). When I stayed in Bel Air, I used one of the few pit latrines on the block, managed by Frantzy's landlord. With five adults, three children, and many neighbors using it, it filled quickly. At such times, we had to use neighbors' latrines, or, as many did, resort to defecating in a plastic bag and disposing of the waste in the street with other trash. Under such conditions, it is no wonder then that the sentiment of a "savage development" resonated with Roland. While the urban poor were certainly aware of their increased liberty to participate and rise in democratic politics, they were also aware that this has come at the cost of a way of life bereft of dignity.

In an important way, Roland's reference to a "savage development" played directly on the tendency of civil society groups to label baz/OPs as a "savage politics" orchestrated by "savage people." His point was to not to deny the inhumane conditions affecting the urban poor but to provide the historical and contextual reasons for them, as well as to justify a vehement popular response against them. He had employed similar subversions when he participated in the May 28 counterdemonstration. The urine cocktails, for example, redeployed the people's incivility against the civilized, literally sullying the respectable imagery on which civil society based its moral superiority. And the catapulted projectiles and flaming tires served as threats of more popular disorder, signaling the popular revolution that lay in wait.

"Naturally, it was a big battle, but that's why people joined with our movement," Roland continued. "You see, after Aristide returned [in 1994] baz organizations took the initiative to organize against the high cost of living and the neoliberal plan, which did not work with a popular vision. We realized that the system is for those who can invest, and the state needed a strong plan that had an affinity with the people and respected them, in solidarity, not a neoliberal principle of personal interest and each person an individual, on his own, without a state that fights for the people. With the plan of the people's organizations, all people deserve to have respect and dignity: that means, food, education, pleasure, and work. That was why we made the popular battle. We said, 'We need to fight for the state that can *goumen* [fight] for the people.'"

"OK, I think the problem can be that when you say *goumen* a lot people hear 'violence.'" I interjected.

"You mean *civil society* [hears that]," Frantzy clarified.

Roland continued. "*Goumen,* that means we had to show the groups in civil society that we were ready for a battle. Look, everyone wants to say they are agents of peace, but politics has never been about peace. And the political class has never really been about peace. How can you be about peace when the majority of people live in hunger? That is an agent of misery, not peace!"

"Yes, I countered, "but I could say that's inviting civil war, no?"

"Yes, you could say that. It was a battle, a big battle. We were not for violence but we had to keep fighting. The thing is we had to show civil society that we are here to defend our right to democracy. In Haiti, that means not just what's on paper but also who controls the bayonet. And for us the bayonet is the force of the street."

"I suppose that's politics," I said.

"Yes, that is why we had to make a show of force. Everyone remembers how JPP with TKL [a baz/OP in Lasaline] threatened civil society with the words of Dessalines, but we forget that the system of slavery—minority on top, majority on bottom—has not changed."

As Frantzy later explained, Roland was specifically referring to January 9, 2001, when, a month prior to Aristide's second inauguration, JPP and TKL organized a demonstration to denounce the ISC-backed Convergence for planning to hold a parallel inauguration of its own government. The TKL leader went so far as to accuse the Convergence of plotting another "bloody coup d'état" and warned that "if the opposition plants violence in the midst of the people, who reject them, it is violence they will sow." Invoking the words of Louis Boisrond Tonnerre—Dessalines's secretary who authored, in 1804, Haiti's Independence Act—Roland threatened that those who did not dissociate from the Convergence in three days risked—as the blan did in the nineteenth century—having "their skin used as parchment, their blood as ink, and their skulls as inkwells." He particularly admonished radio journalists who had referred to "disputed elections" on air, and in the aftermath of the rally, a band of pro-Aristide youth attempted to burn down a prominent radio station (Deibert 2005).

Fighting for Democracy

It should by now be possible to recognize the Tonnerre-inspired call and its apparent uptake by popular forces as squarely aligned with an ideology of democracy rooted in the politics of respect. It invoked a nationalist rebuttal to the political opposition and their ties to a foreign political agenda. Referencing the original revolution's incompleteness, it gave meaning to the idea of a second, popular revolution. And modeled on the battle of poorly armed, former slaves against the formidable French army, the call redeemed baz/OPs' counterpower of the street by asserting that they were engaged in not onl reciprocal violence but also an epic challenge against a more powerful enemy. Taken together, the baz/OPs sought to claim democratic legitimacy not by denying the role violence plays in politics but rather by insisting on the necessity of force for usurping an unequal social order. But at the same time, it should be apparent how this call—as an incitement to violently suppress individual liberties, if not life itself—could represent the opposite of a respectable, liberal democratic order. In the attack's aftermath, the ISC released a public address, in which it condemned an insecure environment, where "fear was in the streets and in the hearts" (Civil Society Initiative 2001).

Ultimately, both civil society and political society employed violence in their politics, but they employed it and legitimated its usage through distinct democratic ideologies. Whereas civil society groups often justified structural violence by pursuing democratic policies and institutions that excluded the vast majority of citizens, baz/OP leaders often defended popular violence as a means of founding a more egalitarian, democratic society. Let me be clear: my point in asserting this is not to dismiss baz/OPs as criminal agents devoid of politics, as the politician in the opening scenario with Yves did, nor is it to sanitize their real use of violence, nor is it to reinforce prevailing notions that Haiti is incapable of fostering proper civil society, let alone democratic standards of respectable governance. Rather, I question the presumed separation of violence and democracy, such that the two are understood as distinct moments or contradictory phases in the evolution of a political teleology. "As a result of this contradiction between the democratic ideal of peace and security and the continued reality of insecurity and violence," Enrique Arias and Daniel Goldstein, writing of Latin America, have observed, "a whole range of adjectives—including *imperfect, illiberal, incomplete, delegative, and disjunctive*—have been used to characterize the differences between democracy in Latin America and the supposedly more evolved forms in Western Europe and the United States" (2010, 3).[34] These adjectives, and the extended debate surrounding this taxonomy, they argue, has not provided "the necessary descriptive or analytical tools to conceptualize politics in Latin America [and the Caribbean] today" (Arias and Goldstein 2010, 3). These concepts have no way of grappling with the presence of violence in democratic societies—which is a fact of politics worldwide—other than as an aberration.

In revealing the divides between popular and civil society, the politics of respect and respectability in Haiti, I likewise resist the tendency to recategorize the country's democracy apart from an ideal type presumably present in the countries promoting its democratization.[35] This case instead aids in understanding the manifold and conflicting ways in which *violence*—as a sign and practice—has been part and parcel to imagining, making, and maintaining contemporary democracies. Though from the ideological perspectives of Haiti's opposing political camps, violence figured as an aberration of democracy, from the vantage point of their actual pursuit of democracy, violence materialized as very much entangled in it: as an instrument for the maintenance of class hierarchies, as an element of an elite discourse used to condemn and criminalize popular politics, and as a popular method for challenging structural inequality and making political claims. In fact, the appeal to "fear in the streets and hearts" by the ISC signaled the advent of new campaign by baz/OPs to militantly defend Aristide's rule as well as a concerted campaign by civil society, at home and abroad, to cast these militants as demonic chimè who compromised the core tenets of liberal democracy. The next chapter takes up the escalation of these dynamics, illustrating the political economy that transformed baz leaders into spectral menaces of democracy rather than respected opponents, while also showing how baz leaders counteracted this construction by rhetorically and affectively inverting it.

IDENTITY

The goal of all Vodou ritualizing is to *echofe* (heat things up) so that people and situations shift and move, and healing transformations can occur. Heating things up brings down barriers, clears the impediments in the path, and allows life to move as it should. . . . The opposite of this openness, heat, and flow is the state of being arrested or stopped (*rete*) or, worse, of being bound (*mare*).

—Karen McCarthy Brown, 1991

Tout sa ou wè, se pa sa. (All that you see, it's not what it is).

—Haitian proverb

Yves was a difficult person to get to know, though he always seemed to be around. When I first started coming to Bel Air in 2008, he often stopped by Kal's place as I ate lunch prepared by Sophie. He'd stand sideways in the open doorway, pulling the curtain to the side, and alternate between greeting people in the street and staring at me. After a while, he would ask something like "*Blan an remen diri, huh?*" (The blan likes rice?) or "*Blan an pale Kreyòl?*" (The blan speaks Creole)? "*Wi,*" I would reply. "Huh!" he would say, before saying goodbye to Sophie and walking out the door.

This sort of interaction between Yves and me went on for some time. However, months later, in March 2009, when I was about to ask Sophie why he never used my name, Yves entered the doorway and asked Sophie if I might come with him on a visit to Centrale Autonome Métropolitaine d'Eau Potable, or CAMEP, the public office then responsible for Port-au-Prince's water supply. He planned to follow up on discussions of putting a public water kiosk near Plateau Bel Air under control of OJREB.

Sophie dug through a black garbage bag of clothes and produced a red, button-down, long-sleeve polyester shirt that matched my red sandals. I put the shirt on over my tanktop (which is not permitted in state offices), and Kal and I jumped in Yves's white jeep. CAMEP's office was located only a couple of miles away in the city's governmental district, but traffic made for a long trip. My eyes fixed on the assortment of identity badges hanging from Yves's rearview mirror, and I tried to memorize all the organizations. He was a security guard, city delegate, adviser, and public relations representative with, respectively, Aurore du Bel Air (the local public health clinic), Service Métropolitan de Collecte de Résidus Solides (SMCRS, the city's waste and sanitation office), Ministère de la Justice et la Sécurité Publique, Comité du Carnaval, and Organization National d'Assurance Viellesse (ONA, Haiti's social security program). He also had a badge for the American Red Cross and a nonprofit based in Brooklyn, which ran a school in Bel Air. There was no badge for CAMEP. Perhaps that was the purpose of our trip.

When we arrived at CAMEP, Yves asked Kal to stay in the car and for me to come with him. We walked into the office, and he greeted the receptionist with the enthusiasm of an old friend. He asked to see someone whose title reflected a leadership role with the neighborhood committees that oversaw local water distribution. The committees, usually groups of baz-affiliated men, charged a fee for water (2 goud/gallon, or 5 cents), then paid CAMEP, keeping about a quarter of the profits.

We took a seat on a sticky, faux leather sofa. Soon, a light-skinned, middle-aged man appeared. He was dressed, despite the tropical heat, in a dark suit and tie. He greeted me with matched formality, calling me "Madame" and speaking in French. Yves corrected that I spoke "*Kreyòl*" and then told him that I was "an American anthropologist who loves Haiti."

"She accompanies us in everything we do. She's been with us since last year, and she helps us do things right in the zone. Writing letters and typing up charters for the youth organizations. We call her our *marenn* [godmother]," Yves announced.

"*Bon bagay!* Ok, come now," the bureaucrat said, as Yves gestured for me to stay put.

When Yves returned after a few minutes, he bore a look of disappointment.

As we rushed through the courtyard to his jeep, a group of young employees chided us. "The chimè comes with a white lady! *Depi ou nan labatwa, fòk ou aksepte san vole sou ou*" (If you are in the slaughterhouse, you should expect to get blood on you), they said to uproarious laughter. I ignored the proverbial slight, but Yves, ever the quick-witted, retorted, "*Menm nan lanfè, gen moun pa*" (Even in hell, there are your people).

Once on the road, Yves turned to me.

"See-see," he began, addressing me for the first time by my nickname, "what do you think that word *chimè* means?" I said it seemed the boys thought it meant *move moun* (bad people).

"That's right. They say it to mean criminal, the *san manman* [motherless] who kill people for political reasons, but do you know what it really means?" Yves replied. "In English, people say it means ghost [using the English], what you call *fantom*," I said.

"No, I don't agree!" Yves protested. "It means nèg geto. You know anyone can become chimè. Even the president of Haiti. If he does not find anything that responds to his needs, if he is blocked all the time, he'll be frustrated all the way until he's chimè! So, I have no problem that they call me chimè because, yes, I am frustrated. I live in the geto and I am frustrated."

"*Dako,*" I responded, agreeing with him. "See-see understands! *Pale Kreyòl, komprann kreyòl*" [Speak the Creole language, understand the Creole people], Yves concluded.

Despite my "understanding," I had doubts about Yves's explanation of chimè. The term, I knew, was the name given to those who had engaged in a violent campaign to repress opponents of former President Jean-Bertrand Aristide during the final throes, and beyond, of his second term in office. I wondered if Yves was not playing with semantics to exculpate himself, especially in the eyes of an American whose government largely agreed with the criminal interpretation of chimè. After all, he knew the United States had, through aid blockades, democratization trainings, and diplomatic cold shoulders, helped undermine Aristide's second term and bolster the civil society, and eventually ex-military opposition, that ended his rule.[1] Still, I found his interpretation suggestive, for the times I had heard chimè used in everyday life, it was to describe moments of frustration: a child throwing a fit, a lover consumed by jealous rage, or a drug addict who was tweaking. How much of his identity, I wondered, hinged on the power of a simple redefinition to rewrite his life story?

In this chapter, I contemplate the experience of being blocked, the state of subjugation from which the poor, urban man—nèg geto—attempts to maneuver for a sense of identity, agency, and power while being continually reinscribed through discourses and practices of subjugation. Yves experienced this predicament as *fristrasyon* (frustration), and he often referred to his life as an ongoing struggle to *fè yon lòt jan* (make another way).[2] Primarily an economic struggle, Yves was under constant pressure to *chache lavi,* to make a livelihood and, in turn, a life, under conditions that were far from ideal. He forged his pathways to livelihood across a sociopolitical terrain in which the fact of being nèg geto predetermined his slot within a highly exploitative political division of labor as well as political geography of the urban population. In this way, the struggle to "make another way" was ultimately an existential problem of crafting not just a livelihood but a *life* on one's own terms. As the wordplay around chimè already makes clear, this often came down to insisting on being not *one* but *many* identities. If from the vantage point of his political opponents (and patrons) among the *hommes politiques,* Yves was nothing more than a criminal, what struck me was how he had a way of pulverizing this ontology of criminal singularity into a multiplicity of politicized existences. The ways he tacked between the delinquent and the downtrodden, the criminal and the frustrated, the violent and the militant, and made neither all-defining of his personhood was an intricate two-step that narrated who he was and wanted to be.

The literary scholar Caroline Walker Bynum, working with the magical texts of medieval Europe, has argued that identity construction is best understood as a relationship between story and shape. "Story spreads out through time the behaviors or bodies—the shapes—a self has been or will be, each replacing the one before" (2001, 180). The self is made in the narrative sequence of shape-shifting, of transmuting into new forms, while retaining vestiges of what is left behind. "For my self is my story, known only in my shape, in the marks and visible behaviors I manifest—whether generic or personal" (Bynum 2001, 181). In a similar vein, the anthropologist Karen McCarthy Brown has shown how words in Haiti have the power to act as *pwen* or *wanga*, a kind of magical charm that "captures the essence or pith of a thing" (1987, 151).[3] Just like a doll tied to a chair to correct a wayward husband or a bowl of coconut water placed on an altar to "clear" the vision of a jealous friend, "word *wanga*" exert power over a troubled relationship by imagining it in a particular way and by persuading oneself and others to recalibrate their interpretations to this imaginary. Rather than limit the interpretation of a person, thing, or situation to *one* meaning, then, word *wanga* makes it meaningful in terms of a social relation or conflict—which is to say the word *wanga* always has at least two, but often many more, meanings. Word *wanga* are "competing narratives that are empowered by their various abilities to convince key audiences (including spiritual ones) of their points of view and, therefore, shift problematic situations" (Brown 2003, 242). The polysemic nature of nicknames, baz titles, and political labels, like chimè, provides good examples of the art of word *wanga*—or what in common parlance is called *voye pwen* (sending points). Like the exchange of proverbs between Yves and the CAMEP employees, such word *wanga* serves to intervene in a social conflict and changes how we interpret the players and events involved.

In this chapter, I contemplate Yves's recasting of chimè, as well as other instances of his and others' rhetorical gymnastics, as shape-shifting exercises that reframed the story of himself in relation to the stories others told about him. In some ways, this narrative recalibration unfolded along a linear trajectory, tracing the "sequence, the before or after, of a self," as Bynum writes (2001, 181).[4] The *frustrated* self was a reaction to the *criminal* self. But these selves also existed simultaneously. Yves assumed different shapes as he represented himself and was represented across different social contexts and conflicts. Not limited by the Western dictum of noncontradiction (the rule that two things cannot be true at same time), those conversant in the ritual arts of possession and transmutation retained the possibility for coeval multiplicity.[5] Teasing out this process is one aim of this chapter. Another is to illustrate the central role Yves played at Baz Zap Zap and, in turn, my ethnography of it.

It would be difficult to write about Baz Zap Zap without writing about Yves. He was, after all, its current recognized political leader—so much so that many referred to him as simply "Zap Zap." Yves allows me to contemplate the complexity of this role as well as my relationship to it. My interactions with Yves show how ethnographic knowledge is enabled and shaped as much by the friendships we build in the field as by the ambivalent, often tense alliances we negotiate with powerful actors there. Yves's ultimate acceptance of my company went far to situate me as an insider and enable my research in a charged and volatile sociopolitical milieu. But this was a strategic alliance—from both sides. Our accord arose out of hierarchies of race, class, and nationality that, while enabling the research process, also reinforced our social distance from each other. However, these asymmetries did not always play to my practical or epistemological advantage. Yves navigated relations on the block, in governmental ministries, and with the anthropologist, with ease, fluidity, and insight. The more time I spent with him the more I was able to analyze his political maneuvers—a process that led to increased *konesans* (understanding) but also *mekonesans* (misunderstanding). In attending to this "ethnographic dissonance," as Steven Gregory (2006, 168) aptly calls it, I seek not to diminish Yves's point of view. On the contrary, I hope to avoid the tendency to parse the distanced, objective interpretations of anthropologists from the on-the-ground, subjective ones of anthropologists' interlocutors. For the truths of our accounts commingled as narratives we both were telling about ourselves and the world in which we were likewise implicated.

Stuck on the Bottom

After the earthquake, when I began to focus my sites on baz politics more, I let Frantzy know that I would like to accompany Yves on more of his political errands. Yves was not opposed to the idea. The company of a blan, as he and others often presumed, would ease relations with politicians, making him appear more honest and trustworthy. I remember once after he was denied entry to the Ministère de la Culture et de la Communication, he retrieved me from the car and was then granted access. But my presence could also backfire in the face of someone frustrated with US-Haiti relations or the privileges granted to white people in Haiti. More than once, Yves was told to "leave the blan outside."

My outings with Yves were not organized around scheduled meetings but rather followed the circuitous, spontaneous rhythm of *bwase lari*. The Port-au-Prince version of "hustling," bwase lari evokes racing around town orchestrating all manner of errands. On the days I shadowed Yves, he met up with politicians, friends, acquaintances, and often lovers in pursuit of money, contacts, and favors. He spun tales and made false promises, though he never begged. He balanced his "asks" with giving. Sometimes simultaneously with his own demand, he answered that of others, handing over small change, arranging a private school scholarship, or a gig in the next baz activity. To bwase lari is to live by way of and be in constant pursuit of the next deal. It is associated as much with criminality, with those who take advantage of others, as it is with social skill, smarts, bravery, and the ability to make an unfair world work for you. Bwase lari is a survival strategy: life for the urban poor depends on an exchange of benefits among an ever-expanding network of kindred. Yet it also facilitates empowerment. By displaying command over an endless web of social exchanges, its practitioners attain status and power on the streets.

Our outings began with heaping bowls of *bouyon* at Janice's street-side restaurant. Yves often joked that I was too thin for his taste and would give me tips and mysterious potions for gaining weight. I never drank the tonics, but I did follow one piece of advice: Janice's beef stew for breakfast. When I was with Yves, I usually ate for free. As with most of his relationships, Yves and Janice swapped favors: in exchange for our meals, Janice received jobs cooking for baz events and membership for her two sons in street-sweeping projects and other activities.

On a June morning in 2013, after our meal, we headed to SMCRS. Our visit was timed to coincide with Bel Air's annual patron saint celebration. Festivals were periods of peak activity for baz formations, as they organized the details of the event and its preparation—which inevitably entailed sprucing up the streets. On our way, Yves greeted countless people walking along the curb. "*Respè, blade!*" "*Sa k ap fèt la?*" "*Ki jan manman ou ye?*" "*Tout moun anfòm?*" I was impressed with the breadth of his contacts, extending to statesmen in the corridors of power and the man on the street. He handed out small change to the young boys who wiped the windshield, encouraged me to buy sodas from a young vendor, generously tipped Bel Air's makeshift crossing guard, and offered a ride downtown to two young women. Social largesse also returned to him. A former deputy from his natal district in Léogâne stopped, jumped out of his car, and raced to greet Yves. They hashed out plans for a meeting next week about "a lot of projects." As they chatted, oblivious to the mounting traffic, a police man approached on his motorbike. I feared a ticket, but Yves simply jumped into a routine to which I had grown accustomed. "I am Zap Zap! We created the police. Remember the song we sang in all the streets under the de facto [regime]: 'Army, army, army of thieves. Army, army, zenglendo army. Crush the army and give me the police corps.'"[6] The policeman laughed and told him to get going.

Yves turned to me, "You see the way I am a gwo nèg. It's not the ti nèg of Bel Air that has friends in all places."

When we arrived at SMCRS, Yves was waved through security, parked his car in employee parking, and eased his way upstairs to the executive offices. The main office, a recipient of post-earthquake development funds, was newly out-fitted with imported desks, office chairs, and desktops, many of them still in bubble wrap. Yves announced that he was there to deliver a letter to the director requesting support to help "young people in the popular quarters participate in the festival in a positive way."

We were asked to wait. As we did, Frantzy insisted that I take a photo of him in the state office. "It's not everyday I get to come face-to-face with the state." Unfortunately, when Yves was called back, Frantzy was turned away. He was wearing tattered Adidas sandals. Although he had polished the scruffy white leather until it shined, he was told that he needed to wear dress shoes and not show his *gwo zotèy* (big toes). Such rules—no short sleeves, shorts, caps, or sneakers—were enforced as matters of proper etiquette and decorum, but they often functioned as ways of making the urban poor feel like second-class citizens and locking them out of civil society.[7] No matter how hard they tried, Belairians often fell just short of the norms of respectability. Even Yves, ever the savvy politician, was instructed to take off his New York Yankees cap.

Once we were in the corridors of the main offices, Yves handed a letter detailing his proposal for a street-sweeping team to a secretary, who smiled and asked us to sit again. Hours seemed to pass. Eventually, we were called back and escorted to the desk of a thirty-year-old man. A look of surprise crossed his face as he saw me, and he shuffled some folders on his desk. He told us the director could not see us, but that he had read the letter. "I regret we can't support the project. But *blada*, we'll fight for the work you do to help Bel Air stay calm," he remarked, the street slang for "brother" sitting uneasily on his tongue. It was then that I noticed a small stack of Haitian goud sticking out of a folder on the desk. The director's assistant distracted me with questions about my background and thoughts about Haiti, but I noticed him push the envelope toward the desk's corner. Yves got the hint, picked up the folder, and we headed for the door, with Yves filling the air with boisterous goodbyes.

I expected him to be thrilled with the payout, but when we got in the car, he was clearly perturbed. "Haitians are supposed to respect Haitians. But you see how Haitians treat each other: bad, bad, bad. I follow all the rules: write a letter, type it, print it, put it in folder. That's not easy. And they treat me like a *vagabon* [vagabond]."

"Why do you think that happens?" I asked.

"Ask Frantzy," he said.

"I don't know," Frantzy began. "All people are people. Titid [Aristide] said that. But in reality, when the poor go to a state office, they are treated like an animal. That's crazy, right?"

"And you saw how he thought twice when he saw you," Yves added. "In the country of Dessalines, blan get more respect. Huh! Haitians are discriminatory. We walk on a straight line, but they make us turn and turn, and the line is no longer straight."

"OK, I agree, but you still got something, even if he did not give it in the proper way."

"What other choice do I have? They think they are helping me, and it's true it's a little something, but I back up, back up, back up, and never advance. Let me tell you something: I want to stop fè politik one day. I put my body before the fire for too long. Look, look at all these badges," he said, gripping the lanyards. "Not a single good job, but a lot of people are against me for this reason! I can even die. What will badges do for my children? Nothing!" he said as he ran his index finger across his neck.

We visited three other offices that day, none of which even bothered to grant a meeting.

Yves's complaints point to his frustrations at embodying the complicated status of baz leader—at once a powerful figure who can reach into the corridors of power and manage neighborhood affairs and a mistrusted hustler who is often dismissed or paid off, if not criminalized, by those in power. The saying to fè politik shares semantic terrain with *kriminalite* (criminality), since the latter can imply not merely acts that violate the law but also those that benefit oneself at the expense of others.[8] In this way, all those who hold positions of power in Haiti become prime targets for narratives of criminality that check and challenge their status. But the fact that Yves's power in particular and baz leaders more generally manifested from the purview of the nèg geto made them even more vulnerable to renderings of their identity in criminal terms. While the bribe attested to Yves's political contacts and clout, it also put him in his place as a nèg geto—a man of danger and disorder. He welcomed the financial support but resented its disrespectable delivery. It reminded him of his job. The reason he had time for political errands was that the only real job behind all his badges was the one at the public health clinic, and it was hardly ever open. I only ever saw him work there once. Like the bribe, it showed less an act of incorporation into the state than an exercise in social control and further marginalization. It framed him as someone who is only capable of fè politik. Yet at the same time, Yves was also well aware of how he could rework the category of nèg geto in ways that empowered him to fè leta—make the state in contrast to doing politics.

Yves's entry into politics followed a trajectory at once predictable and seren-dipitous. Yves was born on July 25, 1977, at the General Hospital in Port-au-Prince to parents who resided in a shack on Bel Air's hillside. His parents were part of the Duvalier family dictatorship's large state labor force. His mother worked at the Ministère des Affaires Sociales et du Travail as a cook, and his father was a soldier in the Haitian army. The employment made it possible for Yves to attend Lycée Pétion, a reputable public high school, but he never performed well. In 1994, when the Haitian army was disbanded following Aristide's return to power, his father became unemployed. The job loss disrupted the family and made it impossible for them to afford school fees and materials. Yves dropped out two years before graduation.

This was a sore spot for Yves. When denied state jobs or contracts, he would often protest that it was because the hommes politiques thought he lacked *kompetans* (competency). And I often witnessed how his lack of a diploma and poor literacy manifested in tensions with his followers, including his right-hand man, Frantzy, who had finished high school. Yves often boasted in public about the closeness of their friendship and how it was fated, since both of their families migrated to the city from rural Léogâne. But he once told me how he, in fact, needed Frantzy for his education. Frantzy was charged with navigating state and NGO bureaucracies, including writing and reading all correspon-dence between them and Yves. This was an essential task, and Yves was much appreciative of Frantzy, making him the prime benefactor of his political labors. Yet when he informed the zone about the office job he helped Frantzy secure with Cantine Scolaire, he immediately compared it to his more militant post as a security guard at the local public health clinic, saying, in a high-pitched French accent that mocked elite discourse, "I'm not fit for such *bourgeois* work, because I'm a man of the people!" He also publicly ridiculed Frantzy when he found out that Frantzy delegated his tasks to his baz mate Michel, who not only finished high school but graduated with above average marks. Invoking the image of school kids crowded on wooden benches and Frantzy's less ample frame, he remarked, "It turns out that school did not impart knowledge, just a flat bottom."[9]

Yves's sensitivities around education and his experiences of disrespect by hommes politiques affected our relationship as well. Although Yves allowed me to accompany him on many political errands, he was not exactly open with me. Occasionally, he voiced an opinion about an issue, but we rarely had an open, back-and-forth conversation. He resisted answering my questions directly, often delegating to Frantzy or someone else present. I suspect he had many reasons for this. For one, it seemed to advance his mystique as a powerful figure. He was also wary of letting anyone, let alone an outsider, know too much about his political dealings. But at the bottom I suspected a nagging tension about education that limited our closeness. Yves often joked that if I were to come back, after death, as a Gede spirit and possess someone in ritual, the possessed would grab a pen and notebook and ceaselessly take notes. This drew loud laughs—from me especially. Once, after the laughter settled, Yves remarked, "Everyone laughs, but the pen, the computer, the camera, all of that is also a weapon."

Managing Power on the Block

Despite his ties to the Duvalier dictatorship and his lack of "competency," Yves found a foothold in politics during Aristide's second term. He played the banbou in the Zap Zap rara, participated in pro-Lavalas protests, and frequented political meetings at the Aristide Foundation for Democracy, an organization dedicated to offering the urban poor "the tools needed to participate in the democratic life of the nation," including adult literacy classes, a children's radio, and a medical and nursing school.[10] In early 2000, soon after becoming a party member, Yves started to help plan demonstrations and press conferences for the elections that, later that year, would put Aristide in power again. It was then that he got his big political break—almost sacrificing his life and indebting Aristide to him.

"I was in a car that, while transporting people in Bel Air to vote, got into a serious accident," he recounted. "[Aristide] made the party delegates pay for the hospital, and he compensated us for our injuries, more than normal. And then, after he took power, Aristide asked to meet the injured, and it was then that I met him face-to-face. He gave me a lot of respè, because we discussed the problems in the zone." Aristide, recognizing the sacrifice Yves had made and his enthusiasm for the cause, made Yves a key node in Lavalas's urban political network. "I became part of the team, a delegate for Aristide in Bel Air, and I could elevate the baz. I had a lot of political activities, and people began to see that I have political skills, and we arrive to today, where I am a political force in the geto."

Being a "political force in the geto" meant, among other things, that Yves had the power to acquire and manage state-sponsored projects for the zone. Soon after the SMCRS visit, as I again ate my midday meal with Sophie, Yves stopped by to tell Kal that he kept following up with SMCRS and had secured a new street-sweeping project. He pulled out his black leather wallet. It was stuffed with so many plastic identity cards that it burst at the seams. He slowly and methodically went through all the cards, stacking them on the wooden hutch in two tall piles. Finally, he came to the one he needed and showed it to Kal. Hastily made with a personal printer, it pictured his grainy headshot, the office's acronym, and his newly codified role: head of a local street-sweeping project. The badge meant that

Yves could employ for two weeks fifteen neighbors to clean the street of garbage. Yves offered Kal a post as head of a five-person team at 400 goud ($10) per day (the sweepers would make half as much).

I imagined Kal would jump at the opportunity, but he said nothing and began to eat.

Yves left and went to Kay Adam, where he pulled up a chair curbside, drank a small bottle of Barbancourt three-star rum, and listened to rap kreyòl playing from his jeep's radio.

Soon after, Kal struck up a conversation I found puzzling at the time.

"You are a Democrat, right?"

"Yes," I replied.

"Because your mom and dad are Democrats. You were born in a Democratic family."

"Yes, you can say that," I agreed.

"There are Democrats and Republicans in the United States, is that right?"

"Other parties too. But yes, only two big parties."

"OK, and now you have Obama, and you are happy, you find things. But when George Baby Bush was president, you and your family did not find things, right?"

"You can say that we were not OK with his projects."

"OK, I see. But even though you did not find anything, you did not try to change camps. You did not run behind George Bush. You waited eight long years. You suffered all the time because you are a Democrat. You waited until Obama could come to power. You had your camp, and you stayed with your camp, even if it meant four years of hunger."

"Yes, I don't think I'd ever vote Republican," I replied.

"You see, Sophie, that is a beautiful system. Each person has his camp. Like that, each person knows his place."

"Yes, but the two parties are not so different," I said as I contemplated the many drawbacks of a two-party system. But before I finished, Yves reappeared.

Yves put his hands on his hips and blocked the doorway with his wide frame. "You are part of the Democratic Party, but you are also a good democrat, See-see, isn't that right?" he began. "You walk with all people! You are not konplekse [discriminatory]. You can take the road or the corridor . . . to make another way," he said, as he flailed his arms in excitement.

It was then I noticed he was sporting the pink-and-white bracelet of Foundation Rose et Blanc, the social organization run by Michel Martelly, better known as "Sweet Mickey," the pop music star had won the presidency two years later in 2011. Yves was an unlikely supporter of Sweet Mickey, who was a vocal member of the civil society sector that had opposed President Aristide's second term. Sweet Mickey had headlined the musical acts for several koudyay, or political rallies, at the state university to energize disaffected students for protests against the government. Just as I was realizing that the street-sweeping project probably came by way of a new alliance with Martelly, Yves pulled from the pocket of his t-shirt the electoral card from Aristide's first election in 1990. Pushing the face of the gamecock that symbolized Aristide's FNCD party toward my face, he said, "*Kòk la chante pou toutan!*" (The rooster crows for all time.)

"*E li li ye; li pa ka lwen*" (It is him; he can't be far away), Kal approvingly responded.

I nodded as Yves put the card back in his shirt pocket and batted his chest with his fist.

It was not uncommon for Belairians' political affiliations to be unknown, ambiguous, or replete with contradictions. Despite the fact that Bel Air remained a Lavalas stronghold, there was the practical matter of advocating for oneself and one's social circle by managing multiple, opposing political contacts simultaneously. This was especially the case after the collapse of Aristide's second term, when the two-party system pulverized into several political camps that cut across the old Makout-Lavalas divide. In this political landscape, it became advantageous for baz leaders like Yves to claim control over an urban block and act as gatekeepers for all those who could bring resources or benefits to the zone, including former political rivals. Still, there was the sense that true allegiance ought to lie with Aristide and the Fanmi Lavalas party. Yves's ultimate display of the 1990 electoral card did not assert his one "authentic" political identity, but rather how he organized his multiple affiliations into a nested hierarchy, where they were positioned according to the "sincerity" he felt toward each, to invoke the anthropologist John Jackson's distinction between authenticity and sincerity (Jackson 2005). What was more valued was kept close, what was less treasured held at a distance, but neither affiliation was true or false in an either-or understanding of reality.[11] Yves might wear the pink bracelet, but the card stayed closer to his heart. Furthermore, each was sincerely employed for the context of its use. Wearing the pink bracelet on the outside might very well facilitate the work of the card on the inside—needing to partner with a rival in order to further an ally's agenda. At least, this was what he hoped to convey to Kal, whose discourse on American partisanship was a tutorial in the standards of political loyalty.

Soon after, Kal told him that he would take the post, but he demanded that Jak and Bernie, his two closest buddies, be included in his team. "If the baz does not change, the chèf does not change either," Kal said, again making a plea for loyalty. But Kal also made clear that his agreement was contingent. He complained that the money was not sufficient for the work involved, to which Yves replied that they should also seek contributions from supporters.

"I'll tell everyone that, so we can create more jobs," Yves said.

"Good idea," Kal seconded.

As Yves left, he told me he had something to discuss with me. I followed him outside and into his jeep, where he held many private meetings. I was prepared for what would come next: the reference to contributors included me. But I was still taken aback when Yves asked for 4,000 goud ($100 U.S.)—a large sum on its own terms but exorbitant given that I had just given him the same amount to repair a faulty brake pedal on his jeep. He insisted it was only a loan, and that if this went well, more projects and funds would come. I reminded him that I did not like to *prete* (loan) money but that I would make a *kado* (gift). Thinking of Sophie and the other women who would likely be left off the street-sweeping teams, I preemptively told him I wanted my contribution to pay for Sophie to make a pot of hearty *bouyon* for the team.

The next day, before lunchtime, I went to Yves's house. When I handed him the money, he thanked me, but then quickly handed me back half of it. I wondered if he had thought twice about how the large sum would hinder a future request. But instead he told me it would be better for me to give the money to Sophie directly, since it was a gift. I did not object, and together we walked over to her house. When we arrived, he proudly announced that I had "loaned the project 2,000 goud" and had also "made a gift so that everyone can eat after the day's work."

It then dawned on me that the message Kal had conveyed via US party loyalty was not only about political sincerity but also the ethics and norms of reciprocity that governed social relations and exchanges between politicians and the baz, and between the baz and people in Bel Air more generally. Yves earned his position at the helm of Baz Zap Zap through the sacrificial gift he made to Aristide (putting his body on the line), and he maintained it through a chain of gifts to his local supporters in Bel Air. The onus on the gift—a sense of communal mutuality and obligation more generally—was heightened in an urban environment of mass unemployment and intermittent earnings from informal labor. Few would get by without the imperative to share earnings. But on another, moral level, the plea for my contribution was a key mechanism by which people were incorporated and retained as members of the baz. By requiring that I contribute to the endeavor, Kal and Yves inserted me into the constant circulation of debts, never fully compensated, that bound the urban poor together.[12] In fact, far from an act of generosity, my policy on "gifts" was an attempt to exit this sense of communal obligation. I knew that, given the vast wealth differentials at stake, my loans were unlikely to be repaid, at least monetarily, and I wished to avoid the tense relations that often resulted from unreciprocated loans. I also hoped gifting would relieve me from the stifling pressure and accounting headaches of owing and being owed by an ever-expanding network of people.

In other words, I was hopelessly reaching for a "free gift" that required no reciprocity. Yet as Mary Douglas (1990) long ago asserted, the free gift was not only an unattainable ideal but a flawed social exchange, precisely because it lacked reciprocity (see also Mauss 1954 [1990]).

Yves's ultimate acceptance of my "gift" only made this point more obvious. One arena in which a free gift was imaginable was the collective meal. "*Manje kwit pa gen mèt*" (cooked food has no master), goes the Haitian proverb, implying prepared food is not a commodity in the same way as dry goods. Although cooked food is regularly sold on Bel Air's streets, the saying comes from a rural past, when a pot of stew was said to be for sharing with the community, not for sale. Still, the meal only approximated a free gift. I would also eat and enjoy it. It was more like a collective loan, entering a realm of noneconomic gift exchange, freed from the demand to account for its transactional value but not from the norms of mutual exchange.

Beyond reinforcing my social positionality, my offering also participated in Yves's efforts to manage perceptions of his status as a respected local leader who abided by the terms of redistribution. Part of the reason he kept me at some distance was that affiliating too close with the blan might suggest a lucrative source of money that was not being duly reallocated. In the days following the announcement of the street-sweeping project, grumblings surfaced on the block: several women, older men, and others who occupied spaces on the periphery of baz networks, as well as those locked in competition with Yves, approached the endeavor with skepticism and disapproval, knowing that they were not likely to reap the same benefit as Yves and his baz mates, if any at all. By accepting half the money in private, while handing over the other half in full view of others, Yves was allaying concerns that he was employing my services for his own enrichment rather than that of the group. Likewise, his job offerings to Kal skirted the public/private line, with most of the jobs being allocated among friends in private, while the potential for additional ones and other benefits was made public. A panoply of secrets and disclosures, navigating the politics of redistribution in Bel Air proved difficult. It often collapsed under its own pressures.

"Vagabon! Kal blurted out when we were again left alone. "They always give a little more, but do we see any of it? No! He's supposed to make the state, but he'd rather act like a vagabon. Disorder!"

I hesitated, thinking Kal knew I had given more money than he witnessed. It turned out, however, that Kal had learned via Frantzy that, as before, some cash—in addition to the project funds—had been secretly delivered to Yves at his latest visit to SMCRS. This accusation of vagabondage and the threat of disorder raised the troubled history of corruption, criminality, and violence that underlay both the operations of the state and the baz's quest to assume state duties on the block. This was the problem that made it hard for Yves to fully shake the criminal connotations associated with the chimè label and become a recognized homme politique.

The Power to Suffocate and Resuscitate

A good starting point for analyzing the contradictory valences of the chimè label is the tale of Baz Zap Zap's conflict with Baz GNB that played out during President Aristide's second term. Like Zap Zap, whose name can be rendered as "affairs of the people, affairs of the country" as well as an onomatopoeia that mimics the sounds of a swiping machete, GNB signaled a compound, contradictory identity. In its more benevolent guise, it stood for "Gran Nèg Bèlè," calling to mind the "big man" who settled disputes, found jobs, shared earnings, or otherwise offered help to his followers. In its more malevolent guise, it meant, "Grenn Nan Bouda," literally "testicles in the butt" and implying the "strongman" who is primed for battle against his enemies. One of the mottos of the group was "Ling Di" (the hard line), suggesting how it cordoned off the neighborhood under its control and threatened to retaliate against those who crossed its barrier, or, as people often elaborated, "those who did not walk the *ling dwat* [straight line]." The definitional ambiguity of GNB allowed the group to keep open the possibility of conflicting identities as well as put the onus on interpreters to determine when any one was operative.

Baz GNB took root after Aristide's second inauguration about two blocks from Plateau Bel Air. The group first appeared to incarnate the narrative of the big man. Aristide's second term was severely undermined by an international aid blockade that starved the state budget and crippled the already weak public sector as a result (Schuller 2012b). Garbage went uncollected, blackouts were the norm, and water pipes ran dry. "There was no state at all then!" people often recalled about that period. Within this void, many baz throughout Port-au-Prince began to come together to assume the work of the state that was left undone. Baz GNB, for example, took over control of the most important public water kiosk in the area, located in the high traffic area behind Lycée Pétion. Its members not only organized the distribution of water when CAMEP turned on the pipes, but they also managed to organize several nearby households with access to state water to supplement the meager offerings of CAMEP. As Fred, a Baz GNB leader at the time, recalled: "It was a good thing. We delivered a social service that reached many people." With the intention of boosting service delivery, Baz GNB began to charge tolls for passage into the neighborhood. The practice repurposed older models common among block committees of charging passing motorists to help pay for road repairs. Yet many people recalled it as a perversion of this practice, since it targeted pedestrians of lesser means, passersby who were not using the public service, and residents of the neighborhood. It was this act that began to shift the identity of Baz GNB to the strongman. "They treated us like we weren't Bel Air people! You're not supposed to do that to your neighbors who are just trying to get by, just like you. They became a gang," Sophie once recalled. Other, more egregious abuses of power exacerbated this perception.

A key incident involved Baz Zap Zap directly. As Yves told the story, "GNB stole from Bel Air people. They even stole and raped machann." He went on to detail how a member of Baz GNB approached Marie, a resident of Plateau Bel Air, after a long day of selling water buckets near Lycée Pétion. They asked her to pay a toll of 50 goud as she passed by the water kiosk. Having sold only two buckets that day for 5 goud, she did not have the money to pay the toll. The Baz GNB member let her go, but the next day, she was robbed of all her merchandise by two masked men. That same day, a Baz GNB member targeted another machann and a friend of Yves's wife. He pushed her to the ground, put a foot on her stomach, and threatened rape if the Plateau's machann would not pay her toll. The use of theft and rape against neighborhood women to force compliance overstepped an implicit code of baz operation. Although such actions were recognized as criminal, they could at times be tolerated if they targeted outsiders. Attacks against "Bel Air people," however, were condemned. It was, in fact, often this act of attacking the in group (as opposed to an out group) that differentiated a *gang* from a *baz* in local parlance.

Yves, perceiving just that, retaliated. "I told Fred that he did not respect my people, and that I would make *le police* [de facto police] and go after him if he does not respect that, and to give back the money and buckets he stole." A confrontation ensued, and Fred ended up with a machete cut across his waist. Then, in the middle of the next night, a fire broke out near Petit's gambling hall, where Baz Zap Zap had been organizing its operations. The fire, presumably started by GNB members, burned three neighborhood shacks to the ground, including Petit's residence. An elderly woman died, and a child was severely burned. The fire brought the conflict to the attention of those far beyond the neighborhood. As Yves recalled: "The way things got hot, that arrived all the way to the state, and they paid more than 1,000 *bon* US dollars in damages for us to stop fighting, to make a peace accord. They sent a little fireman to put out the fire before it took over the city. That happened a lot during that epoch. They even sent me a check," referring to a job that he was offered at the public health clinic to quell tensions. "That worked, but it was a "peace *pèpè*." As has become common practice, he used the word for used clothes imported from the United States to indicate that this peace, because neither homegrown nor high quality, would not last. But as such, it would provide more opportunities for the baz's political brinkmanship. "What did that do at the end?" he wondered. "Let me tell you something," pointing to his hulking thighs. "It sent the baz *jarèt* [thighs]!"

This was a story Yves enjoyed telling, in part because it portrayed him as a hero defending the neighborhood from criminals who assaulted "our women." This aspect of the story planted doubts in my mind. The patriarchal provider persona countered my observations of Yves's relations with women in Bel Air, including me. He frequently and openly cheated on his wife, often flaunting his liaisons with teenagers who were financially dependent on him. I disapproved of this behavior, and he knew it. Aggravating the matter was his longing to marry an American for residency in the United States. When he first propositioned me, I readily declined, but he did not drop the matter, often pressuring me to find a friend who would fulfill his request. What bothered me was not his maneuverings for a visa, which were common among my contacts, but the nagging feeling that he saw women as little more than vehicles to advance his personal pursuits. Seen thusly, his story lacked credibility not only because it contradicted his treatment of women but also because it fit a pattern of using women for self-promotion. As I contemplated this point, I wondered how this whole story served to promote an image of Yves and Baz Zap Zap that did not grapple with the less reputable underpinnings of their street sovereignty. But this is precisely the point. Yves's narrative was an attempt to shape his subjectivity as the righteous actor in a charged context of power relations.

Yves also enjoyed telling this story because it showed how—at least at this moment—his political clout extended from the neighborhood into the halls of state authority. The members of Baz Zap Zap, like those of GNB, positioned themselves as informal state agents, administering basic services and implementing informal justice (*le police*), when the real police (*la police*) were absent or ineffective. They were also the point people for rallying the urban population for demonstrations in support of the government and against the opposition. In so doing, they became indispensable cogs in the wheels of Aristide's administration. Because baz formations employed informal, illicit tactics for this work, Aristide could not officially sanction them, but because they controlled highly populous and potentially volatile districts, he also required their allegiance. Hence when disruptive conflicts erupted between baz formations, party leadership was reluctant to intervene in ways that compromised local authority structures, opting to "put out fires" through peace treaties, damage compensation, and more jobs rather than arrests or imprisonment (Dupuy 2007b; Beckett 2008). It was also the case that the act of imprisonment implied a recognition of criminality—a stigmatizing mark that would extend to their allies in power. Over time, however, this practice emboldened baz leaders, sending them "the thighs" that set the stage for them to take on more power in their zones. As the political scientist Robert Fatton wrote in 2002, "The danger was that having begun as a mere political instrument in the struggle for power, the chimè have now become a power unto themselves" (2002, 148).

By the end of 2003, the political battle over Aristide's second presidency had reached its climax with a firm aid blockade, a staunch civil society opposition, and a new source of popular support. The civil society opposition found the popular following that it had been missing in an anti-Aristide university student movement that also took the name GNB. (Many in Bel Air felt they appropriated this name in order to claim the power of the baz and, in turn, weaken it.)[13] The students proved a natural ally for civil society, offering something of a middle ground between the elite minority and poor majority. They mainly hailed from lower and middle-class backgrounds, but they were also among the privileged 1 percent of the population who attended university, and many envisioned themselves as aspiring members of civil society. They also proved a natural enemy to baz leaders like Yves, who resented them for the same reasons. Although some baz did ally with the opposition, most baz formations in Bel Air and elsewhere in the city united under the moniker rat pa kaka.[14] The phrase rat pa kaka—preferred by baz leaders to chimè—was a slice of a longer chant used, during the de facto period, by the Bel Air Resistance Platform and meant to threaten anyone who dared trespass the neighborhood or its political platform, "Rat pa kaka, sourit pa travèse lari, sinon ou shotta" (Rats don't shit, mice don't cross the street, or else you'll be shot).

One of the most significant GNB-led protests against Aristide occurred on Friday, December 5, 2003. As the students rallied for a march inside a university courtyard, several rat pa kaka stood in the street and blocked the entrance. A group from Bel Air, led by Yves, was among the most fervent in the street. Both groups yelled insults and threw rocks at each other through the university gates. Tensions escalated, and eventually, those on the street broke into the courtyard and incited a brawl that resulted in injuries on both sides. For many, the day represented the nadir of the popular movement and the height of chimè terror. It became known in oppositional circles as Vandredi Nwa (Black Friday)—and it ultimately shifted key sectors of national and global civil society from hoping to resolve the political impasse to actively calling for Aristide's ouster.[15] Two months later, on February 29, 2004, Aristide's government toppled.

When Aristide was ousted from power, baz in Bel Air turned the streets of Bel Air into wards under their control and in the service of their political agenda. They imposed tolls and protection rackets, as well as organized kidnappings, to assert their power and buy weapons to fight what became known as Operation Baghdad, another complex word play that invoked the war in Iraq and its competing meanings: an illegitimate US intervention in a sovereign state (the view of baz leaders) or a legitimate war against brutal terrorists (the view of anti-Aristide forces).[16] After Aristide's ouster in February 2004, the UN-authorized Resolution no. 1542, a Brazilian-led peacekeeping force known by the acronym MINUSTAH, which was principally charged with eradicating the pro-Aristide "gangs" so that a new government could take power (Dziedzic and Perito 2008).[17] A month after the coup, police apprehended Yves and imprisoned him for his involvement in Black Friday. He was held without trial for two years, the duration of the interim regime installed by the UN. On September 30, 2004, thirteen years after the first coup against Aristide, baz leaders in Bel Air rallied thousands of disgruntled citizens and staged a protest to contest the coup and the interim regime. Police opened fire at the protest and killed two protesters, which set off weeks of reprisal killings, with several headless bodies, including those of two police officers, found throughout the city (Griffin 2004; Hallward 2007). The daily protests, police killings, and rampant insecurity that lasted until February 2006, when Aristide's successor René Préval was elected president (Deibert 2005, 2017). Over the course of Baghdad a reported seven hundred people died.

In her memoir *Brother, I'm Dying*, the renowned Haitian American novelist Edwidge Danticat (2007), who was raised in Bel Air by her aunt and uncle, recounted the toll Operation Baghdad had on ordinary Belairians. Following the events from Miami, she detailed how her uncle, a pastor of a church down the hill from Baz Zap Zap, was forced into exile after CIMO police and MINUSTAH stormed his church during Sunday service on October 24, 2004. The soldiers climbed onto the roof and shot at a hideout of *drèd* (dreads), as the dreadlocked baz leaders were often called. Two members of Baz GNB died in the gunfire, as did at least fifteen civilians, and countless people were injured. Baz leaders, suspecting her uncle had conspired with the authorities for the steep Haitian ransom (an estimated $15,000) offered for their capture, threatened to kill her uncle. Soon after, he left Bel Air and then Haiti. The memoir ends with a harrowing account of her uncle's captivity at Miami's Krome immigrant detention camp, where he became severely ill and died in custody. The story illustrates, among other lessons about the inequities Haitians must endure at home and abroad, the human toll of living without an authority to trust—whether baz leader, police officer, or immigration officer. Power acts on those in this position unpredictably, contradictorily, and precariously, crisscrossing between what people in Bel Air call *mòde-soufle* (to bite and to blow, to suffocate and to resuscitate), "where those who are most able to obliterate you are also the only ones suffering some illusion of shelter and protection, a shred of hope—even if false—for possible restoration" (Danticat 2007, 204).[18]

The Division of Political Labor

I was not the only one who questioned Yves's heroic narrative over Baz GNB. In fact, another account of the turf war between Baz Zap Zap and Baz GNB cast Yves less in the role of a masculine savior than a crafty politician manipulating the political labor market. "That whole thing was jealousy!" as Petit began the second version of the story. "Yves was frustrated because he did not find the work he was looking for."

Though Yves benefited more than most from his political contacts, there were still, as Petit put it, "bigger chèf with better jobs." Yves and his clique coveted jobs at the Port-au-Prince port. Beyond a good salary, these jobs provided access to lucrative contraband rackets (the arms and drug trade) as well as extortion powers on the trade of mundane goods. It was Baz GNB, however, that oversaw these jobs. Fred, who had served as the port's assistant manager since the mid-1990s, had allocated neighbors several port security jobs, though none to Baz Zap Zap. To add insult to injury, Roland delegated to Baz GNB ten more CAMEP jobs after Aristide's reelection. "The battle really began, what caused all the damage," Petit asserted, "was when Aristide first took power, when the Lavalas boss Ronald came to the zone with CAMEP jobs."

Roland, on that same trip, promised Zap Zap some jobs, but patience was already beginning to grow thin. "We stood before GNB," Petit continued, "but we also stood before the state. We said we could not wait all the time for that, and we began to say that we would turn against this power. They heard the message, because after that, Roland came back with a security job for Yves at Aurore [the public health clinic] and made me an assistant administrator at Teleco. But we still needed jobs for all the little guys in the baz." The group then waged a series of protests—including hijacking the Teleco payroll truck—to pressure the government. "Eventually," as Petit said, "they came with some jobs at Teleco. We were happy with this, but, you know even this was not good work. They were such small jobs."

As an assistant administrator at Teleco, Petit was supposed to earn 6,000 goud (about $150) every two weeks, and as a security guard at Aurore, Yves made about the same. The prospect of such steady and secure income would prove life-changing. As Jak, who took one of the Teleco posts, recalled: "With that job, it was not just a little money I found. Thanks to that job I got a woman and my first baby!" Yves also built a new house in the neighborhood, moved in with his wife, and welcomed two new children. (He is now the father of five.) Yet while these jobs were worth fighting for, they also proved to be a great source of frustration. For one, the state budget crisis meant that the salary was aspirational. The Teleco employees waited months before being compensated, and then they only received a fraction of what was owed. Further, the jobs issued "*zonbi* checks," payments to people who had no official duties or responsibilities. While this may seem like a windfall, many saw it as evidence of their marginal status and as an affront to their worth as employees. They lamented that they were never provided the literacy classes, skill training, and projects that their "Technician" title promised. As Jak put it, "You know what the [Teleco] badge provided us? It was a new space for the baz to *bay blag* [sit around and tell jokes]! They did not give us any responsibility. We got no training to find another job, and then they fired us." Or as Kal put it, "Those jobs were not good work, work that would last. It was social appease-ment! They were afraid we'd turn against Lavalas." To them, the *zonbi* checks suggested less an investment in their social advancement than a calculated politi-cal expediency, unlikely to last beyond Aristide's rule. Indeed, Teleco employees hired in 2001 were abruptly fired when Aristide's government fell in 2004. The local branch was soon shuttered, and in 2010, Teleco was privatized, eliminat-ing 2,800 jobs and any hope for future postings.[19] Despite complaints about the jobs, the loss of them stung acutely, with Belairians founding Asosyasyon Viktim Amplwaye Teleco (Association of Victimized Employees of Teleco, or AEVT). In 2012, nearly a decade after the men of Baz Zap Zap lost their jobs, they dis-rupted a concert held in Bel Air by the newly appointed President Martelly with signs that read, "All of us in Bel Air are the fired of Teleco."

The Teleco jobs and other low-level state employment made available under Aristide were an exception in an otherwise steady trend of privatizing public utilities and shrinking the public workforce. Historically, the Haitian state has been the main source of formal employment in Haiti. This has changed over the past decades as neoliberal reforms have streamlined public offices, privatized national industries, and transferred many state duties and functions to private organizations and NGOs. State jobs are increasingly few and far between, espe-cially for the urban poor. Yet rather than eliminate the urban poor's participation in the state, this restructuration has channeled them into the informal sectors of statecraft. This goes beyond neighborhood groups assuming the work of a compromised government, such as water distribution, trash collection, and elec-tricity. It also includes the dangerous and sometimes lethal work the urban poor perform for hommes politiques in Haiti.

Those in Bel Air conducted work for politicians that put them at risk for arrest, injury, and death. While the nèg geto was often excluded from formal political work because of his reputation for political disorder and disruption,

FIGURE 13. Rally held by President Michel Martelly in Bel Air in 2012, where Baz Zap Zap members held signs protesting the loss of Teleco jobs.

he was also, paradoxically, useful for politicians precisely because of this reputation. Politicians and state agents with whom I spoke routinely shared the view that baz leaders were essential for their political success but also a dangerous force that could easily lead to their demise. Regardless of party or ideology, they tended to view the nèg geto as best suited for the volatile and sometimes violent work of "doing politics." These perceptions drew on a long history of politicians subcontracting the violent work of the state to the poor in general, from Emperor Soulouque's zenglen in the nineteenth century to the Duvalier family's makout and their zenglendo spin-offs in the twentieth.[20] Yet it is also important to recognize that under conditions of massive urbanization and the "ghettoization" of the city (Laguerre 1976b; Manigat 1997), the association of the urban poor with "street" toughness, danger, and militancy has intensified and increased the tendency for them to be employed for this kind of political labor only. Monsieur Belcourt, a middle-class man and aspiring senatorial candidate who worked on two campaigns with Baz Zap Zap, once told me, "Bel Air people are so skilled at *fè manifestasyon* [making protests]. They have *tèt cho* [hot heads]. I didn't know how to do that. It's not something you learn in school. You learn that on the street [*lari*]. For a well-formed person, it is not easy to turn into a *tèt cho*." For

Monsieur Belcourt, a knack for protesting among the urban poor derived from "the street," an arena foreign to educated hommes politiques. Following a logic of contagion (Douglas 1966), those born and raised in the geto were infected with the qualities of danger and disorder that dwelled there, defining the *geto* resident as hotheaded and well suited for the activities of the street.[21] In this sense, the nèg geto articulated an ontology of race-class-space that constructed the urban poor as a particular kind of person rooted in a particular place.[22] In a conflation of body and place, the nèg geto's penchant for protest thus appeared as an ingrained corporeal and emotional trait that set, at a fundamental level, those from the geto apart from others in the city.

As "hotheads," Belairians were, in this view, well suited to making protests, a genre of politics encompassing a range of activities grounded in the street, including organizing marches to the center of power; placing flaming-tire barricades at busy intersections to block traffic and force a general strike; throwing urine-filled bottles to break up opponents' press conferences; launching rocks at cars, businesses, or other sites of elite wealth; or, in the most extreme example, going underground to attack, kidnap, or assassinate political enemies. The idea of hotheadedness also extended beyond protest to limit the urban poor's participation in other kinds of political labor as well, such as *zonbi*-check jobs or short-term development projects such as street sweeping, construction, or block party organization. When Kal referred to the Teleco jobs as "social appeasement," he was implying that they depended on a perception of the urban poor as primed for protest. In fact, when I thanked a politician who had just awarded the group with the street-sweeping project, he told me: "It's just a little social appeasement. You know, because if we don't do that, they'll take to the streets. It's like that in Haiti." In a similar vein, a senator who sponsored the paving of a dirt corridor behind Kal's house, for which he and fifteen friends did the hard labor, remarked to me in confidence: "Better I put some money in their pockets now! These people are so poor they call them *san manman*. They'll do crimes for money."

The phrase *san manman* is complex, implying those who have not been raised properly, with adherence to the rules and ethics of society, as well as those who act without shame, because they are bereft of a mother before whom they would feel guilty or remorseful. In the mouth of the senator, it portended innate criminality. This was not the identification of someone who broke the law but the kind of person who lacked a moral compass or ideological affiliations and was driven by a purely economic calculus.

Many scholars and journalists have likewise trafficked in this interpretation. Of the youth who carried out the lethal attack on pro-Aristide Saint Jean Bosco parishioners in 1988, for example, Amy Wilentz reported, "According to all accounts, the men with red armbands were paid seven dollars plus a bottle of

Barbancourt rum worth three dollars to do their damage" (1989, 353). Years later, the political scientist Alex Dupuy, writing of the chimè, similarly emphasized the economic dimension. "Insofar as the chimè were mercenaries with no ideological convictions," he writes, "their loyalty to Aristide and their willingness to do his dirty work depended primarily on the monetary and other concrete benefits they derived from the government" (Dupuy 2007a, 155). The Haitian sociologist Alain Gilles (2008, 2012), who has conducted fieldwork in baz strongholds, has similarly argued that residents in marginalized sectors of urban Haiti are unable to develop class consciousness and a unified political movement. The conditions of extreme poverty, coupled with the fact that many slums are inhabited by recent migrants, cultivates neighborly distrust, a generalized opposition to society, and a willingness to act on the political begging of any political patron. The baz I observed did at times exemplify a milieu of agonism, with internal rivalries impeding a sense of community and collective action, but at others the baz seemed to exemplify relations of solidarity. Emerging from and responding to the conditions of the geto, they fostered a context of mutual exchange in daily life and cultivated a collective politics that enabled them to make political claims, both grand and petite. It was also certainly the case that economic benefit was a driving force in the violent political work of the urban poor, but it was also not reducible to it. It is useful to look for a more complex explanation: one that accounts for the economic exigencies of poverty as well as the legitimate grievances and affective experiences of the urban poor. Such an experiential, as opposed to racialized, explanation can help clarify how people in Bel Air *became*, rather than *were*, "hotheads," and why it was an identity both embraced and contested by them.

Being or Becoming Hot

Kal and many others agreed with Monsieur Belcourt's understanding of Bel Air people's protest acumen, but for different reasons. Kal often took on the title Mèt Beton (Master of the Concrete) to express his ability to put the people in the streets, whether for a rara, protest, or both. When he relayed this title to politicians, he often followed it with an accounting of his protest experience. "I organize protests all the time. I cannot even count how many. More than two, three hundred! So many problems we have! I could *revandike* something every day," he once told a presidential candidate. Rather than situate his protest skill in an ingrained hotheadedness, he attributed it to his experience as a protest organizer—an experience nurtured by the economic benefits he derived from it as much as the presence of myriad and unrelenting grievances. The intermingling of economics and politics—as well as the extension of socially integrative debts between the state and citizenry—was even revealed in the banner under which people took to the streets: to *revandike* implies both the correction of a social wrong (vindication) and the retrieval of a debt owed (claim). Still, despite rejecting an ontology of hotness, he was not unaware of the role this racialized understanding of identity played in his own political goals. In fact, he knew that his niche within the protest economy depended on projecting a "hot" identity—an identity he cultivated through the rara band that helped catapult him into the political arena.

Kal's path to become Master of the Concrete recalled Yves's trajectory, although Kal was politicized earlier. As a child, he nurtured Lavalassian attachments as the neglected son of an army soldier and a zealous tag-along in the Zap Zap rara. He served as the band's flag bearer, before graduating to maraca shaker, and, finally, to the central role of banbou player, playing alongside Yves. His aptitude for playing the banbou (an instrument for "those with the most force!" as Kal was fond of saying), coupled with his tireless ambition and skill at relating with people of all stripes, made Kal a good candidate to become the group's pòt pawòl, a public-interfacing role that put him into close contact with politicians seeking to organize demonstrations or protests. I witnessed Kal organize many protests. A typical one was held in late October 2009, to demand severance compensation for recently laid off Teleco employees. Led by the AEVT and sponsored by two former Lavalas politicians, Kal was responsible for mobilizing musicians for the rara band, recruiting additional friends and neighbors as supporters, and securing permission from a rival baz to use the main neighborhood crossroads before L'église de Notre Dame du Perpétual de Secours. For this work, he was paid 10,000 goud ($250), a hefty sum, but one that was quickly depleted. The twelve musicians took just over half, receiving 400 to 500 goud each, another 2,000 goud was spent on transportation, cash gifts, and refreshments, and 1,000 goud was paid as a crossroads toll, leaving Kal with about 2,000 goud ($50) for two full days of nonstop, grueling work. Although this exchange of money was an essential aspect of protests, Kal disagreed that he and others took to the streets because of it. Although he would have considered no compensation an affront, the money, as he saw it, was not payment for services rendered but rather the *moyen* (means) to realize a collective project, with a small *kado* (gift) of appreciation left over for him. Moreover, he knew from experience that it was impossible to make a crowd without the presence of a grievance that tapped into the frustrations of many.

Although the grievance supplied the political basis for which people could become hot, the process of becoming hot largely occurred through the practices and rituals of the protest. At the center of the Teleco protest was the rara band. The twelve musicians were charged with summoning in protesters the physical and spiritual force they needed for a successful manifestation. The Teleco protest began with a pre-protest ritual in which the oungan Rémy built a woodpile of old brooms and plywood, placed a handful of hot peppers, coffee beans, and rock salt inside, and then lit it on fire. Rémy circled the mounting flame, cracking a whip, while stoking the fire with splashes of rum and one spark of gunpowder. The band, playing a jumpy *maskawon* rhythm followed him, with friends and neighbors soon joining, before all took to the streets to march uptown to the Teleco headquarters, where they delivered the demand: "The people are tired of citizenship! And also democracy. Go and vote for nothing? When we must take to the streets!" When I asked Kal about the significance of this ritual, he told me, "It's to *chofe pèp la* [heat up the people], so they have the force to deliver the *revandikasyon.*"

This protest ritual presented a sequence of signs through which protesters recognized their potential to become "hotheads," figuring this identity as a process of becoming rather than a state of immutability. Fire—in its capacity to change, create, and destroy matter—figured as the material agency of heat to make one thing into another. But here was a transformation that was not sui generis but built from latent capacities. Coffee, peppers, and salt represented substances capable of imparting qualities—like energy, spice, and flavor—that unlock and augment potential. As the fire "heated up" participants, they became not different

FIGURE 14. Ritual bonfire intended to "heat up" the Zap Zap rara and participants for a musical outing and protest.

people but empowered versions of themselves. The iconography of slavery and war, of whips and gunpowder, furthered a transmutation from passive citizen to militant protester. The bonfire echoes the one that occurred at the Bwa Kayiman ceremony that, as legend holds, inspired the Haitian revolution, and it was Ogou, the warrior spirit, who was summoned out of the fire and into the minds of the protesters.[23] Ogou both represented and legitimized the complex power of the "hot" protesters, tying their social position, struggles, and goals to those of the vicious yet righteous revolutionary soldiers. Like the soldiers, the heated-up protesters were volatile: they teetered on the edge of explosive rage and manic destruction but, in so doing, were constructive of social change. As Kal explained after the rowdy protest: "We're like a Prestige beer that's become frozen because it fell under, at the bottom of the freezer, under a sheet of ice. It's under all the bottles of Coke, Prestige, Malta, and under all the water packets, and it can't find a way for it to get out. And then, it erupts when taken out from under the ice blocks and into the heat. The fire heats us up. We can even turn chimè. The force of our ancestors is strong. [Those in power] know that and they are always afraid of us because the ones in misery are full of force."

This image of the explosive frozen beer echoed how Yves explained his mood and motivation during the Black Friday protest: "We, our mothers, fathers, reacted, and we knew we had to react like that again. The nèg geto feels he cannot live under this misery, because he is hungry. So, we fight to bring changes. And then they try to put you outside the house . . . because there are two classes in the country of Haiti, and they keep the people of the geto far away. Now, you have no job, no money, no activity, and you are really frustrated, and you say but I am still here. It was me who made this state. It's me who can defend it. You don't need a diploma to know what that means. That day we were very angry. You would not have recognized me. . . . We gathered the baz, and we made a ceremony in the crossroads, and we gathered all the force, all the people, and we became real hot, real angry, now I can say chimè. And I feel I got force and I go and crash and burn the streets."

In the ritual act of being heated-up, Yves and Kal found a way to express how the chimè persona stemmed from real-world frustrations, how economic and social marginalization laid the groundwork for transmutation into an aggressive and ruthless persona. The image identified the experience of misery as, on one level, a baseline of impotency from which extreme change was imaginable and, on another, an affective intensity that became an engine of that transmutation. This interpretation neither found its grounding in an idea of the urban poor's body as "naturally" hot, nor did it preclude the possibility for becoming hot. Rather, it stressed the potential for all humans to tap into the transformative power of emotions and ancestral memory. As Yves had said, "Even the president can become chimè." The metaphor of the beer also did not suggest that the urban poor's political leanings were wholly explained by payments. In a way, the beer drew attention to the circulation of protest moneys, since a case of beer is often invoked as the absolute minimal compensation for a protest rara. Yet the metaphor suggested that it was not economic exigency alone that drove a propensity for protest but, more holistically, the experience of poverty as frustration, of not being able to move out from under the manifold forces of subjugation. As Frederico Neiburg has written, the term *fristrasyon* as used by baz leaders is "a word that indicates individual and collective feelings on the verge of explosion, expressing suffering and uncertainty, and simultaneously threatening or justifying violence" (Neiburg 2016, 121). It is important to see how the metaphor of the beer relied on the revolution's example of the slave turned soldier as a model of and for transmutation, providing both a representation of the transformation and a justification for it. Just as with the different interpretations of the turf war between Baz GNB and Baz Zap Zap, the different ways politicians and baz members explained the latter's proclivity for protest was not about uncovering one's real or true identity but about constructing versions of oneself and others within the structure of social divisions and conflicts. If in one scenario the nèg geto marked an ontological proclivity for criminality and violence, in another he marked a social position that was the basis for political consciousness and reclamation.

In a way, Kal and Yves's ongoing attempts to rewrite the history of their roles as baz leaders revealed an attempt to negate stereotypical thinking of the nèg geto not by denying the reality of their dangerous potential but by recasting the utility of that potential and, in turn, its moral valence. Their resignification of their power also worked by interrogating the seemingly benign power of those beyond the geto, in the corridors of the state, the meetings of civil society, or the halls of academia. What was ultimately revealed was the mòde-soufle, the dichotomy of having both the power to lend a hand and to cut one off, common to all forms of power.

A Home in the Geto

In closing, it is useful to reconsider the origins of the term *chimè*. It comes from chimera, the fire-breathing hybrid creature of ancient Lycia whose body comprised a lion's head, goat's trunk, and snake's tail. Viewed from different perspectives, it was three different animals, and yet taken together, it was all of them. The stories that Yves, Kal, and others told about themselves expressed a compound self that changed in its presentation across temporal spans and in terms of relations of conflict. These shape-shifting stories present an understanding of identity that differs from both essentialist and constructivist analyses that presume a degree of singularity. Neither revealing an ontological identity "on the inside," nor performing a social identity "on the outside," the self, when understood as narrative, is modular. Constructed with attention to others' readings of it, the self can express multiple and competing forms and meanings simultaneously, though it is true that different plot lines carry varying degrees of credibility, depending on the relations of sincerity and power between the teller and audience.

Yves, in particular, was gifted at reframing himself narratively. In the story of his making as a baz leader, he wove together political skill with structural oppression, social acumen with class resentments, personal largesse with political grievances. These narratives constituted, in many ways, an effort to frame his complex personality in the context of the sociopolitical forces shaping it. Through the experience of frustration, his class position as a nèg geto, and his popular democratic ideology, he made opposing aspects of his identity meaningful in terms of broader relations of power that were constricting his prospects for livelihood, plans for the future, structures of feeling, and relations to family and friends. It is telling that he never denied involvement in criminal activity, but rather repurposed this criminal history as not only necessary, given the conditions at stake, but also key to his development as a political force. Of his time in prison, he once told me, "They arrested me and tied me up. March 22, 2004, to August 14, 2006. All of that—they tied up my name, my body, my family—but that made me stronger. I am not well educated, but my mind is very strong!" raising his arms and pointing to his head. In this way, he used his imprisonment to prove his force as a politician. The fact that he made it through the whole ordeal with social influence (not to mention his life) intact proved he had a "strong mind" capable of responding to and even defeating the forces stacked against him—to a degree.[24] Such pronouncements, as I have made clear throughout this chapter, did not go uncontested, and to be sure, Yves knew that for many who observed the baz from afar, his imprisonment proved his criminal nature and the criminal intention of his politics. An American journalist referred to Yves as a "young gang leader" who engaged in an attack on "one of the few institutions that ever gave Haiti's poor any hope of educating and bettering themselves." And when I asked a leader of a prominent NGO about the role of Yves in the popular movement, she replied: "Well, you see how things turned out for him. Time in prison says something. He cannot even get a Certificate of Good Conduct, but he still runs around doing politics."

At the root of Yves's frustration was his inability, no matter how craftily he rewrote his story, to fully break free of the stories others told about him. A final

FIGURE 15. View from the second-floor balcony of Yves Zap Zap's house at Plateau Bel Air.

observation illustrates the point. When I asked why Yves was considered a "big man," people in Bel Air often responded, "Look at his house!" Yet when I asked why, given his big man status, he has not left the geto to live in a nicer neighborhood, people oddly gave the same response.

Yves lived in a two-story, concrete building nestled in a corridor just beyond Plateau Bel Air. The house had many of the luxuries of modern life: a refrigerator, freezer, and television. Standing on its second-floor balcony, gazing at the jigsaw puzzle of dilapidated hillside shacks below, while drinking an iced beverage, it was easy to grasp Yves's elevated social standing. But the house also lacked a flush toilet, running water, and metered electricity. Without the latter, he was unable to set up an inverter that would power the house when the state electricity was not running. That meant the appliances worked only sporadically and cold soda was a rare occasion. The house was also haphazardly built, with jagged holes forming windows and rebar jutting out from half-finished walls, which crumbled with each storm. In the 2010 earthquake, a whole wall collapsed and has yet to be rebuilt.

Despite his efforts, Yves's ambitions for a house to match his status fell short. Part of the reason was that he had his eyes set beyond Bel Air, but was, as he often remarked, "tied up in the geto." For some time, Yves has been investing his occasional surplus income into building another home in his parent's natal village outside Léogâne. Over the six years I have known him, however, the project has remained unfinished. When I last visited in 2016, it was a shell of a house, with none of the furnishings of his Bel Air home. He often told me how he was building this house so that he could move his family away from the "geto life" and "the bandits." In fact, he rarely visited it without a contingency of Bel Air baz mates. The second house, it seemed, was more for showing off to people in Bel Air than for leaving the neighborhood. As he once remarked, "See-see, in Bel Air I am a gwo nèg, but I know in the society outside the geto, I am a chimè forever."

DEVELOPMENT

That Haiti is a veritable graveyard of development projects has less to do with Haitian culture and more to do with the nation's place in the world. . . . The decay of the public sector—through aid cutoffs and neoliberal policies—is one of the chief reasons that Haiti, unlike neighboring Cuba, is unable to respond to hurricanes with effective relief.

—Paul Farmer, 2008

Geto pèp di viv devlopman ak lapè! **(People of the geto say: long live development and peace).**

—Graffiti in Bel Air

On Tuesday, January 12, 2010, I was sitting in the courtyard of a restaurant that doubled as an office for the mayor's Carnival committee. It was a mild yet sunny afternoon, almost 5 pm, in the center of Port-au-Prince. Kal was on his way to meet me. He wanted to make sure the Carnival bands, which use rara musicians like him, were forthcoming with payments this year. The first step was knowing how much the bands would be allocated by the Carnival committee.

I ordered a Coke and struck up conversation with Kamal, a leader of a Bel Air baz called Pale Cho (Talk Tough) and a Carnival band renowned for setting off fireworks in the dense crowds of the Champs de Mars plaza during the annual Carnival processions. He burst into a tirade—within earshot of the committee chair—about how Bel Air people are fundamentally honest but are always double-crossed. "They still treat us like that even when you are present, See-see. You see everything too!" he said, slapping his hands together boisterously.

Just then the ground rattled beneath me. A dramatic sound effect to Kamal's angst, I surmised. But the shaking got stronger. I straightened up. It sounded like the subway. A slow rumble that escalated into a resounding roar. My chair teetered. But there is no subway here, I thought, as I fell to the ground.

I crawled toward the tallest palm tree in the lot and held tight to its trunk.

"*Trembleman de terre!*" echoed all around me.

A child of the Midwest, I had no idea what to do in an earthquake. All I could think was to hold the tree and ride the waves of shaking earth.

I watched someone fall to the ground and move over to me. A dust bowl surrounded us. I wiped my face, but still I was blinded. I had lost my glasses.

The tremors soon settled, and I let go of the tree and fell to the ground.

"Ale, ale [Go]!" Kamal yelled.

I clawed around for my glasses, finding them bent out of shape. Holding them to my head, I ventured into the street.

The scene was surreal. Two-story houses, the floors ripped from underneath, the walls pulled apart, were now heaps of cinder block. Three nursing students ran frantically through the street, their white uniforms covered in concrete powder. A woman held a sheet across her naked body and screamed for someone lost. Everyone looked shell-shocked—eyes wide with disbelief and confusion.

As I walked the few blocks to my house, a dust-covered woman in an S.U.V. assured me that I would make it home.

I did, ultimately. But it was months before I would awake from the foggy shock of it all.

I did not stay in Haiti long. I left four days after the earthquake aboard a Coast Guard plane bound for the Dominican Republic, before flying to New York. The decision to leave was agonizing. I was pulled between the drive to witness and the need to take care of my shaken self. The decision ultimately came down to my friends in Bel Air. "You can be of more help if you take care of yourself," I remember Kal telling me. "We can organize activities across the water." He said this as he held back the tears from the loss of his good friend, Berman, who died along with five others under the weight of a house where members of Baz Zap Zap often gathered. "When you come back, we'll do something for Berman."

I returned to Haiti six months later, in July 2010. Among the first things I did was lay a wreath of flowers where Berman had died. Then I took a ride on the back of Kal's motorbike to survey the city. The signs of loss and destruction were everywhere. Countless had died under countless fallen buildings and houses.[1] Kal made the sign of the cross as we passed a mound of rubble that was once a supermarket where I shopped and where several people died. We drove by the house where I had stayed the year before. The second floor was even with the ground, my first-floor apartment deep beneath it. I thanked God that my roommate knew to huddle under a desk and that the house fell away from her. I greeted my friend Hans, who had sold me a nightly Prestige for over a year. He offered a smile and a warm greeting, but his cousin was silent. She had lost her two-year-old son. I recalled her deafening wails of grief and attempts to run away from relatives who tied a rope around her waist and held her down against the street where her son, draped in a white sheet, lay lifeless. Apparently, she had yet to regain the will to speak.

Every open lot in the city was a campsite, and our final destination was among the biggest: the Champs de Mars plaza, where collapsed governmental ministries surrounded parks dedicated to revolutionary leaders. Kal hopped the curve of Place Dessalines and parked his motorbike near the tent of a trusted friend. We walked in zigzag fashion through the tents, hopping over puddles of stagnant water and shielding our faces from the dust. I caught the eyes of a woman bathing, who turned away at the embarrassment. The emergency relief tents were already badly damaged. Odd pieces of plastic, wood, and tin patched the roofs and sides that seemed defenseless against strong rains and wind. The whole scene made me wince with grief.

But I snapped out of this mood as soon as my eyes landed on the tent claimed by displaced members of Baz Zap Zap. A proverb was spray-painted across the Styrofoam door: *Pitò ou manje yon pèn chèch anpè ke ou pè manje nan yon kay ki plen vyann.* (Better to eat some dry bread in peace than eat in a house full of meat). Typical, I thought: a self-effacing joke that also stressed what is important in life. The good humor only increased when Frantzy and Michel appeared from under the USAID-stamped gray tarp. "Kal, good things are happening here!" they exclaimed. They embraced me with great enthusiasm but skipped the usual round of inquiries about my family's health, to delve into some good news. "We have so much activity, a lot of projects right now! Good, good things!" Michel said, as he gestured for us to enter the tent.

The tent revealed difficult living conditions at the same time that it boasted signs of youth, masculinity, and hipness. A poster of Bob Marley, another of Che Guvera, and the Haitian flag hung above the two beds where seven men and one woman slept in alternating shifts. There was no electricity, but batteries powered a laptop computer that streamed the Jamaican film Shottas and a boom box that drowned out the film with rap songs by Bel Air Masif, a rap group started by Michel's brother. Most striking of all was that the tent was literally filled with platters of meat—belying the proverb on the door. Michel and Frantzy had arranged a feast for my arrival. They had just been paid for their participation in a Cash-for-Work rubble removal program, and they were also the recipients of some leftover fritay. Sophie started selling the fried meat and veggies after Yves was able to provide some start-up capital from his role as a coordinator for these programs. "Look how big I've become," Michel quipped, as he grabbed his belly. "I eat all the time these days. It can be midnight, and I can eat something. And I can offer it to others too. I'm eating so much and having so much fun that sometimes I even forget to go to see my mother. She's in a tent too, but it's not nice at all," he said teasingly.

I realized then that I had completely misinterpreted the proverb. It was less a message about valuing the peace of poverty than a warning about the dangers of pursuit. I should have known. To one side of the proverb were the letters OJMOTEEB, the acronym of the group's development organization, and to the other the bible verse: "2 Roi [Kings] 6:16." I knew the bible verse because it had adorned the headquarters of many baz in Bel Air: "And He answered: 'Fear not: for they that be with us are more than they that be with them.'"

"We write the slogans because we make so much money," Michel explained, "but it's because we know how to speak about social work, in the language of development, not politics. In full transparence. We're completely legal," a reference to the organization's state certification.

"Look," he continued, "we're alive, our hearts don't race because this is a house without bandits. The bandits stir up the streets every day, but here we sleep in peace."

The inscriptions were an exercise in "word wanga" (Brown 2003), a rhetorical sleight of hand aimed at presenting the self in a particular way. On one hand, they carried a message to neighbors or others who might judge the group, suggesting that this tent was full of honest people pursuing "social work" despite its appearance as a house full of meat gathered through immoral politicking. On the other hand, they delivered a boast to potential rivals also engaged in development work. An expression of popular sovereignty, the bible verse communicated that the group could not be undermined because they enjoyed a strong social following. The complex messaging did not always work, however. As Michel continued: "We used to not even have to put a lock on the door, but the house was so beautiful people got jealous. They came at night and slashed the tarps. But that did not bother us. We would just tell Yves to send us Styrofoam siding to make it sturdier. So then we made it even better. But we had to call the MOG guys and make a brigade that can walk alongside our projects."

As we walked back to his motorbike, Kal seconded, "They say that Haiti is not developed because it has ensekirite, but I see that it is development that brings ensekirite—tèt chaje [bizarre]!"

In this chapter, I explore how baz leaders' projects to defend the zone intersected with the broader sociopolitical field of development. Their abilities to gain access to development projects entailed transforming their militant brand of politics into a nonconfrontational, less partisan, and overall tamer brand of organizing—the "social work" that appealed to the civil society norms advanced by elite politics and international NGOs. In this way, the baz's remodeling as development organizations echoed the reasons James Ferguson (1990) famously called development an "anti-politics machine." To him, development programs recalled the antigravity machines of science fiction novels that, with the flip of a switch, suspended gravity. With the reframing of an acronym, adoption of a new vocabulary ("transparency"), and the acquiring of official certificates, the baz could perform just as good a trick: "the suspension of politics from even the most sensitive political issues," (Ferguson 1990, 256) such as the allocation of food, shelter, and work. Yet Michel and others recognized that their abilities to attain and implement development projects depended on how well they defended against other groups likewise engaged in the field of development. This is why I speak, following Bourdieu (1984, 1993), of a "field"—in order to illustrate how baz leaders apprehended development as a terrain of power relations, where people staked out territory, position, and advantage in a competition for wealth, resources, and respect. By engaging with development as a "space of positions and [a] space of position-takings" (Bourdieu 1993, 30), baz leaders implicitly challenged the familiar—what Bourdieu would call "doxic"—story of development as an inevitable march of progress pursued by disinterested, apolitical actors (Escobar 1995; Ferguson 2005). Far from a neutral zone of peaceable organizing and technical interventions, they saw development as a field rife with competition, risk, and the potential for violence. Hence alongside their concerted efforts to rebrand their groups as peaceable development organizations, they retained vestiges of their earlier incarnations as militant organizations that defended against political foes, criminal threats, and outsiders—performing shape-shifting practices honed over years of political organizing.

I take this bifurcated identity as a starting point for revealing the many sides of doing development in urban Haiti. This refashioning work showed how Belairians embraced the call for development and innovated successful organizational forms capable of accessing the development field and implementing projects in the neighborhood. But at the same time, the specter of militancy at play in these organizational forms underscored the limitations and challenges of pursuing development work from the margins of the development field. As street sovereigns whose authority did not extend beyond the block or into the legal corridors of power, baz leaders' development endeavors were largely limited to small-scale, fleeting projects that lacked institutional power or legitimacy. Consequently, the benefits of these projects were minimal, mainly offering temporary windfalls for a small group of influential men. Graver still was the risk these pursuits engendered. Rather than reducing the ensekirite that many, at home and abroad, felt drove underdevelopment, these pursuits often served to exacerbate it.

Becoming an Organization in the Specter of the State

When reflecting on the reason insecurity lurked in the project of development, many in Bel Air often blamed not the cornucopia of NGOs that occupied the center of the development field but *leta*, the state, which was largely on the side-lines. This frustrated me, since it failed to grapple with the global forces on which the state was dependent.[2] Yet it began to make sense as I saw the way the state was present yet absent in the lives of the baz. The state was absent in that the governance work of the state was increasingly assumed by NGOs in partnership with local groups. But the state was also newly present in people's lives through its ability to sanction and authorize their participation in the development field. While NGOs often sidestepped the government when working in Haiti—neither registering nor working with state offices (Schuller 2012b), local groups were gen-erally barred from development if they did not fit the model of the NGO and attain accreditation from the Ministère des Affaires Sociales et du Travail (MAST) as a "social organization." This accreditation enabled baz formations to partner with NGOs for development projects, ironically furthering the divide between the state and citizens, leaving the latter to feel abandoned by the former. What frustrated baz leaders about this conjuncture was that it meant they had to rein-vent themselves for the benefit of a government that had largely delegated the work of development to others, however unwittingly. How well the baz adopted and manipulated development lingo and symbols was policed by the gatekeepers of civil society, namely the NGOs with whom they partnered and the govern-ment ministries that authorized their participation as social organizations in the development sector. When I witnessed the members of MOG complete MAST registration in 2008 and 2009, I learned how difficult it was, requiring significant funds, time, organizational know-how, and political contacts.

MAST required members to obtain a Numéro d'Immatriculation Fiscale (Tax Identification Number), which cost 250 goud ($6.25), and a Certificate de Bonne Vie et Moeurs (Certificate of Good Conduct), which also cost 250 goud. The group also needed to prepare an Acte Constitutif (Constitution), which listed the organization's founders and the date of its founding; a Procès-Verbal (Record of Proceedings), which detailed the circumstances of the organization's founding and the members of the organizing committee; a Charte (Charter), which outlined the organization's objectives, rules, and decision-making pro-cedures, and a cover letter for the entire dossier. All of these documents needed to be typed, copied, and delivered to MAST, along with a registration fee of 600 goud ($15). Michel, in his final year of high school at the time, was the most lit-erate of the group. Still, he spent months preparing the documents, first drafting them longhand and then slowly typing them at a cyber café, which charged 20 goud per hour. In total, he estimated that he spent 5,000 goud ($125) finalizing the dossier.

Part of this expense was owed to the group's difficulty in obtaining approval from MAST. Five times Michel was sent home and asked to amend the documents: once for a missing document (cover letter), twice for minor typo-graphical errors; and twice to fix problems with the group's formulation. The first problem concerned its all-male committee. The MAST official who took Michel's dossier suggested that the group would have better luck with NGOs if they had women on the committee. "The international community wants to see that the organization is encouraging the participation of women," he said. Michel agreed. He had, in fact, suggested this earlier but was rebuked by the other baz members. At MAST's urging, Michel added two women, though not in leadership roles. He added his sister and a classmate in the typical feminine role of konseye fèt (party planner), with the responsibility to organize the food, cleaning, and decorations for group activities and festivals.[3] The second problem concerned its name. When not capitalized, MOG spelled mòg (morgue), and this word referred to the slogan: "If you don't respect us, we'll put you in the morgue!" In an attempt to remove such violent connotations from the social organization, Michel redefined the acronym as Moral Optimists for the Grand Renaissance of Bel Air. However, MAST rejected this name. "They could still see 'morgue,'" he explained. He then reconfigured the name entirely, adopting an eight-letter acronym OJMOTEEB that translated as Youth Organization of Moral Optimists for the Educational Enrichment of Bel Air. This new title exemplified Michel's acumen with development lingo. It incorporated the key development terms "youth" and "education," targeting this organization for the slew of development projects aimed at providing wayward youth with educational training sessions, including the NGO Viva Rio's Tanbou Lapè project, which had a prominent role in Bel Air. OJMOTEEB sought to position themselves to be involved in the language and technology courses Viva Rio offered to rara musicians. As Michel put it, "We are young and need better education, and, well, NGOs—look at Viva Rio—love to do trainings."

The group celebrated their legalization by printing identity badges with mem-bers' names and photographs next to the organization's acronym and logo. These badges, simple plastic cards printed with a bare-bones design and barely there ink, carried an outsized importance in a place where most people held few, if any, citizenship papers, like birth certificates, identity cards, or passports. Engaging in a bit of hyperbole, Yves once remarked, "The badge says I am a person that can enter all the halls of power and speak with any person, even the president." Michel, more modestly, remarked when printing OJMOTEEB's badges: "The badge says that we are part of civil society. With it, you can make the state with some little projects and have a job for a few weeks. It's important because here it's every firefly lights his own way." The way people talked about badges reminded me of how chanpwèl secret society members spoke of the spiritual passports that allowed them to go on nightly journeys, flying through the sky and traveling to distant lands. The badges bore similar powers: elevating the social status of their holders and opening doors to arenas from which they were otherwise barred. As a nascent organization, OJMOTEEB usually ran small projects that lasted no more than a few weeks and entailed little overhead costs, such as street cleaning, food or aid distributions, vocational trainings, or seminars, such as one educating residents about the health dangers of cell phones. Yet despite their small size, they received funding from a wide range of sources, such as MAST, Viva Rio, the Ministère de la Culture et de la Communication, American Red Cross, Haitian Red Cross, Concerne International, Digicel, and Ede Yo, among others. Though these projects far from developed the zone in terms of meeting residents' needs, they did provide some benefit to group members. It often seemed that the only way in which these projects were "making the state" at all was in providing the organizers with some income, a sense of purpose, and a degree of authority on the block. Several of these partnerships rewarded Michel and Frantzy with badges displaying titles such as "Community Leader," "Project Liaison," or "Project Delegate," which they proudly showed me. "Look at how I am becoming an organized person," they'd say, often following it with a dismissal of neighbors' organizing activity as banditry or vagabondage. There was clearly social power and legitimacy to be gained from laying claim to a social organization and becoming an "organized person."

In calling development an "anti-politics machine," James Ferguson did not mean that it was apolitical but rather that it had a depoliticizing effect. By framing poverty as a technical problem to be addressed with technical solutions, development plans whisked political issues—such as class interests and conflicts—out of sight. But the execution of these plans actually facilitated "sensitive political operations involving the entrenchment and expansion of institutional state power, under cover of a neutral mission, to which no one can object" (1990, 256). The case here presents a related yet unique scenario, one where it becomes necessary to differentiate the forms of power associated with the state. By outsourcing development projects to NGOs and street organizations, the Haitian state has become increasingly absent and defunct in Bel Air as a public service provider and protector of public welfare. And yet, by managing, to great extent, baz formations' abilities to execute these projects, the state has become overly—indeed, onerously—present to the urban poor as a bureaucratic power. When leta made itself present to neighborhood residents, it was usually not through its governance activities but its "legibility effect," its ability to make citizens readable to the state and nonstate actors who govern and to subject them to various forms of regulation—through, for example, identity cards, good-conduct papers, and civil society accreditation (Scott 1998; Trouillot 2001).[4] In this way, the state revealed itself as a kind of phantom power—a power that is present in its absence, absent in its presence (Goldstein 2012; see also Beckett 2010). Its preeminent role was to authorize the outsourcing of its work, delegating governance without assuming responsibility for it. The result, however, was not so much the elimination as the relegation of politics—and political conflict—to baz organizations who competed to claim a piece of the development sector, often with devastating consequences. This is what I took Michel to mean by the proverb "every firefly lights his own way." The image called to mind the ingenuity and resourcefulness of someone who fended for himself, amalgamating piecemeal projects into the semblance of a life and livelihood. But it also conveyed a feeling of abandonment and risk, presupposing the specter of a state that ought to, but was not, providing for the people and that had, in turn, precipitated internecine feuds as groups fought each other to enact governance for themselves—feuds that unfolded most violently outside the halls of state or NGO offices on the streets of the neighborhood.[5] For this story, we must go down the block to Baz Zap Zap's rival: Baz Grand Black, the baz that has exercised chief authority for the neighborhood since the mid-2000s.

Meeting Grand Black at Development's Door

From the first time I entered Bel Air, I was told that I should meet with a man named Ti Snap, the leader of Baz Grand Black, and let him know what I was doing in the neighborhood. Over and over again, people told me that as a blan interested in development, I had to meet with Ti Snap. My friend Marc, an employee at Viva Rio, was the first to explain why this was the case. It was, he said, an important sign of respè, and if I disrespected Ti Snap, he could prove an obstacle to my work. The suggestion alarmed me, but it was hard to worry in the company of Marc.

Marc had a petite frame but a huge personality. He often served as an *animatè* (animator) for Viva Rio's youth programs, making children laugh with funny voices and corny jokes. Ti Snap, in contrast, rarely spoke, preferring to let others deliver messages for him. But Ti Snap, as Marc told me, was a fun-loving child and had become like this to protect himself. To prove it, Marc showed me a picture of them as adolescents dancing in the streets as the local Carnival band prepared for a parade. "He's not a bad person. He won't do anything to you," Marc assured me. "But I don't think he'll be your friend."

Marc eventually arranged for me to meet Ti Snap at the Popular Sector, then Grand Black's local political office.[6] When we arrived, Ti Snap's friend came to greet us and told us we would have to wait as their "development foundation" had to attend to some project business. I was led into a dark back room, and the door was shut. In the corner of the room on a cinder block were two handguns, what I later learned were Beretta 92s, presumably kept there for safekeeping. The time passed—just, I should note, as it did when I scheduled meetings with NGO directors—and I became aware that Ti Snap was sending me multiple messages about his power and influence.

When he eventually invited me into the front room, Ti Snap asked why I was there. I told him that I wanted to do research on local politics and that I wanted to teach an English class. He said the class was a nice idea, and then asked if there was any money involved. "Who is sponsoring that? What organization is sponsoring this? What NGO do you have? Who is giving the money? Is this with MINUSTAH, the peacekeepers?" I told him it was just something I wanted to do, that there was no sponsor. He let out a big laugh and called to his friend: "The blan comes to talk to me, and she has no money!" He turned to me and said, "Look, we do development, we fight to defend the interests of Bel Air in the area of development, so the zone can find projects and programs. If you don't do development, what can I do?" Ti Snap then told me that we would talk later because he had a meeting with the state disarmament commission, CNDDR. He got into a red Isuzu Tracker and was off.

After that I spent some time talking with his friend who greeted me. His name was Manno, and he was the mayor's popular delegate, a political post he had been given because, as he put it, "I can manage the baz in the *geto*." He told me that the meeting had gone well—just that if anyone took an interest in my project (by which he meant gave money) that I should come back and see Ti Snap. In what I would learn was a common sentiment, Manno told me: "Here, everything is organizations and projects. It's them who control everything. Look, we have so many organizations, you can't even count them all. You have to defend your rights . . . Everyone has rights. That's democracy. But you can't wait for someone to give them to you. You must organize to get respect. So everyone makes an organization. Now you have a problem. You've got to fight organizations with organizations. That can create disorder if you don't have the force to keep a hard line." The term "hard line" was a direct reference to the name of an armed baz called Ling Di that acted, much as MOG did for Baz Zap Zap, as the armed brigade of Baz Grand Black.[7] "There are people who say we are a gang," Ti Snap told me on another occasion, "and it is neither true nor not true. But here it is us who makes the law, so we have to defend our project all by ourselves."

Ti Snap and Marc agreed to help me locate a classroom, the outdoor kitchen behind Marc's house, and recruit students from the neighborhood, selecting equal numbers from their and Zap Zap's social circle. Since I charged no tuition, I was freed from paying Ti Snap to run the class, though I did work out a gift arrangement, purchasing snacks from the boutique and rum shop run by George, a Grand Black member. Ti Snap and Marc championed the class, helping me buy a chalkboard and borrow benches and desks. They often spoke of it as a part of their development activities and of me as an "American they welcomed to the zone to provide a service to the people." Eventually, Marc introduced me to Viva Rio, and I soon took another post as an English teacher for their training program for rara musicians.

Ultimately, my adventures as an English teacher went far to show me how Baz Grand Black authorized and managed development projects and served as promotors for additional opportunities. Although my first encounter suggested their development work was nothing but a protection racket, it actually went beyond that. They not only protected but also directed, sponsored, and promoted my neighborhood English class. Ti Snap called us "partners." He was even pleased that there was no money to be gained from it, as it freed him from the pressures of brokering the transaction and enabled him to speak of the project as a benevolent endeavor. "It's development with our little army only," he would say, implying it was a nonprofit and collective achievement. "We're soldiers who are defending the right of the zone for development," was another of his favored expressions. Such comments reflected an effort to legitimize his role as a local authority, to present his group as engaged in the social improvement of the neighborhood instead of as a "gang" that profited from development projects at the expense of the neighborhood. But he also did not hide the fact that development work entailed projecting, and at times embodying, a militant identity. One day, as I spoke with Marc and Ti Snap during snack time, I asked about Baz Grand Black's involvement in development and if it was really about helping the neighborhood because some people think it is about "doing politics"—code for profiteering and violence.

"When you make the state," Marc said, "there are two things: political things and social things. Development is part of the social things, but there's politics inside it. There are many NGOs, the blan, that don't see the political things. And they say Haitians are too political. 'You speak of the state too much!' they say. But you look at the world, and development is not a meal that is distributed to everyone. Haiti is not developed; your country is developed. There are babies in the world who survive. Others who do not. Not all grow the same. That is a natural thing, but it depends on food in the house too. Haiti was born not long after the United States, but it has grown under its hand, and it is still undeveloped.

"Look, we know you are a student, but we also know it is not free to live here. You have things to pay for, and that means someone gives you money to do your project. So, life for you, like for us, is not free. It's even worse for NGOs that have big accounts to do their projects. My vision is to speak loudly so that Bel

Air finds some advantage in projects, that the Bel Air people get some work and some benefit too."

"OK, I see that. But can Haiti find development if each and every person defends their interests in it?" I asked.

"Development is no small thing; it's a big state project for the state, but when we hear talk about development it is a little latrine or corridor project only."

"When I think about why the United States is developed," Marc continued, "that is because the United States did a better job defending itself than the Haitian state, and it became a big power. It's the same in this little geto. Grand Black is about defending itself and the neighborhood. I don't see that as a bad thing. The problem is that it's one little team against the other. Each has ambition, and then they get frustrated. That is why there are times that development follows a bad route and we have more violence."

The Good and the Bad of Local Development

In speaking of defense, Grand Black members offered an important critique of international development. They did not subscribe to the neutral, civil rhetoric of international development where first-world organizations are thought to be altruistically sharing expertise with undeveloped societies and helping them advance to the modern era. Instead, Baz Grand Black members turned to the language of competition and conflict. They configured development as a field of coeval actors with competing interests, a field where it was necessary to stake claims for the goods and services constituting the modern, developed life. Differences in nations' development status were, in this view, the result of how well they fared in this battle, how well they were able to defend their interests against others with similar pursuits. In short, the fact of undeveloped nations pertained, for Baz Grand Black, to their slot in an uneven field of power relations rather than merely a lack of access to technical solutions—a point that echoed critiques of international development advanced by several anthropologists.

"Development," as Arturo Escobar explains, "fostered a way of conceiving of social life as a technical problem . . . to be entrusted to that group of people—the development professionals—whose specialized knowledge allegedly qualified them for the task" (1995, 53). Recalling colonial civilizing missions, international development discourse, he further argues, "assumes a teleology to the extent that the 'natives' will sooner or later be reformed; at the same time, however, it reproduces endlessly the separation between reformers and those to be reformed by keeping alive the premise of the Third World as different and inferior, as having a limited humanity in relation to the accomplished European" (Escobar 1995, 54).

This simultaneous recognition and disavowal of common humanity is logically sustained by denying the global contemporaneous of populations, by positing that the undeveloped nations have been stuck in a pre-modern space-time envelope, albeit one from which they can emerge if provided the aid of the developed nations (see also Fabian 1983; Ferguson 2005; Trouillot 2003). As Marc and Ti Snap made clear, this line of thinking leads to the erroneous conclusion that Haiti's lack of development is independent of the United States—constructing the problems of poverty, illiteracy, dirty water, or blackouts as having to do with the inferiority and backwardness of the people of Haiti and not the country's long-standing marginalization in the global political economy. Instead of a childlike subject in need of the guidance of "experts" from the developed world, they imagined Haiti as a poorly positioned competitor that needed to better defend its stake in the development field. The same was true of Grand Black. Through the language of defense, its members articulated a need for tying together national and local sovereignty over the development process.

Such critiques of development ideology were prevalent in the 1980s, and out of them emerged a concerted reform effort to disentangle the aid industry from its ethnocentrism and to shift control of development from donor countries to the target populations. In the 1990s, international aid agencies like USAID began to rearticulate their mission around the idea of community participation, calling for an end to "topdownism" and extolling "local ownership" of the development process (Gardner and Lewis 1996; Smith 2001; Verhelst 1990). In Haiti, the goal to empower local communities corresponded with a perceived need to remove control over the distribution of aid money from the Haitian government, which was then undergoing an unsteady transition from the Duvalier family dictatorship to a democratic government. Citing the need for local participation—but also government corruption, political instability, and weak public infrastructure—major donor governments limited their bilateral support to the Haitian state for centralized development plans and instead channeled it to NGOs (or the VPOs, Volunteer Private Organizations, as they were called then) for small-scale community projects. While this did facilitate more participation from Haitian villagers and slum dwellers, it did not put control over the distribution of aid money in the hands of Haitian authorities, either local or national.[8] Over the next decades, the number of international organizations engaged in state-like activity in the country skyrocketed—a Haitian scholar, with a nod to the language of national sovereignty and defense, coined it an "invasion of NGOs" (Etienne 1997). By the time of the earthquake in 2010, there were an estimated ten thousand NGOs active in the country (though only about four hundred were registered with the government) (Schuller 2012a). At the same time, the Haitian government had greatly retreated from the leadership of development and governance. In Bel Air, people denounced this phenomenon with the expression "Here there is no state"—pointing to the sense of not merely a lack of governance but the effacement of the government by a multitude of governing actors who did not hold sovereign authority and the replacement of public services with countless development projects that did not met the public's needs (Kivland 2012). Such calls resounded after the earthquake, when 91 percent of development aid went to NGOs or private contractors, the bulk of which were not Haitian (United Nations Office of the Secretary General 2012; see also Katz 2013; Schuller 2016).[9]

Alongside the transfer of governance from state to nonstate agents was a concomitant shift in the geography of governance, from national to local, public to "community" domain. Most NGOs in Haiti have focused their work in discrete locales, such as rural villages or urban neighborhoods, rarely extending to the urban or provincial, let alone national, region. When Haitians spoke of an "NGO invasion," they were not only criticizing the way NGOs circumvent the government but also that they come to hold local sovereignty, producing territorial divisions in the nation and pulverizing the unifying function of public authorities. As a director for a United Nations Development Programme waste management project in Carrefour, another Port-au-Prince neighborhood, reflected, "We could take over Bel Air, the local council needs to decide whether Viva Rio is going to remain responsible for Bel Air or whether we are going to take it over" (Neiburg and Nicaise 2010, 55). Even when NGOs cover a broader region, their interventions have been parsed into specific "projects" that target small-scale areas. Bel Air residents referred to this problem as "little latrine projects." As Nadine once put it at a community forum regarding a Viva Rio project to build shower kiosks in the neighborhood: "I see this as another little latrine project." She went on to clarify: "One NGO puts a latrine here, one puts one there, but it's only a few families that benefit. Why can't we talk about toilets and a [sewage] treatment plant for everyone?" The response offered by the Viva Rio representative highlighted the systemic problem with community-based development: that in its focus on "communities" it can lose sight of the broader public. He responded: "The project area is Bel Air. That would be the responsibility of the state or the mayor"—two offices whose budgets for city sanitation paled in comparison to that allotted to the NGO.

As development and everyday governance took shape in localized projects, a plethora of social organizations appeared in urban neighborhoods to position themselves as the local development representatives. Like NGOs, there were often too many to count. On the single block of Plateau Bel Air, one could find: OJAB, OJREB, OJMOTEEB, OJRAB, KOREBEL, MOREBEL, MABEL, FODBEL, KONADEV, GBFOD, and KABEL, not to be confused with KAABEL. Some of

FIGURE 16.   Dedication plaque of a solar street lamp that announces the joint project between USAID, the city mayor, and "community organizations" in Bel Air; the lamp at Plateau Bel Air worked for one year before it malfunctioned.

these acronyms named new organizations, but many represented the rebranding of long-standing baz formations. As neoliberal structural adjustments limited the state's abilities to provide public services such as education, health care, and security, and as development economies channeled this service work into localized projects, the opportunity emerged for baz leaders to assume the work of governing, positioning themselves as local development leaders with the power to partner with NGO or state development agencies to implement neighborhood projects. The results of such partnerships often proved mutually beneficial, with baz leaders enriching and empowering themselves while also authorizing and legitimizing outsiders' presence in the area. Viva Rio, for example, named baz leaders as "community leaders" and instituted programs grounded in the organization of the baz, such as Tanbou Lapè (Peace Drum), where after month-long periods of no killings in the area, community leaders doled out school scholarships to children, selected rara musicians for educational programs, and put on public concerts by rap and rara groups (Muggah and Moestue 2009).[10] And yet these partnerships far from met the ideals of "participatory development." Even though Viva Rio went beyond other NGOs to integrate neighborhood baz, community participation was still limited. Foreigners occupied the top leadership positions, and control over the planning of initiatives did not extend much beyond a few influential baz leaders with managerial jobs in the NGO. Furthermore, many neighbors felt that working so closely with baz formations reinforced their neighborhood leadership, a position premised on past acts of violence and continued exclusions of large sectors of the neighborhood, including women, the elderly, and others not amenable to the baz. Yet failing to work with baz formations, or doing so without respecting the baz hierarchy, could also precipitate inter-baz rivalries and turf wars.

Many Belairians complained about how Viva Rio worked with "criminals," "bandits," or "vagabonds." "Being honest and staying out of the game of politics does not pay off in the system of development," Sophie once told me, echoing others. Yet at the same time most recognized that NGOs had to respect the baz structure given leaders' level of local power and abilities to disrupt projects. As Ti Snap made clear, Grand Black had the power to authorize and exercise a protection racket over development projects in the area—including those of other groups and the resident anthropologist. "All foreign organizations, before they step on this territory, must work through the baz, and that is Grand Black," as Marc put it. And as a Viva Rio program organizer elaborated in 2008, "People complain that we work with *bandi*. But we have to work with them. They are the leaders for the areas. You can't say that because you don't like the way the leader became a leader, you won't work with him. You have to respect that he is the leader. Anyway, if you don't work with them you'll have problems. It's simple. We need them to do the work."

The role of the baz in the development field invoked clientelist models familiar to political anthropologists, whereby the local "broker" traded political access for political pork, delivering votes in exchange for state jobs or permitting state projects in exchange for payouts. But it also signaled new relations of urban rule prevalent throughout the Caribbean and beyond in the neoliberal era of state retrenchment and community-based development (e.g., Chatterjee 2004; Hansen and Stepputat 2005; Jaffe 2013). In 1956, Eric Wolf famously asserted that anthropologists should direct their critical attention to such local brokers because they "stand guard over the crucial junctures or synapses which connect the local system to the larger whole" (1956, 1075). This is still true, but what has changed in the fifty years since is that such brokers are no longer merely "Janus-faced," facing *two* directions at once: the nation and the community. They are hydra-headed, situated at the nexus of global and national fields of power, serving to integrate a diversity of governing actors operating at these broader levels with the base level of the neighborhood and coping with the consequences of so doing.

The Challenges of the Mad Hatter

"The Grand Black foundation does social not political things," Marc stressed again when I interviewed him about the history of Grand Black's development work. "We had the political office for political things, but we created the foundation for the social things, because we wanted to show the NGOs that we work in development. The state certifies social organizations—as people say, 'racketeer of papers' [*raketè fey*]—but it is not really active in projects. It does some development, like the food distributions, but it is not a chèf in development. We saw that NGOs were making the state, so we wanted to walk in the rhythm of NGOs so the NGOs value us more."

Baz leaders often separated their development organizations from other aspects of their work by claiming that it was a *bagay sosyal* (social thing) and not a *bagay politik* (political thing). The assertion of a social logic carried many benefits: it separated the group from entrenched political conflicts, identified them with development work, and placed them within the confines of civil society, distancing them from criminal connotations of baz politics. Yet as organizations born of political movements and still active in everyday political affairs, it was not as though the baz could just relinquish their more political, militant identities. Nor was this desirable. Indeed, their conceptualization of development as a competitive field necessitated an ability to move between the categories, to reuse Partha Chatterjee's (2004) typology, of civil society and popular society, the civic and the militant, the social organization and the baz. Grand Black members, for example, tacked between competing organizational identities and modalities simultaneously, fashioning the group as, at once, local chèf of a contested neighborhood, vanguards of the revolution and nèg statehood, and civil society leaders engaged in development. "We wear many hats," as they often put it.

Marc went on to explain how Ti Snap became a leader in the zone. Along with many others, Ti Snap joined Operation Baghdad, the two-year neighborhood resistance movement that fought to reinstate Jean-Bertrand Aristide as president after he was ousted in 2004. "[Ti Snap] lost his job, and he had to find another way," Marc said. He went on to explain how after Dread Mackendy, the leader of Operation Baghdad's *lame popilè* (popular army), was killed, Ti Snap sought to establish himself as its leader. In a public spectacle, he shot and killed a former army soldier (and therefore political enemy) and declared himself in charge of the popular army. A quiet and private man, Ti Snap appointed Sanba Boukman as the public spokesperson for the popular army. Sanba Boukman was an articulate and outspoken advocate of Aristide and the movement of geto youth, who identified with Dutty Boukman, the enslaved African who launched the Haitian revolution. From the beginning, Sanba Boukman sought to lend the popular army legitimacy, and he quickly transformed it from a fighting force to a political organization. As Marc reported and Sanba Boukman confirmed, "Grand Black was founded to represent all the great work we had done to defend the zone. Like all the Grand Blacks—Martin Luther King, Malcolm X, Barack Obama—we work for the social amelioration and development of the geto."

When Viva Rio entered Bel Air in 2006, at the tail end of Operation Baghdad, the first order of business was to orchestrate a meeting with Sanba Boukman, the head of Viva Rio, and the captain of the MINUSTAH peacekeeping operation, which was sponsoring Viva Rio. The meeting facilitated Viva Rio's entry to the neighborhood as well as high-ranking jobs for Sanba Boukman, who was appointed head of the UN-authorized Commission Nationale de Désarmement, Démantèlement et Réinsertion (a disarmament and reintegration program, CNDDR), and Ti Snap, who was put in charge of the Popular Sector, the area's political office tied to President René Préval's administration, which took power in 2006. No longer waging a resistance movement, Grand Black positioned itself as the local political headquarters, exercising control over state and NGO activities in the area, which included charging fees for access and having influence over the allocation of jobs. However, despite publicly surrendering and engaging in a disarmament campaign, Grand Black retained vestiges of its former role as a popular army. It had access to a small arsenal maintained by Ling Di, a title that mainly designated one man and his closest buddies who had a history of mobilizing youth to engage in kidnapping, political assassination, and other crimes during Operation Baghdad.[11] Although the group's development work did not always involve the use of Ling Di or the exercise of force (indeed, most often it did not), the threat of violence was ever-present. As Marc concluded the story: "Baghdad made Ti Snap the political chèf, but now he tries to be a development chèf too, and for that, you have to stand on top of the other groups. It's a role that invites jealousy. . . . Development is not simple.[12] People want to do development, but since people have too much ambition, it can bring problems."

This multifaceted identity—as a local political office, popular army, and development organization—was apparent in the imagery displayed at Grand Black's neighborhood headquarters. The group claimed control of the neighborhood's central square and busiest intersection. Most baz formations were situated at crossroads, their sovereign domain radiating, like a spiral, from the core of the crossroads outward to a ring of material, social, and mystical points across the block. In Haitian religious schemes, the *kalfou* (crossroads) is both a spirit and a place of power and judgment, the site where magic is performed, danger confronted, and fates determined. The rara groups affiliated with the baz performed their pre-outing rituals in the crossroads, where they channeled the strength and fortitude of militant spirits, such as Mèt Kalfou, the Master of the Crossroads, in order to safely traverse crossings and confrontations with other groups in less friendly territory (McAlister 2002). Ti Snap and others often sat behind a gated, street-side bench dedicated to their affiliated, and the area's most popular, rara band. From behind its red-yellow-green gates, he could survey the activity at the rum shop across the street and a small drug market around the corner, both run by baz members, as well as keep tabs on through traffic and folks gathered across the intersection at L'église Perpetual, the common meeting place and staging grounds for public festivals, political press conferences, and citywide protests. From the bench, it often appeared that Ti Snap was gazing across the concrete expanse into the eyes of the late militant Dread Mackendy, whose portrait, nestled in a verdant landscape, a pan-African rainbow, and a crown of long dreadlocks, was painted on the church's outdoor stage in 2006. The mural was a study in contrasts, with Dread Mackendy sandwiched between the expressions: "For a Peaceful Haiti" and "Father of the 2004 Revolution," with the bible verse "2 Kings 6:16" underneath.

This militant mural felt particularly out of sorts with Grand Black's other most prominent material symbol on the block: the two-story yellow concrete building that housed the Fondation Grand Black pour le Developpement. On first glance, the building cast aside the militant legacy of Dread Mackendy. A "foundation" engaged in "development" signaled knowledge of and an ability to work with the organizational forms and modalities of civil society, as did the stoplight icon, which aimed to conjure the public infrastructures and utilities of a modern, developed world. "We put 'development' in the name because we see another future and the traffic light shows a developed zone, with electricity and order in the streets," as Marc explained. And yet residents gleaned much more from these symbols. The stoplight, as Kal, situated in another baz, once explained, "says when to enter, when to exit," signaling the way Baz Grand Black controlled traffic in and out of the neighborhood. It also reiterated the pan-African color scheme of red-yellow-green, which worked with the English name Grand Black,

FIGURE 17. Mural of Dread Mackendy on the stage of L'église de Notre Dame du Perpétual de Secours.

to indicate their relationship to a broader, diasporic racial militancy. A translation of the Haitian Creole gran nèg, Grand Black reflected a sense of transnational black solidarity, naming a commitment to elevating the status and power of the nèg underclass worldwide vis-à-vis the intrusion of *grands blancs*, the foreign experts and international development organizations that echoed the former colonial powers.[13]

Together, this symbolic infrastructure illustrated the intricate dance that the baz orchestrated in order to appeal to multiple audiences simultaneously. As Thomas, who sold cell-phone cards from the church stage once remarked, "Grand Black wears the development hat and the baz hat—without problems," pointing to the foundation and the Dread Mackendy mural. "It's like a soccer player that can play all positions. That makes you stronger. Offense and defense together." As he saw it, the group's success depended on its shape-shifting ability, to reframe its empowerment project as development, and to enforce development work through a reputation for militant and racial politics—as well as the specter of violence. Below the stage where we sat was spray-painted the rara lyric/protest slogan, Pa fè fòs (don't attack [us/here]), which affirmed, but also threatened, the group's control of the area through physical, mystical, and social power. As Collette, a peanut vendor next to Thomas, interjected: "Where do you see development? Every time they have a project, the zone has ensekirite."

FIGURE 18.   Headquarters of Fondation Grand Black pour le Developpement.

Collette delivered this assessment in May 2012, just over a month after Sanba Boukman was shot and killed by an unknown gunman as he dropped his eldest daughter off at school. He had just initiated a post-earthquake, cross-city mobilization for development called Geto Ini (All Geto United). The project again put him in contact with Aristide and in conflict with Baz Pale Cho, a rival baz in Bel Air which had organized against Aristide's Lavalas Party in the 2011 presidential election of Michel Martelly and from whose ranks was named the new city delegate for the zone, nullifying the power of the Popular Sector.[14]

Many felt he was killed by political operatives aiming to shift the balance of power in Bel Air. Shortly after Sanba Boukman's assassination, Grand Black refashioned its identity yet again. In an attempt to appease the new president, as well as the development blan, the group removed overt reference to its project in racial or political terms, calling itself "GB Productions for the Development and Advancement of Bel Air." The shift, as Marc told me, "was to say that we are chèf in this area and we are ready to work with anyone who wants to work to develop the area." However, even in this nominal construction the members kept GB as a trace of their more militant and more partisan identity, and few neighbors missed the meaning.

It is tempting to read Grand Black's continued shape-shifting as a failure to master development norms: that the group failed to embody the standards of civil society because of militant dispositions its members could not shake. However, that reading implies a separation of civil society and militant politics that, while central to the ideology of development, is not operative in the way development plays out on the ground. Grand Black's amalgam of civil society and militant politics indicated a fundamental tension in all governance: that the legitimate control of force is a constitutive part of sovereign authority.[15] After all, how different was the baz's embrace of civil society from an NGO's ties to the UN peacekeeping mission, or, for that matter, a government's ties to the military? Nor is it accurate to speak of Baz Grand Black's trajectory as a tale of deception, the "gang" masquerading as a development organization for opportunistic ends. Deception presumes the group wished to conceal one identity over another. Although its members understood that one message might need to be cloaked in another so as to meet the communicative norms of different discourses, they nonetheless recognized how their claims to local authority rested on communicating both messages—and often simultaneously. This was the crucial subtext in Grand Black members' messaging about defense: their project was as much about defending neighborhood interests amid an NGO "invasion" as it was about defending the interests of this baz against others also engaged in development.

The Dark Side of Development Politics

The morning of June 15, 2013, when I walked Bel Air's streets, I noticed a eulogy poster affixed to several lampposts, gallery pillars, and walls. Underneath the posters was tied a black or purple swath of fabric, mimicking women in mourning who tighten a belt around their waists as if to physically manifest the pain of grief. The poster announced the passing of Demo, a thirty-three-year-old man I knew. Demo was killed when he sat with Marc and another friend on the bench next to Grand Black's foundation headquarters. Two masked gunmen sped by on a motorbike and opened fire, fatally striking Demo. His friends fled in fear, and no one called the police. Demo lay in a pool of blood on the concrete for hours before his family brought his body home in a bed sheet.

FIGURE 19. A lamppost affixed with a poster announcing the death of Demo and tied with a black mourning belt.

His abandoned body on the concrete belied how lovable and well-loved Demo actually was—a sentiment corrected by the poster's image of him tossing his long dreadlocks, winking, and flashing a megawatt smile. Demo was gregarious and quick-witted. He liked to make people laugh with comical or irreverent turns of phrase. *Papa-pi-wow* was a phrase he recently coined to express the joys of fatherhood. Seven months ago, he had welcomed a baby girl. I got to know Demo because of his friendship with Baz Grand Black members. He often drank a beer with George, who ran the rum shop near the foundation. The last conversation we had was about his plans for the new baby. Demo came from one of the poorest families in the area, and although close with Baz Grand Black, he never seemed to gain a foothold in the inner circle that received political or development payouts. "*Depi li fèt, l ap viv*" (Once it's born, it lives), he said, signaling that he would find a way to provide for his child. Recently, it seemed Demo was attempting to do so by aligning his allegiances with another group in the area. In the past weeks I had seen him not at George's shop, but hanging out on Baz Pale Cho's block.

The change was noted on the poster. It read, "Courtesy of Palecho. 2 Kings 6:16."

Many Bel Air residents explained Demo's death in terms that echoed the reasons given for the problem of ensekirite in development work more generally: that it was due to an absent state, or rather one that made itself felt in its absence, in the consequential delegation of governance. The problem with was that, as people often said, this deferral of governance caused *twòp divisyon* (too many divisions). "Division" was a phenomenon closely associated with ensekirite—and both were seen to be on the rise with democratization and development. Unlike in the Duvalier era, people often told me, when there was one rivalry (either for or against the regime), now "there are so many divisions"—It is "*youn kont lòt*" (one against the other), they would say, altering the aphorism, *youn ede lòt* (one helps the other). Years before Demo's death, in 2009, when I asked residents about the causes of insecurity in a sixty-three-household survey, many people simply cited bandits or vagabonds, but when asked to explain recent periods of conflicts, they talked about how elections, NGOs, or projects had precipitated a division among or between neighborhood groups. One respondent, a married man and father of two, told me: "[NGOs] come to do development but they just divide people. The only real development that happens is when people in a community come together to solve a problem without stirring up money. One thing NGOs don't understand is that we need jobs but project money causes divisions." Another respondent, a single mother of three, told me: "For me, it's a question of development and the [lack of] volition of the state. This is a poor area, but it is rich in projects. So what do you get? Too many little chèf fight over the little project money. The zone is divided. I understand that it is difficult for the NGOs to control that. We are supposed to have a representative in the state for that." While it is impossible to answer why Demo died, in the remainder of this chapter, I lay out some of the divisive conditions that led to his death and, in so doing, attempt to explain how it is that the project to develop the neighborhood intersected with the problem of ensekirite.

The first key development took root in late 2010 and early 2011, when a group of teenagers in Delmas 2 broke from a more prominent baz there and established themselves as Baz 117 Aslè (malicious), or 117 for short.[16] They took up residence in the abandoned Teleco site, where hundreds of people then lived in tents. People there traced their rise to their leader's ability to acquire management of two post-earthquake Cash-for-Work rubble removal teams.[17]

After the initial wave of medical, shelter, and food aid, disaster relief shifted to a rebuilding and development effort that incorporated the urban poor mainly as the hired hands for the backbreaking work. While major aid investments went to resort and factory developers, people in Bel Air found temporary work digging drainage canals, paving sidewalks, or removing rubble and debris in Cash-for-Work programs. As with street-sweeping projects, these programs used a rotating team model, employing fifteen to twenty people for two weeks and paying each about 200 goud per day ($5). Each team had a leader who was paid twice as much and had the authority to select and manage the team. The team leader was usually a man and someone of influence in the neighborhood or in the camp—for example, Yves and Paul (Ti Snap's brother) headed two Bel Air camp committees and oversaw several Cash-for-Work programs. The whole program could be a boon for baz leaders and those connected to them. But it also worked to the detriment of many in the neighborhood, especially women. Responding to international norms of gender equality as well as to the reality of women as heads of household, international NGOs in Haiti have increasingly made women the target recipients of development and aid programs. While, in theory, this would work to women's benefit, it could also work to their disadvantage when the gendered hierarchies in the distribution of aid were not also addressed. As we saw with MOG's inclusion of women on their committee, the inclusion of women was often less about female empowerment than the organization's strategic efforts to align with NGOs' target populations.[18] Worse yet was that making women the targets of aid—the recipients of food distribution coupons or of Cash-for-Work jobs—could also make them a target for jealousy or violence. Insofar as men exercised control over the distribution of coupons or jobs, women could be compelled to ally with them, sexually or otherwise, in exchange for goods or resources (Bell 2013; d'Adesky and PotoFanm+Fi Coalition 2012; Schuller 2016).[19]

Such was the case with 117. The group used the monies—residents estimated about $300—they earned from the rubble removal projects to purchase a couple of handguns, and they began a spree of muggings, robberies, and rapes in the surrounding area. In one of their initial Cash-for-Work programs, Kal's teenage daughter Kiki, who was estranged from her father despite living a block away, sought work on a team. Her participation came at a cost: she would have to sleep with one of the young men. Desperate for money and, in part, seeking his approval ("I thought he liked me," she told me), she agreed. He brought her to his *cham gason* (man's room), where she found him not alone but with three of his friends. She was raped by all of them, before fleeing to her mother's house. Kal attacked one of the rapists in the days that followed, punching and throwing him to the ground as he passed by him in the street, but no other punishments were meted out. And despite the humiliation, Kiki still participated in the Cash-for-Work team, even becoming close to the initial attacker, in ways reminiscent of how poverty and violence in a context of gender inequality can lead women to look for assistance and protection in predacious men.[20] When Kiki appeared at Baz Zap Zap, whispers would spread about the "117 prostitute." This disturbing moniker spoke to the way in which the gang rape served as a ritual forum for male bonding and group initiation, as well as how the fear and power the group commanded was built on the public shame and humiliation of a young girl.[21]

Despite the suggestion of prostitution, however, men and women throughout the neighborhood resoundingly condemned the rape, seeing it as evidence of 117's incarnation of their *aslè* namesake. It corroborated a series of other rumors about 117's egregious crimes—including the rape and robbery of three women attending a nightly prayer service in a church and the robbery and murder of a four-year-old boy—and contributed to the reputation of 117 as a true gang. "117 names a gang, a gang of bandits. Gang 117 does not have a baz at all," Michel explained, referring to how they did not have any neighborly following that would give them a claim to local authority. "They violate inside their own house! And they'll take anything. They stole everything in the Teleco camp—wires, toilets, chairs, tables, whatever people had made there, and now they do the same in the neighborhood. You can't even leave your sneakers outside. A criminal thing, simple as that."

The fact that members of 117 engaged in predatory crimes throughout the Bel Air region prevented them from establishing any kind of foothold as a social or political organization representing the neighborhood, but it did not prevent them from disturbing those groups that did. By the summer of 2013, as 117 members wreaked havoc in Bel Air, Ti Snap and Grand Black's authority as protectors of the neighborhood came under question. All sorts of smaller groups, like MOG but also others called Al Qaeda and Kolon Blan, mounted brigad vigilans in an attempt to stave off the 117 bandits. At the same time, another prominent group, Baz Pale Cho, began to stake a claim as the development representatives of the area. They launched a new social organization that acquired control of several Cash-for-Work programs, including a major USAID-funded construction project to build and pave area sidewalks. They also acquired leadership of Fèt Pèpètyèl, the neighborhood's annual patron saint celebration, a responsibility that had fallen to Grand Black since 2006. Leadership included managing a neighborhood-wide cleanup (street sweeping and painting murals) and orchestrating a weekend concert, both sponsored by various NGOs, state ministries, and politicians. Soon after this switch became clear, a few members of Baz Grand Black, including Demo, allied with Baz Pale Cho in search of its newfound power and resources.

In response, Ti Snap launched a campaign to reclaim Baz Grand Black's standing—Zam Pale (talking weapons), an alteration of Viva Rio's recently launched nonviolence program Zam Bebe (mute weapons). The campaign began with a series of mass arrests. Over the span of two nights, the police drove through the zone and hauled about fifty young men to jail. It was assumed that Ti Snap was behind the arrests. Many claimed to have seen him in the police van, and his brother worked at the Ministère de la Justice et de la Sécurité Publique and had close ties to the police. What struck residents was that rather than 117 members, the arrests seemed to target the emergent groups and anyone associated with them. When I heard about the arrests, I was told that Ti Snap had in fact allied with 117 to carry them out, a move substantiated by the belief that Ti Snap must be receiving a cut of 117's plunder. "He can't punish them, so he punishes everyone else. The police don't even know who the bandits are. It's disorder!" Kal told me. Then, just days after the mass arrest, Demo's killing occurred. The news circulated quickly, with a who-done-it readily accepted: Ti Snap. In the next days, graffiti appeared throughout the neighborhood denouncing "Ti Snap = chèf of the 117 thieves!" and "Grand Black = gang like 117."

Soon after Demo's killing, Bernie, a childhood friend of Demo, organized folks at Baz Zap Zap for an antiviolence protest. On OJMOTEEB letterhead, he sent a notice to two radio stations, and, with contributions from neighbors, he made posters that read, "We want justice for Demo in Bel Air," gathered a team of young boys to carry them, and rallied a small rara to lead them to the Teleco camp of 117 and then past the site of Demo's killing. On their way back to Zap Zap's home base, a reporter stopped Bernie for a comment. "OK, I have something to say," Bernie began. "What I ask of the Haitian government, as a youth leader, what they can give the community. What we ask of the Haitian state is to offer us a police station in Bel Air, so they can have more control of the zone and the population can live better. Because we have a lot of development in us. We can do real development in the geto. But there is confusion now. People who don't know the zone treat people like chèf who are not chèf. That makes an explosion. We feel we can't live. We, as leaders, ask the press to pass on the message: 'The Haitian state, let's take responsibility.'" When he finished, the reporter asked Bernie if there was a leader or a group behind the violence. Bernie did not name names, continuing to lay blame on an absent state that does not do "real development." Afterward, I asked him if he feared revenge if he named the person behind the violence. "Yes, but what's more important is that the problem runs deeper than one bandit."

The neighborhood unrest threatened to disrupt not only Fèt Pèpètyèl but also the signing of Viva Rio's sixth Peace Accord for Development, which was scheduled to coincide with the patron saint festival. Since 2006, the NGO had used peace accords, signed by a range of local leaders, from baz leaders to school principals to church pastors, to help stop waves of violence and bring peace to the area. To safeguard the peace accord, Viva Rio arranged a community meeting. About thirty residents attended as well as a police officer, a representative from MINUSTAH, and several Viva Rio staff. After opening remarks, residents were given the opportunity to share their thoughts. A woman, who introduced herself as the leader of a women's development organization, began by stating that the problem was that the festival caused groups to fight each other. A man, the leader of the Carnival band affiliated with Baz Grand Black, then stated: "Since the 12th, anyone can find a project. The zone no longer has a chèf." This caused a huge ruckus, with people talking over each other in a debate about the benefits and costs of Baz Grand Black's leadership. Many felt that it was important to have a single leader, but many others questioned if that worked when "the leader" (who went unnamed) was "corrupt," "cruel," or unable to control the "little disorder." The first woman eventually regained the floor and stated that the problem was "always the same." "Where is the state?" she said. "We come and ask the NGO to resolve the problem. But we are citizens of Haiti. The festival is not for a little team. My team versus your team. We must ask for the mayor, deputy, and delegates—the state—to take control of the festival and to do it in the right way, with everyone involved." The comment silenced the room, with many looking at the police officer as the representative of the state. But he did not say anything, and when conversation restarted, the subject shifted to the upcoming peace accord.

Amazingly, the peace accord signing went off without a hitch, held on a beautiful sunny afternoon under a tent adorned with balloons in the colors of the Haitian flag. The priest at L'église Perpetual gave a blessing for peace and goodwill, followed by celebratory speeches by several representatives and sponsors of Viva Rio. Afterward, as they drank soda and ate meat-filled pastries, three leaders of Baz Grand Black and seventeen other community leaders signed the accord. It proclaimed the leaders would "act honestly and justly" in the pursuit of "actions for development and peace in the area." Never a man of many words, Ti Snap silently watched the whole proceeding from a seat at the courtyard's edge. His participation was visible in the new Peace Accord t-shirt he wore over his dress shirt, but he did not partake in the snacks or good cheer. He appeared uncomfortable, as though aware of the contradiction of his presence. I asked him if he would comment on the event for a film I was making about the festival. He agreed, but when the camera rolled, he deferred to George. With Ti Snap behind him, George offered a message neatly aligned with the aims of peace and development. "We don't need violence anymore but peace, for all of Bel Air to become one," he said. "It's my role to speak with the youth so they don't take a bad path. This peace accord is one part. We need Justice, the police, everyone in the world to accompany us. . . . I want the state to accompany our work. Viva Rio does its part. Now the state must also help. For the youth to find security, leisure, work, food, drink. That's what can bring a solution." When he finished, I asked Ti Snap if he thought the peace accord would make a difference in the zone. Off camera, he was more forthcoming. He told me that he wanted the state to establish a local police station and make him a bona fide policeman or what he called a "partner to the police" so that he could better control the disorder. "Without the state in charge, there will just be more insecurity!" he said.

Over the next days, Ti Snap returned to the zone and reasserted a public presence. For Fèt Pèpètyèl, Baz Pale Cho built a stage at Baz Grand Black's crossroads and hired several city and neighborhood groups to play music for the crowd. Yet with funds acquired from rival politicians, Grand Black built another stage down the hill from the main crossroads and rigged it with a generator and huge speakers. When the concert started, Grand Black blasted a loop of pop hits that drowned out the main stage, causing few revelers to populate the street. The problem was not merely the cacophony but what it signaled: the rivalry between Pale Cho and Grand Black. Many would-be revelers stayed home in fear of a gunfight. The year prior, at a Christmas Eve concert hosted by Pale Cho, a shootout, largely blamed on 117, occurred that killed six people and injured many more in the ensuing chaos. For once, Kal refused to accompany me, stating: "The musical war will turn into a real war. You're going alone." Sophie, his wife, did attend, as she had fritay to sell. A war did not happen, but the festivities never took off, a consequence that hit women, like Sophie, particularly hard as they were unable to sell their goods.[22]

However, weeks later, the zone enjoyed a real concert. It was then that Ti Snap truly demonstrated a sense of reconstituted leadership. It was a peace concert hosted by Viva Rio in the neighboring quarter Fort National.[23] Featuring local bands, the concert was well attended by people throughout the area, with Baz Zap Zap's rap group Bèlè Masif among the attendees. Depending on size and level of acclaim, the groups were paid anywhere from one to a few hundred dollars—a cut of which went to Ti Snap. (Bèlè Masif reported paying $20 of $200 to Ti Snap.) Ti Snap watched the concert unfold from the stage, seated behind the drum kit, and accompanied by two bodyguards with bulging backpacks that most suspected contained weapons. When I spoke with Viva Rio's MC for the event about Ti Snap's attendance, he expressed his dismay: "We don't want to be the ones who are known as bringing Ti Snap back to power, but it's how things are. And it appears that things got worse when there was not a clear chèf in the zone."

It was hard to disagree with this sentiment. After Ti Snap was restored as the leader of the zone, a noticeable calm took effect in Bel Air, with no reported killing in July or August.[24] Yet it was a tenuous peace: as election money began to circulate in the fall, violence was again on the rise.[25] Furthermore, it was not as though Belairians relished Ti Snap's revived leadership. Although many residents claimed that he had their respect, they often qualified this as *respè nan pè* (respect in fear) or *respè pa zam* (respect by the gun). He was not an elected or official state representative of the block; indeed, residents' constant pointing to the state to resolve the security crisis highlighted how he fell outside legitimate channels of governance. Ultimately, then, Demo's and others' deaths revealed in the most glaring terms the dark side of outsourcing the work of development, governance, and security to baz leaders. Without deep knowledge of neighborhood dynamics and leadership structures—knowledge often lacked by foreign development workers unfamiliar with the neighborhood—there was great risk that projects would fall into the wrong hands, such as those of 117 members who went beyond social and gendered forms of exclusion common in baz workings to engage in predatory crimes of rape, theft, and murder.[26] More systemically, the distribution of funds precipitated a competition for authority that spawned turf wars between rival groups. Even when project funds fell into the "right hands"—that is, in the hands of those at the top of the baz hierarchy or those willing to recognize it—they still failed to provide residents or, for that matter, these leaders with an enduring sense of security, let alone services, in their lives.

Rethinking the State as the Solution

When baz leaders first spoke of the need for *leta* as the solution to the problems in the zone, I was skeptical. The demand struck me as a glaring contradiction—the fact that baz leaders would long for that which they have replaced. Would not this jeopardize the need for their very existence? I wondered. But as I witnessed conflicts unfold and lives lost, I began to see it otherwise. When Ti Snap and others longed for *leta*, they expressed a desire for a place in the state as a legitimate, legal authority (a "partner to the police," as he said) and a place to point to that was ultimately responsible for the situation in the neighborhood.

The role of "partner" is significant for understanding the kind of sovereignty baz leaders sought on the street. This was not the total autonomy often portrayed in media and academic accounts of gang or vigilante rule but rather a relative autonomy, an autonomy that was recognized and linked up with national and global agents of power. Instead of cordoning off the neighborhood as a separate zone of governance, such relative autonomy would enable it to be the base scale of governance that connected and localized broader fields of power. Yet from the vantage point of the base, these broader fields appeared populated by a hodge-podge of governing actors, many of which were not of the state at all. Hence the idea of *leta* also enabled baz leaders to configure a governing relationship predicated on respect between a recognized sovereign (*leta*) and the public (*pèp la*) it served. Such an idea was, in part, motivated by baz leaders' need to deflect responsibility when things went awry, to lay blame higher up the chain of command, as well as a way for them to imagine an end to the internecine conflicts that threatened their leadership. *Leta* was the imagined overarching authority— the "third-order object, an ideological project" (Abrams 1988, 76)—that would take charge of the area, be able to back up the baz's local authority, and control their rivals, and make them state "partners" providing public goods and services rather than put them in competition over project funds and resources. Rather than jeopardize their existence, this *leta* would safeguard it. To again invoke Wolf on brokers: insofar as the baz leader's *raison d'être* lay in negotiating the relations between local, national, and global development fields, it was also the case that they must "maintain a grip on these relations lest conflicts get out of hand and better mediators take their place" (1956, 1076).

And yet I do not think it is fair to reduce their pleas for statehood to selfish tactics aimed at securing baz leadership alone. Ti Snap's calls echoed many other Belairians', leading me to see how the idea of the state prefigured a shared strategy for "real development," a development, as George remarked, that addressed insecurity as it manifested in the violence of crime and in the violence of joblessness, hunger, and misery. When I observed, in 2013, George lay out the need for a state that provided security, work, food, and even leisure, the Tea Party movement had been established in US politics with a platform that argued against the overbearing presence of the state and for its radical reduction. I mentioned this to him, and he responded with a look of disbelief. "It's only in a place with 24/7 electricity that people could say that," he told me. Faced with the realities of government retrenchment, what Belairians wanted was more state, not less. Though not any kind of state power would do. Instead of a hodgepodge of NGOs that did state-like work but answered to their own donors, or a government that was more accountable to foreign aid than the electorate, they wanted a clear site of authority and one that was accountable to them. And instead of a government that made itself present in onerous and costly paperwork that highlighted its own abstention and dereliction of duty, they wished for a state that fulfilled its mandate to legitimately represent them and serve their interests. In short, residents' demands for *leta* resounded as a call for the social contract, for public unity and sovereign responsibility. This was to be expected—not only because the absence of government was enfolded into their precarious presents and early deaths, but also because the project of the revolution and nèg statehood remained an unfulfilled aspiration, as baz formations' militant symbolism proclaimed between the lines of neutral development discourse.

As a final point, I want to caution against taking my analysis of the "dark side" of development as evidence that Haiti would be better off if there were no foreign aid or development at all. As I write, the Tea Party is extending its message into US foreign policy, with an "America First" platform that condemns foreign aid on the basis of waste and corruption and argues for its severe curtailing.[27] My critique of development should not lead to this conclusion, nor should the Haitians I cited be viewed as nationalistic to the point of isolationist. In their understandings of development and its relationship to their lives, Belairians held complex, contradictory views: at once desiring a developed state and the public services, infrastructure, and welfare it promised and deeply aware of the violence and neglect of actual incarnations of the state; at once longing for a holistic development and experiencing how the work of development played out in shrewd brinkmanship and violent conflicts that compromised their sense of security. Like the vanguards of America First, many in Bel Air agreed that waste, corruption, and disorder were serious problems in aid economies, but they saw these as problems whose onus fell on donors as much as recipients. This was not merely an exercise in exculpation. However irredeemable Ti Snap's actions were, we would miss the larger lessons they hold if we attribute them to his innate avarice, venality, or criminality—prejudices, rooted in long-standing beliefs about Haiti and black statehood, that often surface in international accounts of the country's underdevelopment.

The conflicts that emerged from development projects were not owed to the subjective failings of Haitians or, for that matter, foreigners, but rather the systemic relations between the two, to the ways in which aid was conceptualized, organized, and dispersed. What I consistently took from my experiences witnessing development projects gone awry and listening to Belairians' reflections on the matter was an assessment of the impacts of the government's retrenchment from development, not an argument for abandoning development. Again, what they wished for was *leta*—national, regional, and city government—to hold a more active and empowered role vis-à-vis NGOs in the development field and to exercise that power by structuring, legitimizing, and supporting a clear configuration of leadership in the neighborhood. While some groups would inevitably lose out in such a reorganization, the prospect provided a vehicle—in the ballot box or in public protest—for endorsing or challenging local leadership. As Bernie told me in the wake of the antiviolence protest: "Here there are people for and against Ti Snap, and for and against others, but how can you know where their power resides? If the big powers want to work with leaders, then they should define who is the chèf for which zone so we can rise and stand up and say, 'Yes, we agree!' or 'No, we disagree with your ways and those that support you.'"

GENDER

> The demagogue had sponsored several *koudyay* and popular feasts for the people and all the beggars came running. He had even gone in person to the lower-class sections of town where the lumpen proletariat were cramped. He gave coins to kids and a few pats on the behind to women—and he had a drink with the men.
>
> "Papa Vincent is a good old boy!" sang the drunks.
>
> —Jacques Stephen Alexis, *General Sun, My Brother*, 1955

> *Nan mas la ladann ou jwenn vi an lamò ak plezi a, bwas la, lareyalite a* (In the masses, you find a life of death and pleasure, the hustle, the reality).
>
> —Bèlè Masif Rap Song

The afternoon sun of August 7, 2010, scorched the hilltops of Baz Zap Zap. A candy vendor joked that today Bel Air was literally earning its reputation as a *cho*, hot or dangerous zone. Six months had passed since the earthquake destroyed much of the neighborhood and surrounding city. Aside from rubble and curbside tents, the earthquake was palpable in the heightened activity among the male youth whose political aspirations and ventures I had been following for two years. That day, I had planned to attend a meeting about Bel Air residents' participation in Cash-for-Work programs to clear debris and garbage from area canals. When I arrived, however, the overheated residents were relishing other news. A brightly painted placard announced the annual Beach Day of MLK [Martin Luther King], the name for a youth subgroup within the larger network of friends and neighbors that formed Baz Zap Zap. The placard stood where a two-story house had collapsed and claimed the lives of two dear friends: Berman, then a leader of the Zap Zap rara, and his girlfriend Nerlande. But the placard's message eschewed grief and sadness. Chiding trash talkers and the penniless and welcoming the displaced, it read: "This year MLK brings the stuff. . . . Pay money so you can do it. We await all new, pretty ladies in the zone, all my new brothers. . . . We await all at Baz ZapZap. Those with big mouths, stay home!"

FIGURE 20.   View of a street-side bench in Bel Air decorated with the slogan "Feeling," which is also the name of a Carnival street band (*bann a pye*).

I might have dismissed the beach day if its significance had not been immediately stressed. Echoing the Haitian novelist Jacques Stephen Alexis's fictionalization of President Sténio Vincent in the 1930s, Michel, a twenty-year-old MLK member, explained: "The beach day is a little thing. . . . But it's a big little thing.

FIGURE 21. The poster announcing the 2010 beach day for Baz Zap Zap.

We can't stay sitting every day . . . under tents, under misery, under insecurity. [It's] problems. We must organize a program, a big little koudyay. We'll make feeling for everyone, totally. That takes force, people must respect us . . . but like that, our force grows. . . . They'll say, 'Look, they're doing something!' Like that, a big little thing becomes a big, big force." His friend added: "We must find success in this! Each baz does a beach day. Ours must be more beautiful. The more beautiful, the more force. All the men will find a little feeling in it, without disorder. *Koudyay pa blozay!* [Exuberance, not explosion]. We contacted all politicians, all the chèf, all the blan too. We have a lot of sponsors, and we have made the state before. The nice beach day we did last year—you don't remember?—MLK became a force in the zone!"

Power relations in Haiti have long been characterized by the interplay of violent force and a form of moral force manifested in collective festivity and "effervescence" (Durkheim 1995). This continuum of sovereignty spans from "necropolitics" (Mbembe 2003), through to the management of public welfare or "biopolitics" (Foucault 2009), to what I call "hedonopolitics" (Kivland 2014), and it is true of the Haitian state as well as more localized domains of power like the baz. Political acts of violence, service provision, and festivity are all said to fè leta, whether performed by presidents or local big men. The "little thing" of the beach day bore a "big force" because of its place in this repertoire of sovereign power. Indeed, the reference point for MLK's beach day was the koudyay (from the French *coup de jaille*, "jolt of force"), the age-old political festival in Haiti whereby leaders attempt to garner support by sponsoring feasts and revelry for their popular followers. Likewise, at this beach day, MLK members could fashion themselves as leaders, as those with power and respect, by showcasing and transducing good vibes, or what was called, drawing on the English "feeling."[1] In this chapter, I argue that insofar as political power was embodied in displays of good feeling, the production of feelingful activities— from street koudyay to soccer tournaments to beach days—represented efforts to perform sovereign agency and power.

The localized model of sovereignty that I have elaborated throughout this book is structurally aligned with post-9/11 efforts to theorize sovereign power as located not in states but in bodies and, in turn, as a performative power that is never singular or static but "multiple, provisional, and always contested" (Hansen and Stepputat 2005, 172). "Sovereign power, whether exercised by a state, in the name of the nation, or by a local despotic power or community court," as Thomas Hansen and Finn Stepputat contend, "is always a tentative and unstable project whose efficacy and legitimacy depend on repeated performances of violence and a 'will to rule'" (2005, 3). Reflecting the apocalyptic zeitgeist of the "War on Terror," anthropologists have recently focused on the way sovereign power is enacted through violence against bodies caught in "states of exception" (Agamben 2005) or the "margins of the state" (Das and Poole 2004) caused by war, emergencies, or other conflicts—spaces such as Guantánamo Bay or the West Bank, where people can be killed outside the bounds of law. The mortal bodies of citizens have also been explored as mediums for enacting sovereign power, as cases of self-immolation, hunger strikes, and sui-cide bombers articulate a power over the personal body that can become met-onymic of broader claims for sovereign power by a nation or cultural group (Hansen and Stepputat 2006). Still others have argued that gangs or strongmen harness violence to establish state-like control of urban territory and econo-mies (e.g., Bogues 2006; Hoffman 2011; Roitman 1998). What is surprising about these accounts is that despite the range of actions and instances analyzed, violence and death remain the primary and often only modes of performing sovereignty. Given the interplay of state terror and state Carnivals in places like Haiti, this focus seems limited.

The interplay of feeling and force in acts said to "make the state" bring together the corporeality of sovereignty in ways that complicate the narrow defi-nition of sovereignty as violence. It is not only violence and the use of armed force that grounds the state-like power of the baz, but also the ability of its leaders to embody and transduce pleasure to others throughout the zone. Plea-sure is an affect that facilitates recognition of power's effect on bodily force, and when shared across bodies, of power's effect on the liveliness of the collec-tive body. As even Achille Mbembe (2001), the coiner of necropolitics, would remind us, pleasure is a necessary part of power rather than a mere privilege of it (McNee 2001). Particularly in postcolonies, power, he suggests, operates as much through violence and coercion as through a convivial, carnivalesque "aes-thetics of vulgarity" (Mbembe 2001, 102).[2] In the political repertoire of the baz, sovereign power unfolds as a dialectic between death and vitality, such that the political gesture involves the negation of death through spectacular displays of life force. The emphasis here is on excessive life, not death, which is why killing is one, but not the only, sovereign gesture.[3] Focusing on power's positive and nega-tive aspects, on vitality and becoming as much as death and finality, provides a basis for explaining why sovereignty is a power that is contested and embraced, not only by its wielders but also those on whom it is enacted. Conceptualizing sovereignty does not negate necropolitics. Instead it reveals how the loss and gain of life force interact in the sovereign gesture. Importantly, *feeling* in Creole suggests a gain where there had been a loss: it is semantically opposed to both *mizè* and *ensekirite*, to the deprived state of poverty and the anxious state of liv-ing under threat of violence. To have "feeling" is to be so at ease as to enjoy, and to do so in spite of real and present dangers—such as attacks from rival bases or by the police or UN peacekeepers.

Of additional significance is that feeling, as both a political and gendered affect, raises the ever-present but often underanalyzed issue of masculinity in sovereign embodiments. Gender, as Joan Scott (1986, 1076) long ago asserted, is "a primary way of signifying relationships of power." Interactions between states and citizens, and colonists and colonial subjects have routinely been performed, apprehended, and made legitimate in terms of relations between men and women. Yet classic theorizations of sovereignty, from Hobbes to Arendt, Foucault to Agamben, fail to account for manliness as a crucial aspect of sovereignty—even as they presume a male sovereign.[4] Building on feminist social scientists' long-standing concern with how women's exclusion from political leadership derives from the material and symbolic disempowerment of femininity (Di Leonardo 1991), a more recent body of scholarship has performed the countermove and looked at what Wendy Brown (1992, 26) called the "man in the state" (1992, 19).[5] As the phrase implies, much of this work has focused on sovereignty at the level of the state or government. Inspired by the recent broadening of sovereignty, my analysis extends this analytical move to focus on the masculinization of power in male figures beyond the state, on the streets of Bel Air. A core aim of this chapter is to show how baz members' quest for localized power takes shape through a sovereign repertoire—locally called respè—that articulates gendered, racialized, and class-specific forms of bodily force and pleasure. As Mbembe urged, properly treating the interplay of manhood and power would require a "genealogical analysis of the symbolic systems" that "have historically tied the social worlds of sexuality and of power to the phantasmal configurations of pleasure (*jouissance*) on the one hand, and to structures of subjection on the other hand" (2006, 162).[6] I take up this provocation in what follows.

Responsible Women, Vagabon Men

Although sovereignty is usually discussed in relation to states, state sovereignty is only one instantiation of the idea of sovereign agency, which can also apply to individuals as much as governments. In the broadest sense, sovereignty is agency. It is acting, as Hannah Arendt (1998, 234) put it, with "uncompromising self-sufficiency and mastership," or with what Iris Marion Young (1980), adding a gendered dimension, theorized as the masculine "I can" orientation to the world. And yet sovereignty does not occur in a vacuum but depends on recognition from others. This is why the idea of respè is useful for conceptualizing sovereignty—since it brings to the fore how claims to power entail controlling the will of others. "No man can be sovereign," Arendt wrote, "because not man, but men, inhabit the earth" (1998, 234). Acting in the world with uninhibited independence eluded most men in Bel Air, and it was the strictures of dependence—on politicians, development aid, better-positioned friends, and often the women in their lives—that drove their incessant and vehement quests for respè at the level of the person, the baz, and the state. They understood that their quests for power usually, if not necessarily, depended on curtailing the agency of others—although it was often their agency that was curtailed. The drive for respè arose out of the marginal positionality of these men, taking shape in the culture and sociality of the geto. In using the model of the nèg geto as a mode of empowerment, respè was, in many respects, counterhegemonic, acting against elite norms of respectability. Yet in privileging masculine subjectivities, it was also entangled in the reproduction of gender hierarchies and subjugation. I begin with this contradiction in order to show how the form of power cultivated at feelingful programs must be understood in terms of its invocation of culturally particular gender subjectivities and relations.

It was years before Sophie trusted me enough to tell me about the trying side of her relationship with Kal, and even then, an incident forced her hand. One day in August 2013, I went, as normal, with Kal to eat lunch at their shared house. When we arrived, however, Kal did not enter but took a seat across the street and began a game of dominoes with Michel and some friends. When I entered the house, I noticed Sophie had bruises around her right eye and neck. She did not say anything at first. She served me my meal and began to braid the hair of Nadine, her long-time friend and fellow hair stylist, whose one-year-old son played marbles at our feet. After I finished eating, she grabbed Nadine's son, put him on her lap, began to feed him some mashed plantains, and then addressed us.

"Look at how I give Kal a good punishment," she began. "He will not eat a hot meal for days. Ha! That guy is getting skinny on crackers. He'll lose all his force! My food is good—right, See-see?"

"Yes! *Koupe dwèt* [finger-licking]," I replied.

"You see how Kal loves it too. He's suffering now. I give Kal a punishment. He does not eat! No pleasure, misery! You know why, See-see? You don't know, do you?

"No, why?"

"Because he beats me," Sophie said. "He beats me too much! Am I right, Nadine?"

"Yes! Same as Carl."

Just the other week, Nadine went with friends to a street koudyay on another block, where she ran into a guy she had recently dated. When she came back, Carl slapped her across the face. When I asked Nadine what happened the next day, she said, "He was jealous. He said I was cheating on him, but it wasn't true."

I already knew that many of the men I befriended treated women this way, but hearing it explicitly made me confront it in a way I had not before, a point Sophie drove home.

"See-see, let me tell you something. Kal is a political force in the zone, but being a leader, this is not real work. It is lottery work, some days you win, most days you lose. That cannot send a child to school, run a family. . . . Everyone thinks Kal is a big chèf. The big guy getting loose in the rara—a joke. But it is me who sends our child, Laloz, to school. I get the money from my mother in New Jersey, and I send her to a nice, Catholic school so she can be a proper person. Do you see how she speaks French? That is on my back. I'm going to have you teach her English too. This is on my back. I am a chèf too!"

"So, now," Sophie continued, "he comes and asks for money, I get mad. What does he need to take care of at ten at night? He goes to get some fresh air [see a girlfriend] on Rue Tiremasse. I know you know that, See-see. You can't be with him all day and not see that."

"They say that," I said, trying to avoid taking sides while acknowledging the truth of her statement.

"Now," she continued, "he says he wants me to take money out of the *sòl* [mutual lending society]. Oh oh, my friends! Everyone knows the rules, right?"

"You are in charge of the sòl, yes!" Nadine responded, and I seconded.

Sophie and Nadine were the two women with the most prominent roles in the baz. Nadine was the lead singer for the Zap Zap rara and a guest vocalist for Bèlè Masif's rap group.[7] She was also the girlfriend of Carl—a founding member of the clique MLK, the defense brigade MOG, and Bèlè Masif, and, most importantly, the man who acted as the policeman for the small market on the block, where five women, including Nadine's mother, sold produce, dried goods, snacks, and toiletries. As a fee for using the space and protecting the market, Carl collected a small weekly payment ($2–$3 dollars) from the machann collective, the Asosyasyon Machann Platon Bèlè. Sophie also had important neighborly responsibilities; she was often charged with cooking collective meals for baz activities, and she managed a sòl for eleven neighbors on the block. Sòl, popular throughout urban Haiti, work by all participants paying, on a weekly basis, a sum of money into a common pot, which is then dispersed to a different member each week. The system allows for people to save for large purchases such as school tuition or appliances. Kal's request to take money from the sòl out of turn threatened the savings of a large group of people and undermined Sophie's leadership of it, a role that gave them both considerable standing in the zone.

"Now," Sophie continued, "he acts like his father and thinks he is a soldier. 'I am head of this house,' he says, and he raises his hand and he hits me. . . . "'No!' I say, "That is for the people in the sòl. Vagabon! A vagabon cannot be part of the sòl!"

"Kal becomes a zenglendo, oh oh!" Nadine exclaimed with surprise. "I tell you," as she moved the curtain back from the doorway to reveal Kal's game of dominoes, "All these Bel Air guys are vagabon. They lack principles!"

"Now," Sophie went on, as she also looked across at Kal who was taking a sip of *kleren*. "Look at how he takes his punishment. He gets feeling with his baz. That's life. But I know he suffers. His stomach is empty. Don't buy him food today, See-see. I'm counting on you!"

I didn't buy Kal lunch that day, but I did give him gas money, part of which I know he used to purchase some fried *pate* midday. I felt guilty, even if I knew the street food was not nearly as tasty (or filling) as Sophie's cooking. Later that day, I asked him why he was having problems with Sophie. I expected him to repeat the reason Nadine had given for Carl's abuse: jealousy. Often used to explain domestic violence, jealousy relived a romantic fantasy of rage born of unrequited love. Jealousies were at play, but this reason alone was incomplete. Men's jealousies grew more intense as their sense of independence and usefulness for others dwindled—as they became dependent on their female lovers.[8] Sexual jealousies were compounded by the insecurity of failing to live up to one's end of the relationship bargain—a failure that they knew could lead women to pursue other partners.[9] Kal must have thought likewise. "There's no work," he replied. "In the geto, the reality is all men are vagabon, and all women love vagabon. They call, 'Help!' But what else can they do? They love the vagabon, and so, they resign to it. They think the vagabon can become a proper man. But there's no work, so we take our little cash, and we get our baz, and we smoke *boz* [marijuana], or get feeling with *ti zanmi* [flings]."

This response was complex. The complaint of "no work"—a common refrain for all manner of problems in Bel Air—worked to excuse why he acted as a vagabon, as a cheating lover, nonproviding father, and aggressive partner. But in affirming the attractiveness of the vagabon, Kal also reclaimed this figure as a model of masculine power grounded in a rejection of the norms of "proper" manhood. In the pursuit of pleasures beyond the socially normative—in friends, drugs, and women—lurked both a resignation to and a reclamation of the vagabon.

The Many Faces of the Vagabon

The ways in which Sophie praised Catholic education, French and English, and responsible parenthood while denigrating Kal's participation in a "joke" rara, senseless politicking, and multiple sexual liaisons echoed the symbolic divide between respectability and reputation. To recap, Caribbean societies in the 1970s, according to Peter Wilson, were divided between two competing value systems. On one hand was "respectability," which valorized the colonial system and European, white culture, and on the other, was "reputation" (or what I have been calling respè), which valorized black, lower-class culture. Of special significance is how these value systems correlated with the gendered division of society: women embodied respectability; men reputation.[10] Wilson's ethnography showed that whereas women went to church and associated with high society in order to gain status and prestige, men structured their lives as a quest to get respect by earning reputations among their friendship crews. Through the hard play of neighborly rivalries, men gained the social clout that they could use to rise from the margins of society into political leadership. Hence Wilson saw in men's arts of seduction, guitar strumming, joke telling, and street fighting a "utopian" value system that was the "true nature of Caribbean society" and ought to transform itself into the dominant system (1973, 230). Nonetheless, Wilson argued that these values were neither completely separate nor was their relationship to each other unchanging. A dialectic between respect/respectability played out in the minds of men and women as they occupied different social spheres and entered different stages of life. As such, he acknowledged that young men recognized (and internalized) the value to be gained in respectability even as they rejected it in their everyday lives and social relations.

There are many critiques of Wilson's framework. Scholars have argued that despite recognizing how respect and respectability worked together, Wilson still wrote about the two values as if they were equally accessible to men and women, missing how they were dependent on an entrenched gender hierarchy and sexual division of labor (Besson 1993; Thomas 2011).[11] Furthermore, although Wilson saw the two value systems as operating at the individual and societal level and rightly argued that they were structured by Caribbean nations' colonial history, he failed to acknowledge if and how the systems had changed in the neocolonial present. A more rigorous examination of how race, gender, and class articulate to validate certain ways of being in the Caribbean, Deborah Thomas has argued, "would require that we situate [Wilson's] concern with nation building within a global frame of reference, both historically and in the present" (2011, 145).

On Bel Air's streets, where talk of respè resounded, it often appeared that Wilson's dream of a Caribbean society had taken hold. And yet just as apparent was that obstacles to respectability have intensified, and so has the competition for respè. The dearth of and drive for respè as a social value in urban Haiti has taken place within a Caribbean restructuring of the sexual division of labor that has increased unemployment, foreign dependency, and poverty for most lower-class, urban men (Freeman 2000; Thomas 2011). For much of Haiti's history, men and women labored together in a peasant economy, with men predominantly charged with farming the land and women with selling the produce at market. This gave women, as the handlers of money, a degree of autonomy and influence in the economy that outmatched prevailing gender norms world-wide (Mintz 1996; Sheller 2012).[12] Yet men have historically checked women's economic power with political power, denying women the right to vote or hold political office until 1950, and dominating the ranks of the professional and civil servant classes still today.

The neoliberal economy has continued to favor upper-class men over women for higher-level political and professional jobs. However, lower-class men have struggled to gain a foothold in the new economy. Development programs oriented around urban export industries, rather than agriculture, have shifted the gendered division of labor. The light assembly and service industries have contributed to a "feminization" of low-wage labor (Caraway 2007; Schuller 2012b), generally preferring female employees, who can be paid less and often controlled more.[13] Given their historical role as machann, women have also been the preferred beneficiaries of international microcredit programs. In addition, whereas Haiti used to mainly send young men abroad for work as migrant laborers, today more women, like Sophie's mother, are emigrating in search of jobs as maids, nurses, caretakers, or other feminized (and often marginalized) roles in the growing hospitality, medical, and service industries of the United States and elsewhere in the hemisphere (Terrazas 2010).[14] And, of course, scaling back the government—once a major source of male employment, second only to agriculture—has dramatically curtailed poor men's job prospects. Overall, lower-class men have been increasingly sidelined in the new gendered structuration of labor.[15]

This sidelining has compromised men's ability to get respè in a respectable fashion: as employed providers for their children and their children's mothers. Sophie's comment about Kal's "lottery work" suggested that the activities of the baz might provide the occasional windfall but not the daily earnings needed to maintain a household or raise children. Indeed, most baz-affiliated men were dependent on entrepreneurial women for money and housing. The beating that Kal levied on Sophie underscored how dependent he was on her earnings and how his claim to them as the head of household was exacted through violent extortion.[16] Sophie's accusation that Kal was acting like a soldier—what Nadine called *zenglendo*—when he hit her bared how his struggle to hold onto his father's militant masculinity manifested in a perversion of the power of the soldier: as a figure that hurts rather than protects, steals rather than provides. The same suggestion was apparent in accusations of banditry regularly leveled against Carl's collection of "taxes" from the block's machann. As anthropologists have long argued, the increased limitations placed on men's access to respectability in contemporary urban economies can precipitate caustic forms of masculinity. Philippe Bourgois, writing of Puerto Rican men in postindustrial New York

City, traced how the end of the economic basis for *respeto* engendered a "crisis of patriarchy" that "express[ed] itself concretely in the polarization of domestic violence and sexual abuse" (1995, 215). Such behaviors drove women, like Sophie and Nadine, to chastise the men in their lives as vagabon, as purveyors of an aggressive, criminal masculinity.

In its most jarring usage, the word vagabon denotes violence and banditry. However, the criminal is not the only referent for vagabon. When Nadine followed the accusation of zenglendo with the generalization that "All these Bel Air men are vagabon. They lack principles" and gestured toward a group of men playing dominoes, she was highlighting a less violent but still deviant manifestation of respect: *distraksyon* (distractions), or the homosocial, heteronormative activities that, in the absence of work, dominate men's days: from playing dominoes to circulating the neighborhood on a motorbike to flirting with female passersby. In this more playful usage, the vagabon appeared as a rebellious, fun-loving guy's guy, who seduces women and humors men through his defiance of the pressures of work or social conventions. "*Pa fè konfiyans, m gen mefians*" (Don't trust me; I am devious) goes a saying that Belair men enjoyed using to boast of their sex appeal and promiscuity, the latter enhancing the former and vice versa.[17] And yet the bite of Nadine's comment came in that most Bel Air men were a poor facsimile of this sexy vagabon, whose arts of seduction necessitated the income they did not have. They could neither be respectable men (looking after the children they sired) nor proper vagabon (suitably seducing women with lavish gifts). To her, these guys more closely resembled another meaning of vagabon: vagrants.

And yet underlying the criminal and vagrant is the mark of the populist who resists the dominant ordering of what is valued in society. In its most redemptive version, the vagabon is a figure that employs sexuality, vulgarity, and deviancy as forms of corroboration with *pèp la* (the people). The vagabon flouted elite power by flaunting a power rooted in the popular body—a power to work with corporeal capacities to circumvent or overcome respectable pathways to wealth, success, or power. Like the *tiguere* figure in the Dominican Republic, vagabon were as "much admired, as they [were] feared for their ability to manipulate, if not subvert, a system stacked against the poor and powerless" (Gregory 2006, 42).[18] The vagabon was coded as male, but as a form of popular power women could be referred to as *fanm vagabon* if they displayed such cunning, counter-hegemonic qualities.[19] The vagabon, for example, was present in Sophie's business savvy and capitalization on her mother's migration to New Jersey as much as in Kal's climb from an orphaned childhood to a local political force. Such social feats illustrate how respè has operated as a complex power, a power that is liberating and destructive, venerable and deviant. These feats also demonstrate that the dialectic of respect/respectability is changing not only through struc-tural shifts that have relegated the urban poor to the insecure margins of the global political economy but also through urbanites' abilities to manipulate this dialectic to their advantage—thus exerting a structuring pressure on the forces that have acted on them. Transnational migration, the localization of sover-eignty, and the global popularity of black culture have bolstered the autonomy of poor, urban Haitians, "giving them," to quote Deborah Thomas, "relatively greater ability to eschew conventional middle-class modes of respectability and to define progress and citizenship through their own cultural idioms and repertoires"—such as bold sexuality, rap music, and street politics (Thomas 2004, 2011). In the transgressive acts of young men in Bel Air I want to see beyond the destruction or distraction that results from an out-of-reach respectability to a way of defining a new norm for respect-worthy manhood—one less rooted in the mores of traditional respectability. Belairians aspired to respè because they have been barred from the gains of neoliberal democratization and because they associated respè with the egalitarian aims of a democratic society. Yet, in so doing, it is critical to remember the masculinist nature of the vagabon. The radi-cal power of this new man, like that of the revolutionary soldier (Sheller 2012), all too often operated through the subjugation of women—though to be sure women had ways of manipulating and subverting the power of the vagabon, as was evident at feelingful programs.

Performing the Man

The two-story house that collapsed in the earthquake was once known as Kay Zap Zap. Bernie's family, who lived in southern Florida, owned it. Bernie used a room on the first floor in exchange for his service as the landlord for three families that lived there. His room was a typical *cham gason*, with no furnishings except for a mattress, stereo, and two posters of rap groups. Kal, Michel, Jak, Frantzy, Berman, and Blan Komen, all of whom had yet to establish their own households, often slept there, and they brought their girlfriends there for privacy. When the earthquake struck, the guys were on the outdoor balcony, except for Berman, who was watching music videos with his new girlfriend, Nerlande, in the apartment her mother rented on the first floor. They both raced toward the balcony as the tremors intensified, but neither made it out in time. Nerlande was survived by her mother and young daughter, and Berman by his common law wife and five children, including a newborn.

Two years prior, during a sunny afternoon in late October 2008, I sat on the balcony of Kay Zap Zap with the regular guys. Frantzy, who was then the rara's secretary, kept repeating that he had something important to say. Eventually, Berman, who played the kone in the rara and acted as the group's Sanba, or songwriter, asked him to explain.

"Ever since the foreigners killed the feeling and took our ancestors during the coup [in 2004], I see that the band has lost its force," Frantzy complained. He was referring to the two-year imprisonment of Yves after the coup against Aristide. Frantzy continued: "We need the force of the youth. We won't let them stay sitting. We have to put them on the concrete, make a big activity, give everyone feeling! The first of November we'll make a big koudyay," and then with a smirk, "just like in the Duvalier epoch!"

After stressing the work it would require, Berman added, "On that day, we will *fè the man* for the zone." I had heard the hybrid Creole-English expression *fè the man*, or "make the man," before—usually when women chided the wayward men in their lives to claim household responsibility or provide for their children. Moving from household to baz, Berman invoked a paternalistic political discourse, in which the group embodied "the man" for the zone. Yet here Berman was not suggesting that the group would provide neighbors with life's necessities so much as free them from the burden of the mundane with a raucous good time. It was nonetheless clear that providing a good time was an exercise in masculine leadership and control over the zone.

This was made apparent in the myriad ways the group established the site of the party as a territory under their control. During the day, Bernie began to "rent" street space for local machann to set up shop. The women paid 20 goud ($0.50), a small but significant sum, in exchange for the privilege to sell fried foods, alcohol, and cigarettes at the party. The group also painted a street-side bench and several walls with murals in honor of the rara and development organizations. They then placed several chairs around the bench and in front of the corner store Boutique Mystère across the street. "VIP" signs adorned the chairs, designating them for the presidents of other bands, local businessmen, and party sponsors, including Nathaniel, then Zap Zap's president, the "anthropologist" (me), and Yves, who parked his white jeep in the middle of the intersection, where it would be surrounded by the crowd. They built a stage at the edge of the block, teetering close to Baz Grand Black's zone, and decorated its backdrop with graffiti that proclaimed Baz Zap Zap as Masters of the Concrete. They rigged the stage with a generator-fueled sound system, from which a DJ would blare, from 10 pm until the wee hours of morning, rap kreyòl and studio-recorded Zap Zap songs so loud that the group could claim sonic control of Plateau Bel Air. "The baz is full of people, full of sound" was how Kal described the party at its height.

Even before the party started, the group ritually established the equation between the baz as social group and geographic zone. The pre-koudyay ritual centered on a display of spiritual and ancestral force rooted in the group's territory. Manfred, the then Vodou priest for the Zap Zap rara, buried two white doves alive before a black cross that stood before the house of Zap Zap's deceased founder. He then summoned the band's core spirit, Mèt Kalfou, and asked guests to pay a toll to this power of the crossroads. He stressed how dropping change in the band's *demanbre*, the hut where the spirits reside, would ensure the militant spirit's protection—and thereby designate the protected. Next he placed a drum and kerosene lamp before the cross, then gathered some dirt and brought it into the hut with the bands' core members, who formed Chanpwèl Blada, the secret society. When they emerged, Manfred carried an old beer bottle tied in a red scarf, signaling his capture of the founding member's zonbi, who would now ceaselessly "work" for the band and, again, ensure their protection. He then lit a pile of wood on fire in the intersection, between the black cross and the demanbre. The band circled the fire, their shadows cast on Yves's jeep before the black cross. Twelve or so musicians then marched, loudly and gleefully playing their iconic melodies, down to the next intersection of their rival Rara M and Baz Grand Black, around the block, and then back to the baz locale. Typically, this ritual ensured the band's performative prowess and protection along long procession or protest routes. However, given that they only circled the block, they were more concerned with showing neighbors what they were doing, where they were doing it, and the seriousness with which they intended to execute it. When I asked Manfred why he did the ritual for a party, he replied, invoking a Bèlè Masif rap lyric, "We tighten up so that we can let loose."

Indeed, Mèt Kalfou quickly gave way to the fun-loving spirit Gede, whose annual festival coincided with the koudyay. The Zap Zap rara did not normally take to the streets in early November. The epoch, in fact, belonged to Rara M. This made the koudyay all the more consequential. Gede, a joke-telling womanizer who nonetheless determines the most crucial questions of life—who lives and who dies—was the perfect "man" for turning a party into a scene of masculine competition. Far from a respectable provider figure, the Gede man embraces masculine sociality—virility, promiscuity, fun, and humor—as a model for transgressive claims to power and respect. "There is a clear linkage," as Katherine Smith writes of contemporary urban spirituality, "between Gede and the average man—or, more to the point, the vagabon" (2012, 130).

At various points throughout the night, a *betiz*, or sexualized joke, cascaded off men's lips and brought smiles to partygoers. In typical irreverence to Catholicism, Michel sang: "Where is Mother Perpetual?/We look for the nice *koko* [slang for vagina]./But she's not alone./She's full of *zozo* [slang for penis]."[20] In a similar vein, Bernie and Jak sang, "*Bouzen* [whores] in zone. They love *cham gason*. [They] don't sleep in the family's house."[21] Throughout the night, Berman incarnated a

Gede called Chèf Gran Bwa [great woods], and teased that the women present at the koudyay were "*fanm vagabon* who love vagabon." These jokes appeared to chastise loose women, though, in light of Bernie's actual *cham gason*, they also called attention to the role the jokesters played in turning women into so-called *bouzen*. From their mouths, the lyrics rang out as boasts about their sexual powers to corrupt respectable women. The Zap Zap song the DJ played the most also had a sexual undertone. Its refrain located popular sovereignty, the people's rule of the country, "in the *dada*," meaning butt but comparable to gut. "Don't let them perish. Don't let them be totally destroyed. Their country is for them. Their power is in their gut. They are the Pharaoh's Army. We are the People of Israel."[22] This song stood out from the other jokes in that it was delivered in the voice of Nadine who, during one playing of it, shook her backside on the stage. Nadine's voicing of it projected the feminine body as the site of a popular power that would undermine the seemingly more powerful forces set against the people. In typical fashion, it was ambiguous whether such forces were in the National Palace, a foreign country, or down the block. "In Zap Zap, there was feeling flowing in the blood of all. When our army entered, we gave you feeling. We put pleasure in your dada!" was how Yves summed up the party.

This song brought to the fore how the power of Gede, though gendered male, is a fundamentally human power. As the spirit of sexual reproduction, Gede is common to all—a power even when no other power is present. This makes Gede a good fit for the urban poor, whose most potent exercise of power is to put their bodies en masse in the street. Yet it is not only the popular body that makes Gede a good fit for the urban poor. It is also because the power of Gede resides in a willingness and a craftiness to step outside the pretenses of respectable society and unlock the vitality of the sexual body. Gede's zozo—its size, hardness, pleasurableness—is always a feature of his jokes, which, at their most potent, can bring humor and fun to the worst of circumstances.[23] Gede's carnivalesque humor has long offered the poor and downtrodden in Haiti a medium for mitigating the standing of the rich and powerful by asserting, through jest and jibe, the commonality of human conception and death. "In a country that has known severe and almost constant political repression," as Karen McCarthy Brown writes, "Gede's ambiguous, many-layered humor is often the only safe form of protest" (1991, 363).[24] And yet it was clear that Zap Zap members utilized this form of popular power at the koudyay not primarily to resist sovereign power but also to embody it. The surrogates of Gede posited the male sexual body as not only a "weapon of the weak" (Scott 1985) but also a medium for weaponizing the weak—using corporeal force and pleasure as a basis for empowerment as "big men," however small the scale or moment. As Manfred, echoing others, told me at the koudyay: "Everyone has a Gede for himself. He is the first spirit, the first zozo.

He's there to give you feeling. Gede, big zozo. For that reason Gede is the master of the party. Nice zozo makes feeling multiply. The size of our bwa. They'll hate us."[25] Drawing on the double meaning of *bwa* as "wood" and "penis," the final line, a rara lyric, construed the penis as an armament.

However, read in context, it echoed the other betiz and suggested that women or feminized others, such as their rival baz, desire the big wood/penis, but since they cannot claim it, detest these men out of jealousy (see McAlister 2002, 68). Yet even this nuanced meaning retained the threat of force, as the presumption of jealousy and hatred provided the motivation for attack and defense. Invoking the trope of romantic rivalry, Manfred's comment construed erotic feeling as not only the antidote to partygoers' shared misery but also as a force that could excite their rival's jealousies and help reestablish Baz Zap Zap's control of the zone.[26] In the past, baz-linked rara battles have exceeded sonic competition to spill over into actual violence.[27] That was not the case here, but the threat of violence did undergird the "deep play" (Geertz 1972), or gravity, of the whole event. The song Zap Zap composed for Carnival the following year boasted about how their magical, militant *petwo* power excited their party and destroyed their rival's. This was also reportage, as their rival's party, held in the following days, disbanded after a police-peacekeeping raid that apprehended and temporarily detained Grand Black leader Ti Snap. "It's Zap Zap that passes here./It gives me feeling./It moves in my blood./Our Petwo is our dangerous party [endangers your party]/It's not just talk.[28]

Activating the Man for the Zone

When Frantzy spoke of the street party as an *aktivite* (activity), he highlighted how baz member's production of feelingful programs stood in contrast to the *travay* (work) they did not have. Travay implies regular employment, whereas aktivite entails the generation of income by inventing a job outside the formal economy, such as acting as a moto-chauffeur or putting on a block party. The word *aktivite*, as Frantzy used it, named the income-generating action, but it also signaled the state of being active. For Bel Air men, activeness was a key sign, or rather "qualisign," a quality that "stands to somebody for something in some respect or capacity" (Peirce 1897 [1997], 135)—the something here being a man with street power. The active man had that quintessential masculine "I can" attitude, but this sense of agency was located outside the bounds of respectable society.[29] For nèg geto who are consumed by the sense of being socially and physically stuck in place, power has become increasingly associated with the man who is on the move, connecting with people, and making things happen.[30] Yet this activeness is also premised on the position of the nèg geto insofar as it depends on an ability to work from the margins of power with unconventional means in order to get what one has been denied. To be active in this vagabon way is to make a show of not only manhood but also geto power and, taken together, street sovereignty.

Qualities, as anthropologists have shown, are culturally and socially mediated experiences that can function as currencies of value for the people and things that embody them (Chumley and Harkness 2013; Munn 1986).[31] In Bel Air, being, feeling, and displaying oneself as active was a "value-producing act" (Munn 1986, 8) that participated in building men's reputations as "I can" men of the street. Activeness was allied with other qualities, such as *cho* (hotness), *vit* (quickness), and *dou* (smoothness) and could be made manifest across a range of actions grounded in the street, from *mobilizasyon* (organizing people for action) to *bwase lari* (hustling), *monte desan* (running around town), and *tcheke zanmi* (exchanging favors with friends).[32] What united these actions was that they signaled the power to move or shift people, things, or situations through socially subversive agency. In performing these activities, men demonstrated an agency premised not on a formal post of power but rather on extensions of "intersubjective spacetime" (Munn 1986, 10) or the spiralistic broadening of the self through networks of contacts that connected various domains of power. Feelingful programs proved to be such key mediums for exhibiting activeness because of the way in which they necessitated engagement in forms of action that both presupposed and entailed the organizers' social base and reach. Program organizers called on multiple contacts (including politicians, NGOs, neighbors, baz rivals, and spiritual mediums) in order to produce an event whose value could be redistributed to a wide circle of participants.

The economic, social, and political value to be gained from embodying aktivite was most evident at the street soccer tournaments that baz organized during summer weekends. In June 2009, OJMOTEEB began planning its second annual tournament, again on the gallery of Kay Zap Zap. With all seated around, Berman called an informal meeting. Michel, who was charged with typing out documents for OJMOTEEB, was quickly roused from his nap on the concrete bench tagged with the letters MLK, and called over to chat with the others, including Kal, Bernie, Jak, and Blan Komen. After announcing that this tournament must have "more feeling" than last year's, Frantzy gave Michel a hundred-goud note ($2.50) to draft letters requesting support at a nearby cyber café. He paused before telling him to whom to type the letters, as if contemplating the range of options. "Since no chèf takes responsibility," he said in exasperation, "we'll have to write everyone"—a statement that reflected his frustration with the lack of a state ministry that oversaw such activities. Eventually, he decided on several actors who, as he said, "make the state": the Brazilian NGO Viva Rio, the Ministère de la Jeunesse, des Sports et de l'Action Civique (state office for youth athletic and civic engagement), a USAID-sponsored neighborhood renewal program, the National Palace, President Préval, the district deputy, a local engineer and aspiring politician, and the owner of Boutique Mystère. Frantzy next dictated a six-hundred-dollar budget, which included t-shirts and decorations ($150); DJ ($275); refreshments ($125); and equipment ($50). He wondered aloud if this would allow enough to give the baz members something, and then added another hundred dollars for *mobilizasyon*.

He ended the meeting by telling Michel to print out some extra letters without addressees. These would be for less official sponsors as well as important personages, including Yves, Ti Snap, and the leaders of two other rival baz formations. As funding requests, these letters signaled the group was not (yet) profiting, but also that if they did, these actors would get their cut. The letters thus recognized and integrated powerful actors by requesting their permission and protection. Such gestures of *respè* were critical to ensuring the success of feelingful programs. In effect, obtaining permission from Ti Snap and others stood in for a city permit system.

Once the letters and budget were stamped with the organization's seal, Frantzy, sporting a button-down white shirt tucked into pristinely ironed khakis, went with me to deliver them.[33] We received from each office a small paper affirming the reception of the letter, which enabled Frantzy to follow up on the request. It was the ceaseless *fè swivi* (following up) that accounted for much of the aktivite over the next weeks. Going out, checking contacts, visiting offices with cash and papers in hand, and arranging baz meetings to deliver news of what happened, put on public display that the group was active and engaged in planning an important matter. While baz members would regularly complain about being *okipe* (very busy) when organizing programs, I rarely heard them express fatigue, as they might when toiling away at "women's work," such as doing laundry, fetching water, or cooking. In fact, the pleasure they took in this aktivite was often highlighted. For example, Jak, at the time single and unemployed, usually responded to questions about what he was up to with "*anyen*" (nothing) and that he was "*nan mizè*" (in misery) as always. But in the run-up to the street party, when I asked how he was doing, he responded by pounding his chest and exuberantly exclaiming: "Me myself, I am doing a lot of aktivite today. Oh oh ... a lot of work. Good feeling! *Travay se liberte* [work is liberty]!"

Ultimately, all of the aktivite for the tournament resulted in a check from the state office for youth and a cash payment from the aspiring politician, which I was told totaled $100. No funding came from the NGOs, which Frantzy attributed to the fact that "NGOs don't like our match. They don't see serious things in taking pleasure. They make the state in corridor-paving projects, violence projects only."[34] To make up the difference, Yves then added another few hundred dollars. However, Yves made clear to all that his contribution came not from him alone but from his "several contacts" in the government—indicating that he had followed up on the letters himself. The suggestion reiterated the way in which baz leadership followed a spiralistic logic, where baz leaders' claims to local control were rooted in their abilities to manipulate and harness the power of others rather than rely solely on an autonomous source of power or income. This representation of the self as networked, as having "the capacity to develop spatiotemporal relations that go beyond the self" (Munn 1986, 11) was a significant value parameter that appraised Yves's reputation in the eyes of other baz leaders as well as his underlings. The socially embedded uptake of his leadership also ensured (and insured) the program's success and an ability to claim success: the display of an expansive political network protected the activity at the same time that it protected Yves by mitigating any claim to complete responsibility if the activity should falter.

In 2009, with a budget of only a few hundred dollars, the tournament was scaled down. The refreshments and t-shirts were forgone. Instead, the group collected promotional shirts that NGOs and businesses distributed to residents and outfitted the teams in matching ones. Decorations were limited to blue-and-white striped plastic bags tied to the maze of informal electricity lines hanging above the streetscape. A small generator, boom box, and two large speakers, borrowed from the owner of Mystère Boutique, provided the sound system. Frantzy acted as the DJ. A miniversion of the Zap Zap rara—composed mainly of new, younger members—made a short appearance after the finale. Finally, Fritz volunteered to referee the game.

Despite its small scale, however, news of the tournament spread quickly. As I walked by L'église Perpetual that mourning, Marc, a member of Baz Grand Black, called to me: "See-see, there's a tournament tonight. You must go! All the nèg will be there," with emphasis on nèg. Whereas some women enjoyed the soccer tournament, the players and the bulk of participants were men. This had to do with the fact that soccer was a male-centered social activity as well as the risk of danger at tournaments. As Sophie told me: "My baby counts on me. I don't go looking for disorder. Better I find a little pleasure inside my house." Her concerns were not unfounded. In the summer of 2005, for example, when the coup-era hostility was still active, several tournaments in Bel Air and other pro-Aristide neighborhoods were violently disbanded by armed actors supporting the interim regime.[35] While this violence encouraged the wary to stay home, the association of soccer tournaments with danger and risk also added to their allure as charged events fit for men or those seeking respect as men. "There cannot *not* be shooting at this program!" was a phrase that I often heard used to advertise this tournament's danger but also its social value. Still, women, and Sophie in particular, often did participate in these events, but not for pleasure; rather, they also used them as opportunities to create aktivite and generate income. In the end, Nadine went to the tournament and sold beverages that she and Sophie had pulled cash to buy. I interpreted Sophie's decision as about not only avoiding violence but also enforcing that her daughter, then a preteen, stay home.

Like street koudyay, soccer tournaments were targets of violence because of the way they put on display the organization of rule in the neighborhood and beyond. The 2009 tournament consisted of four five-member teams culled from other nearby youth development organizations that OJMOTEEB had, via a letter, invited to play. Each organization and team was, like OJMOTEEB, connected to particular baz networks and particular neighborhood zones (or sections of zones). Thus the tournament, which brought together four different zones (two teams from the same one plus Plateau Bel Air), modeled the political geography of the neighborhood. It unfolded as a competition between baz. However, it

FIGURE 22.   A view of the soccer tournament hosted by Baz Zap Zap in 2009.

would be wrong to view this competition as playing out through the teams and the game of soccer. The significant match took place among those who organized the feelingful activity.

Throughout much of the tournament, the main organizers sat, or rather stood, before plastic lawn chairs on a balcony even with midfield, where Frantzy was playing rap tunes. While Yves was not present, his white jeep was parked in the crossroads, behind one of the goals. As at the street party, several market women set up shop in spots the group had designated for them, and for which the women made a small contribution. The organizers wore their best, hip-hop fashions, adding jewelry, new caps, and shiny sneakers to their standard attire. When the first match began, they put their arms around each others' shoulders as if to affirm "*We* did this!" Although one might have expected the organizers to then sit back and bask in their accomplishment, they remained standing and active, even busy, throughout the night. They readily greeted incoming spectators by saying respè and bumping fists, and throughout the night, they purchased rounds of fried food, drinks, and cigarettes, which they shared widely among the crowd. A palpable good vibe permeated the nearly all-male crowd, gathered on sidewalks, balconies, and rooftops. It helped that affiliations were shared across teams, with cheers erupting at goals on either side. But this is not to say a competitive spirit was lacking. Before leaving, Kal told me: "Look, at how we make good feeling, give all the people feeling. No person has misery at this hour in our lakou. No ensekirite. It's because it's us who do this, because it's us who represent the baz now."

"As much of America surfaces in a ball park, on a golf links, at a race track, or around a poker table," as Clifford Geertz famously wrote, "much of Bali surfaces in a cock ring. For it is only apparently cocks that are fighting there. Actually, it is men" (1973, 417). This maxim suggests that men in Bali constitute their place in society through the power plays their surrogated gamecocks stage in the ring. But as Geertz's ethnography attests, the competition is not only between the men and kin groups whose birds are fighting but also between which village chief throws the better fight. The same can be said of these Haitian tournaments. Baz leaders were, to draw on a distinction Claude Lévi-Strauss made long ago, "treating a game as a ritual" (1966, 31), in that the competitions waged in the soccer matches were a forum not for determining but for reinforcing a social hierarchy.[36] However, it might be more accurate to say that soccer tournaments were a cross between a ritual and a game. A competition was taking place but at the organizational level. The significant question was which group of men organized and displayed the better activity. And this decision rested on which group orchestrated the best ambiance of masculine action, pleasure, and sociality. Hence, while activities were certainly about generating income, this was not their only or even primary aim. Of related significance was that activities allowed them to make a show of the "I can" qualities of respected men—active, connected, agentive, generous. In this sense, it mattered that these activities participated in a redistributive economy.

Several baz members were engaged in providing social services—water, electricity, garbage—to baz-affiliated residents at low rates. In addition, the development organizations, largely backed by Yves, offered neighborhood residents a variety of gifts, from elementary school scholarships to school supplies, from children's toys to food aid packages, not to mention the occasional cash handout. Feelingful programs also participated in this redistributive economy, although in ways that went beyond it as well. One of the reasons that these programs were thought to be the premier forum for garnering respè was that they produced less conflict among the benefactors than the distributions of goods or services did. For example, many residents resented paying Blan Komen for pirated electricity, which they thought should be free, since it came at no cost to him; and they also, rightly, made accusations that the distributions of goods and the costs of services were skewed toward the well connected rather than the needy. Hence, by trafficking in values that were socially indivisible, feelingful activities could bring people together in ways that mitigated the interpersonal divisions plaguing so many relationships in the neighborhood.[37] The feelingful program functioned as a gift economy and was recognized as such—representing, along the lines theorized by Marcel Mauss (1954 [1990]), a counterpoint to problematic transactional, monetary exchanges.[38] While an extra-economic and more generalized form of gift exchange, the tournament still presupposed debt forgiveness, forming part of Yves's and the other Zap Zap members' larger quests to mitigate their reputation as sources of ensekirite, as participants in the postcoup violence as well as ongoing conflicts within and between baz formations. When successful, they could transform baz leaders' reputations from criminal vagabon to respected leaders of the zone.

The Affectation of Masculine Pleasure

Another focal point of summer was the *jounen lamè* (beach day)—when busloads of Belairians traveled an hour or so outside the city to spend the day at a public beach. Beach days—even more than street parties or soccer games—centered on the display of masculine sexuality. In the imaginary of Belairians, the beach is a space reserved for the rich, *dyaspora* (mainly Haitian-American tourists), and peacekeeping troops or other aid workers. Beach days are, therefore, associated with elite and foreign forms of leisure. Yet people also saw the beach day as an opportunity for violating elite codes of conduct. In a word, men and women went to the beach for *sex*. A trip to the beach was the courting ritual that tipped a flirtation into a relationship. This was not only because going to the beach was seen as a romantic indulgence but also because it afforded new couples—as well as illicit ones—a space to engage in sex acts beyond the view of nosy neighbors. Even at a crowded beach, the sea provided a degree of privacy. Couples embracing in the sea used the murky water as a screen that prevented onlookers from seeing exactly what was taking place underwater. To be sure, onlookers had little doubt as to the *bagay* (thing) underway. What mattered was that the screen allowed couples to deny it. Yet despite this forbidden-fruit atmosphere, actual sex acts occupied a small fraction of social interactions at beach days. In a homosocial yet heteronormative vein, the mainly male beachgoers spent most of their time advertising to other men their potential for engagement in erotic *aventures* (adventures), as they described them, waxing sophisticated in the colonial language but with a satirical ring.

By the time preparations for the 2009 beach day ignited, I had already heard a lot about it. OJMOTEEB had been inviting me to their annual beach day for over a year. In mid-July 2009, they displayed an elaborately painted placard on the corner, and they circulated to friends and neighbors a grainy flyer designed by Michel. It pictured a young, attractive girl in a white bikini and sparkling belly necklace, jumping enthusiastically, her long locks bouncing around a caramel-colored face. "*Chacha* your body, romp your body, good thing!" Around this image radiated the architecture of the baz; the titles of the various groups appeared in graphic displays with the names of the sponsors, Yves and Mystère Boutique, in finer print. The state office for youth, as well as the NGO Viva Rio were also solicited in writing, and the former was added to the placard after issuing a check for about fifty dollars. Both the flyer and the placard advertised the ticket price of 200 goud (about $5) that would be printed on raffle tickets and distributed to attendees—a prohibitive cost for most. In fact, it was largely an empty performance of economic agency, since most attendees were given complimentary tickets by the organizers. Nonetheless, the idea of paying delivered a real social good. It constructed beachgoers as possessing the social connections that enabled one to obtain the economic capital of bona fide men. The placard even announced, "You must work hard for the ticket, or else you'll be ashamed!" On another level, the fact that tickets came in the form of gifts reinforced the hierarchical standing and capital of the organizers. It also, not unimportantly, gave them a pretext for excluding certain people, like Samuel, who refused to pay after a tiff he had with Kal in the run-up to the event.

I arrived the morning of the beach day at "6 am," as the flyer announced. The street bustled with the prideful aktivite and fun ambiance of a feelingful

FIGURE 23. The flyer advertising the 2009 beach day hosted by Baz Zap Zap.

program in the making. A yellow school bus, for which OJMOTEEB would pay $75, was already parked before Kay Zap Zap, next to Yves's jeep. The group members were casually chatting on the gallery, as Sophie and Nerlande finished cooking a huge pot of rice and beans and saucy chicken. It appeared we were ready to go, but the hours kept passing. This delay went beyond the lax concern for punctuality to which I had grown accustomed. The organizers kept retreating to private meetings on the roof. I suspected that there was a problem with the finances, but when I went upstairs, they were sharing a joint and survey-ing the crowd gathered on the street. After assuring me of our "*gwo aventure*," Berman told Michel to go and check if the bus of La Familia (The Family)—another baz that was also doing a beach day—had left and to assess its crowd. Going to the beach was clearly as much about orchestrating a fun adventure for the baz's following as attracting the attention of others in the neighborhood. As with soccer tournaments, organizing the bigger and more feelingful outing vis-à-vis other neighborhood groups was what made the activity fun and the fun socially consequential.

The interactions at the beach unfolded as a montage of attempts by the attendees to display sexualized attractiveness and erotic prowess. There were about three times as many men as women, though all of the core baz members brought along dates. These dates ranged from long-time partners to extramari-tal partnerships to prostitute-like arrangements, where the women were com-pensated for their time. Yves had, for example, financed the dates for Jak and Bernie, who had been rendered broke by all the beach day expenses. Along with these distinctions, the activities of the attendees varied. Jak and Bernie spent the first part of the day taking photos with their bikini-clad dates and flirting with them in front of their friends, before both women retreated to the bus and the men socialized among themselves. Berman, in contrast, used the beach day to socially and sexually consummate his relationship with his girlfriend, Nerlande. With his wife at home with the five kids, they disappeared into the water and embraced in underwater intimacies. Those without dates were consumed with taking cell-phone pictures. They posed for the camera in an assortment of hip-hop tableaus, with low-slung shorts, crossed arms, and gestures borrowed from their imaginations of American gang culture. To be sure, a dance party in which an amateur DJ, hired by the beach, played popular songs and local hits ended up igniting a few of the fun flings publicized in the poster. After the beats of the local rap group caused a frenzy, a loop of slower tunes brought new couples together in tight embraces. However, by day's end, few men had entered the water, spending most of the time engaged in the kind of activities that dominate their days in Bel Air, socializing, playing dominoes, and trying to get a buzz sip-ping strong liquor.

The most exaggerated display of masculine prowess came with the arrival of Yves. He drove in his own jeep accompanied by Carl. Their dates, attractive teenagers, were Bel Air residents but not of Plateau Bel Air or affiliates of the baz, and when they approached Kal, Bernie, Berman, and Jak, they displayed the awkwardness of strangers. Obviously uncomfortable, the women quickly excused themselves, changed into new florescent bikinis (purchased by Yves), took a quick swim, waved to Yves from the water, and then retreated to the jeep, where they spent the rest of the day by themselves. In the meantime, Yves openly joked with Frantzy, Jak, and another friend, as Nadine and I chatted nearby. Kal, with a raised eyebrow and a smirk, remarked that Yves had brought some "fresh air" to the party. Yves, never one to shy away from sexualized boasting, affirmed that he had already "tasted the sweetness" of his date. "Her pussy gives me too much feeling, oh oh, all that [pubic] hair. Now I have to pound her ass," he said with a guffaw, which was met by laughter from the other men. Yves held court for a while, telling us how his sexual feats were costing him dearly. "Sweet pussy is not cheap!" Jak agreed. Yves concluded by sexualizing my presence, joking that his new girl was driving him crazy just like the *youn pa konnen sa k lòt la fè* (the one who doesn't know what the other is doing). This reference to me, a poetic nickname that poked fun at my long-distance relationship, was well played, and we all fell into laughter.

"What is socially peripheral is so often symbolically central" (Babcock 1978, 32). The seeming irrelevance of the female dates at the beach was an example of the way in which performances of manliness, though about women, often happen between and are primarily addressed to other men (Gregory 2003; Sedgwick 1985). The interactions Jak, Bernie, and Kal had with their dates were "theatrically performed so as to incite the collective participation of the men (through laughter, whooping and hollering, and catching each other's eye) and enable the alignment of a shared male gaze" (Gregory 2006, 148).[39] This gaze rested on the momentary yet momentous performance of these men as those with the economic and social power to position these women as sexual objects within a masculine economy of respè. Yves's homosocial performance was a classic example. His monologue did not exhibit sexuality itself but was rather a gesture aimed at giving the impression of sexual prowess without actually achieving anything other than men's emotional excitement through the power of word and boast. This was not the last laugh, however. Having long since found a way of asserting female sexuality in this male group, Nadine countered with another joke in my defense. "You are too ugly, Yves," she said. Grabbing her crotch but indicating mine, she continued, "This beautiful, pink clitoris, if you don't have a beautiful zozo, it'll cost you your car." The joke played on the assumption that desirability and economic agency were two powers Bel Air women often possessed over men. Nadine, like other Haitian women, often referred to her vagina as *tè mwen* (their land), a saying that invokes a long history of dependence on men but also exalts feminine attraction as a power through which women control men's access to the acts that give them respect: sex and virility (Maternowska 2006). In this way, Nadine used female sexuality and economic agency to undermine Yves's claim to manhood as a source of pleasure and provision.

In the wake of the joke, I could not help but think of Yves's two young dates. I knew little about them, but I had seen them at the prior mini-koudyay.

I made a point to go talk to them in the jeep, using the excuse of the oppressive heat. They were shy, but I learned they were cousins and lived in Delmas 2. Having stopped schooling after grade school, they now often helped one's mother sell hair and skin products at the main city market. I bought one of the sunscreens they acquired with some help from Yves and hoped to sell to beachgoers. Although it is easy to read these women as commodified pawns in Yves's game of respect, as was put on bold display in his show for the other men, it was also the case that these women were using the beach day and its commodified signs (bikinis, a ride in the jeep, start-up capital, income) as key assets in their navigation of sexual and social hierarchies in the city. Although not on their own terms, they could use these assets to redefine their relations with men as a mark of their success and independence from men and other women. When I asked why they did not join the other beachgoers, they responded, "Those aren't our people." I made a puzzled expression. "You don't see the difference? Look at how they [the other women] are dressed," one responded as she flaunted her new bikini.

There was also more to men's beach day performances of manliness than simple erotic fantasy. Somewhat surprisingly, the beach day provided an opportunity for some men to embody "the man" in a starkly different way from Yves. Sophie, for example, spent much of the day sitting at the water's edge nestled between Kal's legs, as they supervised their adolescent daughter playing in the ocean. Unable to afford a bikini, Sophie wore a blue Obama tank I had lent her, boxer briefs, and a hair cap, which, after each splash, Kal wiped off and realigned. When I approached them, Kal told me in an elated tone, "I've had time to forget the city, the geto, totally. They call it Bel Air, but it's here I get the feeling of *bèl* air, itself, together with my wife [squeezing Sophie]. OJMOTEEB, a lot of respè! We organized ourselves well. We're mobilizing a lot of men with all this feeling. Good thing!"

This was among the happiest I had seen Kal, who vacillated between depression and anger, and seen him and Sophie together, as their relationship always seemed to be recovering from or on the verge of domestic violence—usually triggered when Sophie accused Kal of cheating or Kal demanded some of Sophie's meager earnings as a hair stylist. His comment thus left me wondering about the personal and social significance of this beach day moment. By way of this program, he and the other organizers were able to momentarily transcend their everyday lives in the socially marginalized neighborhood—the dirty, crowded, insecure Bel Air—and find another, better *bèl* air. This *bèl air* flowed across the success of his organizing activities, but it was no less enmeshed in the portrayal of fatherhood, in the fondness with which he and his partner were looking after their child. As I watched this wholesome intimacy, I was sure that this moment, if not the whole day, provided an arena for Kal to ask forgiveness for past transgressions. It enabled him to show the kind of man he might be under different circumstances. As much as "feeling" was realized in his abilities to act as a respected leader in the zone, it was also expressed by personifying the role that eludes him on most days: that of a respectable man. The fact that this public display of domesticity—of home, marriage, and children—enabled a performance of reputable manliness exemplified how both respect and respectability work on and through women as much as men, and through performed heterosexuality in the context of homosociality. Moreover, it shows how the search for respè was not only defined by deviance but also by the struggle to moralize and mobilize baz activities to meet the norms of manliness that these men imagined they would attain in the state jobs that eluded them.

Becoming a Force, Momentarily

Apre dans la tanbou lou (After the dance, the drum is heavy) is a Haitian proverb that captures how worldly pressures always return once festivity has passed. While providing an escape from daily life in the geto, feelingful programs had a way of highlighting participants' poverty and marginalization. Trips to the beach were overrun with anxieties about exercising mobility in the city. Beach days were often unsuccessful, with buses breaking down, insufficient gas money, or attacks by rival baz impeding the trip. Peacekeepers or policemen with suspicions of kidnapping, theft, or political conspiracy could also stop buses at checkpoints surrounding Bel Air and routes exiting the city. Beyond these anxieties, those who stayed home could also undermine organizers' effort to feel like big men. As we disembarked the bus that day, celebratory gunshots—courtesy of MOG—sounded in the background. Yet the owner of Boutique Mystère was not impressed. He chided sarcastically, "Today they acted like leaders." His wife and shopkeeper then joked: "What'll they do tomorrow? Nothing at all!" While offering an intense display of who ruled the zone, the beach day, like other feelingful events, was by definition an ephemeral and contested consolidation of political power and pleasure.

The emergence of the baz as a key sociopolitical player in the Haitian political landscape affirmed the importance of the scholarly trend viewing the workings of state sovereignty as similar in kind and politically connected to more localized arenas of rule and order. Yet baz leaders' attention to feeling and to its entanglement with force suggests that we rethink the way the urban vernacularization (or "street-ization") of sovereignty has been conceptualized through the power to take life. Theoretically, the entanglement of feeling and force in the construction of baz sovereignty can enable us to reformulate ideas about sovereign self- and collective fashioning beyond the actions of death, injury, or neglect. This does not mean dismissing these acts but rather understanding the sovereign gesture as a dialectical play between the necropolitical and the hedonopolitical. Feelingful activities, by virtue of being bound up with symbolic and material contestations of space and power, constituted critical expressions of pleasure as political power, expressions that were also bound up with symbolic and material relations of gender. The street party acted as a mode of sensualizing power as good, masculine feeling; the organization of neighborly sporting events served as a medium for displaying productive, redistributive activity; and the beach day provided a key script for embodying the sexual persona of powerful men. These activities revealed that pleasure was not merely a privilege of baz leadership; it was a necessary exercise in performing leadership. This was because manifesting feeling necessitated an artful ability to activate political contacts, mobilize resources, organize people, master logistics, and, not least, conjure power and stimulate others to imagine it as well. The affective intensity generated at feelingful activities could then be channeled in all sorts of productive ways: to incite pleasure, articulate manhood, promote reputations, and fortify political standing. These spectacular koudyay enabled men to emerge from the pits of misery, insecurity, and idleness, and cast themselves as "the man" who savored their power by transferring its pleasures to those of the zone they claimed to represent. Against the fragile and fraught political platform of the baz, feelingful programs provided a stage on which young men could perform, if only momentarily, the contours of sovereign power and become a force in the zone.

Before I end this discussion of feeling, I want to disclose that I took up this topic with considerable reservation. Like violence, gender and sexuality in Haiti are sensitive subjects, not least because people who look like me have often constructed Haiti and black people more generally as hypersexualized. "The sexual life of Africans," as Elizabeth McAlister (2002, 60) writes, "have been the object of fascination of foreign writers," with eroticization serving as a key medium for exotification (Blackwood and Wieringa 1999). I worry that my frank discussion of masculinity in urban Haiti risks creating a platform for outsiders to blame, demean, or shame Haitians. This is why I placed this discussion in its historical and political context. By analyzing gender in relation to evolving regimes of sovereignty within and beyond urban Haiti, I hope to have provided an explanation that usurps cultural essentialism with an understanding of how cultures of sexuality (and sexual critique) are structured by and structure power relations. This is also why I brought up, with some embarrassment, my own sexuality—to reiterate that the ethnographic gaze goes in two directions and to demonstrate that my sexuality factored into the power games shaping sociopolitical hierarchies at the baz and across the water.

In a related way, I worry that a discussion of how masculine pleasure garners respè might glorify the patriarchy or, which is the same, blame women and their entrepreneurial drives for the crisis of respect and its deleterious outcomes. As has been the case all over the world, the process by which women are staking out new influence in political economies is rife with contradictions and suffering, not least because the fundamental templates for empowerment are often still masculinist (Bourgois 1996; Butler and Scott 1992). Such tensions are evident in Haiti, but since women have long been economic players there, the country may also prove instructive of another way forward. Because there is less cultural angst about a switch from "domestic woman" to "working woman," it is easier to see how in Haiti the problems derive from the pressures that poverty, insecurity, and a retracted state have put on men and women. There is no definitive solution, but the lesson to be learned is that the particularly cruel manifestations of masculinist forms of respè—such as rape and abuse—are not inherent to Haitian culture but symptomatic of extreme social and political inequities. Behind even in the most harmful incarnations of respè often lurks an unfulfilled quest to be respectable, or to carve out a new kind of respected manhood.

Conclusion

THE SPIRAL

The spiral visualizes the movement of life in an upward motion, from the bottom to the top, the base to the superstructure. . . . The political power of the people was born in the reality of marginalization, that they have been fighting against multiple forces, seen and unseen, from all directions. Connecting one with another is a matter of living in the face of death.

—Interview with Frankétienne, 2009

Lespwa fè vlv **(Hope makes one live).**

—Haitian proverb

At the border of Bel Air, along a wide thoroughfare, where a high concrete wall cordoned off a prestigious high school from the uneasy streets of the neighborhood, stood a mural. It was a surrealist scene, depicting distorted faces encircled by red, yellow, and orange spirals. The fiery coils engulfed open mouths and burrow into skulls. The first impression was of embodied chaos, of senses arrested by the whirlwind of forces overwhelming them. In fact, residents' most common interpretation of the mural was that it represented how difficult it was to think or act when your head was spinning from poverty and hunger. "*Tèt chaje*," as people routinely said, in an effort to capture the myriad, unwieldy forces "crowding the mind." But others gathered something different. For some, these spirals appeared to expand outward rather than inward, shifting the impression that their force field was not arresting the otherworldly figures so much as the onlooker who was unaware of their surreal power. I once asked Kal what he thought was the artist's message. He responded, "You know, he's from Bel Air, so he was trying to say this is a zone *tèt anba* (upside-down), that has a lot of problems. But at the same time, it has a lot of force. It can lead the country. It's like Bel Air is the base of the country, and whoever is the base of this zone rules the country. Vive Haïti, Vive Le Bel Air!" As the end and departing point for this book, I offer this street mural as a window into the potential and challenges of imagining the world from the perspective of the baz.

The mural was painted by Frankétienne, the Bel Air native and renowned artist whose Xeroxed photo is affixed to the mural. He painted it in late 2010,

FIGURE 24.   Mural by Frankétienne, painted in 2010 in Bel Air.

nearly a year after the earthquake, as a message of inspiration for his beloved natal quarter.[1] The mural exemplified the Haitian Surrealist art movement called *Spiralism*, which he helped found. Emerging in the 1950s under dictatorial repression, Spiralism took the spiral as its key symbol, using its dynamic, fluid, and open-ended properties to critique dominant ways of ordering the world. In some ways, the spiral represented a universal image of life. "The spiral," as Frankétienne (1992, 389–90) wrote, "defines the perpetual movement of life and of all evolving things; it is the characteristic of the dialectic." Yet the spiral is also an image with particular resonance in Caribbean natural, political, and spiritual worlds: in the "bands of the hurricane winds that regularly ravage the country," "in the structure of conch shell, an object that functions symbolically to recall the rallying cries of Haiti's revolutionaries," and "in the form that decorates the entire length of the *poteau-mitan*," the central pillar of Vodou temples (Glover 2010, viii). It is no surprise, then, that Haitian and Caribbean thinkers more broadly have been drawn to models, such as chaos theory, that theorize history, politics, and society through spiralistic movements, relations, and tensions, through that which "repeats, reproduces, grows, decays, unfolds, flows, spins, vibrates, seethes" (Benìtez-Rojo 1997, 2–3).[2] In spiralistic models Caribbean thinkers have found a way to recognize and appreciate the force of the small man and tiny island: "The emphasis on each and every infinitesimal movement as having potential import . . . is precisely what requires a careful look at 'diminutive poles' and not only dominant narratives" (Murray-Román 2015, 26). As I contemplated the mural on my daily walks in Bel Air, I began to see in the spiral a paradigm of power that could serve as a heuristic for thinking through the baz project, of pointing out its unique and novel temporal, geographic, and ideological frames, and its implications for the current political moment.

First, the spiral, with its circling back to go forward, complicates a linear theory of history and enables a reading of the past as entangled in the present, a swirling of the time of the colonial and postcolonial, dictatorial and democratic, and crisis and postcrisis (Murray-Román 2015; Thomas 2016). On one level, the baz was another instantiation of the militant popular forces, populated by marginal youth, that have long enforced Haiti's political systems (Dupuy 2007; Fatton 2007). The baz took inspiration from the revolutionary leaders who fought for popular redemption against more powerful outsiders and from peasant resistance movements who allied with powerful politicians to defend local territory. The baz also constituted itself in the stead of dictatorial power, reworking the political infrastructure and repertoires that solidified the Duvalier family dictatorship. The baz went on to found its militant footing and habitus in the long and horrific battle to overcome the repressive violence of the dictatorial legacy that lingered in the aftermath of the dictatorship. Yet if the baz pointed to the entrenchment of a historic political scenario, it also highlighted a process of evolution. In replicating the past in the present, the baz redefined the politically possible and productive. On another level, then, the baz constituted a continually evolving response to emergent structures of neoliberal democratization and development: governmental retrenchment, electoral politics, and "community-based" development, not to mention rapid urbanization. The baz mastered the art of shape-shifting, developing into new forms to meet the reigning conditions, while still retaining vestiges of previous incarnations. My history of the baz traced how they constituted multiple organizational forms, including music groups, defense brigades, and development organizations, as well as how they both alternated between and simultaneously integrated militant and civil personas, to stake their claims to local representation and respect in the contemporary era.

Second, as a balance between centripetal and centrifugal forces—of the opposing pressure to at once pull inward and push outward—the spiral inspires a reading of the baz as an inversion of traditional spatializations of sovereignty— margins mix with centers, the people with the chèf, the geto with the state, the "below" with the "above" (Ferguson and Gupta 2002). In many ways, baz leaders affirmed the newfound clout of the neighborhood broker in a context proliferated by multiple, ill-defined, competing governing agents. The baz constituted its inclusion in this novel political configuration not in lieu of but on the basis of its "base" position of its power, its ability to belong to and claim control over the geto, a space positioned both within and below the state.[3] Although this spiralistic model of power configured neither hierarchy nor centralization, it was also not centerless. It was rather polycentric. Imagine a dispersed yet nodal network that linked the street-based centers of baz formations to each other and to broader centers of power such as state agents, politicians, and NGOs. The spatial and political dispersion of those who govern prompted a dialectical play of centripetal and centrifugal forces. The baz built a street-based center that both pulled it into broader centers of power and pulled these broader centers into the center of the zone.

In this way, the spiral illuminates what set street sovereignty alongside as well as apart from other models of sovereignty. It may seem incongruous or incorrect that I have used the language of sovereignty to discuss what is, after all, a very localized endeavor. I do so to highlight how the baz was at root a project to assert control over an area as well as to show how this occurred through a historically and culturally particular repertoire of performance premised on state mimicry and self-fashioning as urban "big men." I locate the baz's sovereign project in the ways in which baz members put on display—for themselves and others—their leadership of the micro-polity of the zone. Spanning the necropolitical, biopolitical, and hedonopolitical, I have traced how they "made the state" through the embodiment of sovereign heroes from the revolutionary past, through the mounting of a popular army that protected against the incursion of a dictatorial army, through the militant machinations of the brigad vigilans that warded off neighboring criminal threats, through the management and distribution of public services, through the brokerage of community development projects, and through the hosting of collective recreation.

These performances of sovereignty surfaced in momentary displays of leadership rather than in the highly formalized disciplinary power that Michel Foucault associated with high-functioning, modern statehood. Yet this performative model of sovereignty is anything but archaic. Insofar as the telos of Foucauldian political history is in question, it is not because Haiti is behind the curve of modern forms of power, but because those modern forms of power are in retreat across the globe, as states relinquish the responsibility to provide for the public to nonstate entities, which compete for local control (see Comaroff and Comaroff 2006a). Haiti puts forth a picture of this sovereign future. In contrast to classic Hobbesian sovereignty in which a singular Leviathan (or king) stands above and incorporates the people, what has emerged is an organization of sovereignty in which multiple big men serve as nodes in a web of localized sovereignties that spiralistically link micro and macro domains of rule, without any clear ordering of ultimate power. Indeed, behind the claim of "making the state" is the assertion that the street leader is not only performing the state in the zone but also bringing the capital-s State into being by activating a network of political connections.

Such adventures in street sovereignty gave the urban baz leader newfound political clout and leverage, but they were not without consequence. The image of the spiral can also invoke the contradiction of potential and pressure that defines the eye of the whirlpool or hurricane, two prominent images that baz leaders often used to describe their place in the configuration of those who govern. When Kal spoke of both the "problems" and the "force" of Bel Air as the "base" of the state, I took him to be reflecting on the simultaneous experience of being catapulted forward and driven asunder by broader social-structural forces. Insofar as baz leaders were empowered by their role as political brokers at the base of a fragmented configuration of global and national agents of governance, they were also burdened by occupying a role in which they assumed the responsibility for governance and conflicts over it without formal status or adequate resources, rendering them vulnerable to internecine rivalries and persistent insecurity. In addition to revealing the baz as a platform of organizational innovation and productive leadership, I have also shown the inefficacious and often destructive outcomes of baz politics and its agonistic habitus. The actual, on-the-ground manifestations of state making by the baz (as with other sovereign entities) often channeled the opposite of the public servant: the aggressor or bully. The delegation of state resources or development projects to neighborhood baz formations instigated rivalries between and within groups. Such rivalries were exacerbated in a context of scarcity, in a context where what was to be distributed—weeklong jobs, one-off aid distributions, some petty cash—could neither reach everyone nor satisfy the needs of the lucky recipients. The rivalries quickly turned deadly when those responsible for implementing governance made claims to authority that were informally constituted and not collectively recognized.

Beyond such cataclysmic outcomes, baz politics regularly reinforced forms of gendered and generational disrespect and exclusion on the block.[4] The redistributive political economies of the baz often privileged those tied to the baz through membership, social networks, or cohort groups, which were composed of young men. This was as evident in the youthful male crowds of street parties as it was in the allocation of spots on sweeping teams to a rotating cast of baz members. While baz leaders were continually engaged in a quest for respè from those in power, they were also continually battling accusations that they were conduits of disrespect for those they claimed to be defending. Indeed, the basis of baz leaders' claims to authority and legitimacy on the block depended on how well they mitigated perceptions of exclusionary, unfair, or miserly behavior and demonstrated relations of mutual respect with those in their overlapping social spheres. A good deal of baz leaders' time and energy was dedicated to presenting themselves as "*youn ki bay*," one who gives to all.

This brings me to the final insight gleaned from the mural. For Kal, the spirals on the wall expressed the force of the marginalized to turn the hierarchy of things upside-down, despite their lack of resources, daily setbacks, and informal power. His and other leaders' focus on charting legitimate lives and livelihoods from marginalized sectors and via unofficial paths situates street sovereignty as a personal and social project of becoming someone of consequence. Throughout this book, I have cited a number of Haitian proverbs that capture both a profound sense of being disrespected and a profound aspiration to be respected as a human, a citizen, and a leader: *analphabèt pa bèt* (the illiterate is not a beast), *pa fòme pa vle di sòt* (the uneducated is not stupid), *travay pou ou manje ak lòt* (work for yourself, eat with others), and *nou lèd, nou la* (we're ugly, but we're here), among others. In the recitation of these proverbs, people were expressing a desire to be taken account of, to be treated as party to the collective project of making a society, to be considered as worthy as those with more wealth, better houses, or foreign passports. Such aspirations were most palpable in the organizing efforts of those that occupied the bottom rungs of Haitian society, but they are also comparable and connected to the way all Haitian leaders experience the denial of sovereign agency. Disrespect is the issue when Haitian leaders protest their relatively minor role on the post-earthquake Interim Haiti Recovery Commission, when the Haitian government is forced to accept neoliberal polices favored abroad but unpopular at home, and when the Haitian parliament is overrun in diplomatic deals between foreign contractors and the Haitian president (Kivland 2017).[5] The disrespect experienced by the baz was often viewed as the last manifestation of disrespect in a long line of slights of Haitian leaders by outsiders.

Here I am reminded of the teachings of Frantz Fanon, the Caribbean philosopher inspired by Surrealism. Fanon is perhaps best remembered for his complex view of the link between sovereignty and violence, where the latter was constitutive of the former. While Fanon exhaustively chronicled the violence at work in the colonial government's sovereignty over the colonized, he reserved "true sovereignty" for the colonized subject who took up arms against the colonists. For him, true sovereignty was palpable in the respect gained by defying the assigned colonial status and founding a new political order. "Dignity and sovereignty," he wrote, "were the exact equivalents" (Fanon 2004, 139). I ultimately read the baz as a Haitian institution that has emerged in order to refute the structural disposability and disrespect imposed on residents of a marginal urban zone of a marginal state in a global racial and economic hierarchy of nation-states. "Since 1804 to the democratic movement, we fight against the exclusive system for a state that gathers the people," was how Michel articulated what the baz meant to him. However, quite unlike the postcolonial state envisioned by Fanon, baz leaders did not seek the reclamation of dignity in the establishment of a separate or isolated polity freed from the structures of the state or the global order. In some ways, they imagined a "non-sovereign future," one premised not on a complete break from but rather a "strategic entanglement with the dominant system" (Bonilla 2015, 62; see also Jaffe 2015). Yet alongside efforts to "temporarily break, circumvent, or contest the norms of a system from which they cannot fully disentangle" (Bonilla 2015, 42), baz leaders were also focused on finding points of entry, bases for inclusion, and positions of leverage for strategic integration into the multilayered political order.

Another proverb baz leaders were fond of reciting, especially in the context of protest movements, was, "*ou siyne nòn mwen, men ou pa t siyne pye m*" (you signed my name, but not my feet). This proverb is often understood to exemplify *mawonaj*, or maroon politics, invoking "a knowing agent who goes along with the formalities of signing a contract, but who then asserts the freedom to leave when the time comes," to walk off the plantation or away from the state (Sheller 2012, 167). "Moving beyond the reach of the state is one of the few means of resistance in situations in which freedom is seemingly won, yet self-determination remains elusive; it is the art of not being governed," as Mimi Sheller writes (2012, 185–86), quoting James Scott. However, as with all proverbs, multiple interpretations prevail. A key one speaks more to the power of vindication than evasion. Indeed, when Belairians spoke of mawonaj, it was often in the context of their grievances about uncollected garbage, an unfilled pothole, or spotty electricity. They were chastising the state's mawonaj—its absence, neglect, and abdication of responsibility—not the people of the zone. Rather than flee state-making projects, they were calling on those in power to act, in some small way, as providers of governance, as makers of statehood. To locate the force of the people in the feet is, then, to invoke the counterpower of the street, the power not to run from but to show up at the gates of the National Palace. "The only time anything changes in Haiti is when the people take to the streets," as Roland once told me. In calling on state agents to install electrical meters, on NGOS to delegate community development projects, on state agents to allocate government jobs, the baz sought representation and inclusion in the state, as a micro-polity within a broader network of power holders, both national and global. And significantly, despite an emphasis on gaining a seat at the table, they were not asking to have the same seat as state or NGO agents. Their claims to baz leadership depended on a power hierarchy that positioned those with wealth, resources, and power as responsive and accountable to the demands emanating from leaders of the urban poor. This is perhaps the most important meaning behind the expression, "*Nou fè leta*": to summon a responsible state into being and action.

A final anecdote illustrates not only baz leaders' perpetual difficulties in rendering their claims to street sovereignty but also their perpetual commitment to the principle of respè as the foundation of a proper polity. Let us return to the community meeting, discussed in chapter 3, that Yves held in the wake of a street party and toy distribution hosted by a politician for whom the baz had engaged in electioneering work. Soon after the distribution, grumblings had surfaced about how it unfolded, and, in an attempt to address them, Yves called, without much warning, for people to gather in the former community school-turned-gambling hall run by Petit.

I followed him to the hall and watched as he draped a well-worn card table with a white, lace-patterned table cloth, hung a Haitian flag on the gray concrete wall, and arranged a half-circle of white plastic chairs, so "people look me in the eyes," he said. He placed a vase of plastic flowers on the table "for color and beauty." The carefully arranged décor recalled the meetings of state officials or businessmen I had seen broadcast on the nightly televised news. The air of formal respectability softened the ambiance, even as Yves, in a Lionel Messi soccer jersey stretched across his broad shoulders and large stomach, struck an imposing figure behind the table. About fifteen friends and neighbors quietly shuffled in and took their seats. "Thanks, because you came today. I have something to discuss with you. Since the days of the French colonists, people have said democracy is *liberté, égalité, fraternité*," he began the meeting. "But to me, maybe because they never lived under colonists, they forgot what is most important for democracy. . . . That is respè."

He went on to speak about the need for mutual respect between the international community and the state, the state and the people, the leader and the community. As he did, I looked around the room and noted the disapproval of women, older men, and others who occupied spaces on the periphery of baz networks, as well as those locked in competition with Yves. They seemed to express both skepticism and disagreement, knowing full well that they were not likely to benefit and might be neglected or maltreated because of his promises.

Yves climatically punctuated his opening address with an emphatic "*Dakò?*" (agree), to which everyone answered together, "*Dakò!*" However, Petit immediately stood up and shook his head. Petit had reason to dissent. He had recently missed out on the job he desired in a project managed by Yves and OJREB and sponsored by USAID, via Wyclef Jean's NGO Yéle Haiti. The project was to dig a drainage canal to channel rainwater down the dirt mountaintop, and Petit, a senior member of the group, felt he should have been awarded a job as a team leader and not one of the diggers, receiving less pay for more difficult work. The basis of his complaint was the need to open a space for such grievances to be aired.

"You speak of respè, but this whole thing lacks a little respè. It is necessary for us to say something!" Petit said. "We are not on board with how things are being managed." The comment ignited a deluge of complaints, with several people reiterating that the toy distribution had also not been properly managed, asserting that Yves had excessively profited and that he had not advocated well for the zone. "They gave little toys, but did anyone ask what the children needed? It was notebooks!" Nerlande, a young mother of a preschooler, commented. Samuel then added, "Better to give cash to buy what they need. A lot of people need uniforms!"

Rather than back away from the debate, Yves encouraged it. "What do you have to say?" he asked those who had not yet spoken. A cacophony of voices filled the tight space, with several people rising from their seats to address Yves up close. Standing his ground, Yves repeated, "I'm listening, but I'm not in agreement." He directed his stance toward Petit, who had become, in the course of the discussion, the leader of the dissenters. Petit faced him back and allowed the complaints that echoed behind him to amplify his own grievances about the drainage and distribution projects. "The thing lacks leadership," he repeated.

At points in the discussion, people seemed so agitated that I feared a brawl, but once everyone had their say, tensions settled. "Now, the thing has become democratic!" Petit asserted.

Yves, smiling widely, responded, "A lot of respè!"

With an air of humor and humility, Petit countered, "A little respè today, more tomorrow!"

Although perhaps not fully realized at the meeting (or ever), the essence of respè took shape in the minds of the participants as the feeling of speaking up and being heard, of being in charge of one's own opinions and having those opinions heard as a matter of consequence. What led Yves and Petit to remark that this was a good discussion was not that the participants reached agreement or consensus—indeed, that did not occur—but rather that he cultivated a debate where participants were treated as legitimate and substantial opponents, with ideas and opinions that rivaled his own.[6] Yves stoked the debate in the room because acknowledging others' opinions was a prerequisite for the respè he needed from residents to participate in political circles as a local leader, easing, if not resolving, the political chasm between the individual and community as well as between hierarchy and equality. By letting grievances be aired, he could mitigate conflict and soften tensions.[7] He could also create the feeling of a committed collective.[8] And by demonstrating respè for others in such forums, he could also earn respè from them, which would enable his legitimacy and influence in larger spheres of power—an exchange of respè that, when working, extended spiralistically downward and outward to connect a network of people and spheres of power.

As we walked back up the block after the meeting, Yves jokingly mimicked my worried look and remarked, "See-see, don't worry! You were scared—ha! That was a good *diskisyon*. Next time you must speak too!"

I began this book by reflecting on what it might mean to engage in *fas-a-fas* (face-to-face) ethnography, a method of ethnography grounded in a model of robust, lively, and even contentious discussion, where the anthropologist's interlocutors are positioned not as objects of study but as parties to a collective endeavor to debate what matters to us. I often fell short of this ideal, as my muteness at the meeting reminds me, but I still heed the lesson. When Yves stressed that I also must say something, he was not only expressing interest in my opinion but also letting me know that failure to participate was its own kind of privilege. I hope that in striving to write an ethnography grounded in the ethic of respectful *diskisyon*, I have offered a fuller picture of the words and ideas through which those at Haiti's urban margins shape their visions for a better society, and one that can help all those concerned with making that possible. Although these visions were replete with contradictions and far from being realized, there is something to be said for the risk it takes to put them out in the world. Through the continual effort to found a state in which they were included as consequential participants, the baz offers a poignant lesson for political thought and movements for social change: one that counters prevailing modes of thinking about the state as that which should be flouted, escaped, or dismantled. Ultimately, the baz project reminds us that when the government has largely disappeared from the political landscape and where the revolutionary project awaits its due, statehood—or more pointedly, the social contract—resurfaces as the bedrock of a good society and an aspiration for those vying for a good life within it.

Notes

PREFACE

1. To retain the many valences of the term *geto*, I use the Creole term in the book rather than the English translation *ghetto*.

2. Because of the ubiquity of its usage, the term *baz* is henceforth not italicized. This rule is also followed for other Creole terms that are used frequently.

3. In Haiti, there is a tendency for social divisions of any kind to sort along the lines of a duality or rivalry, or what I call "agonistic dualism"—a phenomenon that played out between bazes, raras and other music groups, youth organizations, neighborhoods, political parties, and individual big men, among others. In fact, it is this rivalry that gives the competition its social significance and lends its participants a degree of legitimacy as competitors.

4. Although widespread in anthropology, there is much debate about the use of pseudonyms. Nancy Scheper-Hughes, for example, has criticized the practice as futile and excessively liberating. Those familiar with the field site can easily decode the "where" and "whom" of the text. Moreover, these masks can turn anthropologists into "rogues—too free with our pens, with the government of our tongues, and with our loose translations and interpretations of village life" (2000, 128). I likewise worry that total anonymity can lead ethnographic writers to forgo the ethics they employed in the field, where their work depended on the cultivation of friendships. However, I am also acutely aware of the dangers of exposure in a country where people are routinely imprisoned or killed for their political stances. It seems to me that striking a balance between anonymity and disclosure is best worked out between researchers and researched, in dialogue with but not determined by disciplinary convention and Institutional Review Board approval processes.

5. All personal names in this book are pseudonyms, with one exception. The deceased are referred to by the names with which they were commonly known. I am aware that the need to protect our collaborators should be extended after death, especially in a context where the ancestors walk among the living. Yet in consulting with family and friends, we agreed that naming those who have passed was one way to memorialize them.

6. Clifford Geertz, to be sure, was interested in how cultural actions can be read as both primary and secondary texts by anthropologists. As he noted, culture was already an interpretation of social life: the cockfight was "a Balinese reading of Balinese daily experience, a story they tell about themselves" (1972, 26). However, for the purposes of the ethnography, "the Balinese may not know—and need not know—that the cockfight is a story they are telling about themselves" (Trouillot 2003, 131). Rather than partners in interpretation, the Balinese were positioned in the ethnography as producers of texts to be interpreted by the anthropologist.

7. Part of the reason this debate has arisen is that it has become increasingly difficult in the era of globalization to separate the world of anthropologists from those we study. This means that anthropologists must, if they are to truly decolonize the field, acknowledge shared participation in the modern world and shared interpretation of it. For models that have influenced how I understand this approach, see Beckett 2013, Bonilla 2015, Lins Ribeiro and Escobar 2006, Scheper-Hughes 1995, and Smith 2001.

8. Beyond Gayatri Spivak, many in anthropology and allied disciplines have shown how academic scholarship is part of the machinery by which non-Western understandings of the world (and, therefore, non-Western people) are subjugated. See, for example, Abu-Lughod 1991, Asad 1995, Fabian 1983, and Said 1978. My point is not to deny this process of subjugation but rather to grapple with the prior move by which structural differences affect access to academic expertise, which then perpetuates social inequality.

9. See, for example, Haraway 1988, Knorr-Cetina 1999, Latour 1999, and Mannheim 1936 (1997).

INTRODUCTION. THE BAZ

1. I have elaborated another instance of neighborly angst against Frantzy in Kivland 2012, which further discusses the contradictory outcomes of baz organizing.

2. Working with the NGO Viva Rio, Frederico Neiburg and his research team, including Pedro Braum, have written extensively about the baz as a key social form in the geto, defined as "a moral and geographic space of affects, belonging, and protection" (2017, 130). For more, see Braum 2014, Neiburg 2016, 2017; Neiburg, Nicaise, Braum 2011; and Muggah and Moestue 2009.

3. The most distinctive instrument of rara bands is the indigenous wind instrument known as banbou (sometimes called *vaksin*). Originally made of hollowed-out bamboo tubes, the instruments in urban Haiti are now fabricated from PVC piping with a mouthpiece fashioned on one end. Because banbou playing takes a great deal of strength and lung capacity, it is usually played by large, robust men; and those who play it well are seen as endowed with exemplary physical strength and stamina.

4. In 2009, I surveyed ninety-four households in Bel Air about their access to social services; sixty-three of these households also agreed to participate in a follow-up interview. When asked about their main worry or concern in the neighborhood, nearly all respondents (58/63) cited ensekirite.

5. I have developed a more detailed discussion of perceptions of statelessness and the context of governance that has given rise to them in Kivland 2012.

6. Accounts of "gangs," "mobs," "thugs," and even "monsters" appeared in mainstream and fringe news stories, with the appellations being applied to both anti- and pro-Aristide forces. See, for example, a CNN-broadcast associated press article titled "Street Gangs Hijack Food Aid in Haiti" (Associated Press 2004), a *New York Times* editorial titled "In Haiti, Mobs Are Easy Part" (Cain 2004), and an article in *The Telegraph* titled "Monsters and Cannibals at War in Haiti" (Warren 2003).

7. Haitians, as subjects of a black nation born of the enslaved at a time when slavery was still enforced in the United States, have historically occupied a place of danger and disorder in the American imaginary (see Dubois 2004; Polyné 2013; Ulysse 2015), which is little more than an intensified rendition of a common American "script" about racially marked immigrants (Molina 2014).

8. See *Daily Mail* Reporter 2010; Delva 2010; and Padgett 2010.

9. Although I avoid the term *gang*, I hope that readers will use the baz as an opportunity to rethink and critique the gang label in the United States and other places. The political entanglements of the baz can shed light on the ways in which gangs elsewhere are political entities. While it has become commonplace to view US and transnational gangs as purely criminal organizations, many were founded and continue to operate as local governance organizations that defend the neighborhood against criminality in ways similar to the baz, as John Hagedorn (1988, 2009), among others (Davis 1990; Venkatesh and Levitt 2000; Wacquant 2002), has argued. On this note, I have long been struck by how organizations of white, middle-class youth are deemed "cliques," whereas those among youth of color are called "gangs." These labels ostensibly distinguish between whether the

group is criminal or not, violent or not, but they are also profoundly racialized categories. The gang label, in Haiti and elsewhere, often functions first as a marker of race/class and second and derivatively as an evaluation of criminality. It goes without saying that this racial, criminal stigma has far-reaching repercussions for those that bear it.

10. The term *culture of poverty* became popular in the 1960s mainly through the ethnographies of Oscar Lewis, who detailed the life histories of the slum dwellers in the urban United States, Puerto Rico, and Mexico. The concept, which attributed poverty to presumed cultural deficiencies, circulated widely as a theory of reproduction that also explained other social problems among the poor, such as violence and drug addiction. Reduced of ethnographic complexity, such culture-of concepts circulated widely in media and popular accounts and came to influence the development of US antipoverty social policies targeting people of color in the United States and beyond, such as those set forth by Daniel Patrick Moynihan's report on the "Negro family" (1965). Rather than economic redistribution or social-structural change, the resultant programs, as Bourgois (2001) chronicled, mainly focused on addressing the culture of poor children and individuals through educational and self-help programs (e.g., Head Start and job training).

11. While certainly mired in racist presumptions of Western cultural superiority, it is important to acknowledge that some Haitians also share Brooks's viewpoint. For example, in the 1930s, François Duvalier and his fellow intellectuals of the Griot cultural movement stridently maintained that it was a particular Haitian *mentalité* that both explained and held the key to resolving Haiti's social problems—an assertion still common among politicians and laymen alike. See Nicholls 1996; and Trouillot 1990b for supplementary discussion.

12. Following Luke Lassiter (2009) and others (e.g., McGee and Warms 2004), I hold holism to be a key organizing principle for anthropology. The holistic methodology privileges explanations of human behavior that account for the fullest range of social influences, including historical, cultural, biological, and psychological factors, among others.

13. Here I am inspired by Lucas Bessire's adaptation of Didier Fassin's (2011) concept of "biolegitimacy" to cultural politics. For Bessire, "the sociolegal figure of culture operates as a regime of [biolegitimacy]," or "the specific kinds of late liberal governance instantiated through policing the constricting limits of who should live and in the name of what" (2014, 21). However, unlike in Bessire's case, where an indigenous population's merit derives from their possession of a purported worthy culture, the Haitian case shows how a society can just as easily be devalued on the basis of a presumably unworthy culture.

14. In tracing this history, it is important to remember that the Haitian nation established itself in a time of slavery and a global context hostile to its existence, making it necessary to maintain a strong military. Out of this grew a symbolic attachment of the soldier to the nation. Because the valiant force of its soldiers "elevated the black man out of the depths of slavery into his rightful place as father, leader, and protector of his own people" (Sheller 2012, 148), the soldier held a central place in society. Soldiering not only afforded men their freedom, it also determined their pathways to citizenship and political participation (Laguerre 1993). After independence, the heads of the revolutionary army seized the plantations and apportioned property based on military rank, with generals acquiring large plantations.

15. In Haiti's early years, the landholding military generals competed for control of the Haitian state, as did others brave enough to mount an army. Throughout the nineteenth century, the *gran nèg* (big men) of regions or districts—often appointed *chefs de section*, or section chiefs, by regional army generals (Comhaire 1955)—organized peasant armies that effectively controlled local territory and were regularly mobilized by politicians to overthrow state power (Trouillot 1990a). Until the consolidation of the army during the US occupation (1915–1934) and the militarization of the state during the

Duvalier dictatorship (1957–1986), these localized armies provided key checks on power and alternative sources of political leadership and community.

16. I am indebted to David Scott's (1997) writing on the role of historical explanation in what he calls the "culture of violence fallacy" in Jamaica. See also Thomas 2011.

17. Interestingly, Haitian exceptionalism can be mobilized to define Haiti's virtue as much as its vice, with the two often inextricably intertwined. The literary critic J. Michael Dash, writing of the revolution's legacy, has argued that Haiti serves as a kind of "chimera" in the Caribbean imagination. Rather than symbolizing radical universalism, which the revolutionaries sought to represent, "the island disappears under images of racial revenge, mysterious singularity, and heroic uniqueness" (2004, 3). The chimera of the slave revolution, and the tropes of unimaginable success and subsequent failure that accompany it, remain central to contemporary discourses about Haiti, to its dueling identity as both the first black republic and the poorest country in the Western Hemisphere. See Bonilla 2013; and Ulysse 2015 for more discussion.

18. Of interest here are those studies that have sought to understand urban gangs in Haiti and in particular the chimè as an example of the Haitian state's long-standing use of paramilitaries and other informal armed actors. Notable examples include Dupuy 2007; Dziedzic and Perito 2008; and Fatton 2002, 2007.

19. In line with Mikhail Bakhtin (1981), I describe the street as a chronotope because it marks a particular space-time that frames the interpretation of its meaning and valence. Twentieth-century urban studies have regularly drawn on "the street" to conjure the presence of poor, marginal, disobedient youth as located in a distinct and separate context from a purported mainstream society. A few notable examples include Anderson 1999; Bourgois 1995; and Whyte (1943) 1981.

20. The scholarly literature on Westphalian sovereignty is too vast to cite here. A selection of works that have informed my thinking include: Crawford 2006 and Philpott 1997 for understanding the role of the Westphalian model as a fixture of international law; and Agnew 2008; Biersteker and Weber 1996; and Krasner 1999 for grasping how state sovereignty and the Westphalian model act as an unsustainable ideal.

21. C. Wright Mills (1956 [1999], 6) specifically applied his concept of the "power elite" to American society, but it is useful to describe the way "the state" names and defines a certain consolidation of power in Haiti among political *and* economic actors.

22. Early political anthropologists focused their analyses on indigenous societies that organized power around chiefs, tribal councils, or other "big men."

23. See Arias and Goldstein 2010 for a fuller discussion of the rise of these monikers.

24. Bare or naked life is the translation of *bios*, the most basic form of life, as theorized by Giorgio Agamben (1998, 2000). Distinguishing between *bios* (the way in which life is lived) and *zoe* (the biological fact of life), Agamben argues that modern political orders are mainly concerned with bare life rather than with the quality of the life lived. Several scholars have argued that the production of bare life among the poor is particularly salient in contexts of neoliberal systems of governance, humanitarianism, and development. See, for example, Biehl 2005; Biehl and Locke 2010; Redfield 2013; and Sylvester 2006.

25. For more examples that have informed my thinking, see Arias and Goldstein 2010; Comaroff and Comaroff 2016; Humphrey 2008; Misse 2018; Richani 2007; and Rodgers 2006.

26. I draw my analysis of the *marenn* from Sidney Mintz and Eric Wolf's (1950) seminal treatment of godparenthood in its European beginnings and Latin American application. They note how in communities defined by high inequality, choice of godparents will proceed "vertically," aiming for a higher status or wealthier benefactor.

27. "How did I manage to study men *as a woman*?" is a question readers often pose about my research. Such queries strike me as problematic on several fronts: reflecting the naturalization of sex/gender difference, the assumption of natural affinity among

sex/gender groups, and the long-standing pattern of ethnographers and subjects sharing the same gender. Though in highly sex-segregated societies cross-gender ethnography may prove impossible, the assumption that this is the case everywhere strikes me as rooted as much in the heteronormative cultural mores of the societies from which anthropologists hail as in those anthropologists study.

CHAPTER 1. DEFENSE

1. Lisa Malkki has argued that this anthropological tradition of mapping the field-site has erroneously reinforced the idea of a "naturalized identity between people and place" and promoted a fixed "national geographic" ordering of the world (1992, 28, 26). A great deal of recent scholarship has furthered this critique. See Appadurai 1988; Clifford 1988; Malkki 1992; Ong 1999; and Rosaldo 1989. The counter-map I offer here follows recent efforts to capture geographies of the imagination (see Chu 2010).

2. For more on Baghdad, see chapter 4.

3. This joke turned out to be prescient. A couple of days after the 2010 earthquake, I made my way to the US Embassy in Port-au-Prince, where I awaited a spot on a Coast Guard plane evacuating US citizens from the country. I passed the time watching CNN and had the surreal experience of my photograph appearing on the television screen. As I watched my parents talking about their missing daughter in Haiti, I could not help but wonder how I, among the forty-five thousand Americans in Haiti after the earthquake, was chosen for a feature profile. Although there were probably many reasons, I am certain one had to do with the way I as a white, blond female resonated with the stereotypical portrait of an American victim in ways that the black bodies of Haitian Americans (who accounted for the vast majority of Americans in Haiti) did not.

4. The two brushes with violence I have endured in Haiti—a mugging and what I presumed was an attempted kidnapping—happened far from Bel Air, in the wealthier, uptown district of Pétion-Ville. The mugging occurred in the back of a tap-tap bus on its ascent to Pétion-Ville via Route Frère, and the possible kidnapping occurred while leaving an up-scale restaurant in Pétion-Ville. I was walking with my white, female friend, who was visiting from the United States, to hail a motorbike when a white van stopped and a light-skinned man offered us a ride to our destination. When we politely but insistently declined, the van door swung open and revealed an armed man. We quickly ran away before I could discern whether it was a kidnapping or an offer of assistance from a member of Haiti's elite, who often carry weapons in their vehicles.

5. It is important to understand Haiti's current insecurity within a broader regional pattern that reflects urbanization and, in particular, ghettoization. Haiti has a homicide rate below regional averages: 10.2 per 100,000 people, about half the rate in the Dominican Republic (22.1 per 100,000 in 2012) and a quarter that in Jamaica (39.3 per 100,000 in 2012), which had, in 2012, the highest rate in the Caribbean (UNODC [United Nations Office on Drugs and Crime] 2013). However, this must be seen in the context of Haiti's lower rate of urbanization. When viewed at the urban scale, Haiti fits within regional norms. On average, nearly 80 percent of Haiti's murders take place in Port-au-Prince, giving the city a murder rate in 2011 of 40 per 100,000—a rate midway between Santo Domingo (29 per 100,000 in 2012) and Kingston (50 per 100,000 in 2012) (UNODC [United Nations Office on Drugs and Crime] 2013). The picture is even grimmer for those living in the so-called geto. UN officials have estimated that 90 percent of Port-au-Prince's murders occur within or in areas surrounding the three densest and poorest districts: Martissant, Cité Soleil, and Bel Air (Dade 2007). Moreover, the figures for these areas are likely to be underestimated—only about 4.3 percent of violent crimes in greater Bel Air were reported to the police or peacekeepers in 2007, for example (Fernandez and Nascimento 2007b).

6. The international discourse around gang violence has much to do with an entrenched understanding of criminal activity in the region as an outgrowth of the transnational drug trade. As noted in the introduction, this bias can obscure the phenomenon of the baz. Haiti is a trans-shipment point for cocaine and other drugs, but this market, since its inception in the 1970s, has been mainly controlled by political and economic elites (Dziedzic and Perito 2008; Kemp, Shaw, and Boutellis 2013). Some armed baz in the city have established links with elite drug traffickers, but most baz formations' involvement in the drug trade is confined to overseeing small-scale, local markets. The main income-generating activity of baz in urban geto remains political brokerage and racketeering, but some baz—what residents distinguish as the actual *gang yo* (gangs)—are involved in thievery as well as kidnapping rings, the latter often linked to rival groups of elites.

7. In teasing out the meanings of *ensekirite*, I seek to unpack the term not merely in its sociocultural particularity but also its analytical applicability—after all, insecurity, as anthropologists have shown (Arias and Goldstein 2010; Auyero, Bourgois, and Scheper-Hughes 2015; Thomas and Lewis 2011), is a popular idiom not just in Haiti but throughout Latin America and the Caribbean.

8. Though a pseudonym, Kal retains the signification of the person's actual nickname, as do other nicknames used in the text.

9. People often use the labels *Ginen* and *Maji* to distinguish between two opposing forces in Vodou ritual: the former referring to spirits and rites brought by the ancestors from Africa ("Guinea") and the latter as sorcery and the class of rites classified as *Petwo*. Where *Ginen* represents tradition, community, and legitimate authority, *Maji* represents pursuit, foreignness, and corrupt power. However, Karen Richman (2005, 151–52), among others (Brown 1991; Deren 1953; Larose 1977), has shown that in actual practice this dichotomy plays out not as two distinct pantheons but as "complementary ideologies": "they exist only in relation or in opposition to each other." In everyday language, the labels provide a vocabulary for assessing moral persons and action. "*M se moun Ginen*" (I am a person of Guinea), for example, is used to assert adherence to proper social ethics and to dispel accusations of the opposite.

10. Examples of foundational works that have developed the concept of structural violence and influenced my thinking include Bourgois 2009; Bourgois and Scheper-Hughes 2002; Farmer 1996, 2004; and Scheper-Hughes 1992.

11. The tendency to construct a direct relationship between structural conditions and violence has much to do with how structural violence theory can appear as an omnipotent machine of oppression that predetermines, or overdetermines, individual agency and action (Parsons 2007; Ralph 2014). My resolution of this problem is threefold. First, by unpacking misery as an economic, social, and psychological condition, I follow James's (2010, 52) call to explain violence by analyzing "structural conditions" alongside personal factors of "identity, fantasy, desire, and reputation" (see also Biehl and Locke 2010). Second, I employ, following Bourgois (1995, 2002), a dynamic approach that accounts for how people contest social milieus of misery and insecurity in ways that both challenge and reproduce the forces that act on them. Third, and moving beyond others, I follow the ways in which people maneuver within the structural field in ways that are unpredictable, innovative, and original and can influence the workings of the field.

12. The existence of agonism in Haitian political and social life is a matter of deep concern and debate in Haiti and among those who study or work in Haiti. Citizens, academics, aid workers, politicians, and policy writers routinely blame Haiti's social ills on this deeply rooted habitus—citing proverbs such as *de kòk kalite pa ret nan menm baskou* (two fighting cocks cannot stay in the same yard) and *crab nan panye* (crabs in a basket) that attest to social division. Indeed, some academics have gone so far as to argue that

the popular rhetoric around unity, equality, and mutual aid—*youn ede lòt* (one helps the other), *men anpil, chay pa lou* (many hands make the load light), *yon sèl dwèt pa manje kalalou* (one finger does not eat okra)—is only a mask for this more sinister cultural substrate, and that this substrate must change before Haiti can achieve economic development (see Smucker 1983). In pointing out the agonism of baz politics, I do not mean to situate the baz as an example of some ingrained or permanent cultural flaw. Rather, my aim is to recognize agonism as a product of social and political marginalization and as a force with which baz leaders must continually contend in their organizational and activist activities. The values of equality and division can then be seen as mutually constituted, as the products of a history characterized by staunch inequalities and a legacy of contesting them. For more discussion on this topic, see Averill 1997; and Smith 2001.

13. In framing misery as structured and structuring, I revisit the question of whether, and to what extent, Pierre Bourdieu's social theory allows for social change. Many have read the concept of habitus as inert and deterministic, but in fact, he balances social reproduction and social change. He writes, "because the habitus is an endless capacity to engender products—thoughts, perceptions, expressions, actions—whose limits are set by the historically and socially situated conditions of its production, the conditioned and conditional freedom it secures is as remote from a creation of unpredictable novelty as it is from a simple mechanical reproduction of the initial conditionings" (Bourdieu 1977, 95). To speak of misery as generative of an agonistic habitus is neither to deny that people facing oppression are capable of envisioning or organizing for social transformation, nor to romantically endow them with the capacity to shift the structures that have limited her agency. Instead, it is to understand that their maneuverings are both motivated and limited by the social and historical conditions of their enactment. I understand Paul Farmer's reference to "structured and stricturing" as a way of articulating this dual structuration and conceptualizing it as conditioned by one's sociopolitical location in society. But readers of Farmer will note that I have avoided using the language of "victims," which suggests a degree of helplessness and impotency I am unwilling to grant my socially marginalized but engaged informants.

14. In a similar vein, Philip Bourgois and Nancy Scheper-Hughes (2002, 1) have argued for understanding violence along a continuum that recognizes the ways in which "like produces like" and "violence gives birth to itself" yet also refutes a fixed causal chain or cycle.

15. In the conclusion, I go into detail about the Haitian literary and art movement called Spiralism and how it can inform the study of politics in Haiti generally and for the baz in particular.

16. Trouillot has pointed out that since, in the Haitian language, the word *leta* can mean "state" or "bully," references to those who "make state" (*fè leta*) suggest that these actors are seen "as a site of power equal to and capable of challenging the state, but also as potential bullies" (2001, 132n22). This is certainly the case, but I also observed people use the expression *fè leta* to call to mind a very different idea of state power—as a site of advocacy. Indeed, the fact that fè leta could signify both a bully and a godparent spoke to the way Haitians recognized how the state was constituted by its embodiment of both forms of power.

17. I have much more to say in subsequent chapters about the gendered exclusions and masculine mediations resonant in the baz (see especially chapter 6).

18. This notion has relevance for the literature on urban black communities in the United States. To counter culture-of-poverty theory, William Julius Wilson argued to great effect that the problems of these communities had to do with the way residents have become "increasingly socially isolated from mainstream patterns of behavior" (1987, 58). This notion of isolation, especially as utilized by scholars less attentive than Wilson to

structural factors, has been critiqued by theorists of North American gang violence and urban poverty attentive to the "mutually reinforced tensions between local communities and their broader social and historical contexts" (Ralph 2014, 14). Such tensions include the way in which people shut out of mainstream society respond with violent practices of opposition that further their suffering and marginalization (Bourgois 1995); how street gangs respond to the collapse of the manufacturing economy and rise of unemployment by creating jobs through the drug trade (Venkatesh 2000); and how when the drug trade collapses, people can redeploy the structure of the gang and gang competition to rob each other of their meager profits (Contreas 2012).

CHAPTER 2. HISTORY

1. In Creole, the lyrics are *Tout moun se mmm./Se mmm.*

2. In Creole, the lyrics are *La famille Schiller./Si nou la, Schiller pral mouri./Se nan plan li ye./Demen a 4h, mache a patriyòt./Al devan Saint Jean Bosco, w ap jwen Schiller.*

3. See also Mbembe 2001 on the "entanglement" of past and present in the postcolony.

4. I thank Deborah Thomas for directing my attention to Diana Taylor's conceptions of repertoire and scenario for understanding the history of political violence in Haiti and the Caribbean. Like Thomas in *Exceptional Violence* (2011, 90), I want to think through the repertoires of political violence as "techniques of performance that have developed over time and that are made available through a variety of public forums for improvisatory citation or reprisal."

5. Members of Baz Zap Zap often sang, in daily life and regular outings, rara songs from the mid-1990s that referenced the US occupation. A most popular one went: *Peyizan Peyizan m yo, se pa konsa peyi nou te ye./M sonje lontan lè peyi m te bèl nou te rele l Perles des Antilles./Nou pa gen dwa janm bliye jou sa./1915 blan te anvayi n./Se koreksyon ak divizyon yo simen nan peyi nou.* (My countrymen, this is not how our country was./I remember long ago when my country was beautiful./They called it Pearl of the Antilles./We don't have a right to forget that day./1915 blan invaded us./It's punishment and division that they sowed in our country.) Attesting to its forceful message, singers often assured me mid-stanza that despite my US citizenship, "they did not have a problem with me."

6. This is my own translation of the lyrics cited in Laguerre 1976a, 35: *Dépi sé Fignolé mété li sou coeur moin. Apa li papa.*

7. For more on Daniel Fignolé's downfall and François Duvalier's rise to power, see Bellegarde-Smith 2004; Diederich and Burt 1970; and Smith 2009.

8. Covering the elections, the *Nation* reported that "the latest estimate of dead reaches 476. The actual estimate cannot be known because all but the few bodies taken to the morgue were loaded into lorries and buried in the plain. . . . Many demonstrators and people dragged at random from their homes were dumped without food or shelter on La Gonâve" (Smith 2009, 182).

9. It is difficult to know the full scale of violence carried out by François Duvalier, but for a partial accounting, see Moïse 1988; and Pierre-Charles 1973, 2000.

10. Roots of the baz can be found in the rural form of communal living known as the lakou. The lakou was founded by the first generations of Haitians who set up their households mainly in the countryside (Bastien 1985; Woodson 1990). The lakou echoes the baz in that it was a mechanism for the "auto-regulation" of social and political life, with the head of the lakou overseeing inheritance, ritual activity, and family relationships (Barthélémy 1990, 30). The lakou system protected the family's claim to the land, especially against encroaching state leaders and landholders who desired to reinstate the

plantation system. In addition, many lakou, often in concert with others, organized mili-
tias to defend against local disputes and national repression or to join larger armies com-
missioned to overthrow those in power at the regional or national level. Some have argued
this tradition of regionalism is what "acted as a brake on the development of political
centralization" until Duvalier (Dubois 2013; Trouillot 1990, 97). In some ways, then, the
baz is a return to this earlier mode of dispersed localities of sovereignty.

11. Laguerre 1983, citing Pierre-Charles 1973, notes that some of the Bel Air makout
participated in attacks against rebels in August 1963.

12. These wages reflected an equivalency between the US dollar and Haitian dollar.
The Haitian dollar, or five goud, was calibrated to the US dollar in 1912. This lasted until
1989, when the currency was floated as a part of the structural adjustments implemented
by the international community. For more, see Neiburg 2016.

13. There is a tendency, especially among foreign observers, to explain the Duvalier
dictatorship's rise and longevity through excessive brutality rather than its elaborate system
of patronage. There is no doubt that the regime was brutal, but such lopsided portray-
als reflect a pattern of portraying Haiti as a demonic, pathological country incapable of
democracy. As Trouillot writes (1990a, 192), "Foreign journalists and scholars in search
of exotic buffoons have enjoyed painting François Duvalier as an incoherent madman, a
black Ubu, a tropical Caligula who would spout any amount of nonsense at any time" (see
also Dubois 2004; and Nicholls 1996). This perspective misses how the regime established
the consent of the population, which was a necessary part of its claim to power for so long.

14. Although this book takes urban organizations as its focus, it is important to note
that during the postdictatorial period a swell of organizing took place in the countryside as
well. These groups, generally known as *gwoupman peyizan* (peasant groups), have roots in
older forms of agricultural and religious collectives but developed in relation to democratization and development programs. Like the *komite katye*, they were "central to the widespread consciousness-raising and persistent mobilization that led to the 1986 overthrow of
the Duvalier regime" (Maguire 1990; Smith 2001, 142). What sets the baz apart from these
groups is their emplacement in the geto, the attachments it has shared with Aristide's movement, and the particular history of their militantization, as developed in this chapter.

15. In the 1970s, the Peruvian priest Gustavo Gutiérrez (1973) defined liberation theology in his book *A Theology of Liberation: History, Politics, and Salvation*, and its teachings quickly captivated the poor throughout Latin America and the Caribbean. For more
on its adoption in Haiti, see Dupuy 2007, Farmer 2014, and Gogol 2015.

16. Classic liberation theology infuses Marxist political theory with Christian theology, positioning the working class as the agents of the emancipatory struggle for a com-
munist society. However, Aristide followed a current of liberation theology in which the
dehumanizing experience of poverty and suffering rather than the capitalist class position
of the proletariat defined the class to be emancipated (see Dupuy 2007).

17. The portrait of diverse members of the Haitian polity eating around a table was a
key image on Lavalas party posters.

18. A group known as Solidarite Ant Jèn still exists in Bel Air.

19. Fanmi Selavi also means the Selavi Family. The center was also named after a
child's nickname, which was Selavi (That's Life).

20. Amy Wilentz, who chronicled Aristide during this time, noted how the youth
came seeking meals, conversation, friendships, and small change but also the thrills of
being a part of the democratic movement. "Aristide did not hesitate to emphasize the
political underpinnings of Lafanmi Selavi," Wilentz reported (1989, 214). He pointed
out that the condition of these children was the result of "a society in which the rich were
utterly rich and the poor impossibly poor," and he championed the youth center as one

of the few programs in Haiti that "raised the consciousness of those it intended to help, rather than just feed them" (Wilentz 1989, 214).

21. In Haiti, as in many other places, men are expected to demonstrate an ability to provide for a family prior to marriage. Given today's rates of male unemployment, this is rarely the case—a predicament that leads many aging young men to proclaim that they are stuck in their youth. Securing a job and a place to live is usually the first step in entering a more serious relationship with a woman, in either formal or *plasaj* (common law) marriages. See, for more discussion, Maternowska 2006.

22. Rumors of Madame Max Adolphe's escape abound. The journalist Mark Danner (1989) reported accounts that she left the country disguised as a nun or hidden in a mango crate for an exile on Long Island.

23. When recounting this story, several people highlighted how this makout "used to be abusive" (*konn fè abi*), in contrast with Ti Bout, who was not.

24. Aristide captured 67 percent of the vote, with 51 percent of eligible voters casting ballots—a turnout and victory margin that have yet to be repeated. For more on the popular groundswell that catapulted Aristide to the presidency, see Wilentz 1989 and Dupuy 2007.

25. See Farmer 2003 for more discussion of the 1991 inauguration.

26. The lyrics in Creole are *Pèp la enosan, Abraham!/Rele san manman yo, vin pale yo!/ Nou p ap pran yon lòt kou deta.*

27. In the sixteen months after the coup, nearly forty thousand people seeking refuge from repression and hunger took to the high seas, beginning the crisis that would lead to Haitian migrants becoming the first people detained at Guantánamo Bay (French 1993; Kahn 2013; 2018).

28. Before an expanded UN arms and oil embargo went in effect in 1993, the United States turned a blind eye to oil sales that fueled the light assembly industry and allowed subcontracted companies to export apparel and other goods, therefore shielding elite business investments and protecting elite wealth from the worst of the embargo.

29. The term *zenglendo* is often understood as a riff on an ancient paramilitary: in the nineteenth century the second and last self-styled emperor of Haiti, Emperor Faustin I Soulouque, organized his poor, black, youthful followers into armed bands called *zenglens*, who defended his rule against an opposition of army officers from the elite *milat* (mulatto, or mixed race) social class (Nicholls 2013).

30. People first employed the label *zenglendo* in the aftermath of the dictatorship as a way of condemning excessive or illegitimate offenses by the army. But during the de facto it came to signify a new deviant type operating under cover of the army. At face value, the term condemned the nonstate criminals, the bandits and thieves, who emerged when the dictatorship lost the monopoly on violence and flourished in the absence of a functioning government. Most zenglendo, however, were former soldiers or makout who used their guns, networks, and training to engage in crime for personal gain. Some were working for the army as its *attachés*—proxy gunmen "attached to" the army—who killed, stole, and intimidated on its behalf. These associations were formalized in September 1993, when the regime integrated zenglendo and attachés into a formal paramilitary: Front for the Advancement and Progress of Haiti, or FRAPH, a play on the Haitian word *frap*, meaning "to hit." In an example of reprisals from those targeted by the dechoukaj, the FRAPH paramilitary was founded by Louis Jodel Chamblain, an army officer who engaged in the preinaugural coup against Aristide and lost his pregnant wife in counterattacks, and by Emmanuel "Toto" Constant, the son of a general who served as François Duvalier's chief of staff. For more, see Halward 2007; Deibert 2005.

31. In Creole, the lyrics are *M ap rele yo, LONU./Kapitèn Chèlton minote yo./Nou pa pè gwo zam lame a./N ap toujou minote yo./Ale devan bay sove./Lom a grenad yo panike./Sa k pa lavalas ap panike./M ap rele yo, Titi./Minote yo, Signor.*

32. The rara groups in the greater Bel Air area that emerged during this period as affiliates of the Resistance Platform included Zap Zap, Avili, Anvayi, Laflè Ginen, Chaba, and Rara M, many of which still exist. For more on rara as a religious, cultural, and sociopolitical performance practice, see McAlister 2002 and Bien-Aimé 2008.

33. The rara groups of the resistance platform circulated the same basic songs, but each group was known to create modifications in the lyrics or melodies that made them its own, as is characteristic of rara groups (McAlister 2002). The songs included here are versions I recorded with Zap Zap.

34. As Karen Richman has documented, choral singing is a privileged medium for delivering coded political critiques, since "under the transparent veil of nondirected, public discourse, singing serves as a vehicle for persuasive maneuverings and verbal aggression" (2005, 17).

35. In Creole, the lyrics are *Tout moun se mmm./ Nou pa ka pale./Lame vle touye nou./ Korridò korridò korridò.*

CHAPTER 3. RESPECT

1. For more discussion on categorizations of democracies as "failed" as a result of rising levels of social and political violence, see Arias and Goldstein 2010; Caldeira and Holston 1999; Glendhill 2000; Goldstein 2012; Koonings and Krujit 2013; and O'Donnell et al. 2004.

2. In 2012 Haiti registered a GINI index of 60.8, which was the highest in the world (United States Central Intelligence Agency 2013).

3. See Michel 1992 for the full text of the 1987 constitution.

4. The state paper, titled Strategy of Social and Economic Reconstruction, was what Aritside agreed to issue as a condition of his reinstallment as President of Haiti in an international military intervention led by the United States. The paper expresses his commitment to impose neoliberal reforms, which went against the consensus among his supporters. See Dupuy 2007; and Fatton 2002.

5. I recorded this chant among the repertoire of street slogans remembered by Fritz. It is also cited by Aristide in his autobiography (Aristide and Wargny 1993).

6. With the phrase "trickle down," I invoke US President Ronald Reagan's iconic phrase and his administration's role in popularizing the neoliberal agenda as a long-term solution to equality. As Jane Guyer (2007, 414) has written, the politics of neoliberalism relies on an orientation to time that "concentrates on choice, in the very short run, and the anchoring notions of the distant future." The adherents of this ideology invoke a preternatural faith in individuals' pursuit of profit in the market to reach the poor in the distant future.

7. See the introduction for more on the tendency to posit popular politics against the state in anthropological scholarship.

8. My focus here differs from symbolic anthropology, which has analyzed honorifics in ritual and other sacred venues as markers of social hierarchy. Nevertheless, my thinking is influenced by interpretive approaches that have grappled with how the value of respect plays out in rituals of everyday life, especially when an effort is made to balance hierarchy and equality. See, for example, Geertz 1961; and Goffman 1967. I am also inspired by work that has shown how ideas of democratic, egalitarian models of respect run up against religious forms of respect, where the value is "conjoined to the valorization of hierarchy and elders" (Hartikainen 2017, 88). However, in my context, I see the tension between hierarchy and equality play out not across religious and political milieus but within the latter as it pertains to various ideas of democratization.

9. Importantly, since the inception of human rights discourse, there has existed a tension between civil rights and socioeconomic rights. Leaders in the United States,

beginning with Ronald Reagan, have consistently claimed that social and economic rights are inconsistent with liberal theory and values and thus cannot be endorsed as foreign policy. These rights, in contrast to civil rights, tend to necessitate a large and powerful state apparatus that intervenes in society to inhibit individual choice and liberty, especially among the elite class. See, for a fuller discussion, Farer 1989; and Allen 2013.

10. The significance placed on holding a community meeting was, in many ways, why Yves denounced elections in the context of a discussion about respect and democracy. While residents' voices could certainly be expressed via the ballot, there was no guarantee they were heard, let alone heeded. An abundance of candidates often impeded face-offs between opposing options, and fraud was a major concern, with meddling from competing parties and international delegates commonplace. Moreover, voting lacked the kind of face-to-face exchange that demonstrated ownership of one's viewpoint and investment in the consequence of what others have to say. Jean Comaroff and John Comaroff raise a similar point, recalling how, in a seminar at the University of Chicago, Wayne Booth "observed that freedom of speech is guaranteed in America only to the extent that no one is listening; that while everybody has a right to talk, nobody has an obligation to pay attention; that democracy disempowers by encouraging the kind of cacophony in which voices cancel each other out" (Comaroff and Comaroff 1997, 126).

11. It is significant that conversations about respect and dignity so often pivot on distinctions between humans and animals. Greg Beckett (2017) has shown how people in urban Haiti use the idea of being treated like a dog to express and critique the disrespect they experience in aid economies, where they are relegated to a position of dependency. I also witnessed how the figure of the dog, as well as animals more generally, were called upon to articulate the experience of being "pushed beyond the limits of the human, to be radically excluded, to be stripped bare of all that makes you a person" (Beckett 2017, 42)

12. There is an important gendered dimension to Peter Wilson's framework of respect and reputation, which is further discussed in chapter 6.

13. Foreigners often wonder why people in Haiti often go back to 1804 when explaining what ails them today. I have witnessed many diplomats, aid workers, and missionaries roll their eyes as Haitian interlocutors respond to a query about the country's poverty, instability, or underdevelopment with, "Well, it began in 1804." In this gesture is the belief that, as Laurent DuBois put it, "The Haiti of today cannot be understood without knowledge of its complex and often tragic history" (2013, 13).

14. The phrase *mò pale* (talking dead) is a common sentiment expressed at funerals of victims of political violence in the city. It is often offered as a condolence, affirming the common mortality faced by all who partake in political actions that have as a consequence the enmity of those in power and their allies on the street.

15. Jeremy Popkin (2007) includes an account by Peter S. Chazotte, one of the few French whites who survived the massacre. Writing about it from exile in the United States, his account attests to how Dessalines's brutal reputation dominated the minds of white planters and forced their exodus.

16. The saying "crab antics" was a local term in Providencia, where Peter Wilson (1973) did his fieldwork. The related saying, "crabs in a barrel," is a popular proverb throughout the English-speaking Caribbean. In Haiti, the same idea is rendered as "crabs in a basket" (*krab nan panyen*) or, reflecting today's usages of plastic buckets, "crabs in a bucket" (*krab nan bokit*).

17. The policy of militarized agriculture appeared during the war of independence, with revolutionary generals, including Toussaint Louverture, instituting the policy to maintain the lucrative plantation economy. It was then institutionalized in independent Haiti by Dessalines. For more on this policy, see Trouillot 1990a; Fick 1990; and DuBois

2013. For more on how debates about the policy circulate in everyday discussions among Haitians, see Brown 1991.

18. Since their inception, development plans have centered on an understanding of Haiti's place in the global economy as defined by two comparative market advantages: proximity to US markets and the lowest wages in the region. In 2009, following the devastating 2008 hurricane season, the British economist Paul Collier (2009) issued a policy report that became the blueprint for reconstruction after this catastrophe as well as the 2010 earthquake. Emphasizing the need for job creation above all else, he wrote, "From the important perspective of market access, Haiti is now the world's safest production location for garments. . . . Of course market access is not enough. . . . In garments the largest single component of costs is labour. Due to its poverty and relatively unregulated labour market, Haiti has labour costs that are fully competitive with China, which is the global benchmark" (Collier 2009, 5).

19. Aristide had run for president in 1990 under the Front National pour le Changement et la Démocratie (FNCD), a broad coalition of left-leaning political parties. Prior to taking office, Aristide created his own party, Organisation Politique Lavalas, or OPL, which claimed a majority in Parliament after he returned in 1994. Following the founding of Fanmi Lavalas, OPL, now without Aristide, changed the definition of its acronym to Organisation du Peuple en Lutte. Today, there are countless parties in Haiti with ancestral ties to Lavalas, many of which claim to best represent the original ideals of the movement.

20. Adam Przeworski (1991, 2000), following Joseph Schumpeter (1950), has put forth a minimalist definition of democracy—elections in which outcomes are uncertain and candidates abide by results—that has become the international policy standard for labeling whether a country is "democratic" or "authoritarian." The model takes into account the regime's impact on economic well-being, yet not as a criterion for democracy but rather as an indicator of a democracy's longevity: higher per capita incomes predict if and for how long democracy will survive. The irony is that this model, although overlooking economic parity as a condition of democracy, can have far-reaching consequences on the political economy (Wedeen 2008). As an international policy assessment tool, it was used, in the 2000s, to classify Haiti as an inadequate democracy, which curtailed the international grants and aid the country received (Dupuy 2005b).

21. For more on the role international democratization and development organizations played in the formation of the Civil Society Initiative, see Schuller 2012b; and Sprague 2012.

22. Rosny Desroches, minister of education under Jean-Claude Duvalier, founded and led Fondation Haïtienne de l'Enseignement Privé (FONHEP).

23. For more detail on the controversial election cycle in 2000, see Carey 2002; Deibert 2005; and Dupuy 2005a, 2007.

24. For a fuller discussion of the founding of Group 184, see Beckett 2010; Bogdanich and Nordberg 2006; and Sprague 2012.

25. Charles Taylor (1990) has argued that the modern idea of civil society, coined in Adam Ferguson's 1767 *Essay of the History of Civil Society*, emerged in light of increasingly absolutist, despotic states in Europe, where it came to articulate an autonomous public with its own opinion and the independent domain through which the state would be held accountable to public opinion. At this time, Europe was transitioning from an aristocratic to a capitalist political order, a point Karl Marx and Friedrich Engels (1970) stressed in their analysis of civil society as the domain that represented to the capitalist state the interests of bourgeois society. But, as Comaroff and Comaroff (2006b, 4) point out, the term, whether denoting a public or bourgeois sphere, still maintained traces of its earlier usages as a code for civilization. It was defined, as they put it, by contrast to what it was not: "the

uncivil, 'prehistoric,' condition of mankind living in nature (without any rational government), under the domination of divine authority or under the thrall of savage despotism." On these points, it is important to recall that Thomas Hobbes suggested that, aside from the "civill Warre" in England, the state of *warre* was present among "the savage people in many places of *America*" (1968, 187).

26. The phrase *Jan l pase, l pase* was adopted from a song released by pop music group System Band in early 1997. The refrain goes, "*Sa l fè, l fè l!/Jan l pase l, l pase!/Ou kwe m ap sove?/Ou kwe m ap chape?*" (What he does, he does it!/The way it goes, it goes!/You believe I'll be saved?/You believe I'll survive?).

27. Feeding and eating are central metaphors in Haiti for illustrating respectful relations between people. The act of *separe manje* (distributing food) is to recognize and place others within the family or community; conversely, to hoard or deny others food is an act of exclusion (Brown 1991; Richman 2005; Stevens 1995). As Samuel illustrated with the proverb—*travay pou ou, manje ak lòt* (work for yourself, eat with others)—the act of sharing food both elevates one's status as a productive person and bestows on others a sense of membership in the sharer's network. Yet, as the empty plate protest illustrated, to eat well while others go hungry is to enrich or empower oneself at the expense of others. *Manje* (to eat) is the verb used to describe sorcery—the paradigmatic act of killing someone for one's own gain.

28. The market for rice provides a key example. Already reduced in 1987 from 150 percent to 50 percent, the tariff on imported rice was lowered to 3 percent in 1995, far below the Caribbean average of 20 percent. Around the same time, former US President Bill Clinton signed into law the Federal Agricultural Improvement and Reform (FAIR) Act, which shifted US farm policy from subsidies to direct payments to farmers, catapulting US rice exports. Underselling Haitian rice by about 25 percent, US rice, nearly all from Clinton's home state of Arkansas, soon overtook the domestic rice market. Self-sufficient in rice production in 1980, by the late 1990s Haiti imported 80 percent of its rice (Lundahl 2013). Despite its original low price point, the cost of so-called *diri miyami* (Miami rice) steadily escalated. In 2006, when I first traveled to Haiti, a *gwo mamit* (coffee tin) of Miami rice went for $1.25 (fifty goud); a mere two years later, a *ti mamit* (soup can) cost that much. Such price increases also elevated the cost of local rice: by 2008, a *gwo mamit* of Haitian rice cost $3.10, or 85 percent more. To make matters worse, rice is the primary food staple for the urban poor. Although most Haitians had eaten a diet diverse in root crops when residing in the countryside, since moving to the city the diet has shifted toward cheap food imports, with the related health consequences of obesity, hypertension, and diabetes, among other illnesses (Kivland and Sosin 2018; World Bank 2010).

29. In April 2008, after two neighborhood children died of hunger, hundreds from Bel Air joined with thousands of other urbanites to demand an end to *lavi che à* and *klowòks*. Following a week of protests, in which five protesters were shot and killed by police, the price point was reduced, but by summer, it had surpassed previous highs.

30. Annual estimates suggest that women consistently account for around 65 percent of factory workers (Better Work Haiti 2013; Schoepfle and Pérez-López 1992). For more on how development policy has instituted a noted feminization of low- and middle-income jobs in the circum-Caribbean, see Freeman 2000; Mendez 2005; Schuller 2012b; and Thomas 2011.

31. A survey conducted by Viva Rio in 2007 reported that, after accounting for those making a living by selling a good, service, or labor in the informal economy, the unemployment rate in Bel Air dropped to 44 percent (Fernandez and Nascimento 2007a). See Fass 1988 for a more in-depth discussion of how official employment figures misrepresent the realities of work in urban Haiti.

32. It is common in scholarly and lay discourse for Haiti to be identified as a predominantly rural country. However, as early as 2009, over 50 percent of the population lived in cities. See, for reference, United States Central Intelligence Agency 2015.

33. It is impossible to know the exact population of Bel Air. The neighborhood is not an official urban district, and the city and state do not keep official records for the majority of residents who live beyond the street on dirt hillsides. However, the 2007 Viva Rio survey of Greater Bel Air—an aerial estimate using Google Earth and household survey data of the neighborhoods of Bel Air proper and its surrounding environs—provides reliable figures. In my observations, the demographics of the neighborhood did not dramatically shift following the 2010 earthquake, despite changes in housing stock and household composition.

34. The various neologisms used in academic accounts to qualify democracies like Haiti's are too vast to cite here. However the most influential terminology includes: "illiberal democracies" (Diamond 1996); "disjunctive democracy" (Holston 2008); and "delegative democracy" (O'Donnell, Cullel, and Iazzetta 2004; Zakaria 2003).

35. The tendency to separate violence and democracy among scholars of Haiti can also be observed in debates over the allusions to Pè Lebrun, or necklacing, that Aristide made in speeches to his followers at the end of his first term. To justify these usages, which were criticized for inciting violence, Peter Hallward (2007, 25), drawing on reporting by the journalist Kim Ives, has argued that the allusion to necklacing was not a call to violence but a "code or shorthand for 'popular power,' 'street power,' or 'popular vigilance'" (see also Sprague 2012). There is some truth to this, but categorically separating violence and populism, as well as violence and democracy, appears misguided, especially when it was an appeal to the potential of popular revolution that gave the references their punch. More in line with my reasoning are those who have defended popular militancy on the basis of its necessity and, therefore, legitimacy in the absence of the rule of law or constitutional order—a point Aristide made when, in one reference to necklacing, he added the proviso "you may never use [necklacing] again in a state where law prevails." Alex Dupuy (2007, 2009) and Nick Nesbitt (2009) mobilize this reasoning, though they diverge on when such necessity existed. I also disagree, however, with the way these analyses maintain an adherence to an ideal form of democracy devoid of violence. It is true that the recognition of this necessity does indicate a degree of failure on the part of those who govern to address and protect the needs of the population. But rather than evaluate the utility and justification of violence on the basis of whether the state has failed at democracy, I am concerned with analyzing the role that violence—as a political discourse and tool—has played in both maintaining and challenging the competing faces of democracy in Haiti.

CHAPTER 4. IDENTITY

1. The involvement of the US government in the downfall of Aristide's second term and the subsequent coup d'état has been well documented by Sprague (2012) and Dupuy (2007b), among others. While there was notable dissent from pro-Aristide groups in the United States (including Democratic congressmen and congresswomen), the then administration of George W. Bush was vocal and active in its distrust and disapproval of Aristide's government.

2. For an excellent discussion of frustration in the life of the baz, see Neiburg 2016. See also Braum 2014.

3. See, for examples and elaborations of the definition of *pwen*, McAlister 2002; and Richman 2005.

4. For another framework for understanding the self as "becoming" in and through history, see Biehl and Locke 2010. I am here specifically drawing attention to the narrative construction and conflict that shape perceptions of the self.

5. Anthropologists (e.g., Bernstein 2012; Sharp 2007) have argued how Western suppositions of identity are based on an understanding of the body as individual, unchanging, and nonporous. In this understanding, the transgression of physical boundaries, as in possession, becomes possible only as an act of violation and finality rather than transmutation and potential becoming.

6. The full lyrics in Haitian Creole are *Lame, lame, lame, lame volè./Lame, lame, lame zenglendo./Kraze lame zenglendo ban m kò polis./Yo pat al lekòl./Yo pa fè reto./Yo pa fè filo./Yo gen foli jeneral./Kraze lame zenglendo a./Banm kò polis la.* The lyrics to this song were recorded on multiple occasions between 2008 and 2013, though it was originally performed in 1994.

7. Rules of dress in the government offices, banks, the church, and other spaces have long functioned in Haiti as a way of discriminating against the poor. Under Duvalier, people were required to wear shoes outside the home, a practice that effectively policed the mobility of the rural (and often urban) poor, who, out of habit and means, often went barefoot. In fact, the poor in general were—and continue to be—often derogatorily referred to as *gwo zòtèy* (big toes). See Smith 2001 for a fuller discussion.

8. The semantic equivalence between crime and politics exposes the way those who have controlled the Haitian state have a long history not of serving the majority of Haitians but profiting from them, from nineteenth-century predatory taxation policies (Trouillot 1990a) against the peasantry to today's exploitative political labor of the urban poor. See chapter 1 for more discussion on the meaning of *fè politik* and its differentiation from *fè leta*.

9. These jokes referenced an entrenched economic and racial division in Haitian society, between the lighter, wealthier, more educated *milat* minority and the darker, poorer, less educated *nèg* majority. The division between *milat* and *nèg* classes has historically shaped the division of political and economic power in the country, with the former controlling the economy and the latter the state. There is an expression *politique la doublure* (politics of the double), which describes how the *milat* class would put a *nèg* president in power who was a puppet controlled by their directives and interests. However, both classes have also battled for control of the state. In the late nineteenth century, a political party division took shape between the *milat*-dominant Parti Libéral and the *nèg*-dominant Parti National, whose respective slogans were "Power to the most competent" and "The greatest good to the greatest number." For more, see DuBois 2013; Fatton 2007; Nicholls 1996; Schuller 2012b; and Smith 2014.

10. For more about the Aristide Foundation, see http://www.aristidefoundation fordemocracy.org.

11. John Jackson argues for understanding race as a "subject-subject model, not subject-object model" (2005, 15). In other words, racial ways of being are not authentic objects that can be verified by others but rather subjective embodiments that are evaluated intersubjectively and contextually. I likewise use the notion of political sincerity to illustrate how people grappled with conflicting affiliations not by determining which ones were real or fake, but by evaluating them as relational stances in accordance with the exigencies of the social situation.

12. I am concerned with understanding debt in terms somewhat apart from most contemporary anthropology. Many scholars in anthropology and allied disciplines have argued how the history of debt in modern society traces a change from relating to fellow humans as a "unique nexus of relations with others" to quantifiable commodities that can be tallied and compensated (Graeber 2011, 208). Studies of microfinance development programs, in particular, have shown that recipients of loans often become entangled in cycles of indebtedness, and this leads to individuals who, in struggling to overcome debt, abide by neoliberal principles of individualism and self-help, rather than collectivity and mutual aid. However, other studies, from which I take inspiration, have begun

to show how credits and debts—when understood as components of transactional and moral economies—continue to be important links that bind a social group and reinforce notions of communal reciprocity. See, for example, Chu 2010; Schuster 2014; and Watanabe 2015.

13. Yves, in particular, subscribed to this narrative. As he told me, "Chimè, that is something in everyone's blood. See, the GNB movement gave us that name *chimè*—it made everyone afraid of us, made them look at us like malefactors. They took our name [GNB] and then gave us another name. I am a person of Ginen, but they say that they worked that name *chimè* with Maji . . . a devilish thing. Anyway, it consumed the baz after they called us that . . . because they started to see us as animals, even devils."

14. For a thorough history of *rat pa kaka*, see Braum 2014. As Aristide's hold on power waned, some baz formations allied with the civil society opposition, which proved critical to the end of Aristide's rule. See Beckett 2008; Deibert 2005; Hallward 2007. The Zap Zap rara coined a song about this: "In our house a small criminal group of fake leaders is conspiring to sell the country./In our house a small criminal group of *restavèk* [child servants] is conspiring for a visa./But when the popular masses take to the streets to defend the country they curse us *chimè*." The song referred to how some baz formaations (*restavèk*) had allied with civil society groups (fake leaders) in order to stake their political fortunes in the opposing camp or negotiate opportunities to leave Haiti. The lyrics in Creole are *Yon ti gwoup fò lidè kriminèl la kay nou k ap fè konplo pou vann peyi a./Yon ti gwoup restavèk kriminèl la kay nou k ap fè konplo pou visa./Men lè mas pèp la pran lari pou defan peyi k ap kraze yo joure nou chimè.*

15. FOKAL (Fondasyon Konesans ak Libète), a Haitian NGO, highly respected among civil society in Haiti and abroad, whose offices were located down the road from the site of the event, reported that they witnessed "groups of pro-governmental militia, called *chimè* or OP (Popular Organization), regroup in front of our building, visibly preparing to attack the student demonstration scheduled for that day. . . . Within two weeks of the bicentennial of our revolution, we are revolted by the use of children and youth made by the government, teaching them violence and hatred and driving them to the dead-end paths of destruction and chaos. We renew our confidence in knowledge and learning . . . because we are convinced of the primordial role of education and culture in the construction of a free, united and democratic Haiti" (FOKAL 2003).

16. Naming this movement "Operation Baghdad" exemplified the use of word *wanga* within a social conflict. While political opponents and intervening forces insisted that the name was coined by Bel Air baz to announce their brutal campaign of beheadings (acts performed by the putative terrorists in Iraq), most Belairians offered other explanations. Some said it was, in fact, coined by them to announce their justified resistance; others said it was applied to them to cast them as the ultimate criminals; most, however, said its origins are unclear but that they used it to signify the unlawful role foreign powers played in ousting Aristide from power.

17. See Greenburg 2013; Higate and Henry 2009; Mobekk 2017; and Lindenmayor et al. 2009 for a critical discussion of MINUSTAH in Haiti.

18. The idea of *mòde-soufle* resonates with how the political scientist Charles Tilly likened state making to organized crime in the sense that state power issues the impression of safeguarding the people from the violent threats the state itself has manufactured. "Protection," he wrote, "sounds two contrasting tones": the "shelter against dangers provided by a powerful friend, a large insurance policy, or a sturdy roof" and "the racket in which a local strongman forces merchants to pay tribute to avoid damage—damage the strong man himself threatens to deliver" (Tilly 1985, 170).

19. In May 2010, the Haitian government completed the sale of 70 percent of its controlling stakes in Teleco to the Vietnamese company Viettel.

20. See, in particular, Nicholls 1996 on zenglen; Pierre-Charles 1973 and Trouillot 1990a on makout; and James 2010 and McAlister 2002 on zenglendo. See also the discussion in chapter 2.

21. Mary Douglas (1966) long ago argued that an overarching binary organizes human societies: purity and danger. Purity identifies order, civility, and holiness; danger articulates dirt, disorder, and evil. "Dirt," she further argues, follows a logic of contagion, whereby its (perceived) presence in a space can make the persons and objects within it "dirty" as well. When mapped onto the space of the city, this logic is present in perceptions of poor neighborhoods as disorderly as well as labeling other places as "hot" or "disorderly" when those residents are present beyond the neighborhood—in street protest, for example.

22. Many anthropologists have criticized the common presumption that racial identities are rooted in biological differences that result from the connection of people to particular places. See, for example, Appadurai 1988; and Malkki 1992. Urban studies scholars have similarly criticized the widespread tendency to map race and class onto "the ghetto" in ways that presume a fixity between kinds of people and kinds of spaces (Jaffe 2012b; Omi and Winant 1990; Wacquant 2004; Wirtz 2017).

23. Ogou, like the protesters, straddles the lines of the archetypal social groups that characteristically define constructive and destructive power in Haitian spirituality: family members and strangers, insiders and outsiders, the oppressed and the oppressors: "Ogou cannot easily be assimilated into either group because, as a soldier, he must necessarily be in between, defending the one from the other" (Brown 1991, 101). The "hot" protester entered this liminal border zone between good and bad power. The fire imparted in them the force and courage needed to complete the protest route and withstand attacks by political enemies or police agents, yet this protection worked by inciting fear of the protesters' power.

24. The notion of a "strong mind" (*mynd fò*) is a spiritual and social concept, referring to a level of mystical power and social understanding (*konesans*) that allows one to exert control over the world and the myriad malevolent forces within it. In Yves's rendering, he was referring to the power of his strong mind to counteract political enemies, social-structural forces, and illness—subsuming all to the logic of the social. For more on *konesans* and the mind as a powerful defense mechanism, see Brown 1991; Farmer 1992; and Gregory 2006.

CHAPTER 5. DEVELOPMENT

1. Estimates of how many died in the earthquake vary widely. A USAID-commissioned report provided a range of 46,190 to 84,961 (O'Connor 2012), and the Government of Haiti provided an estimate of 316,000. There are political reasons for over- and underestimating death tolls, as the numbers affect the amount and expediency of aid money distribution (Wilentz 2013). By comparing household surveys before and after the earthquake, a team of researchers estimated that the number of those killed in and around Port-au-Prince was closer to 158,000 (Kolbe et al. 2010). However, the exact number will probably never be known.

2. Many have pointed out that despite the Haitian government's limited resources and political clout vis-à-vis donor countries, the people of Haiti lay the blame for Haiti's problems on the Haitian government (Katz 2013; Schuller 2016). It is possible to read this as false consciousness, as ignorance about how little control the government has over aid or development allocation, but it is also possible, as I do here and elsewhere, to see it as an indictment of this system and an aspiration for state control (Kivland 2012). As Katz documented, in the aftermath of the earthquake, focus groups assembled for a donors'

conference shared a desire that reconstruction "benefit the nation as a whole" and "reinforce self-sufficiency and sovereignty" (2013, 146).

3. Such roles for women were typical among the groups I knew. Though women were nominally included on organizational committees, they were rarely a part of the inner circle that planned projects or reaped their payouts, unless it was a "women's organization." However, women's roles as party planners were not inconsequential either, as parties were significant events and, as planners, they often exercised some control over the distribution of money.

4. This goes far toward explaining why Belairians at once complained of there being no state and of being oppressed by the state. People rarely encountered state agents unless it was at their own initiative, either because they needed a document or were in search of some project or service for the neighborhood. These encounters were usually costly, time-consuming, and unsatisfying, not to mention degrading. Most Belairians were treated with the exaggerated form of indifference that Michael Herzfeld (1993) associated with modern bureaucracies, as matters of race, class, language, and criminality interacted to construct Bel Air residents as less than worthy citizens. Even the most powerful political actors in Bel Air were often treated with expediency and dismissiveness, signaling a need to placate or appease them.

5. In the introduction and elsewhere (Kivland 2012), I have detailed some of the conflicts that have jeopardized a sense of order and security for the leaders of OJMOTEEB and their ally/rival OJREB. For example, I witnessed Frantzy, the leader of OJREB, have his door beat down, his television smashed, and his house ransacked over a street-sweeping project whose funds were deemed unjustly distributed by OJMOTEEB members. The incident led Frantzy to denounce the lack of security and absent state in the area, though, in its aftermath, he doubled down on his own state-making project, employing a defense brigade to protect the next street-sweeping project.

6. On taking office, President René Préval established Popular Sectors in the major geto of Port-au-Prince and other cities to integrate the baz/OPs active under Aristide.

7. Readers attentive to the politics of naming will recognize Ling Di as the slogan of Baz GNB in Bel Air, operative during Aristide's second presidency. The reuse of this name signaled the change in the power hierarchy of baz formations as Baz Grand Black seized control of the neighborhood.

8. Jennie Smith has offered a compelling critique of participatory development during the 1990s in Haiti. She wrote, "participating meant little more than carrying rocks on one's head or being present at a community governance meeting in which development agency staff asked people to define local needs, and then presented them with prêt-à-porter project possibilities (each with its own pre-formulated set of regulations for 'local contributions'" (2001, 35).

9. The Action Plan for National Recovery and Development of Haiti, issued in March 2010, was a ten-year development plan signed by the Haitian government but largely authored by experts of the UN and international financial institutions. In line with previous development plans, it listed "strengthening the state" as a priority but ultimately called for further privatization of the public sector by outsourcing public services to businesses and NGOs (Republic of Haiti 2010; see also Bell 2013; Schuller 2016). The United Nations Office of the Special Envoy for Haiti (2012) has reported that of the $6.43 billion in aid money disbursed by donors from 2010 to 2012, the Haitian government received 9.1 percent; Haitian nongovernmental organizations received 0.6 percent.

10. Viva Rio's project Tanbou Lapè incorporated many components as it evolved over the course of its implementation, including scholarships for school children, motorbike and laptop prizes for baz leaders, language and professional classes for rara musicians, and peace concerts.

11. I rarely encountered the leader of Ling Di, who did not walk the streets or attend public events. I mostly heard of his presence after the fact, when he, for example, visited Michel in December 2013 to ask if he'd like for him to "punish" (read: kill) the person Michel once suspected of ensorcelling him.

12. In a Vodou ritual context, the expression *pa simp* (not simple) suggests sorcery, or more specifically, that an action or thing is not natural or benign but purchased by someone with malevolent intent. This meaning is resonant here. Although people do not equate sorcery and development, both are seen to be undertaken by those in pursuit of wealth and power over others. Many anthropologists have shown how people faced with the contradictory outcomes of democracy and development—such as economic growth amid rising inequality—revive the occult cosmologies that have long served as moral assessments of social equilibrium. See, for example, Comaroff and Comaroff 1999a; Geschiere 1997; and West 2003.

13. The phrase *grands blancs* was the colonial term for the wealthiest of the colonists, those who owned large sugar plantations and enslaved on them hundreds of Africans.

14. Martelly's appointed city delegate was the descendant of a leader of a political bureau under François Duvalier. Although many baz, including Baz Grand Black, have, to some extent, moved beyond a strict competition between Lavalas and Makout, this division remained a salient organizing principle for baz geography and conflicts in the area.

15. It is useful to recall Max Weber's well-known definition of the state as a "human community that (successfully) claims the *monopoly on the legitimate use of physical force* within a given territory" (1946 [1998], 78). Several anthropologists have revitalized this conception of statehood by focusing on the key role of violence in sovereignty (see Das and Poole 2004; Hansen and Stepputat 2005; and Mbembe 2003). While I agree with these readings to an extent, I am interested in reading force, especially as semantically coded in Haiti, as a constructive and destructive force.

16. Though the group had only a few members, the name *117* was a boast that claimed a network of 117 members.

17. As noted in the introduction, several international commentators and analysts predicted that criminal gangs would take over the city in the aftermath of the earthquake. Alongside emergency medical aid, the United States sent twenty thousand US troops and the UN added an additional three thousand peacekeepers (bringing the total to twelve thousand) to police the disaster zone (Bell 2013; Ulysse 2015). Yet these fears were unfounded. Amid the initial chaos and uncertainty of the earthquake, when Haiti appeared most vulnerable, criminal gangs did not overrun the city. In fact, the rate of kidnapping and murder declined (Kolbe and Muggah 2012; Wilentz 2013). However, as the disaster cemented itself in makeshift camps and haphazard aid distributions, the story began to change, with people reporting increases in incidences of rape, theft, and killings (MADRE et al. 2011; Muggah and Kolbe 2011; Schuller 2016). According to data gathered by Viva Rio's Biwo Analyiz Kominotè (Community Record Office) and reported by Commission Episcopale Nationale Justice et Paix (JILAP), homicide rates increased in 2011 as the presidential elections were underway and continued to rise in certain encampments and popular quarters of the capital afterward. In Bel Air and its surroundings, the homicide rate went from 40 in 2010 to 138 in 2011 and 164 in 2012. See JILAP 2014.

18. There has been much debate about how women are addressed in international development policy. Critiques in the 1970s and 1980s regarding the exclusion of women in development economies brought about the "Women in Development" mandates of global institutions, such as the United Nations Development Program, that stipulated women's involvement as a condition of funding. However, in response to feminist critiques, this framework has since been revised to incorporate a more relational approach to gender (considering men and women in terms of each other) and making gender

equality a goal of development (Antrobus 2004; Cleaver 2002; Schuller 2012a, 2016). Still, it remains the case that many development initiatives in Haiti stipulate women's participation without adequate attention to the gendered ramifications of that involvement (Schuller 2012a).

19. It is important to note that positioning men as the distributors of aid and women as the recipients of aid reinforced a gendered division of labor, with men seen as responsible for political, organizational work and women as the benefactors of this leadership. Such an organizational structure worked to further women's marginalization in leadership roles. See James 2010; Schuller 2016; and Selby 2015 for a fuller analysis.

20. Many early media reports attributed the increase in rape and sexual violence after the earthquake to an overall climate of lawlessness driven by the collapse of Haiti's National Penitentiary and other jails and the escape of an estimated four thousand inmates. However, subsequent studies suggested that this assumption was wrong. Following patterns of sexual violence worldwide, the vast majority of assaults were committed by individuals known to the victims, such as acquaintances or neighbors (Bell 2013; MADRE et al. 2011). The climate of the disaster probably contributed to the increase in rape not by unleashing a climate of lawlessness, but moreover, by disrupting social networks, creating gendered dependencies, and enabling power grabs by men.

21. Research on gangs and sexual violence has established the role that gang rape plays as a ritual in coming-of-age sequences, male bonding, and group formation (Bourgois 1996; Sanday 2007; Wood 2005). In this context, the gang rape and the talk it engendered was also a key vehicle by which the group promulgated a fearsome reputation and, as Bernie once put it, "held the community hostage."

22. Sophie's predicament was not unique, attesting to how women in Bel Air were particularly affected by violence at street parties—by putting them in harm's way and affecting their livelihood.

23. Viva Rio peace concerts were to be held as a reward for periods of no killings; however, despite the wave of violence in Bel Air and three killings in Fort National over the summer, the peace concert was still held.

24. This data was gathered from JILAP and Viva Rio's Biwo Analyiz Kominotè. During this time, I volunteered with Viva Rio's Biwo Analyiz Kominotè, which also tracked homicides in the area. As a part of this work, I cross-referenced Viva Rio's and JILAP's accounting of homicides

25. According to Viva Rio's Biwo Analyiz Kominotè, there were four killings in Bel Air in September 2013 and eleven in the surrounding areas. Similar numbers were reported through the end of that year.

26. The problem of delegating to local organizations the authority for aid disbursement without adequate knowledge about the area of intervention worsened in the disaster context of the earthquake. The Humanitarian Accountability Project and International Organization of Migration, in an assessment of post-earthquake camp committees, noted that NGOs gave such committees great decision-making power even though they and the wider camp population knew little about member roles and responsibilities and did not have a mechanism for redressing wrongdoing on the part of members (Humanitarian Accountability Project and International Organization of Migration 2010). The same can be said of the social organizations, which formed the basis of camp committees.

27. The America First platform is, in some ways, a response to the ideas of the Tea Party, especially in terms of its oppositional stance on free trade and globalization. However, in terms of foreign policy, President Donald Trump's administration has adopted the Tea Party's call to curtail US involvement in the world and to focus on the domestic economy, exemplified by his first year's budget proposal, which aimed to reduce foreign aid expenditures from $59.1 billion to $40.5 billion. As the budget proposal explained,

"It is time to prioritize the security and well-being of Americans, and to ask the rest of the world to step up and pay its fair share" (Trump 2017).

CHAPTER 6. GENDER

1. The spelling in Creole would be *filing*. I avoid this spelling here because of its orthographic similarity to the English word for sorting and storing documents.

2. *Pace* Mikhail Bakhtin, Achille Mbembe (2001) appeals to the carnivalesque body as a way to define not only popular contestations of state power but also enactments of that power.

3. I am particularly indebted to Achille Mbembe's suggestion that I read Georges Bataille as a theorist who locates the sovereign gesture at occasions of festivity and in acts of lavish generosity, such as at the potlatch when the tribal leader bestows lavish gifts on tribesmen. Bataille (1988) locates sovereign excess in acts of both death and pleasure, bringing into play how festive occasions of social largesse reverberate in the staider acts of redistribution that characterize modern, disciplinary states.

4. For a study of how the masculine ideal of autonomy, conceivable by virtue of men's position in the family and society, figures in the works of Thomas Hobbes, Karl Marx, and John Stuart Mill, see di Stefano 1991. For more on Hannah Arendt's constructions of the sovereign, see Mann 2014. On Michel Foucault's omission of a gendered analysis of the manly sovereign, see Diamond and Quimby 1988.

5. Much of the analysis of how masculinity plays into state formation has focused on the states of North America and Europe (Cohn 1987; Dudinik, Hagemann, and Clark 2007; Dudinik, Hagemann, and Tosh 2004; Mann 2014; Nelson 1998). Other notable works on gender in colonial state formation include Luhrmann 1996 and Sinha 1995. See also Leacock 1981 for a discussion of the myth of male dominance cross-culturally, as well as examples of societies with alternative gender and power relations.

6. It is important to note that Achille Mbembe raises this point in response to a critique by Judith Butler (1992) regarding his failure to account for how the "theatricalization of power is first and foremost a theatricalization of the masculine body through which the state is ritualistically ratified" (Mbembe 2006, 162).

7. When the Zap Zap rara recorded its songs in studio for circulation on the radio, they used a female lead singer. When they performed in the streets, men and women sang in chorus.

8. Philippe Bourgois wrote about how poor Puerto Rican women who were entangled in relationships with abusive men used the romantic idiom of sexual jealousy to excuse both the abuse they endured from their partners and their own abuse of men. "Romantic love," he wrote (1995, 223), "enables a subordinated woman to assert her individual needs while at the same time binding her to the principle of a male-dominated nuclear household." I extend this discussion to Haiti and the particular social-structural pressures driving jealousy-inducing behavior and resultant jealousies.

9. Women's complaints of men being overly jealous ignored a context in which women were often compelled to forgo monogamy. Men's unemployment often led women to form multiple sexual unions in search of a stable provider (cf. Maternowska 2006). This was, in fact, the case with Nadine, who after Carl failed to provide for his son took up with other men in the neighborhood in search of the funds that often flowed at the beginning of relationships.

10. Peter Wilson's account derived from a novel methodological move that I have also followed in this book: rather than analyze, as had become the anthropological norm, the household as a microcosm of the social structure, Wilson explored how people socialized as an index of the deep structure, the "principles of thought and sentiments" that guided

behavior and produced the "groupings and segments of the society"—within and beyond the household (Wilson 1973, 7).

11. An understanding grounded in the mutually constitutive roles men and women have held historically would have revealed that women did not so much as "choose" respectability—a choice Wilson erroneously attributed to "the preferred status of women in the colonial structure, a status they have enjoyed since slavery" (1973, 234)— as respectability chose them. For example, women were not privileged in colonial society, even if they attained certain privileges (Reddock 1985). Rather, their privileges were—and often continue to be—gained through relationships with men, from being manumitted through marriage to free men in the time of slavery to inheriting land from a father's or husband's decree post-independence (Geggus 1996; Madiou 1847; Stinchcombe 1996). However, recognizing this does not mean women were, or are, defined by men. By focusing his ethnography on men, Wilson missed many of ways in which women subverted the system of respectability to their advantage or embraced a politics of reputation in order to carve out a space of agency and empowerment in society (Besson 1993; Sutton 1974).

12. Sidney Mintz quoted an American traveler and journalist in Haiti who, in 1854, observed "a strange inversion of the ordinary relations between husband and wife," where a machann "was the head of the house . . . the capitalist of the concern, and does all the business. [The husband] has no more to do with the direction of affairs, in or out of the house, than if he were a child" (1996, 239). As Mintz points out, the American's infantilization of men trafficked in hegemonic masculinity and cast Haitian men's dependence on women as socially backward. Mintz argued that part of what was interesting about the American's account was that it showed how the Haitian husband did not perceive the wife's economic independence as a loss of status for him. Mintz goes on to suggest that the "supplantation of such non-Western values by Western values may, in some cases, eventuate in a regressive social direction for women—or, at any rate, for some women" (1996, 239). The passage is telling in light of the increased influence of global power in Haiti and the forms of masculinist control exercised over lower-class women as men increasingly view their dependence on women as a loss of power and respect.

13. The NGO Better Work estimated in 2013 that women held 64 percent of jobs in the export industry (Bell and Erkert 2013).

14. For a detailed report on the feminization of immigration throughout the Americas, see Pessar 2005.

15. I use the language of sidelining to highlight how poor Haitian men are not divorced from but marginalized within the global economy. The development industry depends on the production of places like Bel Air as spaces of poverty and insecurity, the latter of which is attached to male bodies in particular.

16. The question of who is the head of household is difficult to assess in Haiti. It has been estimated that women head about 30 percent of households (Gardella 2006). However, this figure is misleading. Even when women contribute the bulk of money to the household, men can claim to head it. This was the case with Kal and Sophie. Although she supported the household financially, she and Kal recognized Kal as its leader and public representative when they were approached by surveyors, missionaries, or anthropologists, for example.

17. This saying derives from the 2007 song "Vagon 4 Life" by the pop music group Kreyol La.

18. There are many other analogues throughout the African diaspora: for example, the *rude bwoy* in Jamaica (Stolzkoff 2000), the *stick man* in Trinidad (Rohlehr 2004), the *débouillard* in the French Antilles (Browne 2004), and the *gangsta* in the United States (Rose 1994). See Smith 2012 for discussion of these varieties.

19. It is significant that when used for women, the gender of vagabon is marked: *fanm vagabon*. This suggests that although women can access this mode of power, it is viewed as the purview of men. Hence the gender hierarchy remains in place even as women might be empowered through manipulations of it. It is much more difficult for women to position themselves as vagabon in a positive way—for example, the term *fanm vagabon* can also mean *bouzen* (whore) (Smith 2012). This usage is telling, not only because of the gender marker but also because of how vagabon and fanm vagabon are mutually constituted—that is, the behavior of men as vagabon (as disrespectable men) that often turn women into fanm vagabon (nonmonogamous partners).

20. In Creole, the lyrics are *Kote Manman Pèpètyèl/N ap chache bèl koko./Men l pa sèl./ Li plèn zozo.*

21. In Creole, the lyrics are *Bouzen nan zòn an./Yo renmen cham gason./Yo pa dòmi kay fanmi.*

22. In Creole, the lyrics are *Pa kite yo fin peri./Pa kite yo fin detwi./Peyi yo pou yo/Pou-vwa yo nan dada yo./Yo se lame Phararon./Nou se pep Israel la.*

23. A good example of Gede's healing humor came as I awaited a ride home late that night. Berman cut right through my fatigue and impatience when he quipped, "I am a vagabon before and above all vagabon," he said. "I make babies without looking back. My zozo has no master. It has no ears. It'll slap you so hard, you'll cry for help."

24. Elizabeth McAlister has grasped the betiz of rara lyrics in similar terms: as "a series of lyrical revolts against gender roles and economic structures on the part of '*ti nèg*'" (2002, 68). Building on this insight, I want to highlight how the machismo figure also constituted a mimicry of state-like moods and vitalities that did not merely critique but also generated sovereign structures of belonging, authority, and feeling.

25. In Creole, the lyrics are *Mezi bwa nou./Y ap rayi nou.*

26. The entanglement of feeling and force at street parties and musical events in general resonates with the way ethnomusicologists have theorized the embodied process of "getting into the groove." Gage Averill has written about how musically and kinesthetically energized crowds at Carnival and carnivalesque koudyay in Haiti are described as *anraje* (enraged)—a sensation of being "worked up" to such an extent that they were on the verge of upheaval or revolt (Averill 1994). Steven Feld (1988) has likewise theorized this process in Papua New Guinea as "hardness." He writes, "Hardness is force, the attainment of that evocative, charged, energized state (where to extend the notion into English one is 'knocked out' or 'blown away')" (1988, 89). This force is not akin to violent domination or controlling others through fear of death, yet it is nonetheless intensely powerful and persuasive and can be channeled into all kinds of actions, aggression and violence among them.

27. In 2007, during Raranaval, a procession of rara bands in greater Bel Air, Baz Grand Black was in conflict with a baz in Fort Touron. When the baz-linked rara in Fort Touron mounted Bel Air, masked gunmen in Bel Air shot into the group and killed seven people. It was following this event that Viva Rio initiated its program Tanbou Lapè, which began with baz and rara leaders from rival zones signing a peace accord. Rara groups have long seen themselves (and are seen by others) as "armies," or "statelike entities involved in diplomacy and warfare," who represent the people and territory affiliated with them (Averill and Yih 2003; McAlister 2002, 136). But the potential for violent confrontation was heightened in the current era when urban rara are linked to baz fomations that are often armed.

28. In Creole, the lyrics are *Se Zap Zap k ap pase la./Li ban m filing./Li mache nan san m. Petwo nou se malè fèt nou menm./Se pa pale.* This sanguineous imaginary is telling, for it tweaked conventional models of national community, positing blood not a marker of

descent so much as an affective bond. Yet like descent markers, this model also facilitated solidarity as well as division (Marcelin 2012). Those with common feeling in the blood formed an agentive and righteous "army" of kin, neighbors, and acquaintances that was different and better from that of their rivals. Baz members often qualified rivals as not merely vagabon but *vagabon san sal* (dirty-blood vagabonds)—a term that deemed their blood flow both weak and immoral.

29. See Mann 2014 for a related discussion of Young's conception of the "I can" attitude as a masculine model of sovereign agency, as a model that depends on the social construction of the male body as, in contrast to the feminine body, capable of intentional and superior motility in the world.

30. Several anthropologists have recently applied the concept of qualisign to show how newly formed attachments to certain qualities are emblematic of societal formations and shifts in power relations (e.g., Harkness 2013; Ralph 2013; Reyes 2017). Julie Chu's (2010, 13) suggestion that "mobility is a privileged qualisign of modern selves and relations" in contemporary China is particularly apropos of my discussion. Chu traces how this "much-touted feature of being modern" (2010, 13) has propelled desires to migrate abroad. My discussion here also resonates with how Jeffrey Kahn (2015) has presented the changing paradigms of power in Haiti through the different malevolent spirits, or *dyab* (devils), that represent them, moving from an older *dyab* figured in the body of an obese, sedentary landowner who fed off the productivity of the peasantry to a more modern *dyab* figured in a speedy, light mobile spirit who accompanies people in their migration journeys. I build on these analyses of migration to explore how mobility has also figured in the production of modern selves and power in the city, with particular attention to its masculine dimensions.

31. See also the articles included in the special issue *Qualia* in *Anthropological Theory* edited by Lily Hope Chumley and Nicholas Harkness (2013), and those of the special issue *Qualia and Ontology: Language, Semiotics, and Materiality* in *Signs and Society* edited by Lily Hope Chumley (2017).

32. My attention to how activities take shape among other qualities and through various mediums builds on Nancy Munn's ethnography about the production of "fame" in Gawa. As she showed, a culturally significant quality, such as lightness, can be embodied in water, boats, and dance, to name a few examples (1986; see also Harkness 2013).

33. In an expectation of me that had by then become common, Frantzy insisted on my company because he anticipated that my privileged status as a white foreigner would help him get by the front desk to a meeting. In this case, it did not, though he told me that, without me, "the thing would have lacked respè totally."

34. It was significant that the group did not receive sponsorship from the NGOs they contacted. In suggesting that feelingful activities contrasted with NGOs' agendas, Frantzy's comment posited an idea of the state and its duties as beyond the biopolitical management of "bare life" or the calculated minimums of food, water, shelter, and security that govern what aid organizations determine is needed to keep a population alive. Baz leaders regularly singled out opportunities for collective pleasure and enjoyment as key to what a good leader and just state would provide (cf. Smith 2001). Beyond a critique of NGOs' biopolitical agendas, Frantzy's comment also criticized how local organizations had to shape their activities to fit the specified target areas of the main NGOs in Bel Air to receive funding. For more on the standard of bare life at stake in humanitarian aid, see Redfield 2005, 2012. For related discussions about the politics of life in international humanitarian aid in Haiti, see Beckett 2017 and Minn 2016.

35. The most lethal incident occurred on August 20, 2005, in Martissant, another geto in Port-au-Prince. According to eyewitness reports, dozens of machete-wielding men,

accompanied by police officers in uniform, entered a soccer stadium in Martissant where a USAID-sponsored game was under way. They stabbed and shot at least six people to death—and precipitated the injuries of many more as spectators rushed to escape (Beeton 2008).

36. Claude Lévi-Strauss used the example of the Gahuku-Gama of New Guinea who have "learnt football but will play, several days running, as many matches as are necessary for both sides to reach the same score. This is treating a game as a ritual" (1966, 31–32). Thanks to Greg Beckett for pointing me in this scholarly direction.

37. At the soccer tournament in 2011, for example, the group organized a food distribution in order to secure support from the NGO Food for the Poor. Although some residents benefited, the distribution was remembered for its disorder. To begin with, the food coupons were distributed mainly to women connected with baz leaders or their friends. When a group of excluded women protested and attended anyway, a skirmish broke out in the line. To make matters worse, Yves then began to throw the bags, which contained such heavy items as sacks of rice and cans of tomato paste, into the crowd, injuring several people. The whole thing, as many said, "lacked respè," and although Yves could have undoubtedly organized it better, I was left with the belief that the food distribution's logic fundamentally clashed with the objective of communal good feeling. As Yves said in its aftermath, "We should have instead had Janet make a big pot of *bouyan!*"—an eminently more shareable meal.

38. In her discussion of value-producing acts in Gawa, Nancy Munn (1986) builds on the work of Marcel Mauss. As she shows, it is through the circulation and exchange of objects that people in Gawa accrue "fame." The objects are endowed with cultural significance, but in addition the manner of exchange endows the exchangers with value.

39. Steven Gregory uses the term "imperial masculinity" to illustrate how sex tourists in the Dominican Republic "both registered and reinscribed the sociospatial hierarchies of the global division of labor" through their relations with Dominican women (2006, 133). He recounts a memorable scene in which a group of male sex tourists at a bar "spend more time interacting with each other than they do with women" (Gregory 2006, 148).

CONCLUSION. THE SPIRAL

1. Like many socially mobile Belairians, Franketienne has since left the neighborhood. He remained involved with a school and cultural center there after leaving, but these closed during Baghdad in 2004.

2. Examples of Caribbean authors inspired by chaos theory include Antonio Benítez-Rojo, Edouard Glissant, and Wilson Harris. See Murray-Román 2015 for an overview of their work.

3. This is why baz formations are not rhizomatic war machines in the ways theorized by Deleuze and Guattari (2002). "Bands in general, even those engaged in banditry or high-society life," they wrote, "are metamorphoses of a war machine formally distinct from all State apparatuses or their equivalent, which are instead what structure centralized societies" (2002, 358; see Mazzarella 2017). Such a view negates how the baz both mimics and seeks to summon the state into being.

4. In a related discussion, Greg Beckett (2017) has illustrated how older men in particular feel disrespected by the organization of development labor in poor neighborhoods. In the case of cash-for-work development programs, jobs tend to be allotted to men and women in their teens and twenties—a preference that is due to the hard labor involved and the control of the labor market by baz networks. In my observations, older men are also unlikely to accept these jobs due to the disrespect they entail in working for or alongside younger men.

5. For reporting on the Interim Haiti Recovery Commission and Haitian leaders minor role on it, see Sontag 2012. For an analysis of how the Haitian government reluctantly accepted unpopular neoliberal reforms in the mid-1990s in order to obtain crucial aid funds, see Dupuy 2005b. A recent example of Parliament being overruled concerns Haiti's minimum wage policy. In 2009, after Parliament passed a law raising the minimum wage by 60 percent (from 125 to 200 goud), President René Préval, facing pressure from the US State Department and foreign apparel executives, vetoed the law and instituted a two-tier wage structure that maintained the low wage for export assembly workers. For more information, see Bell 2013.

6. Deliberative democracy theorists such as John Rawls (1971) and Jürgen Habermas (1962 [1989]) have grounded democracy in the practice of rational deliberation. The "ideal speech situation" is one where free and equal interlocutors (by virtue of their constitutional liberties of free speech, press, and assembly) attain consensus on political issues through reasoned, peaceful discussion. Among others (e.g., Fraser 1992), Chantal Mouffe has offered a compelling critique with her idea of "agonistic pluralism": "the aim of democratic politics is to construct the 'them' in such a way that it is no longer perceived as an enemy to be destroyed but an 'adversary,' i.e., somebody whose ideas we combat but whose right to defend those ideas we do not put into question" (2000, 15). See also Bhrigupati Singh's related idea of "agonistic intimacy," which provides an image of neighborliness that is not "overwritten either with a wholly negative valence of hostile contradictions" or "with entirely affirmative hopes of trust, community, and social capital" (2011, 21). My discussion of baz agonism likewise aims to see connection in conflict and to balance communitarianism with competition.

7. The emotive, impassioned styling of this debate also evidenced residents' beliefs in the ill effects of keeping certain feelings inside rather than bringing them to the surface to be discussed, dealt with, and controlled. Letting emotions fester was one cause of *move san* (bad blood), or an nervous, anxious state, that compromised personal and communal wellness (Brodwin 1996; Farmer 1988).

8. The role of conflict as a basis of social solidarity is well theorized in social thought. Georg Simmel famously argued that conflict expressed and was aimed at restoring social connection: "If every interaction among men is a sociation, conflict—after all one of the most vivid interactions, which, furthermore, cannot possibly be carried on by one individual alone—must certainly be considered as sociation" (1955, 13–14).

Bibliography

Abrams, Philip. 1988. "Notes on the Difficulty of Studying the State." *Journal of Historical Sociology* 1 (1): 58–89.

Abu-Lughod, Lila. 1991. "Writing against Culture." In *Recapturing Anthropology: Working in the Present,* edited by Richard G. Fox, 137–62. Santa Fe, NM: School of American Research Press.

Agamben, Giorgio. 1998. *Homo Sacer: Sovereign Power and Bare Life.* Stanford, CA: Stanford University Press.

Agamben, Giorgio. 2000. *Means without End: Notes on Politics.* Translated by Cesare Casarino and Vincenzo Binetti. Minneapolis: University of Minnesota Press.

Agamben, Giorgio. 2005. *States of Exception.* Chicago: University of Chicago Press.

Agnew, John. 2008. "Sovereignty Regimes: Territoriality and State Authority in Contemporary World Politics." *Annals of the Association of American Geographers* 95 (2): 437–61.

Alexis, Jacques Stephen. 1955 (1999). *General Sun, My Brother.* Charlottesville: University of Virginia Press.

Allen, Lori A. 2013. *The Rise and Fall of Human Rights: Cynicism and Politics in Occupied Palestine.* Palo Alto, CA: Stanford University Press.

Anderson, Elijah. 1999. *Code of the Street.* New York: W. W. Norton.

Antrobus, Peggy. 2004. *The Global Women's Movement: Issues and Strategies for the New Century.* London: Zed Books.

Appadurai, Arjun. 1988. "Putting Hierarchy in Its Place." *Cultural Anthropology* 3 (1): 36–49.

Appadurai, Arjun. 1996. *Modernity at Large: Cultural Dimensions of Globalization.* Minneapolis: University of Minnesota Press.

Appadurai, Arjun. 2007. "Hope and Democracy." *Public Culture* 19 (1): 29–34.

Arendt, Hannah. 1998. *The Human Condition.* 2nd ed. Chicago: University of Chicago Press.

Arias, Enrique Desmond, and Daniel Goldstein, eds. 2010. *Violent Democracies in Latin America.* Durham, NC: Duke University Press.

Aristide, Jean-Bertrand. 1990. *In the Parish of the Poor: Writings from Haiti.* Translated by Amy Wilentz. Maryknoll, NY: Orbis Books.

Aristide, Jean-Bertrand, and Christophe Wargny. 1993. *Aristide: An Autobiography.* Maryknoll, NY: Orbis Books.

Asad, Talal. 1995. "Introduction." In *Anthropology and the Colonial Encounter,* 9–19. London: Ithaca Press.

Asad, Talal. 2000. "What Do Human Rights Do? An Anthropological Inquiry." *Theory and Event* 4 (4). http://muse.jhu.edu/article/32601.

Asad, Talal. 2003. *Formations of the Secular: Christianity, Islam, Modernity, Cultural Memory in the Present.* Stanford, CA: Stanford University Press.

Associated Press. 2004. "Street Gangs Hijack Food in Haiti." *CNN,* September 28.

Auyero, Javier, Philippe I. Bourgois, and Nancy Scheper-Hughes, eds. 2015. *Violence at the Urban Margins.* New York: Oxford University Press.

L

250 **BIBLIOGRAPHY**

Averill, Gage. 1994. "Anraje to Angaje: Carnival Politics and Music in Haiti." *Ethnomusicology* 38 (2): 217–47.
Averill, Gage. 1997. *A Day for the Hunter, a Day for the Prey*. Chicago: University of Chicago.
Averill, Gage, and Yuen-Ming David Yih. 2003. "Miltarism in Haitian Music." In *The African Diaspora: A Musical Perspective*, edited by Ingrid Monson, 267–93. New York: Routledge.
Babcock, Barbara A. 1978. *The Reversible World: Symbolic Inversion in Art and Society*. Ithaca, NY: Cornell University Press.
Bakhtin, M. M. 1981. *The Dialogic Imagination: Four Essays*. Translated by Michael Holquist. Austin: University of Texas Press.
Barthélémy, Gérard 1990. *L'univers rural Haïtien: Le pays en dehors*. Paris: L'Harmattan.
Bastien, Rémy. 1985. *Le paysan haïtien et sa famille: Vallé de Marbial*. Paris: Kharthala.
Bataille, Georges. 1988. *The Accursed Share: An Essay on General Economy*. 3 vols. New York: Zone Books.
Beckett, Greg. 2008. "The End of Haiti: History under Conditions of Impossibility." PhD dissertation, University of Chicago.
Beckett, Greg. 2010. "Phantom Power: Notes on Provisionality in Haiti." In *Anthropology and Global Counterinsurgency*, edited by John D. Kelly, Beatrice Jaregui, Sean Mitchell, and Jeremy Walton, 39–52. Chicago: University of Chicago Press.
Beckett, Greg. 2013. "Thinking with Others: Savage Thoughts about Anthropology and the West." *Small Axe: Journal of Caribbean Criticism* 17 (3): 166–81.
Beckett, Greg. 2017. "A Dog's Life: Suffering Humanitarianism in Port-au-Prince, Haiti." *American Anthropologist* 119 (1): 35–45.
Beeton, Dan. 2008. "Bad News from U.S. Press Misses the Story." *North American Congress on Latin America*, September/October.
Bell, Beverly. 2013. *Faultlines: Views across Haiti's Divide*. Ithaca, NY: Cornell University Press.
Bell, Beverly, and Alexis Erkert. 2013. "A Hard Day's Labor for $4.76: The Offshore Assembly Industry in Haiti." *Truthout*. https://truthout.org/articles/a-hard-days-labor-for-476-the-offshore-assembly-industry-in-haiti/.
Bellegarde-Smith, Patrick. 2004. *Haiti: The Breached Citadel*. Toronto: Canadian Scholar's Press.
Benìtez-Rojo, Antonio. 1992. *The Repeating Island: The Caribbean and the Postmodern Perspective*. Durham, NC: Duke University Press.
Berggren, Gretchen. 1993. "Sanctions in Haiti: Crisis in Humanitarian Action." Cambridge, MA: Harvard University Center for Population and Development Studies.
Bernstein, Anya. 2012. "More Alive Than All the Living: Sovereign Bodies and Cosmic Politics in Buddhist Siberia." *Cultural Anthropology* 27 (2): 261–85.
Bessire, Lucas. 2014. *Behold the Black Caiman: A Chronicle of Ayoreo Life*. Chicago: University of Chicago Press.
Besson, Jean. 1993. "Reputation and Respectability Reconsidered: A New Perspective on Afro-Caribbean Peasant Women." In *Women and Change in the Caribbean: A Pan Caribbean Perspective*, edited by Janet H. Momsen, 15–37. Bloomington: Indiana University Press.
Better Work Haiti. 2013. "Better Work Haiti: Garment Industry." Washington, DC: United States Department of Labor.
Biehl, João Guilherme. 2005. *Vita: Life in a Zone of Social Abandonment*. Berkeley: University of California Press.
Biehl, João Guilherme, and Peter Locke. 2010. "Deleuze and the Anthropology of Becoming." *Current Anthropology* 51 (3): 317–50.

Bien-aimé, Kesler. 2008. "Musique Racine et Mouvement Social Populaire, 1986–2000." Licence, Département de sociologie et anthropologie, Faculté d'éthnologie, Université d'état de Haïti.

Biersteker, Thomas J., and Cynthia Weber. 1994. *State Sovereignty as a Social Construct.* Cambridge: Cambridge University Press.

Blackwood, Evelyn, and Saskia Wieringa. 1999. *Same Sex Relationships and Female Desires: Transgender Practices across Cultures.* New York: Columbia University Press.

Bogdanich, Walt, and Jenny Nordberg. 2006. "Mixed U.S. Signals Helped Tilt Haiti Toward Chaos." *New York Times,* January 29.

Bogues, Anthony. 2006. "Power, Violence, and the Shotta Don." *NACLA Report on the Americas* 39 (6): 21–26.

Bonilla, Yarimar. 2013. "Ordinary Sovereignty." *Small Axe: Journal of Caribbean Criticism* 42: 152–65.

Bonilla, Yarimar. 2015. *Non-sovereign Futures: French Caribbean Politics in the Wake of Disenchantment.* Chicago: University of Chicago Press.

Bourdieu, Pierre. 1977. *Outline of a Theory of Practice.* Cambridge: Cambridge University Press.

Bourdieu, Pierre. 1984. *Distinction: A Social Critique of the Judgement of Taste.* Cambridge, MA: Harvard University Press.

Bourdieu, Pierre. 1992. *The Logic of Practice.* Translated by Richard Nice. Stanford, CA: Stanford University Press.

Bourdieu, Pierre. 1993. *The Field of Cultural Production.* New York: Columbia University Press.

Bourgois, Philippe I. 1995. *In Search of Respect: Selling Crack in El Barrio.* Cambridge: Cambridge University Press.

Bourgois, Philippe I. 1996. "In Search of Masculinity: Violence, Respect, and Sexuality among Puerto Rican Crack Dealers in East Harlem." *British Journal of Criminology* 36 (3): 412–27.

Bourgois, Philippe I. 2001. "Culture of Poverty." *International Encyclopedia of the Social and Behavioral Sciences*: 11904–7.

Bourgois, Philippe I. 2002. "U.S. Inner City Apartheid: The Contours of Structural and Interpersonal Violence." In *Violence in War and Peace: An Anthology,* edited by Nancy Scheper-Hughes and Philippe I. Bourgois, 301–7. Malden, MA: Blackwell.

Bourgois, Philippe I. 2009. *Righteous Dopefiend.* Berkeley: University of California Press.

Bourgois, Philippe I., and Nancy Scheper-Hughes, eds. 2002. *Violence in War and Peace: An Anthology.* Malden, MA: Blackwell.

Braum, Pedro. 2014. "Rat pa kaka: Politicia, violéncia, e desenvolvimento no coráçio de Porto Principe." PhD dissertation, Antropologia Social do Museu Nacional, Universidade Federal do Rio de Janeiro.

Brodwin, Paul. 1996. *Medicine and Morality in Haiti: The Contest for Healing Power.* New York: Cambridge University Press.

Brooks, David. 2010. "The Underlying Tragedy." *The New York Times,* January 14, A27.

Brown, Karen McCarthy. 1987. "Alourdes: A Case Study of Moral Leadership in Haitian Vodou." In *Saints and Virtues,* edited by John Stratton Hawley, 144–67. Berkeley: University of California Press.

Brown, Karen McCarthy. 1991. *Mama Lola: A Vodou Priestess in Brooklyn.* Berkeley: University of California Press.

Brown, Karen McCarthy. 2003. "Making *Wanga*: Reality Constructions and the Magical Manipulation of Power." In *Transparency and Conspiracy: Ethnographies in the New World Order,* edited by Harry G. West and Todd Sanders, 233–57. Durham, NC: Duke University Press.

Brown, Wendy. 1992. "Finding the Man in the State." *Feminist Studies* 18 (1): 7–34.

Browne, Katherine E. 2004. *Creole Economies: Caribbean Cunning under the French Flag.* Austin: University of Texas Press.

Burr, Lars. 2005. "The Sovereign Outsourced: Local Justice and Violence in Port Elizabeth." In *Sovereign Bodies: Citizens, Migrants, and States in the Postcolonial World*, edited by Thomas Blom Hansen and Finn Stepputat, 192–217. Princeton, NJ: Princeton University Press.

Butler, Judith. 1992. "Mbembe's Extravagant Power." *Public Culture* 4 (2): 1–30.

Butler, Judith, and Joan Scott. 1992. *Feminists Theorize the Political.* New York: Routledge.

Bynum, Caroline Walker. 2001. *Metamorphosis and Identity.* New York: Zone Books.

Cain, Kenneth. 2004. "In Haiti, Mobs Ate the Easy Part." *New York Times*, March 2.

Caldeira, Teresa Pires do Rio, and James Holston. 1999. "Democracy and Violence in Brazil." *Comparative Studies in Society and History* 41 (4): 691–729.

Camilleri, Joseph A., and Jim Falk. 1992. *The End of Sovereignty? The Politics of a Shrinking and Fragmenting World.* Brookfield, VT: Edward Elgar.

Caraway, Teri L. 2007. *Assembling Women: The Feminizaion of Global Manufacturing.* Ithaca, NY: Cornell University Press.

Carey, Henry. 2002. "Foreign Aid, Democratization and Haiti's Provisional Electoral Council, 1987–2001." *Wadabagei* 5 (2): 1–47.

Chatterjee, Partha. 2000. "Two Poets and Death: On Civil and Political Society in the Non-Christian World." In *Questions of Modernity*, edited by Timothy Mitchell. Minneapolis: University of Minnesota.

Chatterjee, Partha. 2004. *The Politics of the Governed: Reflections on Popular Politics in Most of the World.* New York: Columbia University Press.

Chu, Julie. 2010. *Cosmologies of Credit: Transnational Mobility and the Politics of Destination in China.* Durham, NC: Duke University Press.

Chumley, Lily. 2017. "Qualoa and Ontology: Language, Semiotics, and Materiality; an Introduction." *Signs and Society* 5 (S1): 1–20.

Chumley, Lily, and Nicholas Harkness. 2013. "Introduction: Qualia." *Anthropological Theory* 13 (1/2): 3–11.

Civil Society Initiative. 2001. "Civil Society Appeal for a Solution to the Crisis." Port-au-Prince: Civil Society Initiative.

Clastres, Pierre. 1987. *Society Against the State: Essays in Political Anthropology.* Translated by Robert Hurley and Abe Stein. Cambridge, MA: MIT Press.

Cleaver, Francis. 2002. *Masculinities Matter! Men, Gender, and Development, 2002.* London: Zed Books.

Clifford, James. 1988. *The Predicament of Culture: Twentieth Century Ethnography, Literature, and Art.* Cambridge, MA: Harvard University Press.

Clother, Charles. 2001. "Fonction des comités de quartier dans la lutte contre la pauvreté." Licence, Département d'anthropologie et sociologie, Faculté d'éthnologie, Université d'état de Haïti.

Cohn, Carol. 1987. "Sex and Death in the Rational World of Defense Intellectuals." *Signs* 12 (4): 687–718.

Collier, Paul. 2009. "Haiti: From Natural Catastrophe to Economic Security. A Report to the Secretary General of the United Nations." Oxford: Oxford University.

Comaroff, Jean, and John L. Comaroff. 1997. "Postcolonial Politics and Discourses of Democracy in Southern Africa: An Anthropological Reflection on African Political Modernities." *Journal of Anthropological Research* 53 (2): 123–46.

Comaroff, Jean, and John L. Comaroff. 1999a. "Occult Economies and the Violence of Abstraction: Notes from the South African Postcolony." *American Ethnologist* 26 (2): 279–303.

Comaroff, Jean, and John L. Comaroff. 2006a. "Criminal Obsessions, after Foucault." In *Law and Disorder in the Postcolony*, edited by Jean Comaroff and John L. Comaroff, 273–98. Chicago: University of Chicago Press.

Comaroff, Jean, and John L. Comaroff. 2006b. "Law and Disorder in the Postcolony: An Introduction." In *Law and Disorder in the Postcolony*, edited by Jean Comaroff and John L. Comaroff, 1–56. Chicago: University of Chicago Press.

Comaroff, John L., and Jean Comaroff. 1999b. *Civil Society and the Political Imagination in Africa: Critical Perspectives*. Chicago: University of Chicago Press.

Comaroff, Jean and John L. Comaroff. 2016. *The Truth about Crime: Sovereignty, Knowledge, and Social Order*. Chicago: University of Chicago Press.

Comhaire, Jean L. 1955. "The Haitian Chef de Section." *American Anthropologist* 57 (3): 620–24.

Contreas, Randol. 2012. *The Stickup Kids: Race, Drugs, Violence, and the American Dream*. Berkeley: University of California Press.

Crawford, James. 2006. *The Creation of States in International Law*. Oxford: Oxford University Press.

Dade, Carlo. 2007. "Haiti: Economic Growth and Violence." *Focal Point: Spotlight on the Americas* 6 (1): 1–3.

D'Adesky, Anne-Christine, and PotoFanm+Fi Coalition. 2012. "Beyond Shock, Charting the Landscape of Sexual Violence in Post-Quake Haiti: Progress, Challenges, and Emerging Trends, 2010–2012." Port-au-Prince: PotoFanm+Fi Coalition.

Daily Mail Reporter. 2010. "Haiti Earthquake: Machete-wielding Gangs Roam Streets as Fears Grow Death Toll Could Hit 200,000." *Daily Mail*, January 16.

Danner, Mark. 1987. "The Struggle for a Democratic Haiti." *The New York Times Magazine*, June 21.

Danner, Mark. 1989. "Beyond the Mountains." *The New Yorker*, November 27.

Danticat, Edwidge. 2007. *Brother, I'm Dying*. New York: Knopf.

Das, Veena, and Deborah Poole. 2004. *Anthropology in the Margins of the State*. Santa Fe, NM: School of American Research Press.

Dash, J. Michael. 2004. "The Disappearing Island: Haiti, History, and the Hemisphere." The Fifth Jagan Lecture and the Third Michael Baptista Lecture, York University, March 20.

Davis, Mike. 1990. *City of Quartz: Excavating the Future in Los Angeles*. London: Verso.

de Certeau, Michel. 1984. *The Practice of Everyday Life*. Translated by Steven Rendall. Berkeley: University of Califormia Press.

Deibert, Michael. 2005. *Notes on the Last Testament*. New York: Seven Stories Press.

Deibert, Michael. 2017. *Haiti Will Not Persih: A Recent History*. London: Zed Books.

Deleuze, Gilles, and Félix Guattari. 2002. *A Thousand Plateaus: Capitalism and Schizophrenia*. London: Continuum.

Delva, Joseph Guyler. 2010. "Gangs Return to Haiti Slum After Quake Prison Break." *Reuters*, January 17.

Deren, Maya. 1953. *Divine Horsemen: The Living Gods of Haiti*. London: Thames and Hudson.

DeWind, Josh, and David Kinley. 1988. *Aiding Migration: The Impact of International Development Assistance on Haiti*. Boulder, CO: Westview.

Di Leonardo, Micaela. 1991. *Gender at the Crossroads of Knowledge: Feminist Anthropology in the Postmodern Era*. Berkeley: University of California Press.

Di Stefano, Christine. 1991. *Configurations of Masculinity: A Feminist Perspective on Modern Political Theory*. Ithaca, NY: Cornell University Press.

Diamond, Irene, and Lee Quinby. 1988. *Feminism and Foucault: Reflections on Resistance*. Boston: Northeastern University Press.

Diamond, Larry. 1996. "Democracy in Latin America: Degrees, Illusions, and Directions for Consolidation." In *Beyond Sovereignty: Collectively Defending in a World of Sovereign States*, edited by Tom J. Farer, 52–105. Baltimore: Johns Hopkins University Press.

Diederich, Bernard, and Al Burt. 1970. *Papa Doc: Haiti and Its Dictator*. London: Bodley Head.

Douglas, Mary. 1966. *Purity and Danger: An Analysis of Concepts of Pollution and Taboo*. New York: Praeger.

Douglas, Mary. 1990. "Forward: No Free Gifts." In *The Gift*, edited by Marcel Mauss. New York: W.W. Norton.

Dubois, Laurent. 2004. *Avengers of the New World: The Story of the Haitian Revolution*. Cambridge, MA: Harvard University Press.

Dubois, Laurent. 2013. *Haiti: The Aftershocks of History*. New York: Picador.

Dudinik, Stefan, Karen Hagemann, and Anna Clark, eds. 2007. *Representing Masculinity: Male Citizenship in Modern Western Culture*. Manchester: Manchester University Press.

Dudinik, Stefan, Karen Hagemann, and John Tosh, eds. 2004. *Masculinities in Politics and War: Gendering Modern History*. Manchester: Manchester University Press.

Dupuy, Alex. 1997. *Haiti in the New World Order: The Limits of the Democratic Revolution*. Boulder, CO: Westview.

Dupuy, Alex. 2005a. "From Jean Bertrand Aristide to Gerard Latortue: The Unending Crisis of Democratization in Haiti." *Journal of Latin American Anthropology* 10 (1): 186–205.

Dupuy, Alex. 2005b. "Globalization, the World Bank, and the Haitian Economy." In *Contemporary Caribbean Cultures and Societies in a Global Context*, edited by Franklin W. Wright and Teresita Martinez-Vergne, 43–70. Chapel Hill: University of North Carolina Press.

Dupuy, Alex. 2007. *The Prophet and Power: Jean-Bertrand Aristide, the International Community, and Haiti*. Lanham, MD: Rowman and Littlefield.

Dupuy, Alex. 2009. "Indefensible: On Aristide, Violence, and Democracy." *Small Axe: Journal of Caribbean Criticism* 30: 161–73.

Durkheim, Emile. 1995. *The Elementary Forms of Religious Life*. Translated by Karen E. Fields. New York: Free Press.

Dziedzic, Michael, and Robert M. Perito. 2008. "Haiti: Confronting the Gangs of Port-au-Prince." Washington DC: United States Institute of Peace.

Escobar, Arturo. 1995. *Encountering Development: The Making and Unmaking of the Third World*. Princeton, NJ: Princeton University Press.

Etienne, Sauveur Pierre. 1997. "Haïti: l'Invasion des ONG." Port-au-Prince: Centre de recherche et de formation économique et sociale pour le développement.

Fabian, Johannes. 1983. *Time and the Other: How Anthropology Makes Its Object*. New York: Columbia University Press.

Fanon, Frantz. 2004. *The Wretched of the Earth*. Translated by Richard Philcox. New York: Grove Press.

Farer, Tom J. 1989. "Elections, Democracy, and Human Rights: Toward Union." *Human Rights Quarterly* 11: 504–21.

Farmer, Paul. 1988. "Bad Blood and Spoiled Milk: Bodily Fluids as Moral Barometers in Rural Haiti." *American Ethnologist* 15 (1): 62–83.

Farmer, Paul. 1992. *AIDS and Accusation: Haiti and the Geography of Blame*. Berkeley: University of California Press.

Farmer, Paul. 1996. "On Suffering and Structural Violence: A View from Below." *Daedalus* 125 (1): 261–83.

Farmer, Paul. 2003. *The Uses of Haiti*. Monroe, ME: Common Courage Press.

Farmer, Paul. 2004. "An Anthropology of Structural Violence." *Current Anthropology* 45 (3): 305–24.

Farmer, Paul. 2014. "Sacred Medicine." *Sojourners*, January1.

Fass, Simon. 1988. *Political Economy in Haiti: The Drama of Survival*. Piscataway, NJ: Transaction Publishers.

Fassin, Didier. 2011. *Humanitarian Reason: A Moral History of the Present*. Berkeley: University of California Press.

Fatton, Robert. 2002. *Haiti's Predatory Republic: The Unending Transition to Democracy*. Boulder, CO: Lynne Rienner.

Fatton, Robert. 2007. *The Roots of Haitian Despotism*. Boulder, CO: Lynne Rienner.

Feld, Steven. 1988. "Aesthetics as Iconicity of Style or "Lift up over Sounding": Getting Into the Kahluli Groove." *Yearbook for Traditional Music* 20: 74–113.

Feldman, Allen. 1991. *Formations of Violence: The Narrative of the Body and Political Terror in Northern Ireland*. Chicago: University of Chicago Press.

Feldman, Allen. 1994. "On Cultural Anesthesia: From Desert Storm to Rodney King." *American Ethnologist* 21 (2): 404–18.

Ferguson, James. 1990. *The Anti-Politics Machine: "Development," Depoliticization, and Bureaucratic Power in Lesotho*. Minneapolis: University of Minnesota Press.

Ferguson, James. 1993. "The Duvalier Dictatorship and Its Legacy of Crisis in Haiti." In *Modern Caribbean Politics*, edited by Anthony Payne and Paul R. Sutton. Baltimore: Johns Hopkins University.

Ferguson, James. 2005. "Anthropology and Its Evil Twin: 'Development in the Constitution of a Discipline.'" In *The Anthropology of Development and Globalization: From Classical Political Economy to Contemporary Neoliberalism*, edited by Marc Edelman and Angelique Haugerud, 140–54. Malden, MA: Blackwell.

Ferguson, James. 2006. *Global Shadows: Africa in the Neoliberal World Order*. Durham, NC: Duke University Press.

Fernandez, Rubem César, and Marcelo de Sousa Nascimento. 2007a. "Demographic Census of Bel Air." Rio de Janeiro: Viva Rio.

Fernandez, Rubem César, and Marcelo de Sousa Nascimento. 2007b. "Violence in Bel Air, Port-au-Prince: Household Survey." Rio de Janeiro: Quisqueya University, Viva Rio.

Fick, Carolyn E. 1990. *The Making of Haiti: The Saint Domingue Revolution from Below*. Knoxville: University of Tennessee Press.

FOKAL. 2003. "Press Statement in Regards to the Aborted Student Demonstration of December 5, 2003." Port-au-Prince: FOKAL.

Fouard, Jean. 1972. *Les marrons de la liberté*. Paris: Edition de l'Ecole.

Foucault, Michel. 2009. *Security, Territory, Population: Lectures at the Collège de France 1977–1978*. Edited by Michel Senellart. New York: Picador.

Frankétienne and Mohamed Taleb-Khyar. 1992. "Interview with Frankétienne." *Callaloo* 15 (2): 385–92.

Frankétienne. 1968 (2014). *Ready to Burst*. Translated by Kaiama Glover. New York: Archipelago Books.

Fraser, Nancy. 1992. "Rethinking the Public Sphere: A Contribution to the Critique of Actually Existing Democracy." In *Habermas and the Public Sphere*, edited by Craig Calhoun, 109–42. Cambridge, MA: MIT Press.

Freeman, Carla. 2000. *High Tech and High Heels in the Global Economy: Women, Work, and Pink-Collar Identities in the Caribbean*. Durham, NC: Duke University Press.

French, Howard. 1993. "Few Haitians Tempt U.S. Sea Barricade." *New York Times*, January 21.

Fuller, Anne, and Amy Wilentz. 1991. "Return to the Darkest Days: Human Rights in Haiti since the Coup." New York: Americas Watch, National Coalition for Haitian Refugees, and Physicians for Human Rights.

Galtung, Johan. 1969. "Violence, Peace, and Peace Research." *Journal of Peace Research* 6 (3): 167–91.

Gardella, Alexis. 2006. "Gender Assessment For USAID/Haiti." Washington, DC: United States Agency for International Development.

Gardner, Katy, and David Lewis. 1996. *Anthropology, Development, and the Postmodern Challenge.* Chicago: Pluto.

Geertz, Clifford. 1972. "Deep Play: Notes on the Balinese Cockfight." *Daedalus* 101 (1): 1–37.

Geertz, Clifford. 1973. *The Interpretation of Cultures: Selected Essays.* New York: Basic Books.

Geertz, Hildred. 1961. *The Javanese Family: A Study of Kinship and Socialization.* Glencoe, IL: Free Press.

Geggus, David. 1996. "Slave and Free Women in Saint Domingue." In *More than Chattel: Black Women and Slavery in the Americas,* edited by David Berry Gasper and Darlene Clark Hine. Bloomington: Indiana University Press.

Gerth, Hans Heinrich, and C. Wright Mills, eds. 1946. *From Max Weber: Essays in Sociology.* New York: Oxford University Press.

Geschiere, Peter. 1997. *The Modernity of Witchcraft: Politics and the Occult in Postcolonial Africa.* Charlotteville: University of Virginia Press.

Gilles, Alain. 2008. *Etat, conflit et violence en Haïti.* Oslo: Peace Research Institute.

Gilles, Alain. 2012. "Lien social, conflit, et violence en Haïti." Oslo, Norway: Peace Research Institute.

Girard, Philippe R. 2004. *Clinton in Haiti: The 1994 U.S. Invasion of Haiti.* New York: Palgrave Macmillan.

Girard, Philippe R. 2011. *The Slaves Who Defeated Napoleon: Toussaint Louverture and the Haitian War of Independence, 1801–1804.* Tuscaloosa: University of Alabama Press.

Glendhill, John. 2000. *Power and Its Disguises: Anthropological Perspectives on Politics.* Sterling, VA: Pluto.

Glick Schiller, Nina, and Georges Fouron. 2001. *Georges Woke Up Laughing.* Durham, NC: Duke University Press.

Goffman, Erving. 1967. *Interaction Ritual: Essays on Face-to-Face Behavior.* Chicago: Aldine.

Gogol, Eugene. 2015. *Utopia and the Dialectic in Latin American Liberation.* Leiden: Brill.

Goldstein, Daniel. 2012. *Outlawed: Between Security and Rights in a Bolivian City.* Durham, NC: Duke University Press.

Graeber, David. 2011. *Debt: The First 5,000 Years.* New York: Melville House.

Greenburg, Jennifer. 2013. "The 'Strong Arm' and the 'Friendly Hand': Military Humanitarianism in Post-earthquake Haiti." *Jounal of Haitian Studies* 19 (1): 60–87.

Gregory, Steven. 2003. "Men in Paradise: Sex Tourism and the Political Economy of Masculinity." In *Race, Nature, and the Politics of Difference,* edited by Donald S. Moore, 323–55. Durham, NC: Duke University Press.

Gregory, Steven. 2006. *The Devil behind the Mirror: Globalization and Politics in the Dominican Republic.* Berkeley: University of California Pres.

Griffin, Thomas M. 2004. "Haiti Human Rights Investigation: November 11–21, 2004." Miami: University of Miami School of Law, Center for the Study of Human Rights.

Gros, Jean-Germain. 2012. *State Failure, Underdevelopment, and Foreign Intervention in Haiti*. New York: Routledge.

Gutiérrez, Gustavo. 1973. *A Theology of Liberation*. Maryknoll, NY: Orbis Books.

Guyer, Jane. 2007. "Prophecy and the Near Future: Thoughts on Macroeconomic, Evangelical, and Punctuated Time." *American Ethnologist* 34 (3): 409–21.

Habermas, Jürgen. 1962 (1989). *The Structural Transformation of the Public Sphere*. Cambridge: MIT Press.

Hage, Ghassen. 2015. *Alter-politics: Critical Anthropology and the Radical Imagination*. Melbourne: University of Australia Press.

Hagedorn, John M. 1988. *People and Folks: Gangs, Crime, and the Underclass in a Rustbelt City*. Chicago: Lakeview Press.

Hagedorn, John M. 2009. *A World of Gangs: Armed Young Men and Gangsta Culture*. Berkeley: University of California Press.

Haiti Commission. 1991. "Haiti Commission for Inquiry into the Sepetember 30 Coup d'Etat: Preliminary Report from the Delegation Trip to Haiti." New York: Haiti Commission.

Haïti Progrès. 1999. "Anti-Violence Demonatration Sparks Clash." *Haïti Progrès*, June 2–8.

Hallward, Peter. 2007. *Damming the Flood: Haiti, Aristide, and the Politics of Containment*. New York: Verso.

Hansen, Thomas Blom, and Finn Stepputat, eds. 2005. *Sovereign Bodies: Citizens, Migrants, and States in the Postcolonial World*. Princeton, NJ: Princeton University Press.

Hansen, Thomas Blom, and Finn Stepputat. 2006. "Sovereignty Revisited." *Annual Review of Anthropology* 35: 295–315.

Haraway, Donna. 1988. "Situated Knowledges: The Science Question in Feminism and the Privilege of Partial Perspectives." *Feminist Studies* 14 (3): 575–99.

Harkness, Nicholas. 2013. "Softer Soju in South Korea." *Anthropological Theory* 13 (1/2): 12–30.

Hartikainen, Elina. 2017. "A Politics of Respect: Reconfiguring Democracy in Afro-Brazilian Religious Activism in Salvador, Brazil." *American Ethnologist* 45 (1): 87–99.

Herzfeld, Michael. 1993. *The Social Production of Indifference: Exploring the Symbolic Roots of Western Bureaucracy*. Chicago: University of Chicago Press.

Higate, Paul, and Marsha Henry. 2009. *Insecure Spaces: Peacekeeping, Power and Performance in Haiti, Kosovo and Liberia*. London: Zed Books.

Hobbes, Thomas. 1968. *Leviathan*. Edited by C. B. Macpherson. Baltimore: Penguin Books.

Hoffman, Danny. 2011. *The War Machines: Young Men and Violence in Sierra Leone and Liberia*. Durham, NC: Duke University Press.

Holston, James. 2008. *Insurgent Citizenship: Disjunctions of Democracy and Modernity in Brazil*. Princeton, NJ: Princeton University Press.

Honneth, Axel. 2007. *Disrespect: The Normative Foundations of Critical Theory*. Cambridge: Polity.

Hooper, Michael, Jocelyn McCalla, and Aryeh Neier. 1986. "Duvalierism since Duvalier." New York: National Coalition for Haitian Refugees and Americas Watch.

Humphrey, Caroline. 2008. "Sovereignty." In *A Companion to the Anthropology of Politics*, edited by David Nugent and Joan Vincent, 416–36. Malden, MA: Blackwell.

Human Rights Watch. 1999. "Haiti: Human Rights Developments." New York: Human Rights Watch.

Humanitarian Accountability Project and International Organization of Migration. 2010. "Camp Committee Assessment: A Tool for Deciding How to Work with Camp Committees." Port-au-Prince: Humanitarian Accountability Project.

Hurbon, Laënnec. 1979. *Culture et dictature en Haïti: L'imaginaire sous contrôle*. Paris: L'Harmattan.

Hurbon, Laënnec. 1995. *Voodoo: Search for the Spirit*. New York: H. N. Abrams.

Ibekwe, Chinweizu. 2010. "On Negrophobia: Psychoneurotic Obstacles to Black Autonomy (or Why I Just Love Michael Jackson)." *Afrikan Consciousness*, December 31, https://afrikanconsciousness.wordpress.com/.

Jackson, John. 2005. *Real Black: Adventures in Racial Solidarity*. Chicago: University of Chicago Press.

Jaffe, Rivke. 2012a. "Crime and Insurgent Citizenship: Extra-State Rule and Belonging in Urban Jamaica." *Development* 55 (2): 219–23.

Jaffe, Rivke. 2012b. "Talkin' 'Bout the Ghetto: Popular Culture and Urban Imaginaries of Immobility." *International Journal of Urban and Regional Research* 36 (4): 674–88.

Jaffe, Rivke. 2013. "The Hybrid State: Crime and Insurgent Citizenship in Urban Jamaica." *American Ethnologist* 40 (4): 734–48.

Jaffe, Rivke. 2015. "From Maroons to Dons: Sovereignty, Violence, and Law in Jamaica." *Critique of Anthropology* 35 (1): 47–63.

James, Erica Caple. 2004. "Political Economy of Trauma in Haiti in the Democratic Era of Insecurity." *Culture, Medicine, and Psychiatry* 28 (2): 127–49.

James, Erica Caple. 2010. *Democratic Insecurities: Violence, Trauma, and Intervention in Haiti*. Berkeley: University of California Press.

Jefferson, LaShawn, Regan Ralph, Dorothy Thomas, and Evelyn Miah. 1994. "Rape in Haiti: A Weapon of Terror." Washington, DC: Human Rights Watch and National Coalition for Haitian Refugees.

Jensen, Steffen. 2005. "Above the Law: Practices of Sovereignty in Surrey Estate, Cape Town." In *Sovereign Bodies: Citizens, Migrants, and States in the Postcolonial World*, edited by Thomas Blom Hansen and Finn Stepputat, 218–40. Princeton, NJ: Princeton University Press.

JILAP. 2014. "Jè wè, bouch fèt pou pale: Vyolans nan lari zòn metwopolitèn nan." Port-au-Prince: JILAP, Commission épiscopale nationale justice et paix.

Kahn, Jeffrey Sterling. 2013. "Islands of Sovereignty: Haitian Migration and the Borders of Empire." PhD dissertation, University of Chicago.

Kahn, Jeffrey Sterling. 2015. "Smugglers, Migrants, and Demons: Passages of Wealth in the Haitian Caribbean." Department of Anthropology Colloquium, Dartmouth College, May 8.

Katz, Jonathan. 2013. *The Big Truck That Went By: How the World Came to Save Haiti and Left behind a Disaster*. New York: Palgrave Macmillan.

Kemp, Walter, Mark Shaw, and Arthur Boutellis. 2013. "The Elephant in the Room: How Can Peace Operations Deal with Organized Crime?" New York: International Peace Institute.

Kivland, Chelsey. 2012. "Unmaking the State in 'Occupied' Haiti." *PoLAR: Political and Legal Anthropology* 35 (2): 247–69.

Kivland, Chelsey. 2014. "Becoming a Force in the Zone: Hedonopolitics, Masculinity, and the Quest for Respect on Haiti's Streets." *Cultural Anthropology* 29 (4): 672–98.

Kivland, Chelsey. 2017. "Street Sovereignty: Power, Violence, and Respect among Haitian Baz." In *Who Owns Haiti? People, Power, and Sovereingty*, edited by Robert Maguire and Scott Freeman, 140–65. Gainesville: University of Florida Press.

Kivland, Chelsey, and Anne Sosin. 2018. "Why Climate Change Is Worsening Public Health Problems." *The Conversation*, January 25. https://theconversation.com/why-climate-change-is-worsening-public-health-problems-86193.

Knorr-Cetina, Karin. 1999. *Epistemic Cultures: How the Sciences Make Knowledge*. Cambridge, MA: Harvard University Press.

Kolbe, Athena R., Royce A. Hutson, Harry Shannon, Eileen Trzcinski, Bart Miles, Naomi Levitz, Marie Puccio, Leah James, Jean Roger Noel, and Robert Muggah. 2010. "Mortality, Crime, and Access to Basic Needs before and after the Haiti Earthquake: A Random Survey of Port-au-Prince Households." *Medicine, Conflict, and Survival* 26 (4): 281–97.

Kolbe, Athena R., and Robert Muggah. 2012. "Haiti's Urban Crime Wave? Results from Monthly Household Surveys." Rio de Janeiro: Igrarpé Institute.

Koonings, Kees, and Dirk Kruijt. 2013. *Organised Violence and State Failure in Latin America*. London: Zed Books.

Krasner, Stephen D. 1999. *Sovereignty: Organized Hypocrisy*. Princeton, NJ: Princeton University Press.

Laguerre, Michel S. 1976a. "Bel Air, Port-au-Prince: From Slave and Maroon Settlement to Contemporary Black Ghetto." *Contributions of the Latin American Anthropology Group* 1 (1): 26–38.

Laguerre, Michel S. 1976b. "Black Ghetto as an Internal Colony: Socioeconomic Adaptation of a Haitian Urban Community." Ph.D. dissertation, University of Illinois, Urbana-Champaign.

Laguerre, Michel S. 1983. *Urban Life in the Caribbean: A Study of a Haitian Urban Community*. Cambridge, MA: Schenkman.

Laguerre, Michel S. 1993. *The Military and Society in Haiti*. Knoxville: University of Tennessee Press.

Langer, Erick, and Elena Munoz, eds. 2003. *Contemporary Indigenous Movements in Latin America*. Lanham, MD: Rowman and Littlefield.

Larose, Serge. 1977. "The Meaning of Africa in Haitian Vodu." In *Symbols and Sentiments: Cross Cultural Studies in Symbolism*, edited by Joan Lewis, 85–89. New York: Academic Press.

Lassiter, Luke Eric. 2009. *Invitation to Anthropology*. Lantham, MD: AltaMira Press.

Latour, Bruno. 1999. *Pandora's Hope: Essays on the Reality of Science Studies*. Cambridge, MA: Harvard University Press.

Leacock, Eleanor Burke. 1981. *Myths of Male Dominance: Collected Articles on Women Cross-culturally*. New York: Monthly Review Press.

Lévi-Strauss, Claude. 1966. *The Savage Mind*. Chicago: University of Chicago Press.

Lewis, Oscar. 1959. *Five Families: Mexican Case Studies in the Culture of Poverty*. New York: Basic Books.

Lindenmayor, Elizabeth, Sean Blaschke, Andrew Lucas Cramer, Marcy Hersh, Carina Lakovits, Leila Makarechi, and Alejandro Gomez Palma. 2009. "Haiti: A Future beyond Peacekeeping." New York: Columbia University.

Locher, Huldrych Casper. 1978. "The Fate of Migrants in Urban Haiti: A Survey of Three Port-au-Prince Neighborhoods." PhD dissertation, Yale University.

Luhrmann, T. M. 1996. *The Good Parsi: The Fate of a Colonial Elite in a Postcolonial Society*. Cambridge, MA: Harvard University Press.

Lundahl, Mats. 2013. *The Political Economy of Disaster: Destitution, Plunder, and Earthquake in Haiti*. New York: Routledge.

MacIntyre, Alasdair. 1981 (2007). *After Virtue: A Study in Moral Theory*. Nortre Dame, IN: University of Notre Dame Press.

Madiou, Thomas. 1847. "Histoire d'Haïti." Port-au-Prince: Imprimerie de Joseph Courtois.

MADRE, Komisyon Fanm Viktim Pou Viktim, Fanm Viktim Leve Kanpe, Kodinasyon Nasyonal Viktim Direk, and The International Human Rights Clinic at the City University of New York School of Law. 2011. "Gender-based Violence against Haitian Women and Girls in Internal Displacement Camps." Port-au-Prince: MADRE.

Maguire, Robert. 1990. "The Peasantry and Politcal Change in Haiti." *Caribbean Affairs* 4 (2): 1–18.

Malkki, Liisa H. 1992. "National Geographic: The Rooting of Peoples and the Territorialization of National Identity among Scholars and Refugees." *Cultural Anthropology* 7 (1): 22–44.

Manigat, Leslie F. 1977. "The Relationship between Marronage and Slave Revolts and Revolution in Saint-Domingue-Haiti." *Annals of the New York Academy of Sciences* 292 (1): 420–38.

Manigat, Sabine. 1997. "Haiti: Popular Sectors and the Crisis in Port-au-Prince." In *The Urban Caribbean: Transition to the New Global Economy,* edited by Alejandro Portes, Carlos Dore-Cabral, and Patricia Landolt, 87–123. Baltimore: Johns Hopkins University Press.

Mann, Bonnie. 2014. *Sovereign Masculinity: Gender Lessons from the War on Terror.* New York: Oxford University Press.

Mannheim, Karl. 1936 (1997). *Ideology and Utopia.* New York: Routledge.

Marcelin, Louis Herns. 2012. "In the Name of the Nation: Blood Symbolism and the Political Habitus of Violence in Haiti." *American Anthropologist* 114 (2): 253–66.

Marx, Karl, Friedrich Engels, and C. J. Arthur. 1970. *The German Ideology, Part One.* New York: International Publishers.

Maternowska, M. Catherine. 2006. *Reproducing Inequities: Poverty and the Politics of Population in Haiti.* New Brunswick, NJ: Rutgers University Press.

Mauss, Marcel. 1954 (1990). *The Gift: Forms and Functions of Exchange in Archaic Societies.* Glencoe, IL: Free Press.

Mazzarella, William. 2017. *The Mana of Mass Society.* Chicago: University of Chicago Press.

Mbembe, Achille. 2001. *On the Postcolony* Berkeley: University of California Press.

Mbembe, Achille. 2003. "Necropolitics." *Public Culture* 15 (1): 11–40.

Mbembe, Achille. 2006. "On the Postcolony: A Brief Response to Critics." *African Identities* 4 (2): 143–78.

McAlister, Elizabeth A. 2002. *Rara! Vodou, Power, and Performance in Haiti and Its Diaspora.* Berkeley: University of California Press.

McGee, R. Jon, and Richard Warms. 2004. *Anthropological Theory: An Introductory History.* New York: McGraw Hill.

McNee, Lisa. 2001. "Review of *On the Postcolony* by Achille Mbembe." *The International Journal of African Historical Study* 34 (1): 164–65.

Mendez, Jennifer Bickman. 2005. *From the Revolution to the Maquiladoras: Gender, Labor, and Globalization in Nicaragua.* Durham, NC: Duke University Press.

Michel, Georges. 1992. *La constitution de 1987: Souvenirs d'un constituant.* Port-au-Prince: Le Natal.

Miller, Daniel, Michael Rowlands, and Chris Tilley. 1995. *Domination and Resistance.* New York: Routledge.

Mills, C. Wright. 1956 (1999). *The Power Elite.* New York: Oxford University Press.

Minn, Pierre. 2016. "Components of a Moral Economy: Interest, Credit, and Debt in Haiti's Transnational Healthcare System." *American Anthropologist* 118 (1): 78–90.

Mintz, Sidney. 1996. "Black Women, Economic Roles, and Cultural Traditions." In *Caribbean Freedom: Economy and Society from Emancipation to the Present. A Student Reader,* edited by Hilary Beckles and Verene Shepherd, 238–44. Princeton, NJ: Marcus Weiner.

Mintz, Sidney W. 1974. *Worker in the Cane: A Puerto Rican Life History.* New York: W. W. Norton.

Mintz, Sidney, and Eric R. Wolf. 1950. "An Analysis of Ritual Co-Parenthood (Compadrazgo)." *Southwestern Journal of Anthropology* 6 (4): 341–68.

Misse, Michel. 2018. "Violence, Criminal Subjection, and Political Merchandise in Brazil: An Overview from Rio." *International Journal of Criminology and Sociology* 7: 135–48.

Mobekk, Erin. 2017. *UN Peace Operations: Lessons from Haiti, 1994–2016.* New York: Routledge.

Moïse, Claude. 1988. *Constitutions et luttes de pouvoir en Haïti, 1804–1987: La faillite des classes dirigeantes.* Vol. 1. Montréal: Éditions du CIDIHCA.

Molina, Natalia. 2014. *How Race Is Made in America: Immigration, Citizenship, and the Historical Power of Racial Scripts.* Berkeley: University of California Press.

Morton, Alice. 1997. "Haiti: NGO Sector." Washington DC: World Bank.

Mouffe, Chantal. 2000. "Deliberative Democracy or Agonistic Pluralism." Vienna: Institute for Advanced Study.

Moynihan, Daniel Patrick. 1965. "The Negro Family: The Case for National Action." Washington DC: Office of Policy Planning and Research, United States Department of Labor.

Muggah, Robert, and Helen Moestue. 2009. "Social Integration Ergo Stabilization." Rio de Janeiro: Viva Rio.

Muggah, Robert, and Athena Kolbe. 2011. "Securing the State: Haiti before and after the Earthquake." Geneva: Small Arms Survey.

Munn, Nancy D. 1986. *The Fame of Gawa: A Symbolic Study of Value Transformation in a Massim Society, Papua New Guinea.* Cambridge: Cambridge University Press.

Murray-Román, Jeannine. 2015. "Rereading the Diminutive: Caribbean Chaos Theory in Antonio Benítez-Rojo, Edouard Glissant, and Wilson Harris." *Small Axe: Journal of Caribbean Criticism* 19 (46): 20–36.

Nagengast, Carole. 1994. "Violence, Terror, and the Crisis of the State." *Annual Review of Anthropology* 23: 109–36.

Neiburg, Federico, and Natacha Nicaise. 2010. "Garbage, Stigmatization, Commerce, Politics." Rio de Janeiro: Viva Rio.

Neiburg, Frederico. 2016. "A True Coin of Their Dreams: Imaginary Monies in Haiti." *HAU: Journal of Ethnographic Theory* 6 (1): 75–93.

Neiburg, Federico. 2017. "Serendipitous Involvement: Making Peace in the Geto." In *If Truth Be Told: The Politics of Public Ethnography,* edited by Didier Fassin, 119–37. Durham, NC: Duke University Press.

Neiburg, Federico, Natacha Nicaise, and Pedro Braum. 2011. *Leaders in Bel Air.* Rio de Janeiro: Viva Rio.

Nelson, Diana. 1998. *National Manhood: Capitalist Citizenship and the Imagined Fraternity of White Men.* Durham, NC: Duke University Press.

Nesbitt, Nick. 2009. "Aristide and the Politics of Democratization." *Small Axe: Journal of Caribbean Criticism* 13 (3 [30]): 137–47.

Nicholls, David. 1996. *From Dessalines to Duvalier: Race, Colour, and National Independence in Haiti.* New Brunswick, NJ: Rutgers University Press.

Nicholls, David. 2013. "Rural Protest and Peasant Revolt." In *Haitian History: New Perspectives,* edited by Alyssa Goldstein Sepinwall, 180–96. New York: Routledge.

Nugent, David. 2004. "Governing States." In *A Companion to the Anthropology of Politics,* edited by David Nugent and Joan Vincent, 198–215. Malden, MA: Blackwell.

O'Connor, Maura R. 2012. "Two Years Later, Haitian Earthquake Death Toll in Dispute." *Columbia Journalism Review,* January 12.

O'Donnell, Guillermo, J. Vargas Cullel, and O. M. Iazzetta. 2004. *The Quality of Democracy: Theory and Applications.* Notre Dame, IN: University of Notre Dame Press.

Omi, Michael, and Howard Winant. 1990. *Racial Formation in the United States: From the 1960s to the 1990s*. New York: Routledge.

Ong, Aihwa. 1999. *Flexible Citizenship: The Cultural Logics of Transnationality*. Durham, NC: Duke University Press.

Ong, Aihwa. 2006. *Neoliberalism as Exception: Mutations in Citizenship and Sovereignty*. Durham, NC: Duke University Press.

Padgett, Tim. 2010. "Will Criminal Gangs Take Control in Haiti's Chaos." *Time*, January 14.

Paige, Jeffrey. 1975. *Agrarian Revolution: Social Movements and Export Agriculture in the Developed World*. New York: Free Press.

Pallares, Amalia. 2002. *From Peasant Struggles to Indian Resistance: The Ecuadorian Andes in the Late Twentieth Century*. Norman: University of Oklahoma Press.

Parsons, Kenneth. 2007. "Structural Violence and Power." *A Journal of Social Justice* 19 (2): 173–81.

Peirce, Charles S. 1897 (1997). *The Collected Works of Charles Sanders Peirce*. Vol. 2. Edited by Charles Hartshorne and Paul Weiss. Cambridge, MA: Harvard University Press.

Pessar, Patricia. 2005. "Women, Gender, and International Migration across and beyond the Americas: Inequalities and Limited Empowerment." Mexico City: United Nations Secretariat.

Philpott, Daniel. 1997. "Ideas and the Evolution of Sovereignty." In *State Sovereignty: Change and Persistence in International Relations*, edited by Sohail H. Hashmi, 15–48. University Park: Pennsylvania State University Press.

Pierre-Charles, Gérard. 1973. *Radiographie d'une dictature: Haiti et Duvalier*. Montreal: Editions Nouvelle Optique.

Pierre-Charles, Gérard. 1988. "The Democratic Revolution in Haiti." *Latin American Perspectives* 15 (3): 64–76.

Pierre-Charles, Gérard. 2000. *Haïti jamais plus: Les violations de droits de l'homme à l'époque de Duvaliers*. Port-au-Prince: Editions du Cresfed.

Plummer, Brenda. 1988. *Haiti and the Great Powers, 1902–1915*. Baton Rouge: Louisiana State University Press.

Polyné, Millery. 2013. *The Idea of Haiti: Rethinking Crisis and Development*. Minneapolis: University of Minnesota Press.

Popkin, Jeremy. 2007. *Facing Racial Revoluton: Eyewitness Accounts of the Haitian Insurrection*. Chicago: University of Chicago Press.

Przeworski, Adam. 1991. *Democracy and the Market: Political and Economic Reforms in Eastern Europe and Latin America*. Cambridge: Cambridge University Press.

Przeworski, Adam. 2000. *Democracy and Development: Political Institutions and Well-being in the World, 1950–1990*. Cambridge: Cambridge University Press.

Radcliffe-Brown, A. R. 1940 (1955). "Preface." In *African Political Systems*, edited by Meyer Fortes and E. Evans-Pritchard. London: Oxford University Press.

Ralph, Laurence. 2013. "The Qualia of Pain: How Police Torture Shapes Historical Consciousness." *Anthropological Theory* 13 (1/2): 104–18.

Ralph, Laurence. 2014. *Renegade Dreams: Living through Injury in Gangland Chicago*. Chicago: University of Chicago Press.

Rawls, John. 1971. *A Theory of Justice*. Cambridge, MA: Belknap.

Reddock, Rhoda. 1985. "Women and Slavery in the Caribbean: A Feminist Perspective." *Latin American Perspectives* 44 (12): 63–80.

Redfield, Peter. 2005. "Doctors, Borders, and Life in Crisis." *Cultural Anthropology* 20 (3): 328–61.

Redfield, Peter. 2012. "Bioexpectations: Life Technologies as Humanitarian Goods." *Public Culture* 24 (1): 157–84.

Redfield, Peter. 2013. *Life in Crisis: The Ethical Journey of Doctors without Borders.* Berkeley: University of California Press.

Republic of Haiti. 1994. "Strategy of Social and Economic Reconstruction." Paris: Government of Haiti.

Republic of Haiti. 2010. "Action Plan for the National Recovery and Development of Haiti." New York: Government of the Republic of Haiti.

Reyes, Angela. 2017. "Ontology of Fake: Discerning the Philippine Elite." *Signs and Society* 5 (S1): 100–127.

Ribeiro, Gustavo Lins, and Arturo Escobar, eds. 2006. *World Anthropologies: Disciplinary Transformations within Systems of Power.* New York: Berg.

Richani, Nazih. 2007. "Caudillos and the Crisis of the Colombian State: Fragmented Sovereignty, the War System, and the Privatization of Counterinsurgency in Colombia." *Third World Quarterly* 28 (2): 403–17.

Richman, Karen E. 2005. *Migration and Vodou.* Gainesville: University Press of Florida.

Rodgers, Dennis. 2006. "The State as a Gang: Conceptualizing the Governmentality of Violence in Contemporary Nicaragua." *Critique of Anthropology* 26 (3): 315–30.

Rohlehr, Gordon. 2004. "I Lawa: The Construction of Masculinity in Trinidad and Tobago Calypso." In *Interrogating Caribbean Masculinities: Theoretical and Empirical Analyses,* edited by Rhoda E. Reddock, 326–403. Mona: University of the West Indies Press.

Roitman, Janet. 1998. "The Garrison-Entrepôt." *Cahiers d'études africaines* 35 (150–52): 297–329.

Rosaldo, Renato. 1989. *Culture and Truth: The Remaking of Social Analysis.* Boston, MA: Beacon.

Rose, Tricia. 1994. *Black Noise: Rap Music and Black Culture in Contemporary America.* Hanover, CT: Wesleyan University Press.

Sahlins, Marshall D. 1963. "Poor Man, Rich Man, Big-Man, Chief: Political Types in Melanesia and Polynesia." *Comparative Studies in Society and History* 5 (3): 285–303.

Said, Edward. 1978. *Orientalism.* New York: Pantheon.

Sanday, Peggy Reeves. 2007. *Fraternity Gang Rape: Sex, Brotherhood, and Privilege on Campus.* New York: New York University Press.

Sassen, Saskia. 1996. *Losing Control? Sovereignty in an Age of Globalization.* New York: Columbia University Press.

Scheper-Hughes, Nancy. 1992. *Death without Weeping: The Violence of Everyday Life in Brazil.* Berkeley: University of California Press.

Scheper-Hughes, Nancy. 1995. "The Primacy of the Ethical: Propositions for a Militant Anthropology." *Current Anthropology* 36 (3): 409–40.

Scheper-Hughes, Nancy. 2000. "Ire in Ireland." *Ethnography* 1 (1): 117–40.

Schoepfle, Gregory, and Jorge F. Pérez-López. 1992. "Export-oriented Assembly Operations in the Caribbean." In *Trade Issues in the Caribbean,* edited by Irma Tirado de Alonso, 125–58. Philadelphia: Gordon and Breach.

Schuller, Mark. 2009. "Gluing Globalization: NGOs as Intermediaries in Haiti." *PoLAR: Political and Legal Anthropology Review* 32 (1): 84–104.

Schuller, Mark. 2010. "Mister Blan, or, the Incredible Whiteness of Being (an Anthropologist)." In *Fieldwork Identities in the Caribbean,* edited by Erin B. Taylor, 105–30. Coconut Creek, FL: Caribbean Studies Press.

Schuller, Mark. 2012a. "Haiti, an Island Luminous: The NGOs." http://islandluminous. fiu.edu/part11-slide15.html.

Schuller, Mark. 2012b. *Killing with Kindness: Haiti, International Aid, and NGOs.* New Brunswick, NJ: Rutgers University Press.

Schuller, Mark. 2016. *Humanitarian Aftershocks in Haiti*. New Brunswick, NJ: Rutgers University Press.

Schumpeter, Joseph Alois. 1950. *Capitalism, Socialism, and Democracy*. 3rd ed. New York: Harper.

Schuster, Caroline. 2014. "The Social Unit of Debt: Gender and Creditworthiness in Paraguayan Microfinance." *American Ethnologist* 41 (3): 563–78.

Scott, David. 1997. "The 'Culture' of Violence Fallacy." *Small Axe: Journal of Caribbean Criticism* 1 (2): 140–47.

Scott, James C. 1985. *Weapons of the Weak: Everyday Forms of Peasant Resistance*. New Haven: Yale University Press.

Scott, James C. 1990. *Domination and the Arts of Resistance: Hidden Transcripts*. New Haven: Yale University Press.

Scott, James C. 1998. *Seeing Like a State: How Certain Schemes to Improve the Human Condition Have Failed*. New Haven: Yale University Press.

Scott, James C. 2009. *The Art of Not Being Governed: An Anarchist History of Upland Southeast Asia*. New Haven: Yale University Press.

Scott, Joan Wallach. 1986. "Gender: A Useful Category of Historical Analysis." *The American Historical Review* 91 (5): 1053–75.

Sedgwick, Eve Kosofsky. 1985. *Between Men: English Literature and Male Homosocial Desire*. New York: Columbia University Press.

Selby, Lynn. 2015. "'Let Us Forge One Path Together': Gender, Class, and Political Subjectivities in a Haitian Popular Neighborhood." PhD dissertation, University of Texas.

Shamsie, Yasmine, and Andrew S. Thompson, eds. 2006. *Haiti: Hope for a Fragile State*. Waterloo, Canada: Wilfrid Laurier University.

Sharp, Leslie. 2007. "Commodification of the Body and Its Parts." *Annual Review of Anthropology* 29: 287–328.

Sheller, Mimi. 2000. *Democracy after Slavery: Black Publics and Peasant Radicalism in Haiti and Jamaica*. Gainesville: University of Florida Press.

Sheller, Mimi. 2012. *Citizenship from Below: Erotic Agency and Caribbean Freedom*. Durham, NC: Duke University Press.

Simmel, Georg. 1955. *Conflict and the Web of Group Affiliations*. New York: Free Press.

Singh, Bhrigupati. 2011. "Agonistic Intimacy and Moral Aspiration in Popular Hinduism: A Study in the Politcal Theology of the Neighbor." *American Ethnologist* 38 (3): 430–50.

Sinha, Mrinalini. 1995. *Colonial Masculinity: The "Manly Englishman" and the "Effeminate Bengali" in the Late Nineteenth Century*. New York: St. Martin's Press.

Smarth, Luc. 1997. "Popular Organizations and the Transition to Democracy in Haiti." In *Community Power and Grassroots Democracy: The Transformation of Social Life*, edited by Michael Kaufmann and Harolodo Dillo Alfonso, 102–25. London: Zed Books.

Smarth, Luc. 1998. *Les organisations populaires en Haïti: Une étude exploratoire de la zone métropolitaine de Port-au-Prince*. Port-au-Prince: CRESDIP/Bois Caiman Press.

Smith, Jennie Marcelle. 2001. *When the Hands Are Many: Community Organization and Social Change in Rural Haiti*. Ithaca, NY: Cornell University Press.

Smith, Katherine. 2012. "Atis Rezistans: Gede and the Art of Vagabondaj." In *Obeah and Other Powers: The Politics of Caribbean Religion and Healing*, edited by Diana Paton, 123–48. Durham, NC: Duke University Press.

Smith, Matthew J. 2009. *Red and Black in Haiti: Radicalism, Conflict, and Political Change, 1934–1957*. Chapel Hill: University of North Carolina Press.

Smith, Matthew J. 2014. *Liberty, Fraternity, Exile: Haiti and Jamaica after Emancipation*. Chapel Hill: University of North Carolina Press.

Smucker, Glenn. 1983. "Peasants and Development Politics: A Study in Haitian Class and Culture." PhD dissertation, New School for Social Research.

Sontag, Deborah. 2012. "Rebuilding in Haiti Lags after Billions in Post-Quake Aid." *New York Times*, December 23.

Spivak, Gayatri. 1988. "Can the Subaltern Speak?" In *Marxism and the Interpretation of Culture*, edited by Cary Nelson and Lawrence Grossberg, 271–313. Champaign: University of Illinois Press.

Sprague, Jeb. 2012. *Paramilitarism and the Assault on Democracy in Haiti*. New York: Monthly Review Press.

Stevens, Alta Mae. 1995. "Manje in Haitian Creole: The Symbolic Significance of Manje in Haitian Creole." *Journal of Haitian Studies* 1 (1): 75–88.

Stinchcombe, Arthur. 1996. *Sugar Island Slavery in the Age of Enlightenment: The Political Economy of the Caribbean World*. Princeton, NJ: Princeton University Press.

Stolzkoff, Norman C. 2000. *Wake the Town and Tell the People: Dancehall Culture in Jamaica*. Durham, NC: Duke University Press.

Sutton, Constance. 1974. "Cultural Duality in the Caribbean." *Caribbean Studies* 14 (2): 96–101.

Sylvester, Christine. 2006. "Bare Life as a Development/Postcolonial Problematic." *The Geographical Journal* 172 (1): 66–77.

Taylor, Charles. 1990. "Modes of Civil Society." *Public Culture* 3 (1): 95–118.

Taylor, Diana. 2003. *The Archive and the Repertoire: Performing Cultural Memory in the Americas*. Durham, NC: Duke University Press.

Terrazas, Aaron. 2010. "Haitian Immigrants in the United States." Washington, DC: Migration Information Source.

Thomas, Deborah A. 2004. *Modern Blackness: Nationalism, Globalization, and the Politics of Culture in Jamaica*. Durham, NC: Duke University Press.

Thomas, Deborah A. 2011. *Exceptional Violence: Embodied Citizenship in Transnational Jamaica*. Durham, NC: Duke University Press.

Thomas, Deborah A. 2016. "Time and the Otherwise: Plantations, Garrisons and Being Human in the Caribbean." *Anthropological Theory* 16 (23): 177–200.

Thomas, Kedron, and Kevin Lewis O'Neill. 2011. *Securing the City: Neoliberalism, Space, and Insecurity in Postwar Guatemala*. Durham, NC: Duke University Press.

Tilly, Charles. 1985. "War Making and State Making as Organized Crime." In *Bringing the State Back In*, edited by Peter Evans, Dietrich Rueschemeyer, and Theda Skocpol, 169–91. Cambridge: Cambridge University Press.

Trouillot, Michel Rolph. 1990a. *Haiti, State against Nation: The Origins and Legacy of Duvalierism*. New York: Monthly Review Press.

Trouillot, Michel Rolph. 1990b. "The Odd and the Ordinary: Haiti, the Caribbean, and the World." *Cimarròn: New Perspectives on the Caribbean* 2 (3): 3–12.

Trouillot, Michel Rolph. 1995. *Silencing the Past: Power and the Production of History*. Boston: Beacon.

Trouillot, Michel Rolph. 2001. "The Anthropology of the State in the Age of Globalization." *Current Anthropology* 42 (1): 125–38.

Trouillot, Michel Rolph. 2003. *Global Transformations: Anthropology and the Modern World*. New York: Palgrave Macmillan.

Trump, Donald J. 2017. "America First: A Budget Blueprint to Make America Great Again." Washington, DC: Office of Management and Budget: Executive Office of the President of the United States.

Turner, Victor. 1967. *The Forest of Symbols: Aspects of Ndembu Ritual*. Ithaca, NY: Cornell University Press.

Ulysse, Gina A. 2015. *Why Haiti Needs New Narratives: A Post-Quake Chronicle*. Middletown, CT: Wesleyan University Press.

United Nations Office of the Secretary General. 2012. "Lessons from Haiti." New York: Office of the Secretary-General's Special Adviser on Community-based Medicine and Lessons from Haiti.

United States Central Intelligence Agency. 2013. *The World Factbook 2013–14*. Washington, DC: Central Intelligence Agency.

United States Central Intelligence Agency. 2015. *The World Factbook 2015*. Washington, DC: Central Intelligence Agency.

UNODC (United Nations Office on Drugs and Crime). 2013. "Global Study on Homicide: Trends, Contexts, Data." Vienna: UNODC.

Valdman, Albert. 2007. *Haitian Creole-English Bilingual Dictionary*. Indianapolis: Indiana University Creole Institute.

Venkatesh, Sudhir Alladi. 2000. *American Project: The Rise and Fall of a Modern Ghetto*. Cambridge, MA: Harvard University Press.

Venkatesh, Sudhir Alladi, and Steven D. Levitt. 2000. "Are We a Family or a Business? History and Disjuncture in the American Street Gang." *Theory and Society* 29 (4): 427–62.

Verhelst, Thierry. 1990. *No Life without Roots: Culture and Development*. Translated by Bob Cumming. London: Zed Books.

Viveiros de Castro, Eduardo. 2010. "The Untimely, Again." Introduction to Pierre Clastres, *Archaeology of Violence*, 9–52. Translated by Jeanine Herman and Ashley Lebner. Los Angeles: Semiotext(e).

Wacquant, Loïc. 2002. "From Slavery to Mass Incarceration: Rethinking the 'Race Question' in the U.S." *New Left Review* 13: 41–60.

Wacquant, Loïc. 2004. "Decivilizing and Demonizing: The Remaking of the Black American Ghetto." In *The Sociology of Norbert Elias*, edited by Steven Loyal and Stephen Quilley, 95–121. Cambridge: Cambridge University Press.

Warren, Marcus. 2003. "Monsters and Cannibals at War in Haiti." *The Telegraph*, December 13.

Watanabe, Chika. 2015. "Commitments of Debt: Temporality and the Meaning of Aid Work in a Japanese NGO in Myanmar." *American Anthropologist* 117 (3): 468–79.

Weber, Max. 1946 (1998). "Politics as a Vocation." In *From Max Weber: Essays in Sociology*, edited by Hans Heinrich Gerth and C. Wright Mills, 77–128. New York: Oxford University Press.

Wedeen, Lisa. 2008. *Peripheral Visions: Publics, Power, and Performance in Yemen*. Chicago: University of Chicago Press.

West, Harry G. 2003. "'Who Rules Us Now?' Identity Tokens, Sorcery, and Other Metaphors in the 1994 Mozambique Elections." In *Transparency and Conspiracy: Ethnographies of Suspicion in the New World Order*, edited by Harry G. West and Todd Sanders. Durham, NC: Duke University Press.

White, Robert E. 1997. "Haiti: Democrats vs. Democracy." *International Policy Report*. Washington, DC: Center for International Policy.

Whyte, William Foote. 1943 (1981). *Street Corner Society*. Chicago: University of Chicago Press.

Wilentz, Amy. 1989. *The Rainy Season: Haiti since Duvalier*. New York: Simon and Schuster.

Wilentz, Amy. 2013. *Farewell Fred Voodoo: A Letter from Haiti*. New York: Simon and Schuster.

Wilson, Peter J. 1973. *Crab Antics: The Social Anthropology of English-speaking Negro Societies of the Caribbean*. New Haven: Yale University Press.

Wilson, William Julius. 1987. *The Truly Disadvantaged: The Inner City, the Underclass, and Public Policy*. Chicago: University of Chicago Press.

Wirtz, Kristina. 2017. "Mobilizations of Race, Place, and History in Santiago de Cuba's Carnivalesque." *American Anthropologist* 119 (1): 58–72.

Wolf, Eric R. 1956. "Aspects of Group Relations in a Complex Society: Mexico." *American Anthropologist* 58 (6): 1065–78.

Wolf, Eric. 1969. *Peasant Wars of the Twentieth Century*. New York: Harper and Row.

Wood, Kate. 2005. "Contextualizing Group Rape in Post-Apartheid South Africa." *Culture, Health, and Sexuality* 7 (4): 303–17.

Woodson, Drexel. 1990. "Tout Moun Se Moun, Men Tout Moun Pa Menm: Microlevel Sociocultural Aspects of Land Tenure in a Northern Haitian Locality." PhD dissertation, University of Chicago.

World Bank. 1996. "Memorandum of the President of the International Development Association to the Executive Directors on a Country Assistance Strategy of the World Bank Group for the Republic of Haiti." Washington, DC: World Bank.

World Bank. 2010. "Promoting Nutrition Security in Haiti: An Assessment of Pre- and Post-Earthquake Conditions and Recommendations for the Way Forward." Washington, DC: World Bank.

Young, Iris Marion. 1980. "Throwing Like a Girl: A Phenomenology of Feminine Body Comportment, Motility, and Spatiality." *Human Studies* 3 (2): 137–56.

Zakaria, Fareed. 2003. *The Future of Freedom: Illiberal Democracy at Home and Abroad*. New York: W. W. Norton.

Index

CPSIA information can be obtained
at www.ICGtesting.com
Printed in the USA
LVHW011933230322
714108LV00012BA/618